Glossary of Revenue and Allied Terms of South India

Other Books by the same Author

1. (1990) Agrarian System in South India : Some Aspects
2. (1992) British Historiography Eighteenth Century Punjab : Their understanding of the Sikh Struggle for Power and Role of Jassa Singh Ahluwalia
3. (1994) British In'am Policy & Palegar Resistance in Ceded Districts : Select Documents relating to Narasimha Reddy's Resistance 1846-47
4. (1996) Palegars of South India : Forms and Contents of their Resistance in Ceded Districts
5. Emerging Concepts for Effective Tourism Development (Forthcoming)

Glossary of Revenue and Allied Terms of South India

J. C. Dua

1998
Kaveri Books
New Delhi - 110002

ISBN : 81-7479-017-9

Published by : Rakesh Goel
Kaveri Books
4697/5-21 A, Ansari Road,
New Delhi-110002 (India).
Tel : 3288140, Fax : (011) 7198902

Laser Typesetting by : Om Sai Computers, Vikas Puri,
New Delhi – 110018.

Printed at : Chawla Offset Printers, Delhi - 110052

PRINTED IN INDIA

To

My Teacher and Mentor
Professor B.R. Grover
and
My Daughter
Silky

Acknowledgement

It is to Professor B.R.Grover that I owe this book, in which I have put together the technical terms relating to revenue and allied matters of South India which I came accross in over three decades of research. This work would not have seen the light of the day but for his suggestion and constant reminder that I should keep on noting every technical term along with its meaning and context during the course of my research. Apart from this he willingly spared long hours of his time discussing and clarifying some of the terms.

I have had the privilege of receiving help through long discussions with a wide circle of historians who were instrumental in making me, a person from North India, understand various intricate revenue and economic terms which one has to deal with while studying the history of the region south of the Vindhyas. In this regard I am particularly indebted to late Professor K.A. Nilakanta Sastri, late Professor T.V. Mahalingam, late Professor M. Arokiyaswamy, late Professor K.K. Pillay, Professor N.Subrahmanian, Dr. A.Sarada Raju, Professor Sarojini Regani, Professor K.Rajayyan and many others.

My grateful thanks are due to Dr. V.K. Bawa, the former Director, Andhra Pradesh State Archives for providing me with a Research Fellowship in 1966 which baptized me into a serious study of the South Indian History. To my teachers Professor Bipan Chandra, Professor K.N. Panikkar, late Professor Amba Prasad, Professor Aparna Basu, Professor Suhash Chakravarty, Professor K.C. Yadav, Professor H.A. Phadke and Dr. V.K. Saxena, I express my sincere thanks for their encouragement. I am obliged to Mr. Deepak Malhotra, Principal, Dyal Singh Evening College, New Delhi for sparing me from all extra duties during the course of the finalization of this work.

The Directors and members of the staff of Andhra Pradesh State Archives, Hyderabad; Tamil Nadu State Archives, Chennai; National Archives of India, New Delhi; and Maharashtra State Archives, Mumbai; Deputy Secretary incharge and staff of Karnataka Government Secretariat, Bangalore; Librarian and staff, Oriental Manuscript Library, Chennai; National Library, Calcutta; Delhi University Library, Delhi; and Dyal Singh Evening College Library, New Delhi; and Collectors/Deputy Commissioners of various collectorates were extremely helpful to me and encouraged and facilitated my work. Without their patient assistance and instructions, little of that would have been possible.

I am indebted to my friends Lala Bhagwan Dass Goel, Dr. P.M. Rathnam, Dr. T.R.Vasantha Rao, Dr. M.M.Rathnam, Mr. L.S.Ramaiah, Mr. Zia-ud-din Ahmed, Dr. Prasannakshi Kumari, Dr. G.Niranjan Rao, Dr. Tasneem Ahmed, Mr. A.K.Singh, Dr. Intizar Mirza, Dr. N.M. Narayanan and Mr. Vinod Srivastava for their help at the various stages of the preparation of this work.

It is with great pleasure that I express my thanks to Bhupinder Kumra & Raakesh K. Vaid for preparing the computerised script of this book and Shri Rakesh Goel, proprietor Kaveri Books, New Delhi, for all the pains that he took in not only publishing the book with remarkable speed but also for doing it well.

To members of my family, especially my parents, my wife Anita and daughter Silky, my debt is irredeemable.

J.C. DUA

Preface

Ever since I started working on the economic history of South India in 1966, it has been a very difficult task to decipher many a technical term, and hence the need for an up to date and compact glossary of the revenue and allied terms. This work has undergone a myriad of metamorphoses. Originally my intention was to insert the glossary in my earlier books. However, as my collection of the material progressed, I felt that it would be too exhaustive to be a part of any book. The result is this nucleus now placed in the hands of the readers interested in the economic history of South India.

This Glossary includes the words collected from the inscriptions in Sanskrit and Dravidian languages, and English, Urdu and Persian archival records. Since many of the words have more than one usage in different contexts, an attempt has been made to explain all those usages. Sometimes, in order to understand the exact meaning of particular words, I interviewed some of the eminent historians in South India, knowledgeable persons working in the various archives, and also those involved in the day to day administration in the villages especially those working in and retired from different collectorates and tehsildaris. These interviews were immensely helpful in making out the exact meaning and usage of a particular term/ word.

I am quite conscious of the fact that no glossary of this type can be complete in all respects as I do realize that it is not possible for an individual to collect all relevant words and expressions from all the above mentioned sources. I am also fully conscious of my own limitations as well as possibility of error of judgement and omission and commission creeping into the work. There may be cases wherein I have been misled by earlier writers, or I have accepted their doubtful suggestion as correct, or misunderstood them. Nevertheless, it is still hoped that the work may be of some help to the scholars and students working on the economic history of South India.

Despite being a matter of great satisfaction that I have probably succeeded in explaining a number of terms/expressions, which were previously partly unintelligible or misunderstood, and in cross-referencing in numerous cases, I wonder if it is possible to compile a work of this type without errors, and even more difficult to print it without technical blemishes including misprints.

July 1, 1998

278, Kadambri
Sector IX, Plot No. 19,
Rohini, Delhi -110085

J.C. DUA

System of Transliteration
Tamil

Vowels

ā	ஆ
ī	ஈ
ū	ஊ
ē	ஏ
ō	ஓ
ai	ஐ
au	ஔ

Consonants

k/g	க்
ṅ	ங்
c/ch/s	ச்
ñ	ஞ்
ṭ/ḍ	ட்
ṇ	ண்
ḻ	ழ்
ḷ	ள்
ṟ	ற்
ṉ	ன்

System of Transliteration

Malyalam

ā	ആ	ī	ഈ	ū	ഊ
ṛī	ഋ	ē	ഏ	ō	ഓ
ṅ	ങ	ch	ച	chh	ഛ
ñ	ഞ	ṭ	ട	ṭh	ഠ
ḍ	ഡ	ḍh	ഢ	ṇ	ണ
ś	ശ	sh	ഷ	ḷ	ള
ṟ̤	ഴ	ḷ̤	ഌ		
ḥ	ഃ	ṁ	ം		

System of Transliteration
Telugu

ā	ఆ	ī	ఈ	ū	ఊ
ṛī	ఋ	ē	ఏ	ō	ఓ
ṅ	ఙ	ch	చ	chh	ఛ
ñ	ఞ	ṭ	ట	ṭh	ఠ
ḍ	డ	ḍh	ఢ	ṇ	ణ
ś	శ	sh	ష	ḷ	ళ
ṛ	ౠ	ḷ	ౡ		
ḥ	visarga	ṁ	anusvāra		

System of Transliteration
Kannaḍa

ā	ಆ	ñ	ಞ	ī	ಈ
ṭ	ಟ	ū	ಊ	ṭh	ಠ
ṛi	ಋ	ḍ	ಡ	ē	ಏ
ḍh	ಢ	ō	ಓ	ṇ	ಣ
ṅ	ಙ	ś	ಶ	ch	ಚ
sh	ಷ	chh	ಛ	ḷ	ಳ

Dravidian palatal alvecolar n = ṉ̣
Dravidian palatal alvecolar r = ṟ̣
Dravidian cerebral voiced fricative (i.e. voiced ṣ) = ḻ
anusvāra = ṁ visarga = ḥ
upadmānīya = ḫ jihvāmūlīya = ḣ

System of Transliteration

Hindi

ā	आ	ō, ŏ	ओ	ḍh	ढ
ī	ई	ṅ	ङ	ṇ	ण
ū	ऊ	c, ch	च	ś	श
ṛ, ṝ, ṛi	ॠ	chh	छ	ṣ, sh	ष
ḷ, ḹ	ऌ	ñ	ञ	ḍ	ड़
e	ऎ	ṭ	ट	ḷ	ल
ē	ए	th	ठ		
o	ऒ	ḍ	ड		

System of Transliteration
Arabic, Persian, Urdu

Vowel Sounds

a	ـَـ
ā	ـَا
ē	ـے
i	ـِـ
ī	ـِی
u	ـُـ
ū	ـُو
ai	اَے
au	اَو

Consonants

a	ا
t	ت
ṭ	ٹ
th	ث
ch	چ
ḥ	ح
kh	خ
d	د
ḍ	ڈ
dh	ذ
r	ر
ṛ	ڑ
z	ز
zh	ژ
s	س
sh	ش
ṣ	ص
ẓ	ض
ṭ	ط
ẓ	ظ
C	ع
gh	غ
q	ق
w	و
h	ه
y	ی

A

A'bādāni cultivation, population.

A-chammaṅgālaka, a-chārāsnana-charmāṅgāra the expressions used for land grants that did not carry with them the right to pasturage, hides and charcoal.

A-lavaṇa-khātaka a grant of land with 'freedom from the land being dug out or the trees being pierced for salt.'

A-lavaṇa-klinna kreṇikhanaka this term has been explained as-exemption from the salt-tax-an immunity granted in favour of the donee; also exemption of the donee from fines for extracting salt which was regarded as a royal monopoly.

A-loṇa-guḷa-chchhobha 'freedom from the trouble in respect of salt and sugar.'

A-paramparā-balīvarda freedom of a gift village from the supply of bullocks primarily for the conveyance of royal officers on tour.

A-paramparā-go-balīvarda, a-paramparā-balivarda-grahana a grant of land, 'free from the taking of the oxen in succession,' otherwise it was obligatory on the part of the villagers to supply bullocks for the bullock-carts used by the royal officers when the latter went on tour through the country for revenue collection and other official work; 'no obligation regarding carrying loads free of charge'; 'exemption from providing horses.'

A-prāveśya grant of land with 'freedom from the entry of royal agents.'

A-rāshṭrasāṁvinayika grant of land with 'freedom from the administrative control to which the district was subject.'

A-vāra-siddhika 'no obligation regarding the completion of duty in turn.'

Ā-candr-ārkkam 'so long as the moon and the sun last'; 'in perpetuity.'

Āḍa, aḍḍa (Telugu), a measure of capacity equal to 2 *mānikas* or one eighth of a *tūm*; half, especially of a *fanam* or a certain measure called *kuñcamu;* a weight representing the eighteenth portion of a *varāha.*

Ābhāvya income or proceeds; the income derived from the loads on bullocks going or coming.

Ābhīra member of the cowherd community.

Ābhoga a territorial unit; similar to *bhoga.*

Ābhyantar-ādāya internal revenue income of a village, could be, taxes payable to the village authorities as against those payable to the king. See *bāhya.*

Ācāra a custom or customary laws.

Ācāra-pātra a document relating to customary laws.

Ācāra-sthiti-pātra a charter relating to customary laws.

Ācārya-pūjanā honorarium payable to priests.

Ācāryas a term used in the epigraphs to denote master craftsmen.

Āchu the name of a coin, same as *āsu;* cf. Tamil *accu.*

Āḍha a measure of capacity; same as *āḍhika, āḍhaka*; a land measure also called *āḍhvāpa.*

Āḍāṇaka mortgaged; something

mortgaged, the produce of which will pay of the debt in course of time.

Āḍavallān a type of measure by which the paddy was measured for the purposes of revenue paid as tax.

Āḍhaka a measure of capacity; often regarded as equal to 264 handfuls and one-fourth of a *droṇa*; also used as a shortened form of *āḍhavapa* or *ādhakavāpa*.

Āḍi paccai a tax collected by the temples, choultries and other public institutions.

Āḍi-kārtikai-paccai presents made by the cultivators during *āḍi* (July-August) and *kārtikai* (November-December) to the king in the form of grain or rice.

Ādāna a levy or impost; also see *ādāya*.

Ādāya income or impost.

Ādatta a tax on uncertain import; also, may be, interest or fine on arrears of tax.

Ādeya 'what is to be taken or levied'; a fiscal term meaning same as *ādāya*, *i.e.* income or impost; dues.

Ādhavāpa, āḍhakavāpa an area of land requiring one *āḍhaka* measure of seed grains for being sown; also a land measure which varied during different periods and localities.

Ādirai-ppāṭṭam, attirai-ppāṭṭam (Tamil), tax on cattle.

Āgāmin future income, future benefits; one of the 8 kinds of rights in the property; see, *aṣta-bhoga*.

Āgama-nigama-dāna tax for importing and export.

Āhāras, hāras administrative unit; the most common designation of an administrative district or *tāluk* in the Sātavāhana age; the *āhāra* tends to disappear after the Sātavāhana age, and is rarely met with in the succeeding period, and even when the expression actually forms part of the name of a district it is followed by the term *vishaya*.

Ājñā, Ājñapti, Ājñāpti an order or command, the agency that obtains the command, the executor of a grant; one who communicates, at the order of the king, the details about a land grant to local officers; according to some, a synonym of *Dūtaka*.

Āñjaṣṭa-sabhā, Āñjaṣṭa-śattu-sabhai (Tamil, Sanskrit), village committee of five or eight members.

Āñjuvaṇṇam (Tamil); Sanskrit, *pañca-varṇa*; Kannada, *hañjamāna*, the five artisan classes; also regarded as a form of persian *anjumana*.

Ājīvikas the taxes.

Ājiva-kāśu a type of additional demand on land, over and above the land revenue, charged for the maintenance of temples and brahmans.

Ākāśa-pātāl-otpatti fruits and roots produced in a piece of land.

Ākara-maṇḍalika a term used in the Mysore inscriptions to denote an officer who was the superintendent of mines.

Ākarṣaka the extent (of a piece of land).

Āḷ-vari a term which refers to a tax levied on agricultural labourers : almost identical to *kuṭi-kāṇam* and *kuṭumpak-kācu*

Āḷ-nēl, āṇēl (Tamil), tax payable in paddy.

Āḷamanči a term connected with land revenue used during Chola period in Tondaimandalam; same as *amañci*.

Āḷmañji a custom according to which the *rayats* possessing lands very near the sources of water supply provided the necessary labour at a fixed rate for deepening the river beds or removing the silt; in some localities for every unit of land watered by the channel one cooly was to be supplied.

Āledere a tax on sugar-cane mills;

this term is found in the inscriptions of Mysore.

Āmra mango

Āṇḍārs a homogeneous group with identical functions in the temple and making a living out of the *dēvadāna* lands; they preferred to have separate shares with localized parcels and yield assigned to a group of two.

Āṇimuttu pearls of the finest quality.

Ānanda-nidhi 'a pot of gold'; a kind of gift made in favour of brahmans.

Āndu, andoo in Malabar a cycle of sixty years.

Āni June-July.

Ānita duties on articles of merchandise.

Āpaṇ-ājīvika 'those who live by shops'; *i.e.* shop-keepers in general.

Āpaṇa shops in general

Āpaṇa-paṭṭakāra the shop keeping cloth-dealers.

Āṟṟaṅkarai-ttevai (Tamil), tax for keeping the river-bund in repair.

Āṟṟu-kkulai (Tamil), tax to repair breaches in the river.

Āṟidupadugai the lands lying on the bed of the river between the banks and the edge of the normal water-course; the translation given by some epigraphists as 'arable lands near rivers' does not seem to be sufficiently definite; this land may be covered with water in flood time; at other times, it is usually cultivated, being a very rich soil; another interpretation of the term is 'the land just on the bed of a river which it washes during floods'.

Āraycci, ārāya lit. 'an examination or investigation (of accounts)'; terms used in the epigraphs to denote the officers deputed to inspect the affairs of the country. These officers, in most of the instances, audited temple accounts, and were invariably deputed by the king.

Ārdhika a cultivator who tills other's lands and gets half the crop as his share.

Ārōgyaśātai a term used for hospital (maintained) by the temple.

Āṣṭa-bhāgika '(a village) paying one-eighth of the produce'.

Āśuva-kkāśu, āśuvikaḷ-kāśu, āśuva-kkaḍamais (Tamil), tax payable by Ājīvakas or for the maintenance of Ājīvaka monks.

Āsana 'encamping'.

Āsana-charman hides which villagers had to supply to the wandering officers for their seats.

Āṭṭuppāṭṭam same as *aṟṟup-paṭṭam.*

Ātaṇḍa, Ātoṇḍa, Atanda legendary founder of Vellala hegemony of Toṇḍaimaṇḍalam.

Ātithya land assigned to government officers for public charities.

Āturāvaḍḍi, āntarāvaḍḍi a levy related to the treatment of the king when sick.

Āvāra 'collections to be made from the shops in a market'.

Āvāta a fiscal term referring to the income from lands as a result of changes caused by natural agencies; an income resulting from storms.

Āvaṇam (Tamil) a document; generally, a sale-deed.

Āvesani artisan, pl. *avesanin.*

Āvṛtti an administrative unit like a *pargana.*

Āya a term used in the Kanarese inscriptions to denote remuneration or customary mode of payment either in the allotments of land from the common property, or in fees consisting of fixed proportions of the crop of every farmer in the village or both to the hereditary village servants; each one was also given a house site in the village; the land on which the village servants subsisted varied in a extent from place to place; same as *mēras;* from the term *āyagāṟa.*

A fiscal term meaning 'revenue' 'tax', profit, income, receipt; tribute; corn given by the well-to-do villagers to the hereditary servants of the village as their established fees of office.

Āya daṇḍam penalty.

Āyāga-sabhā administration of a village by a group of officers called *āyāgār* (village officers and servants).

Āyagārs a term by which a body of twelve functionaries of a village were collectively known; they could sell or mortgage their offices; were granted revenue free lands which they enjoyed in perpetuity; they had onerous responsibilities within their locality; were the guardians of the peace within their jurisdiction; no transfer of property could be effected or grant made without their knowledge.

Āyam lit. income or receipts; it was applied in epigraphs to a cess levied particularly on traders and merchandise. During the Chola period in Cholamandalam the term *āyam* was suffixed to other terms, *e.g. canti-āyam* - *i.e.* road cess, *cekkātāyam* - cess on oil press, *kūrait - taraku-āyam* - cess on the sale of roofing materials like coconut or bamboo plaits; few examples could also be cited from Tondaimandalam, *e.g. ēri-āyam i.e.*, cess on using water from tank, *koṭai-āyam*, cess on shop, and *puraṿ-āyam* cess on land. It was also referred as surcharge on all the merchandise inclusive of commodities sold by weight and capacity.

Āyatanam barn; it has also been interpretted as a house or a plot of ground for storing husk or straw; even now in addition to a common threshing floor there is also a common place for the villagers to store husk as straw, in the *samudāyam* villages.

Āyudhīya land granted for supplying troops in lieu of tax. Also see, *amara*.

Áb-kárí, abkari, abkarry a term used for revenue charged on arrack and toddy business; lit. *áb* water, and *kárí* manufacture. Taxes or duties on the manufacture and sale of spirituous liquors, and intoxicating drugs.

Áltamghá, althamga a royal grant in perpetuity; perpetual tenure. An heritable *jagir* in perpetuity.

Ámání, Aamani direct; *aamani* villages were those which were 'properly and indivisibly appertaining to government; 'trust'; management of land revenue direct under government officers as opposed to *Ijára* or farming. It was also called *ására* or sharing system. In Tinnevelly, for instance, for several years such a system was in force on the paddy lands (wet cultivation).

Ámishan, amshom, amsom, amsam, umsom in Malabar, an official division, forming a group of land for land revenue administration purposes, for which there was a headman, and an accountant called *menón*; also smallest revenue administrative division.

Ására sharing system; same as *ámání*.

Áwardah-navis, awurdah novis a writer or recorder of what is brought. The title of certain accountants in the Ceded Districts, to whom the fair accounts of the surveys were delivered.

Aagramandire type vessels (ships) having their cabins towards prows and eminently suited for long voyages and also for naval warfare.

Abayam refuge

Abhayaśāsana a charter granted (by Gaṇapatidēva Mahārāja) to the merchants trading on sea (East Coast) whose vessels used to call at or start from the sea port of Mōṭupalli; the necessity for the charter was that kings of old used to confiscate by force all the cargo of vessels *en route* from one country to another, which, being driven by unfavourable winds, were stranded and wrecked in the sands; under these charters traders were promised protection, and they were freed from all port dues except the authorised customs duties.

Abhidhānacintāmaṇi 'he who enjoyed a comfortable mount'; one of the derivations suggested for the term Sātavāhana.

Abhinava name of a tax

Abhinava-mārgaṇaka name of tax. See *mārgaṇaka, mārg-ādāya* etc.

Abhyantara-Siddhi, Abhyantara-Siddhika, Ābhyantara-Siddhi internal income or revenue, or taxes payable to village authorities as against those payable to the king; also *sarv-ābhyantara-siddhi,* a privilege of the donee of rent-free land, could be privilege of the donee offering full power of adjudication in law suits.

Abohana, agovana waste or uncultivated land.

Abraiaman a term used by Marco Polo for *ceṭṭis* the best merchants in the world, and the most truthful; very long-lived, owing to their extreme abstinence in eating.

Abwáb lit. gates, doors, ways; items of taxation, cesses, imposts, taxes. This term is particularly used to distinguish the taxes imposed subsequently to the establishment of the *asal,* or original standard revenue/rent, in the nature of additions there to. In many places they had consolidated with the *asal,* and a new standard assumed as the basis of succeeding imposition. Many were levied on *zamindars* as the price of forbearance, on the part of government, from detailed investigations in to their profits, or actual receipts, from the lands, according to the *hast-ó-búd. Abwáb-i-kásim khán-abwáb* or cesses imposed by Kásim Alikhan; *abwáb-i-Jáfar Khán-abwáb* or cesses imposed by Ja'far Khan; *abwáb-i-Shujá Khán-abwáb* introduced by Nawab Shujákhán; *abwáb-i-subahdári-abwáb* or cesses of the *subahdári.* New and perpetual imposts levied by the authority of the provincial governors; taxes imposed under the Mohammedan government in addition to the regular assessment on the land.

Miscellaneous cesses, imposts and charges levied by the *zamindars* and public officers.

Acala-pravṛtti a kind of tenure; could be a permanent holding. Also see *vṛtti.*

Acca-taṟi a term used to denote tax on looms. However, significance of the word *acca* is not clear.

Accinaṭankasāla a term used to denote the mint where coins were stamped.

Accu (Tamil) name of a coin.

Accu-pannāya department of taxation or coining.

Accu-taṟi, accu-ttaṟki (Tamil), tax payable on looms.

Accukkaṭṭu land rainfed lands; also *manavāri* lands.

Accupannāyadadhiṣṭhāyaka (Kannada), superintendent of the revenue from mints.

Accutaṟi a professional tax charged from the weavers.

Accuvari (Tamil), the duty payable for minting gold into coins; could be same as *pŏnvari.*

Achandrarkam the term applied to villages in which the lands are permanently apportioned among the different sharers.

Acharyapurusha in'am *in'am* for the service of head priest in a pagoda.

Aḍaiōlai, Aḍaiōlai written engagement; written engagement for the payment of land-dues.

Aḍaipaḍi kaḍamai obligation for tenancy.

Aḍaippar tenants.

Aḍaippu lands held on lease.

Aḍappam the betel bearer, who as per the inscriptions remained always with the king; though only the 'betel page' of the king, his position, dignity and influence in the state was great; Nuniz says that the page who served Kṛṣṇadēva Rāya with betel had 15000 foot and 200 horses; Barradas records that the great Naique of Madura was "a page of the betel of the king of Bisnaga and paid a revenue amounting to 600,000 *pagodas* to the king and had under him many kings and nobles as vassals."

Aḍḍa-cinna name of a coin.

Aḍḍānaka a mortgaged thing; also see, for example, *gṛhāḍdanaka-patra*, deed for mortgaging a house.

Aḍḍavaṭṭa-suṅkamu tax on a herd of sheep and amounted to a kind of property tax on cattle. It is not known whether this term denoted a tax on all classes of cattle or only on certain kinds. If it referred exclusively to sheep, then it would have to be interpreted as an impost relating to industry, since blankets are woven with wool of the sheep, and not as a pure property tax levied on all classes of cattle.

Aḍimai (Tamil), Adumah, Adumy, Adima (Malayalam) **adimai, adami** slave; bondsman; it is significant to note that the term 'slave' is invariably used for describing *cherumans*; in fact the term 'serf' hardly occurs in the literature on Malabar; within Malabar the incidence of servitude for the *adimas* was not uniform, but there were certainly places where they were treated almost exactly like other forms of property.

The word *adimai* was originally used of those who could be transferred separately from the land. However Tamil Lexicon defines *adimai* as 'a slave formerly attached to the land and transferable with it'.

Subordination; subordinate; land less agricultural labourers; some scholars have translated and used this word synonymously with 'slave' or serf. It requires some caution in exercising the choice of such words. Epistemologically *aḍimai* means 'one who is subordinate and whose actions are subordinated.' Thus, it is apparent that this category of individuals were subordinate to all others. Whether such subordination is to be typified as 'serfdom' or 'slavery' is a different matter. It has to be borne in mind that unlike serfs in Europe, the *aḍimai* was not tied to land. Moreover, despite being true that *aḍimais* were saleable, they could as well sell themselves. Whether this constituted 'slavery' is not known. However, it is clearly supported by the evidence that fairly good number of these people were in a states of bondage. The type of relationship that they enjoyed with different members of the society including the *kāṇiyāṭchikārars* would largely neutralise various connotations which might emerge out of such a state. Their rewards were as much parts of the *swatantradittam* as were those of others in the village. As they were represented by powerful collective bargaining bodies, their earnings were negotiated annually. As such, as per the evidence, the resemblance of the *aḍimai* to the slave was contra-indicated by their right to annually negotiate and obtain satisfactory earnings, which averaged around Rs. 7.50 per day at 1976 paddy prices.

Aḍimai-kkāśu fees collected from the temple servants.

Adálat, Adalat justice, equity, a court of justice. The terms, *adálat-i-díwán* and *adálat-i-faujdári* denote the civil and the criminal courts of justice respectively; court of law.

Adamaana chitta (Tanjōre), a deed of land tenure granted, in respect of a part of the land mortgaged for a sum of money taken on loan; the grantee was to enjoy the products of the ground for a specified number of years, at the expiration of which the owner was to engage to redeem the piece of land in question by paying the full sum taken as loan.

Adangal a field register; annual statement of occupation and cultivation, field by field. It shows-the fields (government or in'am, number and letter, revenue-rate (*taram*), single or double crop, area, and assessment) as they appear in the settlement - survey or *mámúl* account. Then follows the name of the holder, the source of irrigation, if any, the occupation, the actual cultivation, and remarks of the *karnam*.

Adangal olungu an elaborate summary of records.

Adavoo saathanum deed of land tenure for the land pledged in lieu of the money taken in Kanara; under this type of deed the owner assigns the land on the condition that he would pay the full assessment to the government and interest (at a specified rate) to the grantee; the owner undertake to pay the full amount taken as loan on a specified date and redeem the ground assigned, failing which he would make over he said ground by the deed of *Kerya Saathanum*, according to the valuation put upon it by 'four intelligent persons,' and if the value should exceed the amount of his debt to receive the surplus; and if the valuation be less, he would engage to pay the deficiency.

Adḍaga, adḍuga (Telugu), half of a *fanam*.

Addhikas 'a labourer receiving half the produce'.

Addhiya-manussas 'men who receive half the crop'; these were the hired cultivators employed for the tillage of the donated land and in return for their labour, these agricultural labourers received half of the annual yield.

Adhaḥ what is below the surface of the ground; root crops.

Adhi-kárí, Adhikari, Adhigari village revenue official; village headman; superintendents, governors, persons of ministerial rank; *adhi* over, and *kárí* agent; a governor or superintendent; or anything relating to superior. A term applied to the villages where an individual holds the entire undivided estate.

Adhika-paḍi (Sanskrit-Telugu), an extra allowance in food (inclusive of grain, salt, vegetables and even firewood-all that was required to prepare a meal), also allowance in money, granted to servants, friends or poor people.

Adhikāra-varttāa customary payments made to an officer at stipulated periods, same as (Sanskrit-Tamil) *adhukāra-pperu, adhikāra-ppon*, etc.

Adhirāṭ, ekarāṭ sole monarch.

Adhyakṣa the head of a department; sometimes mentioned in the list of officials.

Adhyayanam in'am, Adhyayana-vṛtti tax-free land endowed for reciting the Vedas in temples; a grant or perquisite appropriated to Brahmmanas; the grant could be in the form of small lands or whole villages; though almost similar to *brahmadeya* grant which was made usually in recognition of a Brahman's scholarship, or to enable him to impart regular religious or secular instructions to others, it was for the latter purpose that the grant was usually known as *adhyayanavṛtti*.

Adi-kkāśu tax collected from stall-keepers in the markets.

Adirvedi in'am grant for the service of discharging rockets during religious festivals.

Aditi premium, commission.

Adityuñcha local dues; sort of tolls.

Adungul examination prior to the *jammabandi*.

Aerical lit., grinding stones, dues were charged on that; since public mills existed no where in southern India, grinding and preparing the flour they used; this tax, therefore, could not have been paid on the working such stones, but in cutting them in the quarry.

Aga earth or land.

Agahara, agāhara, āgahara rent-free land given to Brahmans; a rent free village; a Brahman village; at times suffixed to names of localities. It was primarily a rent-free village in possession of Brahmans; however, occasional references to *dev-āgrahāra*, *i.e.*, rent-free holding in the possession of a deity, *vaiśyāgrahāra i.e.*, rent-free holding in the possession of the Vaiśyas etc.; sometimes also spelt *agrāhāra*.

Agapat (T) a revenue term designating a channel-fed tank

Agara a corrupt form of *agrahāra* particularly used in Tamil inscriptions.

Agara viniyōgam a term used in the epigraphs to mean the dues distributed among and demanded by the brahman landholders.

Agara-brahmadeya village granted to Brahmans; also called *agara* (*agrahāra*) and *brahmadeya*.

Agara-ppaṛṛu (Tamil) same as *agara* or *agrahāra*; land granted to Brahmans.

Agaram a small administrative unit to which a few villages were attached.

Agaras same as *agrahāra*.

Agathi *sesbania grandiflora*.

Agghāpaṇikaṭṭhāna, agghakāraka an officer in the royal court, whose duties included-estimating the value of elephants, horses, precious stones, gold etc., and paying the owners of wares their proper price.

Agnipuman In'am grant for dancing before the village goddess with a pot containing fire.

Agra, agra-bhāga, agra-pratyaṁśa, agrapratyāya principal share or income, the king's share.

Agráháram, Agrahāra a land-grant revenue-free to Brahmans; land granted to a community of brahmans; F.W. Ellis (*Replies to Seventeen Questions...*, Madras, 1918, p XXV, n. 8) points out that the word *Agrahāra* has a variety of meanings, being sometimes applied to villages held rent-free by Brahmans, to villages paying the full rent, the *Mirasi* of which is held wholly or partly by Brahmans, to streets inhabited by them in large towns, and to alms-houses erected for their use and which they are allowed to occupy without paying rent. The word, however, when applied to the tenure of land, includes all alienations from the public revenue, being derived from *agra-before*, and *harati, it is taken*, meaning land of which the revenue is appropriated *before* it reaches the treasury; such grants by the *mírásidars* could also be an encroachment on the right of the sovereign; it could also signify merely the street of houses which the grantees might have built for Brahmamin a particular town; could have a variety of meanings, hence arises the ancient distinction, preserved in name, of the villages of a district into *agraháravád'ei*, which, though the Brahman holders were in some degree favoured, paid during the British period nearly the full assessment, and *pandára-vád'ei*, those appropriated to the treasury, on which the súdra holders had always paid the full assessment; a village, or a part of one, occupied by Brahmans and held either rentfree or at a favourable rate of assessment; Sanskrit *agra* chief, *hara* a separate allotment.

A royal donation of land to Brahmans, or the village or village site thus given; derives possession and the power of sale from grants of sovereign; that the whole lands of the village appear to be in a manner their property divided in to so many shares; that each holder of a share has the right to sell his share separately, and that the whole community have the right to sell the whole village; that the *agraharums* were originally either *shrotriums or survamaniems;* that under the latter tenure they were entirely exempt from land-tax, and that under the former they paid an easy rent, not depending upon nor proportioned to the annual extent of cultivation, but having the aggregate amount for the whole villages fixed by the grant or *dana shasanum.*

Except that the proportion of *mailwarum* which the sirkar received, was smaller from the *agraharum* than from the *munevet* villages, it does not appear that the sirkar exercised any greater degree of control over the *koodeewarum* of the one or the other, that is as far as regarded those agraharums, which were at first or afterwards became liable to a certain payment to the sirkar. Occasional agents were appointed for the proper security of the *mailwarum* in both, but the management of the *koodeewarum* seems to have been left as equally to the *gramuttan* of the *munevet*, as to the *mahajanum* of the *agraharum* village; land grants generally granted to the Brahmanas when they returned from the *gurukula* after completing studies, in order to help them in settling as *grihasthas.* Practically there was no difference between the rights enjoyed by an *agrahārika* and the donee of a *brahmadeya* grant both enjoying a revenue-free holding; though an *agrahara* was primarily a revenue-free holding in the possession of a Brahmana, we do come across occasional reference to *devāgrahāra* (revenue-free holding in the possession of a deity) and *vaiśyāgrahāra* (revenue-free holding in the possession of a *vaiśya*); usually an *agrahāra* was tax-free, but there were some exceptions also.

Agrahāra-pradey-āmśa a small rent payable for land granted to Brahmans and declared rent-free.

Agrahārīṇa-mahattara headman among the *Agrahārīṇas i.e.* holders of an *agrahāra.*

Agrahārika, Āgrahārika the owner of an *agrahāra*; has also been used for the superintendent of *agrahāras*; village officials.

Agrahārin, Agrahārīṇa the holder of an *agrahāra*; headman or owner of an *agrahāra* village; same as *Agrahārika.*

Agrahara vadakai, Agrahara vadiky *mírási* villages of Brahmans (esp. in Tinnevelly); the tenure of *agrahara vadakai* 'takes its name from the Brahmans, not only from their being inhabitants of the superior caste, but the village being originally bestowed on them, and because they possess the chief authority among the inhabitants'.

Agraharamdar one having a share in an *agraharam.*

Agran patun principal city, used to refer to Seringapatam.

Ahadi member of a select body of noble cavalry troopers.

Ahara territorial sub-division

Ahkám-námah, akamnamah, ahamnamah written orders. Assessment of Tipu Sultan.

Ahasham, ahashaum, ahshám, asham, ahsham retinues, military pomp and parade, the military; matchlockmen in the Mysore infantry. Infantry garrison.

Ahshám-i-amalah, asham omleh retinues of the public officers, whether for protection or parade. An article in the rentroll called *tumar jammah*, consisting of *jagir* appropriations for the support of troops for guards and garrisons.

Ahshám-i-sipáhi, asham sepaye retinues of soldiers, military pomp or parade. Military *jagirs*, or assignments of land, for defraying military expenses.

'Aín (Arabic), essence, the 'thing itself.' The original traditional assessment in the Dakhan, on the basis of which the

Marathás made up their *'kamil'* or full assessment.

Aimbadinmēlagaram a term used in the inscriptions to denote an administrative division; since different terms are referred to in an inscription without any order or sequence, it is difficult to say which kind of division does it signify.

Aimmadaran the grant holders.

Airiṇadurga desert-fort.

Ajnapati the executor; an influential officer who would request the king to allow the land or the village to be made a revenue free gift.

Akhráját, akherjaut expenses, disbursements, charges; charges general.

Akhrájat-i-arang, akherjaut aurung expenses of an *arang* or place where goods are manufactured. Charges for transporting salt to the place of sale; for weighmen, erection of store houses, etc.

Akkam (Tamil), name of a coin; one-twelfth of a *kāsu*.

Akka-Śālā (Tamil-Sanskrit), a mint.

Akkarika-vṛitti free land for the village teacher who taught the three R's.

Akkaśālai-vari charges payable to a mint for minting coins.

Akkasālevari the name of tax that accrued from the villages.

Akṣaya-nīvi, akṣaya-nīvī a permanent endowment.

Akṣayanīkā, akṣaya-nīvikā a perpetual endowment.

Akṣīṇin actual or fixed income; regarded as one of the eight rights of ownership. See for reference, *aṣṭa-bhoga*.

Akshadarśa a revenue official.

Al (Tamil, Malayalam), Alu (Kanarese) person; slave, labourer.

Al-bahr al-kāhil an Arabo-Persian name which means, the sluggish or motionless sea; a term used by Ibn Batuta for the China sea and the neighbouring waters.

Al amanji al, a person, a labourer and *amanji*, 'compulsory service' the assistance the villages are bound to afford to the officers of government, or others travelling on the public account, in the transport of baggage, etc.; the *vettiyán* is particularly charged with this duty, but all are required to aid; it was the practice that existed, but the term and practice were in pre-British days more extensive, including a great variety of services for which the villages were obliged to furnish labourers, artizans, etc., the carriage furnished by the villagers to the officers of government.

Aḷag-accu (Tamil), name of a coin.

Aḻḻāya-mānyam right to receive a handful of grain or the prescribed quantity of an article brought for sale in the market as charges for measuring.

Aḷantapaṭi lit. '(land) as was measured'. It could be taken to imply a revenue survey.

Aḻivu damaged crops and not counted for tax purposes.

Alahida separate, apart, distinct.

Alaktaka a fine dye yielded by the lac gum produced on the leaves and branches of certain trees by an insect both for the covering for its egg and the food for its young; used by women for dyeing the nails and feet.

Alal sherndakally a saltish clay land.

Alavan In'am held by the village officer who measures the grain where the assessment is paid in kind.

Allodium some derive this word from the circumstance of such lands-being lands of "lot or portion," considering it to be derived from 'allot' by adding the Latin termination; the better and no doubt the correct etymology, however, is from *all* and the Saxon *Hod* (whence *hood* in English, as manhood, etc.)

'possession' - 'state of being' - and *allod* (written in English '*allude*,' and by the French *aleud*) or with the Latin termination *allodium*, signifies, therefore, 'entire and absolute possession,' which the meaning of *kániyátchi*; throughout the world the same ideas have ever obtained among mankind, and it is not surprising therefore that they should express them by correlative terms.

Almadia a canoe, or dug-out, a boat made of one entire piece of timber, a ferry boat.

Aloosa diet money.

Alotti In'am grant held for the service of collecting *rayats* for the performance of customary labour.

Alpam-irai (Sanskrit-Tamil), a minor tax payable in grains.

Aṁśa-bṛhadbhogika a share-holder of a big *jāgīr*. Also see *Bhāgika*.

Aṁśapati co-sharer of a gift land.

Amāni, Amáni, aumany, aumani, aumanie (A) something held trust or deposit, applied especially to lands under direct government revenue management.

A settlement under which the government receives its share of produce of the lands from each cultivator in kind, instead of stipulating for a pecuniary commutation; trust, charge. Land in charge of an *ameen*, or trustee, to collect its revenue on the part of government.

In the peninsula the term is particularly applied to a settlement under which the government receives its share of the produce of the lands from each cultivator in kind; instead of stipulating for a pecuniary commutation, or farming them out to individuals by villages, or larger portions of territory. What is in charge of a collector on the part of the government; land directly managed by government officials.

Amadikarambu Long term fallow.

Amal, amulu rule, reign, sway, government, execution, fulfilment, etc.

Amanat in'am certain *in'ams* in Bellary and Cuddapah districts which were not allowed to be enjoyed without the holders furnishing annual security. These claims were not registered at the time of the *in'am* enquiry in *fasli* 1220 owing to the absence of the parties or other causes; but on the subsequent representation of the holders, they were allowed to enjoy the produce of the lands pending investigation, which, however, never took place.

Amañci, Amanci a term connected with land revenue current during Chola period in Tondaimandalam; a term comparable to *veṭṭi,* it was used to denote free labour; free labour; forced labour; unpaid labour; a form of unremunerated service rendered by the holders of land; a service usually demanded for the maintenance of water courses in general. Services rendered, as such, could also be considered as a form of revenue. In other words, instead of collecting payments as tax, the individuals were asked to execute certain public works by the state, and the state was relieved from the burden of collecting taxes and subsequently spending the accrued income for the execution of some public work. This service was generally entrusted with the local authorities and was utilized mostly for maintaining irrigational sources and guarding cities and villages.

Amaniya endowments of pagodas and other religious institution are known by this name in the district of Ganjam.

Amañji labour for communal service.

Amara, Amara-Māgaṇi land or revenue granted by a ruler to his retainers for military service; land assigned to military officers who were entitled to collect only certain revenues with the obligation to raise a contingent of army ready for service whenever called upon and also to pay tribute to the king.

Amara-nāyaka a retainer chief enjoying *amara, i.e.*, land or its revenue, for military service to be rendered to his master.

Amarakar grantee of *amaram* grants.

Amaram 'ease'; to remunerate revenue collecting peons a part of the revenue (royal share) was assigned to them and never raised in amount.

"The most important change which occurred in the agrarian system of south India under the new conditions from the fourteenth century on was the conversion of nuclear areas of the former period in to areas of private jurisdiction (*amaram*) of the warrior - dominated regime.

The *amaram* was not a military service estate, for typically it was not granted by the rulers in Vijayanagar so much as validated by them. Warrior holders of territories designated as *amaram* were most often men who had seized existing settled territories, often the nuclear areas of the former period, or had opened new territories by burning over forest, after conquering the people over there.

The system of military rule which came to maturity under the first dynasty of Vijayanagar after the middle of the fourteenth century, which is described in the inscriptions and by a few European travellers, was what Kosambi has called 'feudalism from belows'. That is, warriors whose private jurisdiction had been forged by the warriors themselves, were recognised by, and submitted to the overlordship of the great warriors of Vijayanagar. The system even under the most powerful of the Vijayanagar warriors, Krishnadevaraya (1509-29), was little more than this." (Burton Stein, 'Integration of the Agrarian System of South India').

The word 'fief' has been inappropriately used for *amaram* by writers like T.V. Mahalingam; the *amaram* never possessed the relatively consistent set of privileges and responsibilities of the European fief.

Land or revenue granted by a chief to his retainers for military service (*Tamil Lexicon*, i,p. 102). Land granted on condition of service (could be even for revenue collection), resumable if stipulated service was not performed.

Amaramāgaṇi estate given to an *amaranāyaka*, an official who represented in the larger council of king.

Amaranāyaka tenure see *nāyankara* tenure system.

Ambalakaram in'am same as *ambalam*.

Ambalam in'am land grants held by the headmen of villages, particularly of villages inhabited by sudras.

Ambalavasis lit. 'dwellers in temples'. A west coast caste intermediate in status between Nambudri Brahmans and Nayars, whose specific caste occupation is temple service. They follow the 'Marumakkattayam' system of inheritance *i.e.* inheritance through the female line of descent.

Ambali in'am for supplying to the poor *ambali* or thick conjee.

Ambaṇam grain-measures.

Ambattam barber; their number used to vary from village to village and from time to time, essential component of most villages; some of them were remunerated in the form of a *mānyam* land and some were given fixed shares of the village output, as a part of the *swatantradiṭṭam* yet others had rewards combining the *mānyam* and the output share principles.

Ambigar in'am *in'am* for ferryman's service.

Amil revenue collector, agent, officer, superintendent of a district or division of a country or *pargana*. (almost same as *amildar*).

Amildar, amal-dár, aumildar a collector of or contractor for revenue, of uniting civil, military and financial powers (a pre 1800 usage in South India); (Hindustani) tahsildar, a revenue officer; agent, the holder of an office. An intendant and collector of the revenue, of uniting civil, military and financial powers. The terms, *ámil* and *amildar* are synonymous.

Ammu-kaḍa-suṅkamu duty levied on each shop or *kaḍa* as a going concern.

Ammubaḍi-suṅkamu the duty collected at some specific rate on sales effected.

Ampu-vari tax levied on a unit of land as a fee for using water for irrigation.

Amṛta-gaṇa, amirta-gaṇattār (Tamil), members of the committee for the management of village affairs; members incharge of the cash-receipts of a temple.

Amṛta-padi, amuda-ppaḍi (Tamil), raw rice; food offering to a deity; *paḍi*- an allowance in food (covering all the necessary commodities to prepare a meal), could be sometime in money as well, and *amuda-paḍi*-an endowment often made in favour of a deity for daily offering of food as *bhoga*, etc.

Amukhyāhāra minor food.

Anubhoga-pparṟ-ōḷugu Sanskrit-Tamil, renewal of title deeds.

An-to-lo the term used to denote Andhra areas.

Anādeśya, aniradeśya 'not to be pointed out (or, ordered)'; epithet of a gift land.

Aṇgāraka pink-lustred pearls.

Aṇai anicut

Aṅkāṭik-kūli, aṅkāṭip-pāṭṭam the terms used for tax on shop.

Aṉṟāḍu-kōmuṟṟavar agents of the ruler.

Aṉṟaḷ-kōvukku 'to the reigning king'; such expression in the inscriptions indicates that the fines, etc. imposed on individuals were also payable to the king.

Aṅga-bhoga usually explained as 'decorations and illuminations of a deity;' a queen is also known to have received a village as an *agrahāra* for her *aṅga-bhoga i.e.* as her pin-money. Sometimes the land granted for the *aṅga-bhoga* of a deity came to be known as the deity's *aṅga-bhioga*.

Aṅga-maṇi property owned by a woman; also, *aṅga-maṇi-dravya*, dowry.

Aṅgāḍi-kkūli, aṅgāḍi-ppāṭṭam (Tamil), tax on bazars, shops, etc.

Aṅgāra, aṅgāraka, a-carm-āṅgāraka charcoal for cooking, which the villagers were obliged to supply to the king or landlord on occasions or to the touring officers.

Aṅgaḍa-siddhāya (Telugu-Sanskrit), fixed revenue from shops.

Aṅgula, aṅguli a linear measure equal to the breadth of the middle finger.

Aṅkāṭi-kūli lit. rent on shops (*aṅkāṭi* = shop; *kūli* = rent). It could have been levied in the form of rent for using the place or for erecting shop and conducting business thereon. Some inscriptions show that it was levied as duty on the merchandise sold in the shop. It can also be understood from the inscriptions that the paddy and rice brought from outside and the commodities sold by heaps were to be assigned for *aṅkāṭi-kūli*. It can also be inferred that this tax was levied on the face value of the goods sold in the shop. The rent on the shops were, perhaps, collected in this manner. It is also clear from some inscriptions that the right of collection of the *aṅkāṭi-kūli* could also be sold. Moreover, since it was levied by the *sabha*, it could very well be held that the duty was of a local import, levied by the local body, the *sabha*. Some inscriptions also show that its collection was effected by the local authorities (*ūravar* = the adminstrators of the *ūr*).

Also known by different terms viz. *kaṭai-iṟai*, and *kaṭai-ayam*.

Aṅkāṭi-pāṭṭam, kaṭai-pāṭṭam, uṟṟaṅkāṭipattam though in substance same as *aṅkāṭi-kūli*, there was a slight difference. They referred to a levy of fee for obtaining licence for establishing a shop for conducting business.

Ana a land measure, one *ana* being equivalent to 7.5625 sq. yards.

Anādi carambu, Anādikarambu long term fallow and; immemorially waste land; some portion of this division of land might be found cultivable; the English Board of Revenue was aware that portions of this land were sometimes cultivated; when given by the *sirkar* for cultivation, the *mírásidárs* would then receive their customary *swatuntrums* from them, in common with the other cultivated lands.

Anāhārya 'unresumable'; epithet of gift land.

Anacchedya 'uncurtailable'; 'not to be resumed;' epithet of a gift land.

Anádi, anadee lit. without a beginning. Old waste land. *Anáthi* could be another spelling-having no lord, master or owner; lands not cultivated within the memory of land.

Anáth-banjar, anad-bunger, anod-bunjer from *anátha* lordless, and *banjar* waste land; waste land without a master or owner; undivided waste or common.

Anaikaṭṭa (Tamil), popularly called *anicut*, a dam or weir over large and perennial rivers, and collecting and regulating the water for distribution through smaller channels.

Anaikkaran in'am held for the service of preserving anicuts or dams in good order and for keeping off cattle, etc., from destroying the reeds growing thereon.

Anakala in'am held by *kattubadi* peons whose duty it was to carry provisions to village and taluk officials; in'am grant to porters and supply carriers.

Anantaravan younger member of the family.

Anavamarśya grant of land with 'freedom from troubles associated with the visit of royal agents'.

Anchana-kabuliyat confirmed estimate of annual produce.

Anchumna, anchumma the name of an order to the village accountants in the Northern Circars to ascertain the quantity of land in tillage and of seed sown; or to value the crops of the cultivators.

Andharia kotha the dreaded dark room once used as a dungeon for recalcitrant tenants.

Andi-samadhi in'am for the support of the tomb of an *andi* or religious mendicant of the siva sect.

Angazala in'am for performing the service of *angazala kattubadi* peons, whose duties consist in distributing waters of the fields, and in collecting *rayats* for the performance of customary labour.

Anicoody people who work in trade, as common workmen.

Anicut a weir across a river or water channel to regulate the flow of water for irrigation.

Aniyukta, niyukt-āniyukta-rājapuruṣa officials of the king, who were not actually appointed by the government, but occupied posts by the virtue of heredity or election.

Añjinānpugalidam lit. asylums for the fearful or oppressed; the term has been used in the epigraphs from the Travancore state to indicate that the rulers demarcated some lands to enable certain classes of weavers, etc., to colonise them and by exemption of the residents from certain taxes and by the grant of other small concessions to them made these colonies what are called *añjinānpugālidam*.

Anjuvannam a body of merchants which represented an organisation of foreign merchants. The earliest known records of the *Anjuvannam* refers to a group of Jewish traders who acquired settlements on the west coast from the Venad (South Travancore) rulers. The term *Anjuvannam*, wrongly interpreted as a group of five different communities or castes, may well be derived from *Anjuman* perhaps first used by early Arab Muslim traders of the west coast, a name surviving down to the 14th-15th centuries on the Kanara coast among Muslim traders as *Hanjumana*.

Anmosha a type of exemption provided to a village and implies that the royal officers were prohibited from taking possession of anything belonging to the village.

Anna sixteenth part of a rupee; anglicised form of *āṇaka* 1/16th of a rupee.

Anna shrotriyam in'am villages in which the interest of the *in'amdar* is defined to be so many. annas out of each rupee of revenue, the rest going to the government. For further particulars see *hissa shrotriyam*.

Annakavadi in'am for collecting boiled rice from door to door and feeding beggers.

Anniyāyavavadaṇḍa viṛai a term used in the Tamil inscriptions which has been interpretted to mean a tax on unauthorized looms in the village.

Anson Banjar waste land put upon rayats cultivating *in'am* lands. Also the lands which the substantial rayats were not permitted to relinuish.

Anta mahāmātra executive officers in charge of the bordering districts of an empire, could also be ambassadors at the courts of neighbouring kings.

Antarāyam, Antar-āya, Antar-āyam, Antarāyām, Antarāyam (Sanskrit) it is a related term to *āyam*; explained as a local tax-*antara* = local; cash levy on the tenants; supplemenal levies; a land revenue term current during Chola rule; 'a tax', 'revenue' or 'a kind of revenue'; same as *antar-ādāya*; also internal revenue or taxes levied by local bodies, same as *uḻvari* in Tamil; internal revenue; taxes levied by a local body.

Antaḥ-kara, antar-ādāya 'excise duty,' 'internal revenue' or revenue income.

Antara-vaniyoga individual share to make up the shortage in the total revenue occasioned by the grant of exemption of *antar-āya* or *uḻvari*.

Antarāya-kkāśu, antarāya-ppāṭṭam Sanskrit-Tamil, 'internal taxes or minor taxes like the profession tax, etc., payable to village assembly.'

Antarāyak-kācu a variant term for *antarāyām* used in some places during the Chola period; it was also levied on land.

Antarāyam-pāṭṭam-uṭpaṭa-iṛaiyiliyāy a term used in the epigraphs to denote that the taxes inclusive of *antarāyam* and *pāṭṭam* were exempted from a piece of land.

Antaralikam the apartment in a pagoda, next to the shrine.

Anuga-jīvita, aṇuga-jīvita, aṇumga-jīvita a fief held by a king's subordinate for his maintenance; also see, *biḻa-vṛitti, biḻānuvṛtti*.

Anumodita ratisfied.

Anuvarttanā a class of contingent dues which came under the head *varttanā*.

Aparāntaka a term used for the Northern Konkan; also a class of cloth.

Apparenjee Pagoda ¾th of Cantaroy Pagoda.

Apradā '(gift land) not to be alienated'.

Apradā-dharma custom regarding

inalienable gift land.

Aprahata uncultivated land.

Apratikara 'without the right of alienation;' without yield of revenue.

Aputra-dhana, aputrika-dhana confiscation of the property of one dying without leaving a son or an heir, which the king could confiscate; escheat of the property of females.

Aputrika-veṇi 'the property of a person who died without leaving an heir;' the same type of expression is mentioned as *aputrā āputraka āputrakadhana, āputrika*.

Aṛaccalai a tenure denoting lands granted to or held by the feeding houses.

Aṛaikāval superintendent of the temple stores.

Aṟṟuk-karai, aṟṟukkulai tax collected for the services demanded for the maintenance of the river bunds.

Aṟṟukkāl-amañci, aṟṟukkāl-veṭṭi tax demanded for the proper upkeep of channels branching from the rivers.

Aṟṟukkāl-veṭṭi a phrase used in the epigraphs which may mean that for raising embankments, as a precautionary measure against floods and seepage of water, the services of the holders of land, who utilised the river water for cultivation were probably commanded.

Aṟṟup-paṭṭam tax levied on water drawn from river sources.

Aṟukūṟinal puravu 'the land revenue from the sixth part.'

Ara spokes

Ara-nír waters the use of which is unlimited; the term is commonly explained to mean water which is allowed to be taken from small tanks, wells, etc. without limitation; water allowed to flow in greater or less quantity in proportion to the abundance or scarcity in the reservoir, usually from the commencement of June to the end of August.

Araghāṭṭa a water lifting machine; current-driven waterlift, consisting of a series of earthenpots lashed to the periphery of a wheel revolving in a stream; the pots were so inclined to the axis that they dipped while passing a trough placed above the shaft. It was not worked in the same way every where; also known as *rahaṭṭa-ghadiya, ghaṭi-yantra* and *udghāṭana*.

Arakkal (Tamil), an instalment of land-revenue.

Aral in'am *in'am* for the service of storekeeper in a pagoda.

Araṇya land jungle land

Araṇya-karshaṇa clearing the forest.

Arang, aurung the place where goods are manufactured.

Araśu svatantaram a tax collected for discharging the police duties. It may here be pointed out that the *kāvalgārs*, after getting the *pāḍikāval* rights and had, in due course, held the office by inheritance, began to collect a tax for discharging the police duties. This tax was called *araśu svatantaram* in some parts of the Tamil country.

Araśukāvalgār chief *kāvalgār*.

Araśy-pēṛu a type of tax that accrued from the villages.

Arasukaval for performing general police duties. The term is used in contradistinction to *grama kaval* or village police.

Aravadaṇḍam lit 'to use harsh words'; a term used in the epigraphs to denote torture, levy of fines or entering any dwelling houses by the state officials for the collection of land-dues; "the harsh words of punishment inflicted by the servants of Yama."

Arcanā-bhoga, arcanā-vṛtti land set apart for meeting the expenses of worship (*arcanā*) in the temple; an endowment created for conducting worship.

Arcanā-vibhava-kāṇi Sanskrit-Tamil, rent-free land granted to temple priests.

Archanabhagam *in'am* for the service of *pujari* in a pagods; see *pujari*.

Arcot Rupee the rupee of the Nawabs of the Carnatic, struck originally at Arcot, was the currency of the Company; retained its name although coined at Madras, or at Dacca and Calcutta.

Ardha-namasya-vṛtti a gift land, taxed at half the normal rate.

Ardhamāanya, Ardhamanyam land grants subject to a fixed rent payable to the state; land half rent-free.

Arikūli (Tamil), dues payable in handfuls of the stalks harvested.

Arimitikōl the stick that is used to remove the corn by beating the hay.

Arimukkai a type of additional demand on land, over and above the land revenue, charged for payments to village officers.

Ariśi-kkāṇam, Ariśi-kāṇam (Tamil), a type of tax that accrued from the villages; a levy for husking paddy in to rice.

Arrack a spirit distilled from toddy or sugar-cane.

Arroba a measure which could be taken as equal to 28 lbs.

Arthāruvā, andhāruvā levy from the money-lenders on the amounts loaned out.

Arudi-carei, Arudikarei, Aṛudikarai (Tamil), **Ardhachandrarkam** (Sanskrit) Division and conversion of land in to separate possession by the Brahmans and under their own ownership; land tenure in Tamil village, of fixed boundary; and *pala-bhogam* in sanskrit, under which each *mírásidar* enjoys the *mírási* of his own particular cultivated fields, and has no interference whatever with those of his neighbours; and when he sells his *mírási*, he transfers to the purchaser not only his common right to participate, to the extent of the share he holds, in the *perumboc, tarisee mírási maunium, marahs*, and other collective property in the village, but his individual right to certain particular and defined cultivated lands.

Supposing him to hold half a share in an *arudi-carei* village of thirty-two shares, he would possess a sixty-fourth *part* of the whole cultivated lands; but if it were a *pasangcarei* village, he would possess a sixty fourth share only in the whole cultivated lands, from 1 to 64 inclusive.

Tenure in which the occupant holds a defined portion of the village lands of which he has the entire disposal, and let or sell them.

A term used for the old *mirásí* village when held in severalty; the division might be perfect or imperfect, *i.e.* the whole cultivable area might be divided, or part might be left in common. Where part was common the land was usually cultivated by tenants whose rents were taken to meet the revenue and village expenses, so that the individual shares received the whole benefit from their own cultivation. If the produce of the common did not suffice, the deficit was made up by a payment from each sharer. In some districts also called *pāla-bhogam* (Sanskrit).

A form of joint land control whereby all cultivable lands were held individually; a variation on *pasungarai*. However, in this system all cultivable lands were permanently distributed, but all other rights and privileges were held in common.

Aruhaṇa, āruvaṇa, aṛuvaṇa a tax of six *paṇas* levied on *mānya* lands.

Aruppampuchi lit. 'harvest insect.' A number of species of insects are included.

Ary koory (kooly) kanum karunum deed of inclosure and tree cultivation.

Aryacut the area of land watered by a

given source of irrigation.

Arz price, market rate.

Aṣṭa bhoga tejah svāmya, Aṣṭa-bhoga, aiśvary-āṣṭaka, aṣṭa-bhūti complete proprietorship of the soil which included the eight fold rights of possession, e.g. *nidhi, nikṣepa, jala, pāṣāṇa, akṣiṇi, āgami siddha* and *sādhya* which may be translated as deposits of buried treasure, water, stones, the *akṣini*, that which may accrue, that which has been made property, and augmentations. Such proprietorship was called at times *kāṇiyākṣi;* eight classes of the privileges of the donee of a rent-free holding.

These privileges are also enumerated as (i) *nidhi* (a treasure or a hoard, *i.e.* a natural board such as a mine). (ii) *nikṣepa* (a treasure hidden or stored up by some one). (iii) *akṣiṇa* (permanent or lasting benefits), (iv) *āgāmin* (future benefits), (v) *sañcita* (benefits already stored up) (vi) *jala* (waters), (vii) *taru* (trees), and (viii) *pāṣāna* (stones). However, *pāṣāna* could also mean 'hilly area.'

The eight kinds of rights are also sometime mentioned as-*vikraya, dāna, vinimaya, jala, taru, pāṣāṇa, nidhi*, and *nikṣepa*, and also as *nidhi, nikṣepa, jalāmṛta, pāṣāṇa, akṣiṇin, āgāmin, siddha* and *sādhya*. However, all these rights vaguely indicate all kinds of proprietary rights.

Aṣṭādaśa-prakṛti all classes of tenants; tenants belonging to all communities.

Aṣṭabhoga-tejaḥsvāmya unbridled ownership endowed with all the rights associated with the enjoyment of property; translated as 'with eight rights of full possession' though term *aṣṭa* may probably mean 'all' and not merely 'eight.'

Aśal a variety of rice

Asadi in'am *in'am* for beating a drum before the village deity.

Asal, assal, asil, ausil, auzil origin, root foundation; capital stock, principal sum. Original rent/revenue, exclusive of subsequent cesses.

Asal-i-tumár jama, assual tumar jamma the original amount according to the rentroll called *tumár*.

Asalminha gardens tenure a description of service *in'am* tenures prevailing in the Gōdāvari and Krishna districts. They were lands exempted from assessment, but not included under the head of *in'ams* in the public accounts. They were usually granted for the purpose of forming topes or gradens, and were sometimes allowed to be cultivated with ordinary crops free of assessment, but were often assessed to revenue when so cultivated. They have been later treated as *in'ams* and enfranchised under the special sanction of government.

Asara sharing; fixed share.

Asaris in most parts of the Madras Presidency the term *Asari* would denote any of the five artisan castes (carpenters, goldsmiths, blacksmiths, masons, braziers). On the West Coast the term was confined to carpenters, who could enter the houses of the higher castes without polluting them.

Ashur-khana in'am for the maintenance of a building in which the bier, banners, and insignia used at the ceremonies of the Moharram are set up.

Askar regular horse in the Mysore army.

Asnad orders, deeds, vouchers.

Asof, Asoph (A) a title given by Tipu Sultan to certain civil officers.

Assāmikadhana property without heirs.

Astamba 'land originally devoid of vegetation which does not yield any revenue to the state.

Asti a mere particle used to introduce the narration of a grant.

Aṭaṅkal, aḍaṅga a term denoting a

register which recorded all information about lands in a village covering-location, owner, area and crop cultivated; register in which all the land revenue accounts of the village were recorded.

This term is still in vogue in the revenue department of Tamilnadu "a detailed account showing certain particulars in regard to the lands in a village namely number of the field, its extent and owner, the nature of irrigation source, the kind of crop raised etc."

Aṭavi (Tamil), this word was used in two different senses, *e.g.* a soldier and a weaver.

Aṭhavana revenue department.

Aṭi one human foot equal to 10.46 inches; a unit of linear measurement; measuring rods of *aṭi* units used to be of varying length from 9 *aṭi* units, approximately equal to 7 feet 10 inches, to 22 *aṭi* units, approximately a rod of 19 feet and 1 inch in length.

Aṭṭagam division of land.

Aṭṭagattar shareholders in a land.

Atalaya a term used for a rowing galley - 'shore boat often used for patrolling;' coast guard, watch-boat.

Atchkutt rice fields. Lands prepared for the culture of rice.

Athalai wild croton or castor.

Athals lands farmed or rented.

Athoonee, athavani revenue servant in the taluk.

Atikārap-poṉ since several types of payments were demanded from the people for various services by the state through its officials, it could be explained as a payment demanded by the *atikari* official, supposed to be the chief executive. However, the real purpose for which it was demanded, is not clear.

Atikāri lit. one who wields authority; may be considered as a top official in the government; as is clear from the epigraph '*perumāṇaṭi-kaḷukku-atikāram-cheykira*,' that this officer was the servant of the king who wielded authority for the king.

Atsu-kavali tenure for guarding a village or tract of country with the obligation of making good the value of any property stolen.

Atti the name of a deed by which the *jenmíkars* or hereditary tenants of the soil in Malabar, pledge their lands, reserving to themselves two thirds of their value, besides a certain interest therein, amounting to about one-third.

Atti kempoorum the name of a contract in Malabar executed when a hereditary tenant has occasion to borrow an additional sum on a mortgage.

Atti kully kanum the name of a contract, or mortgage deed, nearly synonymous with *atti*.

Atti per the name of a deed in Malabar, by which an hereditary tenant transfers the whole of his interest in his land to a mortgagee.

Attipett ola karunum deed of sale of freehold.

Atur in'am in'am for supplying perfumes to the palegar.

Atvani *subedar's* percentage of the revenue collected.

Auavagas a variety of rice.

Audraṅgika collector of the *udraṅga* tax meaning 'tax on permanent tenants or the principal tax.'

Aunakomban a type of paddy crop raised from seedlings transplanted about the beginning of October and reaped at the beginning of March. It is generally grown on channel lands in clay regurs.

Autoopachal (Tamil) a term used to indicate an area irrigated by a river.

Avadāna, āvadāna, āvedana a present; a tax, tax in general.

Avanḍ-āya (Telugu), name of a tax.

Avanaku *ricinus communis.*

Avani-randhra-nyāya the maxim of the fallow land.

Avani-vetana, pādikāval police duties of a village; contribution for such duties.

Avarai in Kanarese this word means the country beams, *Dolichos lablab.* But in Tinnevelly the name is given to a wild shrub, the leaves of which somewhat resemble senna and are used as an adulterant of senna, as well as green manure.

Avarajat abstract accounts showing the collection from each *rayat* as also the total for the village.

Avaram, avarai *cassia auriculate.*

Avasaravarttanai a type of tax that accrued from the villages.

Awaraja a register (of villages).

Ayam surcharge

Ayacret total cultivable land.

Ayacut reputed measurement of land. Land prepared for cultivation; the area of land watered by a given source of irrigation.

Ayakaṭṭu (Tamil), popularly written as *ayacut*; area watered by the tank; the area capable of irrigation from a reservoir or source.

Ayaktakas, ayuktakas headmen of the villages.

Ayyagalu teachers in the *lingayat* household.

Ayyam days, times, period, season, reign.

Azmayish trial, examination, inspection.

B

B'il mukta (Arabic='in the lump'); generally for a lump payment of revenue, etc., to sum of revenue allotted to a village, which the cultivators distributed for payment among themselves. However, the distribution once made lasted as long as the lease or settlement.

Bāda (Kannada), a town or village.

Bāhya, bāhy-ābhyantar-ādāya, puṟavāyam, Puṟa-kaḍamai 'income from the sale of things imported in a village'; 'revenue from external sources (collected mainly in cash)'; 'external taxes' - taxes and fees payable to the state.

Puṟa-kaḍamai is the same as *puṟav-āyam. Bāhya* and *abhyantara* may mean respectively taxes payable to the king and those payable to the village authorities.

Bānisa slaves.

Bághayat, bághát, bagahat, bajyhat, baugayher, baugayut gardens, garden lands; any fields (as a class) cultivated with sugar-cane, vegetables, etc., always irrigated and manured; this land is '*motásthal,*' if watered from wells, the water being raised by buckets, '*mot*' a large bucket; and '*pátásthal*', if from tanks or dams, the water being brought in by small water-courses, '*pát*' a raised watercourse.

Báki, baky remainder; what remains.

Báki kifáyat, baky keffyet remaining profit, or surplus profit. The balance of profit arising from the original selling price of salt, before appropriated to individual benefit; but afterwards resumed, and incorporated with the public revenue.

Báné (in Coorg) holdings of wood-land attached to rice-fields, as an appurtenance, to supply grass, wood and branches to yield ash-manure. In Coorg proper the holder of cultivable land would acquire the use of an appurtenant plot of '*báné*' land-a plot of forest land varying from 4 or 5 to 300 acres, later on it was limited to double the area of the principal holding; located in the slopes above the valley where the rice cultivation was; destined to supply the above things; produce to be strictly use for the supply of the agricultural domestic wants of the holder; if timber, etc., was sold, the tenure was infringed, and the government had a right to demand seignorage on the wood, sandal-wood trees found in *báné* land were always reserved as the property of government.

Bára-balúté the 'twelve' village servants and officials-*patel*, the headman; *karnam* accountant; *shroff* or *notagar*, to examine the coins paid in, a useful functionary in earlier times when coins were so various; *nirganti*, to look after the distribution of the irrigation; *taliyári* or *tóti*, village constable; potter; blacksmith; gold-smith; carpenter; barber; washerman; astrologer, to tell the auspicious days for beginning to plough, harvesting etc.

Báramahál the 'twelve revenue-estates;' acquired by Madras government; now the Salem district.

Báricudu same as *vetti*; he performs menial duties, carries messages, etc.

Bad fixed payments of grain out of the gross produce of a village.

Baḍagá (called '*Burghers*' in the early

reports), tribe, was the latest comer to the Nílgiri (Nílagírí) district, inhabited the settled villages; the only permanently cultivating class of the area. The nature of the area favoured the settlement of small hamlets with a certain area belonging to each. In the immediate vicinity of the hamlet, the manure from the cattle '*kraals*' enabled a limited area of 'home farm' or permanent cultivation to be kept up; for the rest, the poverty of the soil or the habits of the people, or both, induced them to cultivate only bits here and there, over the area attached to the hamlet, the rest lying fallow; it was in fact, a modified form of ***kúmri*** cultivation.

Badai in'am for the service of village carpenter.

Badarkah, budrucka a convoy, or guard upon the road. A tax for conveying goods, protecting the highways, and attending to the inland navigation.

Badernavis special impost levied by Lionel Place during 1793-95, consisting of *wāratundu* and *vilaituṇdu*; a Persian term was "a compound..... word conveying precisely the suppressing of the produce of lands, defalcation, and eccisions from the Government traced by an examination of cultivation, and deeds connected with it....," as opposed to *iyenberiz* which was the actual or normal account of produce.

The *badernavis* consisted of two elements - *wāra thunḍu* ('share deficit') and *vilai tuṇḍu* ('price deficit').

Badi-bad in'am lands held on a favourable assessment generally by persons of the *ratsavar* caste in the Gōdāvari and Krishna districts.

Badulu fees in grain, paid to the village servants before the division of the crop.

Bagayat garden lands; garden.

Bagh-mari in'am granted as a reward for killing tigers..

Bahal enlistment, appointment

Bahattara-niyōg-ādhipati high ranking officer of state (during Kākatīyas); his exact functions are not definitely known-whether he was a mere titular dignity, or an officer ranking only below the king and wielding enormous power.

Bail land yielding three crops.

Baja-wala in'am for the services of musicians in pagodas.

Bajerack ruined (villages)

Bajra a kind of millet; same as *cambu* (Tamil).

Bakshi, Bakhshi (P) a military officer-in-charge for payments of salaries or an officer who kept an account of all disbursements connected with military tenures.

Bali in'am for making sacrifices to the village deities to avert calamities and to promote the common welfare of the village.

Balijas the chief Telugu trading caste, found all over Madras presidency-many of them landowners and cultivators. Their usual caste name is Nayudu, but sometime they take that of Chetti.

Balla a measure, generally being equal to two *seers*.

Banḍi carriages

Banṭula-āyamu a maintenance-rate and formed the allowance paid to foot-soldiers for their support.

Banagar in'ams for making fireworks for pagodas or zamindars.

Band, bund a band, bond or fastening. An embankment against inundation.

Bandaikkai ladies fingers (*Hibiscus csculentus*). The unripe fruit which somewhat resemble small cucumbers, are eaten as vegetable.

Bandaloo the customary fees for the *karnams*; village artificers and servants.

Bandar, bunder a port or harbour.

Bandela in'am held by inferior village

servants for preventing cattle from straying in to the fields and injuring the crops.

Bandiman cartman.

Banjaras itinerant grain merchants.

Bants the word *Bant* means soldier, and the *Bants* are the chief land-owning and cultivating class of South Kanara. Their language is Tulu, but their customs closely resemble those of the Nayars. They are known to be fond of cock-fighting and buffalo racing. Yoked in pairs, the racing buffaloes would draw modified levelling boards over a muddy paddy field. Each pair would race over the course separately and prizes would be given taking into consideration their speed, style, and especially for the height and width of the splash of mud and water.

Bantumana in'am for doing service as peon.

Bapatu' matter, item, affair, head in accounts.

Barața a plant grown for fencing.

Barbast established customs

Bariké (Coorg), grazing ground; some lowlying barren land on which the cattle graze.

Bariki in'am granted to man of low caste who waits upon the village officers, generally assists in measuring land. Also see *toti in'am.*

Bariz rent. A term used in **Dindigul,** same as *jama.*

Barr the regular infantry in Mysore; it consisted of two classes: the *avval barr* or first class, better trained and better paid than the *duyyam barr* or second class.

Barut-goli in'am for supplying the palegar with gunpowder and ball.

Basa oath of service.

Basivi in'am held by prostitutes who have been married or dedicated to Siva, and who attend upon the idol.

Bati a brick kiln; a still

Batta charge on discount against non-standard coin; extra allowance.

Battai, hissa, warum land for which the revenue was paid in kind by the division of the produce between the cultivator and the state.

Batti (in Coorg), a land-measure; a very small land measure, of which 100 equal to three acres; according to another account, twenty five *battis* are equal to ¾ acres.

Bayinidi in'am for singing before the village deity.

Bazí, bazee sundry, various, miscellaneous.

Bazí daf-ah, bazee duffa sundry items; various items of taxation. Revenue derived from fruits, artificers, etc.

Bazí jama, bazee jamma miscellaneous total; aggregate of revenue arising from sundry lands held by brahmins and others.

Bazí zamín, bazee zameen sundry, or miscellaneous lands. The term is particularly applied to such lands as are exempted from payment of public revenue, or very lightly rated; not only such as are held by brahmins, or appropriated to the support of places of worship, etc., but also to the lands held by the officers of government. There formerly existed an office for registering those lands, called *bazí zamin daftar.*

Bazi-kharach, bazeecurtch, bazee-kurch, bazeh kherck sundry expenses, various contingent disbursements, and indemnities allowed to *zamindars,* in lieu of all expenses, otherwise unprovided for.

Be charagh desert, ruined, depopulated.

Bēdige, Bédige taxes on rent-free lands; lit. 'benevolences;' a term used in the inscription to indicate that *bēdige* was collected from the people to use the amount for the service of god; it belonged to the category of taxes usually collected for some specific purposes.

Bedabinugu a class of mean coquetter fond of show (a tax was collected by the state from them also).

Bediga a tax or a favourable assessment; quit-rent on *in'ams*. The word is synonymous with *jodi*. Also see, *Bēḍige* above.

Begari in'am granted for the performance of the lowest offices in a village, as those of a porter, grain watcher, scavenger, etc; the same as *vetti in'am*.

Begayet see *bághayat*.

Beldar in'am held for the service of performing bricklayer's work.

Bellum a type of sugar.

Beríz (Persian), account; the recorded land revenue assessment; total demand against a village or a holding, after adjusting accounts; recorded assessment of Hyder's reign, corrected by comparison with accounts of actual cultivation, and deducting some amount for expenses of servants employed; *'beríz* deduction' - this means, cases where a certain part of the revenue was deducted, *i.e.* not paid into the treasury, but handed to the village headman, who would disburse that for the purpose to which it was to be applied, *e.g.* pay of village servants, or where an amount once consolidated with the revenue was separated and paid to a special purpose, *e.g.* road-cess in the Krishna district. A total of a territorial assessment; revenue settlement; an amount of assessment; the total assessment of a village or district.

Besa-vaga, besa-makkaḷu a term used in the Kanarese inscriptions to denote 'bonded servants' possibly attached to the land.

Bestas a Telugu caste whose hereditary occupation was fishing and hunting, but have largely taken to agriculture.

Bettu land dependent on rain-fall (in S. Ka'nara); there were three classes of land - land was known as *'bail'* when irrigated or yielding three crops; *'majal'* irrigated land yielding two crops; *'bettu'* land dependent on the abundant rainfall only and yielding one crop only.

Betunes, the a class of persons who, according to Barbosa, had the occupation of salt-making.

Bhāga, rājabhāga a fiscal term denoting king's regular and legitimate share.

Bhāṇḍara-pustaka, banḍāra-ppottagam lit. 'account book of the treasury;' a treasury accountant.

Bhágam, baugaum a share, or portion.

Bhaikṣaka land set apart for charity.

Bhakt-āya, bhatt-āya same as *bhaktādāya*.

Bhakta-grāma, bhatta-grāma provision village; village granted for maintenance.

Bhakt-ādāya, pakt-ātāyam revenue in rice or paddy.

Bhale-log a term used to denote persons of rank who were admitted in to the courts of the *zamindars* by virtue of their position. They enjoyed revenue-free lands to enable them to support their dignity.

Bhaṁḍi, baṁdi 'a cart;' really 'a cart load'

Bhaṇḍārin, Bhāṇḍārin officer in charge of the treasury.

Bhandagarika treasure

Bharati in'am for the service of reading Mahabharata in pagodas.

Bharti full; used in South Ka'nara of estates paying a full assessment, as against *'kambharti'* or reduced.

In Nílgiri the term had a different meaning. There under *'bharti'* system each cultivator held from government a *pattá* for the area of land which he ordinarily cultivated each year; but the available land being practically unlimited as compared with the demand for it, and of being of little value to government, the cultivator was permitted to cultivate a different plot each year, shifting from one place to another at will within certain limits, but retaining, by common consent and without payment, a preferential claim, or lien, on the plots formerly cultivated by him, and returning to them in rotation after two, three, or more years, according to the nature of the soil and the period of fallow which was considered necessary to restore its fertility. As such, though the area in a man's *pattá* and for which alone he was charged assessment, might be only ten acres, he was in the habit of cultivating in rotation various plots of land aggregating thirty or forty acres, or even more in poor and sparsely-populated tracts. The '*bharti*' system was abolished as per Secretary of State's sanction in 1863; but no one really paid the slightest attention to the orders, and the practice continued as before. However, later on it came to end.

Bhaṭās armed retainers; members of the police and military forces.

Bhaṭṭa vṛttimānyams land/villages/ perquisites granted to carry on work connected with learning.

Bhaṭṭa-grāma a village owned by learned Brahmans as a rent-free holding; same as an *agrahāra* village.

Bhaṭṭavṛtti, Bhaṭṭa-vṛtti, Bhaṭṭa-bhāga, Bhatta-vritti a general term to denote *in'ams* granted to brahmans/Hindus for charitable purposes. Secular *in'ams* ; a grant for the maintenance of the *Bhaṭṭas* or learned brahmans; grant or perquisite appropriated to brahmans to enable them to impart regular religious or secular instruction to others.

Bhaṭṭavṛtti-mānya tax free land (*in'am*) given for the support of brahmans; same as *bhaṭṭa-vṛtti*.

Bhatraz in'am held by bards for the service of singing the praises of the *zamindar* or palegar.

Bhatta, Batta allowance to troops in the field.

Bhaviṣya-kkiḍai-ppuṛam (Sanskrit-Tamil), tax-free land set apart to enable a teacher to reside permanently in a village for teaching.

Bhikhu-hala, bhikshu-hala cultivated land offered to the Buddhist monks.

Bhōga-āyakam lit. 'mortgage by possession'; lands mortgaged along with their possessions. It may he pointed out that in the Vijayanagar days the lands possessed under *bhṓga-āyakam* were to remain in the name of the mortgagee only for a period of twelve years.

Bhōgam, Bhógam, bhogum, bogum enjoyment; possession; one of the terms used in the inscriptions to denote 'a tax'. It is not easily explicable as there are several terms which signify almost similar ideas and differ only in certain minute details; tax per crop.

Bhōgapatra written deeds

Bhógyádi, bhogyadhi a species of mortgage in Kanara, signifying pledge in possession.

Bhógyam this term which literally signifies that which is to be enjoyed, is given to that species of mortgage in which the produce of the land pledged is *enjoyed* in lieu of the interest on the sum lent.

Bhog-addharaṇika 'the collector of the king's share of the grains'.

Bhoga, Bhogas, bhāgas administrative sub divisions of the *rājya*; at times synonymous with *vishaya;* use; fruition; enjoyment; possession of two kinds-with obstruction, and unobstructed or undisputed; important territorial sub-division esp. under the Pallavas, Vasishtis and Matharas. The incharge, or sometime even referred as ruler, of the *bhoga* was called *bhogika*. During the later periods, the *bhogika* has been referred as a petty officer connected with village administration and enjoyed revenue free land; 'enjoyment'; 'property', a *jāgīr*; also a territorial unit which was generally the subdivision of a district.

Bhoga-āyaka land held as the result of a mortgage.

Bhoga-janapada a free holding in the country-side or a rent-free area.

Bhoga-patra a deed recording conveyance of land; a lease deed; the deed of reconveyance of land.

Bhogapati, Bhogapatika, Bhogikapāla, Bhogikapālaka an *in'amdar* or *jāgīrdār*, or an officer incharge of *in'am* lands or *jāgīrs*, or the officer incharge of a territorial unit called *bhoga*; these officials carried on the revenue administration by revenue-free lands. Their positions were hereditary. Esp. Rashtrakuta period; incharge of an administrative unit (during Rāshṭrakūṭas); their appointments were usually made either in recognition of administrative ability or as a reward for military services. The posts became hereditary in the cases where the original officers had sons who had proved their worth on the battle field or in the secretariat; they carried on revenue administration in co-operation with hereditary revenue officers; they were remunerated by the grant of revenue-free lands.

Bhogapatram a temporary assignment.

Bhogi-rūpa one who enjoys a free-holding as a representative of the real free-holder, or a title-holder who is not in actual possession of the land.

Bhogika, Bhogin, Bhoktṛ the owner of a *bhoga* or *jāgīr*; a *jāgirdār* or *in'amdār*.

Bhogottara, Bhogatrā land granted to the family priest for his services; grant for the enjoyment of a Brahman or deity.

Bhoja, Bhojaka pośar a *jāgīrdār*; title of a feudatory; the faminine form *Bhojiki*; one who enjoys a thing; the possessor.

Bhoy an individual of caste of palanquin carriers; also a fisherman.

Bhū, bhūmi, bhūmī a particular land measure and regarded as equal to four *bhūmāṣakas*.

Bhūmi one of the classes of territorial divisions (*Kākatīya* period).

Bhūmicchidra 'uncultivable land'.

Bhūmicchidra-nyāya lit. 'the maxim of the fallow land'; the principle of the revenue-free enjoyment of land by one who brings it under cultivation for the first time; an old custom of allowing a person, who first brings a plot of fallow or jungle land under cultivation for the first time, to enjoy it without paying any revenue.

Bhūmicchidrapidhāna-nayāya the only difference between this and *bhūmicchidra-nyāya* is that it also means 'the maxim of covering up the hole in the land' referring to the reclamation of fallow land for the first time.

Bhūta-pāta-pratyāya, bhūta pratyāya, bhūta-vāta-pratyāya, bhūtopātta-pratyāya 'the income resulting from storms, earthquakes, changes in the course of a river, elemental or natured changes in the land'; some believe it to be 'excise and octroi duties.'

Bhúdána-patram deed of a gift of land; this type of deeds also afford specimens of one of the modes by which the *mirási* has passed from the original holders, to Brahmans and others, strangers in the land.

Bhúlócam the earth.

Bhu-sakti it was a belief that in the black cotton areas of Rayalaseema the village goddess, called Peddamma, in whom resided '*bhu-sakti*,' which made the earth bring forth crops, while Gangamma ensured an adequate supply of water in tanks.

Bhukta, bugata (Telugu) 'one who

enjoys;'

Bhukti, viṣaya, maṇḍala small territorial unit like a Pargana in South India; an area including a group of districts; a territorial unit; not a province of considerable size, but a relatively small unit comparable to *tāluk* or *tahsīl*.

Bhuktipati a *jāgīrdār*, the officer incharge of a territorial unit called *bhukti*.

Bhumi in the fifteenth century (both in Andhra and Telangana) the basic territorial unit was *sima* which was grouped in to *bhumi* or districts.

Bhumi tottah garden ground.

Bhúmi-vocalu the cultivator of the land; *bhúmi* in Sanskrit means the *earth* generally, and *vocalu* in Kanarese is a *cultivating* inhabitant, an individual of any of the agricultural castes; however, the expression used in some records respecting the other persons stated to be in possession of the lands enumerated, this term seems intended to describe the occupant rather than the proprietor of the soil.

Bhumikreya sadanam deed by which the property right to land is sold (in Kanara); under this deed the buyer is given whole of the said grounds and everything belonging to them, including cocoanut trees, betlenut trees, jack trees, mango trees, earth, or stone, its woods, springs, hidden treasures, good or evil, its every production, and the tanks or wells that might be dug therein; was to pay the *sirkar's* dues, and register the same in his name. The person passing the above deed was required to give a prescribed certificate to the *sirkar's kach'hari*.

Bhumipa, bhūmīśvara protector or master of the earth; a title by which a king was generally known.

Bhuta-bail in'am for making offerings to malignant spirits during the festivals of the village deities.

Bīḻ-ānuvṛtti, bīḻa-vṛtti (Kannaḍa-Sanskrit), land-grant held by a king's subordinate for his maintenance.

Bīsva a land measure equal to 1/20 of a *bīghā*.

Bíbí-nazr, beebee nuzzer *bíbí* a lady, and *nazr* a present. A present to the lady. An annual present to the *Begum* or principal wife of the Cuddapah Nawab.

Biabares, the a class of persons about whom Barbosa writes that they dealt in "goods of every kind both in the sea ports and inland, wherever their trade is of most profit. They gather to themselves all the pepper and ginger from the Nayres and husbandmen, and oft times they buy the new crops beforehand, in exchange for cotton clothes and other goods which they keep at the seaports. Afterwards they sell them again and gain much money." They may be identified with the Ravari Nayres akin to the *Taragan* or *Mūttāns* two mercantile castes in the area.

Bighā, bīghā a land measure

Bíjwár (bíj=seed); old land - revenue assessment based on calculation of seed used and its return (in South Ka'nare).

Bilkoḍe (Kannada), tolls.

Billavas the Tulu speaking toddy-drawers of South Kanara, and the most numerous caste of that district.

Bilmaqta, Bilmakta, Bilmucta by estimate. A term used in the Northern Circars, for a kind of tenure where the land is held at a very low rent; lands held at a fixed rent below the usual standard; a term used to denote stipulated, fixed; the term is applied especially to a tenure by which a *rayat* holds his land at a fixed rate per plough or per *bigha* or to the engagement by which his rent is fixed for a given term without liability to enhancement, a stipulated salary granted to any individual. Also see, *B'ilmukta* above.

Bilvarchana in'am for the service of performing *puja* with the leaves of the *bilva* tree (*aegle marmelos*).

Bissoi tenure, Bissoi, Bissoy a class of hill chieftains in Ganjan who held their lands, sometime whole villages, on the tenure of performing military or police service.

Biswa measurement of land, twentieth part of a *bigha*.

Bittuvaṭṭa, bittukaṭṭe (Kannada), 'a portion of the produce derived from the lands irrigated by tanks, or wet land irrigated by a tank, granted to the person who built the tank or repaired it'. .

Blackgram, Black Pessaloo, oolundoo *Phaseollus mungo*.

'Board-sifárish' reduced holdings favoured by the Board of Revenue (in South Ka'nara), *i.e.* estates disadvantageously situated, which could not be expected to pay in full, were uncertain and were settled annually.

Boddika a currency of foreign country in circulation during medieval South India; it can be thought of as representing 1.625 d.

Boha a kind of tree, the bark of which was used for making ropes.

Boi in'am for service as a palanquin bearer.

Bommalata in'am for the service of exhibiting puppet shows during festivals.

Bovenlanden 'uplands.'

Bowries, Bāolī a large well with stairs descending to the level of the water.

Boyas, Bedars, Bōyas, bedas a race of hardy warriors (occupied the northern marches of the Pallava kingdom corresponding to the present Nellore district); they doubtless took a lower place in the social scale; a caste of hunters and soldiers of Mysore and neighbouring districts, from whom Hyder Ali's armies were largely recruited. Many of the palegars, local military chieftains of South India belonged to this caste. Even after taking up agriculture as their main profession, they continued to remain skillful hunters and fond of wrestling.

Boyavandeloo, Bendars, those who follow hunting as profession same as *Bāōyas, Bedas, Bedars.*

Bṛahdhala 'the big plough'; name of a land measure.

Brāhmaṇa-rāśa (rāja) kkāṇam (Sanskrit Tamil), tax payable by the Brahmans (*Purohita*) to the king.

Brāhmaṇa-vimśati tithe upon villagers for the maintenance of the Brahmans.

Brahm-āṇḍa one of the various forms of gifts given to the brahmans.

Brahmadeya religious donation of land granted to spiritual guides, the priests, and those learned in vedas; this donation implied certain immunities, besides assigning various specific privileges to be enjoyed by the donee, often contained the clause that the grant 'it to last as long as the sun and the moon, etc., shall endure', is to be enjoyed in the lineage of the donee's sons and grandsons; and that 'no one is to obstruct the donee in cultivating the land and causing it be cultivated'; the grant, however, would remain as such if the donees 'donot commit treason against government', 'that they are not guilty of offences of slaying Brāhmaṇs, committing theft, adultery, or acts prejudicial to the king (or) engaged in frays with other villages'.

It was Brahman-controlled circle of villages - a type of settlement under the control of a group of Brahmans. It was, as opined by Burton Stein, a mode of agrarian integration in which several extant settlements were brought together under the management of a group of Brahmans who became the major beneficiaries of the production of the land and who made the crucial decisions about the utilization of resources within the circle of villages. There was a great deal of variations among such settlements, some of which were established on such slender resources or under such difficult conditions that they failed to maintain themselves. In all cases, the establishment of a *brahmadeya* created a comprehensive integration among a circle of established and productive villages under the central direction of a group of Brahmans; a grant or perquisite appropriated to brahmans; the grants were in the form of small lands or whole villages, made usually in recognition of a brahman's scholarship or to enable him to impart regular religious or secular instruction to others; it comprised predominant population of the land-based literati, the brahmans as land-holders or the occupants; land or village given as gift (generally revenue-free) to Brahmans; land to be granted or in the possession of Brahmans; they may in most case, have meant the giving away of rights, economic and administrative, to the donees but instances are not waiting to show that they were not completely exempt from revenue payments to the king.

Brahmadeya-kkiḻavar (Sanskrit - Tamil), sole owner of a *brahmadeya* village; sometime supposed to be the headman or chief of a *brahmadeya* village.

Brahmandaya, Brahmadaya a general term denoting *in' ams* held by Brahmans for their personal benefit.

Brahmapura, brahmapuri, agara-brahmadeya a revenue free village in the possession of Brahmans.

Brattis cowdung cakes.

Bubandu lekka an account of boundaries of fields.

Bulla a large land measure in Coimbatore equal to 3.38 acres.

Bulootch a bundle of corn, to which, in the Northern Circars, each of the *bulootedars*, or village artificers, was entitled.

Burki in'am same as *toti in' am*

Buruj in'am granted as a reward for building a tower or bastion for the protection of a village.

Busa chaff

Busi-bhaṁḍālu (Telugu), stores of unhusked grain.

C

Cālī a system of land revenue.

Cālikar-acca-taṛi, cālikai-taṛi the terms used to denote tax levied on looms possessed by *Cāliyaweavers.*

Cāmara, cavala, cavela name of a coin, 1/8 of a *pagoda.*

Cāṇ a basic unit of linear measurement; a *cāṇ i.e.*, one span was equal to approximately 9 inches; *aṭi i.e.*, one human foot was equal to 10.46 inches, and *piṭi i.e.* one fist was equal to 4.5 inches. However, the measuring rods which were used for the purposes of land survey were formed by the multiples of such units of length. The measuring rods pertaining to the *cāṇ* units used to vary from 12 *cāṇ* units, equal to approximately 9 feet, to 20 *cāṇ* units, equal to 15 feet approximate.

Cāni, Cowny See *Kani.*

Cāturmāsya the season consisting of four months, viz. *grīsma* consisting of the *pūrṇimānta* months of Caitra, Vaiśākha, Jyeṣṭha and Āṣāḍha; *varṣā* consisting of Śrāvana, Bhādrapada, Āśvina and Kārttika; and *hemanta* consisting of Mārgaśirṣa, Pauṣa, Māgha and Phālguna. However, officially year was divided into six seasons, viz. *grīṣma* (Jyeṣṭha - Āṣāḍha), *varṣā* (Śrāvaṇa-Bhadrapada), *śarad* (Āśvina-Kārttika), *hemanta* (Mārgaśīrṣa-Pauṣa), *śita* (Māgha-Phālguna), and *vasanta* (Caitra-Vaiśākha).

Cārikai tax or toll levied on the commodities passing through high roads. Some of the other terms used in the epigraphs for the same purpose are - *cārikai-ceṇvari, canti-āyam.*

Cāvaḍi, śāvaḍi, uśāvaḍi an administrative unit or territorial division.

Cáni-cuppatam fee in kind received by the *mírásidars* after the grain is thrashed.

Cáni-mányam, káni-mányam rent-free lands held jointly by the *Cániyátchicars* as type of their proprietary right; rent-free lands of the *mírásidárs.*

Cáni-mérei grain-fee paid to the proprietors; fee in kind received by the *mírásidárs* before thrashing.

Cáni-peru heritage, hereditary property, and, to obtain; anything obtained, degree, dignity; the whole signifies, the consequence or dignity derived from the possession of hereditary landed property.

Cáni-sudantram all the rights of ownership; the right of hereditary property.

Cabaia a thin cotton linen gown generally worn by brahmans.

Cadjan a term used by the Europeans in the peninsula to denote the leaves of the fan *palmira* tree, on which the natives of the south wrote with an iron style; though the origin of the word is doubtful but is supposed to be of Portuguese origin.

Cadvel, Carvel *Acacia arabica.*

Cairo coir.

Caitya a heap of stone *i.e.* an embankment of stone or any other material.

Cakra-kāṇikkai (Sanskrit-Tamil), profession tax paid by the potters, also called *tirigai-āyam.*

Calavasem marah given in the shape of deductions from the gross produce of all the cultivated lands in the village paying tax to government-generally given to the free labourers, in lieu of hire, and, in some cases, indulgent masters grant it even to their slaves also. Where *pyacarries* cultivate the land, the *calavasem* is appropriated from them, and other *marahs* paid to the *mírásidárs.*

Calingulah sluice for water.

Callapay a kind of small plough.

Calvásám entitlement of the slaves to a share in the produce of every crop, which they receive at various rates and in various modes; also called *sudantram.*

Caṇḍeśvara-pperuvilai (Sanskrit, Tamil) lit. the sale price of *caṇḍeśvara* (the Śiva temple); sale price of land purchased from a Śiva temple.

Candareen equivalent to a weight of about 5 gm., a gold *fanam* was generally reckoned in weight equal to one *candareen.*

Candayem, kandayam land paying money rent.

Candrādittaval, candrādittavar, candrādityavat (Tamil), 'as long as the moon and the sun last'; in perpetuity.

Candy anglicised from of *khaṇḍi,* a weight of different value in different parts; a measure of weight; the Madras *candy* was equal to 500 lb.

Canji rice gruel.

Canti-āyam road cess.

Car in Tinnevelly, the autumnal harvest, beginning with September and ending about the middle of December.

Carah the share of a *pung* or portion of landed property in a village

Carahatonilam the name by which sapphire was known in the kingdom of Calicut.

Coramboo earthern bund put across a water course.

Caray four shares or *pungs* in the village tenure called *agraharahvadiky.*

Careis, carays, carais shares; shares into which the village was originally divided on the formation of the village. "The right of *carai* rarely conveys a right to any proprietor to any specific spot of land in perpetuity, and wherever this practice prevails, it seems a departure from the original institution; the property of the whole village is common to the whole number of proprietors. Every transaction of revenue, every matter of loss and gain, is common to them all, to the extent of their respective shares; and as they are all jointly and separately responsible for the revenue of the village, according to the strict construction of their tenure, so they are all alike equally entitled to any emolument or advantage which may arise therefrom. So tenacious indeed are they of this established rights of every village benefit being in common, that a sort of lottery takes place at stated times to make a new distribution of village lands, by which they change owners for a certain period until the lottery is renewed. By these means they generally continue to pass from one proprietor to another, so as to exclude effectually indeed, the right of any particular spot, but to establish the right of the general body to the whole village in common," wrote S.R. Lushington.

Carī, carī - kṣetra pasture land.

Caroo a crop of rice sown in April and reaped in June-July; in Tinnevelly, the autumn harvest beginning with September and reaped in about the middle of December.

'Carsy crop' a term used for the second crop in the sugarcane cultivation.

Caruveppillai *Murraya koenigii.*

Cash anglicised form of Tamil *kāśu;*

name of a small copper coin.

Cassada, cassava *Manihot utilissima.*

Cathavany a ledger.

Caturaka, catvara a public place in a village, or a police station, a tax for the maintenance of a police station.

Caturi, chaturi a light rowing boat; 'a vessel which goes with a sail and oars... made of one piece, of the length of twelve or thirteen paces each. The opening is so narrow that one man cannot sit by the side of the other... sharp at both ends.'

Caturvēdimaṅgalam (*brahmadēya* village) it used to be consisted of central village to which were attached a large number of small ones. Each village was divided into a number of wards. Each *caturvēdimaṅgalam* had an assembly of a certain number of members. A high standard of qualification was expected of them. They were expected to have studied four Vedas; were expected to have acquired a good knowledge of the conduct of sacrifices and performed them. They were also expected to have besides these cultural attainments a good physique to bear the strain of other work, the term was often denoted by kindred names, *brahmadēya, managalam, agaram, brahmapuram, agrahāra agara-brahmadeya, agara-brahmadēśa, brahmadēśam* and *brahmamangalam.*

It may be emphasised that a brahman village would not include only those who belonged to the community of brahmans, rather it accommodated other classes as well-potters, blacksmiths, goldsmiths, washermen, and village servants all lived there, though in separate *cēris,* close to the *brahman* quarter of the village; it was brahman village in the sense that the land of the village was held by the brahman community.

It is also possible that *caturvēdimangalams* owed their peculiar characteristics to the fact that they owed their origin to kings, who consciously established such villages; it seems more accurate to say that it was a village which was allowed a large measure of control in managing local affairs-made necessary by the fact that the inhabitants of the village, by the terms of the original grant or establishment of the village, were bound to render certain dues and services to the landlord body and the latter was allowed, nay required, to conduct the revenue administration in its own way-and that this landlord body was united by some elements of joint-ownership, either whole or partial; from the economic point of view, it was a community of landholders united together by the fact that they owned all or some land in common, and that they were a landlord body placed over a body of tenants who were bound to render certain services or dues to them, and that the landlord community had a large discretion in managing the affairs of the locality-which they did through a highly developed system of committees, subject to the village assembly; same as *agrahāra*; a village owned by Brahmans, generally revenue free; also called *maṅgala*; written as *śaruppeṭi-maṅgalam* in Tamil; sometimes suffixed to names of localities especially in the Tamil speaking area.

Cauḷūru mahajans.

Cauri, Cāmara, Cavarālu spelt *chowrie* in English; a flywhisk; sometime the right of its use was granted to persons as a mark of honour.

Cavathe, chavathā a levy of one-fourth; or may be a levy of 6 out of a unit of 20.

Cawney, Cawnie, cáni a land measurement equal to 1.32 acres. Also see *káni.*

Cazhani fields of wet land.

Cēris there is a mention in the inscriptions, of separate quarters, called *cēris,* for the habitation of the artisans and other classes of people-the toddy-drawers, the artisans, the untouchables, the washermen etc.; all villages did not have all these *cēris* and only the bigger ones could apparently boast of having them.

Two other *cēris* find mention in the inscriptions-the *talaivāyccēri* and the *taliccēri*; however, they do not refer to quarters of separate communities but rather denote distinction in location; the former means the *cēri* or quarter, or street near the entrance to the village, and the latter, the 'temple-quarter,' generally inhabited by dancing girls.

Cēvakap-pēṟu a term referring to the local officials who were in the service of the people and for that service a payment was demanded.

Cekkātāyam cess on oil press.

Cekkuk-kaṭamai, cekkiṟaip-pāṭṭam, Cekkātāyam a term used for an occupational due, esp. dues on oil press; different terms used to denote tax on the oil-presses.

Ceṉṉīr, nīr-amañci, ceṉṉīr-amañci, ceṉṉīr-vetti, ceṉṉīr-potuviṉai, Ceṉṉir-vetti a service tax demanded for the proper upkeep of the village tank; different terms used to depict the citizens expected to render regular service to the tanks. In certain areas where, in the absence of rivers, rain water was stored in tanks and was utilized for irrigation. The services may include (i) cleaning the tank, (ii) raising and strengthening the bund, and (iii) the proper upkeep of its sluices and branch channels.

Ceṭṭiṟai = *Cheṭṭi + iṟai*, i.e., tax on chetty merchant.

Ceṭṭiṟai-vari duty levied on Chetty merchant community.

Chārāsana pasturage; also according to some 'chāra' and 'āsana' mean respectively 'moving about' and 'encamping.'

Chávadi a small building used for the office of a village officer; resting house for travellers; public place or office of assembly in the village where business is transacted; also *kovil, chauri*, etc.

Chaitya heaps of stone, *i.e.* an embankment of stone or any other material.

Chaityagrhas shrines-for the residence of Buddhist monks.

Chak-bandi in'am an *in'am* with defined boundaries as distinguished from one without any fixed locality, such as an *ivu* or *dittam in'am*.

Chakkiliyans the leather workers of the Tamil districts.

Chakra, chakram a small gold coin in circulation in Mysore; usually equal to 10 *fanams*; a silver coin 12¾ part of a rupee; an ancient coin current formerly in South India, equal to 1/10th of a *pagoda*.

Chali permanently cultivated land of high assessment; land under permanent cultivation; also called *upanum*.

Chalidomma black water, also called 'quarter evil and black leg.' An infectious cattle disease accompanied by one or more swellings most frequently occuring on the hind quarter. The course of the disease used to be rapid and only a few cases would recover.

Chaligéni, Chaligeni (Kanarese) tenancy-at-will, a tenant-at-will (in south Kánara), as opposed to *múlgéní*, a hereditary cult; apparently the tenure does not differ from that of *pahikásht* of northern India or the *parakúdí* of the Tamil areas. However, the holding had a portion of waste attached to that; and cultivation in that waste was not subject to an increased assessment, as it would be in a formally surveyed *rayatwari* tenure.

Chamar in'am the holder of this description of *in'am* is a man of low caste who works in hides and leather, and makes the leather bags for drawing water and any other leather articles required by the villagers.

Champane a small boat later on known as *sampan.*

Chamulu (Samulu), Samai (Panicum miliare) a variety of millet grown on about a million acres in the Madras Presidency.

Chaṇaka *cicer aric tinum.*

Chandanavāri sandalwood water.

Chaudhari in'am (i) for the service of performing revenue duties as the headman of a *pargana* or of a group of villages; (ii) granted to the headman of a trade or profession for settling caste disputes.

Chaudharis tax intermediaries of the revenue system; also headmen (below the head merchants) in each of the commodity markets of the city - could pledge the position of *chaudhari* in one commodity and take over the same post for the other commodity.

Chandrāguru white pearls.

Channel marah in Tinnevelly, the name of a tax.

Channel vary in Tinnevelly, the name of a tax.

Chanta village fair.

Charmakāra leather-workers.

Chaṭāh members of police and military force, and armed retainers.

Chatra, chutter umbrella, shed. The name of an assessment in Kanara, made in the year 1725 by Buswapah Naigue, to defray the expense of erecting sheds and feeding pilgrims.

Chattram a covered place where refreshments are given gratuitously; a halting place for the accommodation of travellers; — *in'am* granted for the support of a *Chattram.*

Chatur bhagam in'am *In'ams* consisting of one-fourth share of the government revenue.

Chauki, choky, chokie customs posts located at the city entrances; a chair, seat; guard, watch. The station of a guard or watchman. A place where an officer is stationed to receive tolls and customs.

Chauravarja it is a fiscal term and stands for certain exemption relating to the land grants; 'with the exception of the right to fines imposed on thieves;' or 'immunity of the donee from the tax imposed upon the villagers for village police;' but probably does not mean that the donee was 'without any right to inflict punishment on thieves and persons committing the crime of treason or to levy fines for them;' other equivalent terms are-*choravarja, choradrohakavarja,* and *choradaṇḍaja.*

Chauth In theory one-fourth, share of the revenue granted to or extracted by the Marathas, in practice could be more or less than one-fourth.

Chavadi same as 'Chattram'.

Chawar a measure of land equal to 120 sqr. *bighas.*

Chazhi a beetle paddy pest. It would appear in the Malabar paddy fields usually about a fortnight before the harvest, and unless blown away by the wind did great damage.

Checári more commonly called *shakili* - the skinner, tanner and leather-dresser; the flesh and skins of all animals, which are killed or die within the limits of the village, are his, and from the latter he is bound to furnish the inhabitants with leather or buckets, etc.

Checcu-muttei dues from oilpresses; an oil press, and an egg; the quantity of an egg-shell full of oil; these dues are always paid in kind, either received by the several *Cániyátchicars* in turn and in proporation to the shares held by each, or sold and appropriated to the general fund for the expenses of the village, *grama-shilava.*

Chennapatam Madras.

Chentasawars, Chenchuvars, Chenchewars, Chenchus A class of people who lived entirely in the jungles and were thoroughly acquainted with tracks and passes unknown to others. They obtained a scanty livelihood from roots, herbs, honey, and a chance elk, or deer that might fall to their bows and arrows.

Cherical crown lands and temple lands.

Cherikallu branches of prominent households in outlying areas which negotiated terms of cultivation with tribal groups.

Cheruman, Cherumar (pl.) a low caste agrestic slave; members of a depressed caste, agricultural labour caste in Malabar.

Cherumas called Pulayas in north Malabar, a numerous caste of agricultural labourers on the west coast. It is believed that they were just like slaves before British rule was established, and continued to be bought and sold openly as such till the Penal Code of 1862 came into force. This made slave dealing punishable with seven years' imprisonment. They were short of stature and dark-skinned. As per the social customs they would pollute superior castes at a distance of 30 feet.

Chety, ceṭṭi, chiṭṭi, sheṭty, saiṭṭi, Chettis (Tamil), merchant; it is the name of a distinct caste, as well as, a title used by many people of other professional castes, *e.g.* weavers, oil pressers etc. to indicate that they make their living by trade. Among the true *chettis* there were many money lenders as well.

Different ways how the word *ceṭṭi* is spelt; it has been derived from the Sanskrit *śrēsti*; the ancestors of the *ceṭṭis* evidently constituted the *vaiśya* caste of the ancient Indian society, and their allotted function was the trade and banking business of the country; and, true to their function, in the middle ages the *ceṭṭis* were the principal merchants.

Cheterys one who carries an umbrella.

Cheṭṭkaḷ-maṇai-iṛai a levy imposed on the places/shops occupied by the *Cheṭṭis*. The term *maṇai* could be explained as a shop. As such, it could be a tax on the shop of merchants.

Chihra identification documents (of soldiers which were checked before paid by the accountants). *Note* : Thousands of *chihra* documents can be found in the vast collection of the Mughal documents in the Andhra Pradesh State Archives, Hyderabad. Most of them are from Aurangabad and other forts in the western Deccan.

Chili (chih-li-pu) a kind of cloth manufactured at Kan-pa-mei identified with modern Coimbatore.

Chillary mānyam sundry *mānyams*, or lands granted to temples, revenue officers, and the public servants of the villages.

Chiller, chillar, chitta small, petty. Sundry small gratuities or *in'ams* in Dindigul.

Chiller in'ams, or enaums sundry small gratuities.

Chilleri petty.

Chinna melam in'am granted to a band of musicians consisting of a dancing girl and her accompanists who keep time, play on the flute and beat the *mrudangam*, a kind of drum. There may be one or more dancing girls in the band, and they sing as well as dance. The term *chinna melam* is used in contradistinction to *melam* or *periya melam* which is a band playing louder music.

Chittah a rough note or account; a memorandum.

Chittari bonded labour prevalent in some parts of Kerala.

Chodi the Telugu name for *ragi*.

Cholam, cholum in Hindustani *juari* (*Sorghum vulgare*) the 'great millet.' It was grown over about five million acres in Madras Presidency, the most important food crop next to paddy; also grown as a fodder crop; a dry crop.

Choudari the headman of a trade, the head merchant who manages a town market. Same as *Chaudhari*.

Choultry, Cháwari a covered public building, generally of hewn stone, often richly carved and ornamented, for the accommodation of travellers; anglicised form of a Dravidian word; same as '*chattram*; see *chávadi*; of which it is a corruption; a *dharma-śālā*.

Chowkie, Chowky, Chokie, a place where an officer is stationed to receive tolls and customs. Same as *chauki*.

Chucker, chuckees extra assessments in Kanara under the pre-British governments; extra assessment of 1720.

Chullaki pot.

Chungadam ferry tax.

Churga roller gin.

Cikāriyap-pēṟu a payment demanded for the officer of the king.

Cil-antarāyam 'a small or miscellaneous tax.' A term somewhat similar to *cillāyam*.

Cillāyam similar to *cilvari* and *cilliṟai*; number of other dues were included in *cillāyam* group, e.g. *aruntōṭu*, *ciṟupātikāval*, *kaṇkāṇi*, *māppatakku*, and *veṭṭi*. From the nature of items included, it may be suggested that services and presents formed the major items in the group. *Cillantarāyam* was another term somewhat similar to it.

Cilliṟai, Cilvari a term somewhat similar to *cilvari*, connected with land tax assessed on a unit of land; a term connected with land tax current during Chola period; it was assessed on a unit of land. A number of other dues were included in the group, e.g. *eccōṟu*, *Kūṟṟarici*, *vetti* and *muṭṭai-al*. From the nature of items included in the group it may be suggested that services and presents formed the major items in the group.

Cina-kkanakam (Tamil), the Chinese gold coin.

Cinna name of a coin; sometimes regarded as a *fanam*; also spelt *sinna* in Telugu; a weight equal to 1/30 of a *tola* and called *canteroy fanam*; one-eighth part of a coin called pagoda; the weight of 4 *guri-giñjas*.

Cintriṇī the tamarind tree.

Ciṟṟaṅkātip the term used in the inscriptions to denote tax on shop.

Ciṟumuṟik-kācu a payment demanded for the delivery of *Ciṟu-muṟti* or a memorandum.

Cira-khila land which was never cultivated.

Cira-khila-śūnya epithet of gift land; fallow land.

Ciravida (Telugu), name of a coin; a special kind of *gadyāṇa*.

Circar (sarkar, government) land lands in the produce of which the *circar* had a clear share; the non-*mānyam* lands were known in the late 18th century by this term. These lands were further classified as *waraput* lands (wherein, the *circar's* share was in kind and constituted a fraction of the gross output) and *teervaput* lands (lands wherein *melwaram* was in cash terms and was predetermined sum). Usually, *waraput* lands were *nanjei* lands with assured irrigation, and teervaput lands where *punjei* lands.

However, the very act of refering to non-*mānyam* lands as '*circar* lands' amounted to a negation of *kāniyāṭchi*, which, in principle, was a dominion over all lands in the village. Indeed, whether such a dominion status was conditional on the *kāniyāṭchikārar's* willingness to meet his obligations to the Company Circar, and hence precisely what action was to be taken against *kāṇiyāṭchikārar* for non-fulfilment of these obligations; constituted the basis of a long drawn out series of battles in the court from 1800 to 1860. Meanwhile, the very acceptance of the term 'circar lands' was the beginning of the abolition of *kāṇiyāṭchi*. The word *circar*, of Persian origin, had no Tamil synonym for it; the village accounts, for all their details, did not have any such concept built into them.

Cirikā, kraya-cīrikā a document; 'a deed of purchase,' a sale-deed.

Ciṭalā, coṭāla, ciṭola a tax or obligation of uncertain import.

Citramēḻi, Citrameḻi, śittirameḻi, Cittirameli the beautiful plough; an organisation of the agriculturists; agricultural corporation of the *Vĕllālas*; the plough which was the emblem of this organisation; the boundary stone with the representation of the plough emblem planted to mark the limits of their land; a term used in the epigraphs to denote a corporation of the agricultural community in the country known as the *vellālas* (*mēḻi* in Tamil and *medi* in Telugu meaning ploughshare). Its members were known as *citramēḻi periyanāṭṭār* and the organisation itself was known as *citramēḻi periyanāḍu*. It appears that the *citramēḻi* organisation had control over the production and distribution of produce from land.

Citraméḻi periyamāḍu, Cittirameli periya nadu an organisation of agriculturists appearing quite early in Chola history.

Cōṇaka-vari duty levied on the foreign merchants, especially on the Arabs (*Cōṇakar* = Arabs.)

Cōṟu, cōṟu-māṭu, eccōṟu-māṭu the terms used to refer to the presents, in which case rice, and bullocks (*māṭu*) were demanded occasionally. The *tiyeṟi-cōṟu* and *arici* would also be included in this tax item.

Cól (large) measured by a rod of 36 feet, the square of which, multiplied by 100 was one *cáni* or 1,29,000 square feet.

Cól (small) measured by a rod of 12 feet, the square of which, multiplied by 100 was one *cáni* or 14,400 square feet.

Cóvil temples, and all other public buildings.

Cody sluice.

Coilumin a variety of ginger mentioned by Marco Polo; a product of the area round Coilum; it was also otherwise known as *colobi* and *columbino*.

Coir coconut fibre.

Colingee *tephrosia purpurea*.

Collei homestead; commonly called-backyard; any small enclosure near the house; the difference between this term and *pizhacadei*, 'backyard,' is that the latter immediately adjoins the dwelling, whereas the *collei* may be at some distance from it.

Colly-chakram a gold coin having a figure of the goddess *kali*, formerly current in South India.

Commewar, combies in Telinga and Orissa, a tribe of husbandmen.

Compte banias in the Northern Circars, retail merchants.

Conicopillies, Kanakkapilla accountant.

Coolie day labour.

Cooll gootah in the Ceded Districts, a term used to denote lands let at low rent to different castes.

Cooll gootah shrotrium in the Ceded Districts, land let at low rent to learned brahmins.

Coolty, kulthee pulse, commonly called grain, on which horses are fed.

Copra dried kernels of coconuts.

Cora-daṇḍa-varjya, cora-varja, cora-varjya a fiscal term which means either that no fines for theft should be collected from the gift village or that the donee was not entitled to fines realizable on thieves in the gift villages.

Corambus, corumboos mud dams; temporary earthern bunds during the summer.

Coray a species of long grass used in manufacturing mats.

Corga for counting piece goods. One *corga* equal to 20 pieces (fixed in 1802).

Cortor broker; also called *lella*.

Cotay, kohti factory.

Cott'adumei from *cottu* a bunch, and *adumei* a slave - it signifies a family of slaves sold at once.

Cottah a land measure, equal to 1.62 acres.

Country plough a heavy country plough used especially in Godavari district. An exceptional thing, as over nearly all southern India the plough used was light one-two of which could be carried by a man of medium physique without apparent difficulty.

Cowgram, thattapair, tuttapire *vigna unguiculata.*

Cowle, Kaul (A) promise, agreement, contract, engagement. An agreement, engagement, or lease of land for the cultivation of land. Generally to large farmers and on favourable terms; authorization to cultivate a prescribed acreage.

Craya-sásanam deed of sale.

Croe equal to .25 to .75 acre.

Cruzado the Portuguese money; its average weight may be taken at about 60 gms.; 9s. 8d. of English money, and the half *cruzado* at 30 grms. or 4 s. 10. 5d.

Cūnā same as Sanskrit *cūrṇa*, lime.

Cūrakāra, Cūṛakāra from Telugu-Kannaḍa *cūṛa* and Sanskrit *kāra*; 'one who has plundered.'

Cucherry, Cusheri see *kach'hari.*

Cuddapah and car, kadappu and kar a small crop on *nunjah* land which 'must be sown and transplanted with the freshes of May-June and July and nourished until October and November harvest with the freshes of August, September and October' (Report by Charles Harris, 15 June 1803). Both are a coarse description of grain.

Cullum a measure equal to twelve *markal* (1 *markal* = 27 lb.); measure of capacity equal to 96 Madras Measures or 220.8 lb.; Tanjore *cullum* was equal to 47.4 lb. or 2 37/64 Madras Marcals.

Cully-chakram a gold coin having a figure of the goddess kali; formerly current in the South.

Cumblies woollen shawls.

Cumbu, cumboo, kumbu *Pennisetum typhoides.*

Cuṅka-mērām toll levied on the commodities passing through high roads.

Cuṅkam toll levied on the commodities passing through high roads....

Cuppam hamlet dependent on town.

Cuppatam it is the *mérei* received by *kániyátchicars* after the grain is thrashed; receiving a share of this mérei or the *káni mányam* is proof of proprietary right in the village.

Curnam, Curnum See, *Karnam.*

Curracut an advance given by the government to the cultivators to cover their expenses for raising the banks of paddy fields. This was recoverable like the *takkavi* loans.

Curudu, kurundu *cinnamon*: as many as ten varieties of *curundu*, namely - rape *curudu* or *pinne curundu*, i.e., honey *cinnamon; nai curundu* or *snake cinnamon; carupu curundu* or camphor *cinnamon*; *cabatte curundu* or astringent *cinnamon*; *swel curundu* or *mucilaginous cinnamon*; *dawul curundu*, that is flat, or broad *cinnamon*; with leaves which resembles the nicacol or *Viitex Migunda* viz., in bearing lanceolate or long and narrow leaves; *caturu curundu, i.e.*, thorn *cinnamon*; *mal curundu* or bloom *cinnamon*; and *tompa curundu, i.e.*, trefoil *cinnamon*, because the leaves are said to divide towards the top.

Cusbah, Cusba (A. Kasbah) A town or township. A town or village with its hamlets.

Cuzhi, kuzhi equal to a square foot english measure, at Madras 2400 *cuzhi* were 1 *manei*, the proper form of which was an oblong 60 feet by 40, and 24 *manei* were 1 *cái* (*káni*), being 57,000 *cuzhi* or square feet the *cáni* and its subdivisions differs in different parts; *Mayilápúr Cáni* was the standard measure throughout Arcot *Subah*, it was measured by a rod of 24 feet, 100 square rods being a *cáni*.

D

Dādaní, dadny money given in advance to weavers and other manufacturers.

Dān-ādhikārin officer incharge of gifts; 'officer in charge of grants (or their writing);' may also mean 'a tolls - collector.'

Dāna-mukha a gift; the principal gift.

Dāna-ppuṛam (Sanskrit-Tamil), land set apart for the purpose of charity.

Dāna-pradānaka all kinds of gifts.

Dāna-śālā a hall for the distribution of gifts.

Dānādāya-dānībhoga explained as 'local cess or road-cess' however, *dāya* is 'a gift to Brahmans or temples', *dāni* is 'land tax' and *bhoga* is 'right of enjoyment;' but *dāṇādāya* should mean excise or custom duties and *dāni-bhoga* a tax for the maintenance of the tax-collector.

Dānam gift or charity.

Dānapuram a tax free land endowed (to facilitate the daily feeding a specified number of ascetics or persons versed in the vedas).

Dāṇi 'the king's dues'; perquisite of the collector of duties called *dāṇa* or *dāna*.

Dānī, Dānin officer collecting tax or corn; officer storing the corn collected as tax from the cultivators.

Dāni-bhāga, Dāṇi-bhoga, dāṇi-bhogabhāga periodical supplies of fruits, firewood and the like by the villagers; also, tax for maintaining the collectors of the tax called *dāna*.

Dāra 'a cleft; gap, hole; a ploughed field; a wife.'

Dāradraṇaka the term probably refers either to some agricultural cess, or to a marriage tax.

Dāśaris, Samayācāra, Samayācārya subordinate officers to minister employed in religious ceremonies among the inferior castes. The custom was that before the ceremony commenced, the customary duty or gratuity was given to them, and they were then at liberty to proceed with the festival whether of marriage or any other occasion. In case the parties neglected the established presents, the *dāśaris* returned to their houses in displeasure, and no other *dāśaris* would perform the office as they would be liable to punishment for interfering.

A class of subordinates of the headman of particular communities in the Vijayanagar empire.

Dāsaka fisherman.

Dāsī a handmaid, slave, concubine, dancing girl.

Dāyādas agnates.

Dánapatram deed of gift.

Dab, dub a small coin of the value of 20 *kas*.

Dadhi curd.

Daffedar, Dafadar, Duffedar (P) the commander of a party of horse and foot soldiers; head peon.

Daftar gardens a term applied to certain *in'am* gardens entered in the early *daftars* or records in the district of South Arcot and enjoyed as private property without being subject to the ordinary lapse rules.

Dahkala in'am a term used to denote *in'ams* which were entered in the *inamat* register of *fasli* 1242 prepared under the administration of the Nawab of Kurnool.

Dak'han-jama-i-kámil a term substituted in the Deccan for *assil toomar jumma* or complete standard assessment began in 1654, on the principle of Todar Mal's original rent roll, and finished by emperor Aurangzeb, in 1687.

Dakhila insertion; entry in an account; verification.

Dakṣiṇāpatha 'the region of the south;' a name for southern India.'

Dakshiṇa Sanskrit word, corrupted as Deccan, which means 'right hand' or 'the south; the term generally designates land that stretches from the Sahyādriparvat, also called the sātmāla, Chāndor, Ajanta, or Indhyādrri range, and the expanse of hill and plateau that connects it with Mahendragiri, and forms the watershed between the Mahānadī and the Godāvarī in the north, to the Krishṇā and the *Tuṅgabhadrā* in the south, and from the Arabian sea in the west to the Bay of Bengal in the east. Historically, the territory included within it embraced the Marāṭhā and Kanarese-speaking districts of the Bombay Presidency, the state of Hyderabad with the southern part of Berār, some adjoining tracts of the Central Provinces, and portions of Orissa and the Madras Presidency lying between Mahendragiri and the *Krishṇā*.

Daksinasimpasandhipati Viceroy of South.

Dalavāy, Dalvai, Dalavay (Tamil : *Talavāy*) (K) the commander of forces; sometimes also enjoying the title *Daṇḍanāyaka*. The commander-in-chief, hence also the prime minister under Vijayanagar and Mysore rulers.

Dalavāy agrahāra village granted for military service.

Dalavāyi (Telugu-Kannaḍa), a general, a chieftain, or the minister of state; also see *Dalavāy*.

Dala-adhikārī, Sainyādhikārin, Senāpati, Dalada-adhikāri, a commander of forces.

Dala-vṛtti the grant for the maintenance of the army.

Damdopat the custom or rule by which the total interest on a loan may not exceed the amount of the principal.

Daṇḍa-āya income from fines; 'a tax'.

Daṇḍa-kkāṇam, daṇḍam-kuṟṟam (Sanskrit-Tamil), amount imposed as fine, a levy of fines; fine and penalty imposed.

Daṇḍa-śulka income from fines and tolls.

Daṇḍanāyaka the commander of forces and officer incharge of administration; title of the provincial governor; one who guided the application of *daṇḍa* to the particular issues at hand, thus a judge primarily, conceivably also a politician and statesman, rather than a general at the head of an army, though the term is indeed elastic enough to include this meaning also; some *sēnāpatis* (generals) were also called *daṇḍanāyakas*, and this was not without good reason.

Daṇḍavāṇi standard gold.

Daṇdege umbali a term used in the epigraphs to denote a grant of revenue-free land for the upkeep of a palanquin or for making arrangements for carrying the king's palanquin; also *palaki umbaḷi*.

Daṇḍa, Suṅka, Śulka fine or tax; a levy or free service; judicial punishment.

Daṇḍikā-jīvita tax-free land given to palanquin bearers for enjoyment during their life-time.

Daṇṇāik originally *Daṇḍanāyaka*; sometimes the designation of a judge at the capital of the Vijayanagar kings.

Dandam punishment.

Dandasi in'am for the service of

village watcher.

Dandiya in'am -held by the headman of the *kattubadi* peons.

Danduga in'am granted by the pre-British governments as a compensation to persons who had suffered from heavy and undue exactions being levied on them for the emergencies of the state.

Dar-ul-jahad when Golconda became the Mughal province of Hyderabad, the latter bore the official epithet 'Dar-ul-jahad' the Muslim term for the 'land of war.'

Darbar (P) The court of a king or chief.

Darbar-Khirch (P) Court charges.

Darbha Bed of grass.

Dargah in'am for performing service at the tomb or shrine of a Muhammadan saint, *Dargah*-shrine of a Muhammadan saint.

Darkhwást (Persian = application, request); for all official requests for transfer, and relinquishment, or for revenue petitions generally; rules for disposal of such, are called the '*darkhwást*-rules'; '*darkhwást* appeals' are also spoken of -meaning an appeal from the order passed on a petition.

Darogha of sa'ir office manager, one of the members of the immediate staff of the *kulkarni* of *sa'ir*, other members being a collector (*amin*), an auditor (*mushrif*), and treasurer (*tahwildar*).

Darśana, tariśana-kāṇikkai a levy; *nazrāna*; presents offered to a king or a chief when one meets him.

Darśana-kāṇikkai a term used in the epigraphs to denote a customary payment made while seeing great personages.

Darzi in'am for the service of tailor to a *zamindar* or to a village community.

Daśa-kriyai a term used in the epigraphs to describe the duties assigned to the architects who were to look after the repairs in the temple.

Daśabandham, Daśabhandha, daśavandha, dasabandham, dasbhandam in South India this term is understood in the sense of a tax or an allowance of land or revenue as compensation for the construction and look-after of a tank, well or channel. According to Wilson it is 'a deduction of 1/10th of the revenue on account of compensation for some public work, as the construction of a tank etc.' Sometimes it also meant the right of collecting 1/10 of the produce of lands irrigated from waters of a tank or well by the persons who repaired the water source. When the water sources were repaired by the state the *daśabandha* was to be paid to the state treasury. It was also collected for keeping the source of water-supply in good repair, (for different meanings of *daśabandha* also see Sircar, D.C., *Indian Epigraphical Glossary*, pp. 84-5).

The *daśabandham in'ams* 'were granted as a recompense to private individuals, who constructed tanks, wells and river channels, by means of which the revenue of the state was augmented. The extent and value of the *inam* were in proportion to the capital expended on work and the out turn in revenue.

In brief it meant one tenth of the revenue set apart for repairs to the tanks and wells for irrigation purposes; land, the income from which would be equal to the amount thus set apart; tax equal to one-tenth of the income of the subject; tax or cess levied to keep the source of water supply like the tanks, etc., in good repair; revenue-free land or land paying only one-tenth of the actual revenue; land granted to a person for repairing or building a tank on condition of paying in money or kind one-tenth or some small share of the produce; land granted at one-tenth of the usual rates to a person in consideration of his constructing or repairing a tank; grants of land free of revenue to support of irrigation works.

An allowance of land (*Khanda Dasbhandam*) or of revenue (*Shamilat Dasbhandam*) given as a compensation for the construction of a tank, well, or channel. The grant generally, though not invariably, carried with it the condition of keeping the work in repair.

Daśavanda grant revenue-free land grant given for the construction, digging and upkeep of tanks, canal, channel etc. for irrigation purposes; as far as possible state encouraged private initiative by making grants to the people or institutions that undertook the work; and such encouragements took the form of *daśavanda* grants, according to which the person who undertook or executed the work was given a piece of revenue-free land watered by tank, canal or well which he excavated; the extent of the grant naturally varied with the importance of the work; a fresh grant would be made if the same tank was to be extended; also called *kaṭṭu kōḍage* grant and *Daśabandham* above.

Dasan slave.

Dasi in'am for the service of a dancing girl in a pagoda.

Dastawiz voucher, document, written instrument.

Dastu chitthas summary statements of total collections; journal of actual total collection.

Dastu kharchu chittha debt and credit account of current collections.

Dastu-zabitas statements of actual collections giving aggregates of *kists* gathered for each year.

Datti a gift.

Daunmuddy seemingly a Tamil corruption of Sanskrit *dhánya-mati*-rice lands.

Davandai in'am held for the service of beating in pagoda a drum called *davandai*.

Daya endowment, gift or donation; *brahmadaya*.

Dayirya koḍage a term used in the epigraphs to denote perhaps a grant of revenue free land for some brave service either in war or in the cow raids which were pretty frequent in the Vijayanagar days.

Dēvāgrahāra a tenure denoting land endowed to the temples.

Dēvadāna land belonging to a temple; land endowed to temples for their maintenance; though in theory it used to be tax free land, some inscriptions point out that a tax was also levied on such lands; sometimes the tax was reduced and while on some other occasions it was confiscated also.

Déva-sthánam in'am, devasthanam in'ams a term applied to *in'ams* held by pagodas, temples and for other religious purposes.

Dévarakádu a sacred grove (Coorg). In Coorg in each *'nád'* there were sacred woods/trees called *dévarakádu*, which were superstitiously reserved as the abodes or hunting-grounds of defied heroic ancestors. A time came when feeling of reverence had given way to the love of profit, and the groves had been surreptitiously cultivated with coffee. In 1887, the government issued rules and these groves were absolutely reserved under government care.

Dega in'am held by falconers in the service of *zamindars* or palegars.

Dehai land revenue.

Dehangi-in'am grant to artisans.

Dekhilu belonging to, together with.

Des-kulkarni the district accountants, one who prepares a general account from the several statements of the village accountants.

Deṣ-ádhíkárí the old term for a headman in an ancient district; the officer who kept the public accounts in a *'nad'* (Malabar).

Deṣ-lekhak see *Deṣ-pándyá*.

Deṣ-pándyá (or-pándé) the accountant of a *deṣ*, in the Hindu state, became the *Qánúngo* of the Mughal empire; the *desmukh* and the *deṣ-pándyá* were to the *dés* or *pargana* what the headman and the village accountant (*lekhak*) were to the village (in Bombay Presidency).

Deṣam under the old Malabar 'Perumáls' (title of the rulers in Malabár and Cochin) there had been a general constitution of small subdivisions called *deṣam*, and the head of each called *deṣaváli*; smallest revenue paying division.

Deṣaválí the head of *deṣam*, see above.

Deś-ādhikṛta, Deś-ādhipati, Deśāyi ruler, governor of a *deśa*, or a province, district, sub-division, territorial or administrative unit.

Deśa a territorial term meaning a small area or a group of villages in some cases but a kingdom, district, tract or country in others; designation of an administrative unit, in the post-pallava period *deśa* was at times used as a bigger unit than a *vishaya*- the Vaṭanagara-*vishaya* was a subdivision of the Nāsika-*deśa*; at times *deśa* and *vishaya* seem to have been used as synonyms; the *āhāra* stood in the same relation to *deśa* as the *vishaya*; while in the early Pallava kingdom an *āhāra* seems to have been converted in to *raṭṭha* or *rāshṭra*, in the Upper Deccan it was usually transformed in to a *deśa* or a *vishaya*; *Deśa*, however, sometimes meant only a country without any administrative significance.

Deśabandham in'am, dasabhandam in'am the *in'ams* of this class are confined chiefly to the Ceded Districts, the western portion of Guntur, Nellore, North Arcot and Salem. They were granted as a recompense to private individuals who constructed tanks, wells and river channels by means of which the revenue of the state was augmented. The extent and value of the *in'am* were in proportion to the capital expended on the work and the out turn in revenue. Of the two descriptions of these *in'am* - (i) *khanda dasabhandams*, were the *in'ams* given in specific localities; and (ii) *shamilat dasabhandams*, were the allowance as *in'am* of a certain proportion of each year's cultivation under the work in question. *In'ams* of the latter description were not brought on the *in'am* registers as they had no locality. In all ordinary cases *dasabhandamdars* are under the obligation of maintaining the works of irrigation in due repairs. In some cases such a condition was either not attached to *dasabhandam in'ams* or it had not been enforced for a long time. Such *in'ams* were treated and enfranchised as personal grants. Also see *Daśabandham, Daśavanda* grant above.

Deśa kával, desha cavel, deshacawel, Desa kaval the same as *menkaval;* district watching fee.

Deśādhikṛita local prefects.

Deśabhōjaka chief executive official of the assembly of elders in the administrative division.

Desai essentially an assessment officer, responsible for the proper assessment and fixation of '*jama*' of the cultivated areas of the villages under him; was next to the *shiqdar* but higher than the other revenue officials like *muqaddams*, *chaudhris* and the *qanungos* who worked under him. - *inam*, for performing the above services; a chief man among lingavant merchants.

Desai in'am for performing the services of the headman of a taluk or *pargana* under the Indian government.

Desaiyan accountants of *parganas*; the superintendent of a *pargana*, the officer of a district, the office was hereditary and frequently recompensed by grants of land so that the *desai* of ten villages became a kind of petty chief in south India. Also see, *Desai* above.

Deṣam region; parish.

Desavazhi - head of a *deṣam*; a traditional authority.

Deshmukh, Desmukh (from S. *desa* a district, and S. *mukha* mouth, face, front) headman or collector of a district or portion of a country; an officer corresponding with *zamindar*, but more ancient.

In Golconda for each of the new subdistricts (*parganas*), the Qutb Shahis appointed a member of a powerful warrior family to act as headman or *deshmukh*. The primary task of the *deshmukh* (or *desai*, Persian, and *deshai*, Marathi) was to maintain an armed body of retainers and assist in the collection of the land tax. (It was originally a Marathi term carried into the eastern Telugu speaking areas by the Muslims.) Royal officials (*hawaladars* or *karkuns*) or tax farmers assigned to the subdistrict could rely on the local authority of the *deshmukh* or *deshai* to help enforce their demands. In return, the king assured the *deshmukh* fixed percentage of the land tax collected (usually 5 per cent), full control of a number of tax-free villages, and hereditary lands with in the *pargana*. Most important, the *deshmukh* gained hereditary tenure in office. The latter assurance-sealed by a royal *farman*-also implied royal support against encroachment by ambitious neighbouring chiefs and families.

In Kondavidu, to quote an instance, the *deshmukh* of the area received 2.5 per cent on annual collection and paid 10 per cent of the total fee for appointment demanded.

In Andhra, south of Godavari much of the administration was in the hands of *deshmukhs*, one for each district, and paid fixed amounts based on a long standing tax assessment on each village and *pargana*.

In Telengana, the majority of the *deshmukhs* were from the dominant military/agricultural castes: *Reddis* (*Kapus*), *valamas*, and *kammas*.

The duties of the *deshmukhs* included (i) enforcement of the details of the assessed or settled taxes on the *pargana* (*haqiqat-i-jama'bandi*) in consultation with revenue officers and *jagirdars*; (ii) prompt collection of the necessary funds in cash (*zar-i wajib*) from the peasantry (*ra'aya*) to the satisfaction of the agents of the *jagirdars*; (iii) prompt and regular transmission of information to the revenue office, including reports on proportion of inhabited and waste lands in the *pargana* and abstracts of the records of the *deshpand*; and (iv) encouragement and conciliation of the peasantry in order to ensure maximum cultivation and population in the *pargana*. The *deshmukh* also promised to meet any orders or demands from the accountants (*mutasaddian*) of the revenue office (*kachahri*). Each *deshmukh* was expected to use his local knowledge, his political influence, and if necessary, his military resources to ensure that all taxes demanded from his *pargana* (or district) were fully assessed and collected. At the same, acting as an official he was to prepare regular reports for the revenue office to conform to the orders of the revenue accountants, and to work in cooperation with other officials or agents of *jagirdars* who had interests or responsibilities in his *pargana* or district. See, J.F. Richards, *Mughal Administration in Golconda*, Oxford, 1975, pp. 140-141.

Deshpande, Deshpandya a clerk, a record keeper, a register; under the Mohammedan government this office was hereditary; the head revenue officer of a district. Registrar of a district, who, in the peninsula, performed the same duties as the *qanungo* of the Mughal empire. The *desmukh* and the *despande* were to the district/*pargana* what the headman and *patwari* were to the village.

Deshmukh in'am for performing the service of *deshmukh*, a hereditary native officer, exercising chief police and revenue authority over a district containing a certain number of villages, and responsible for the revenue.

Despandya in'am for performing the service of *despandya*, the hereditary revenue accountant of a district or certain number of villages.

Deva-bhoga, deva-dāya, devabhoga-hala, deva-dāna, deva-deya, dev-āgrahāra, déva-déyam a revenue-free holding in the possession of a temple; a gift made in the honour of God; land given for the enjoyment of temples, grant of lands to temples for carrying on daily worship and festivals; these grants also contributed much to the economic welfare of the people; also called *tirunāmattukkāṇi;* grants of land for religious purposes.

Deva-vihāra land in possession of temples.

Deva-vṛtti land set apart for the maintenance of temples.

Devāgrahāra revenue free holding in the possession of deity.

Devásthán, dewasthán land granted for support of temple.

Devadāna-iṛaiyili village or land granted to a temple.

Devadasi mānyam the *mānyam* granted to the temple dancer.

Devadayam lit. 'gift to god.' *Ina'ms* granted to or for the support of temples. Religious grants, had several subcategories. Also see, *Deva-bhoga*, etc. above.

Devadurga god's fort.

Devahala, devabhogahala land grants 'with the exception of cultivated lands enjoyed by temples'.

Devakula-puṣkariṇī temples and tanks, the construction of the former and the excavation of the latter requiring the permission of the king or landlord.

Devanga a class of weavers.

Devaswam, devasam property of a temple.

Devata in'am a term applied to *in'ams* granted for the support of the worship of village deities.

Deya periodical offerings to be presented to the king or landlord.

Deya-dharma a pious gift; an appropriate religious gift; an expression used in donative inscriptions.

Deya-meya king's share in kind and in cash.

Deyvamadi in'am held for the service of dancing before the idol as if under the influence of inspiration.

Dhāny-ādāya tax payable in grains.

Dhānya produce of the field, a share of which was payable to the king or landlord.

Dhānya-hiraṇya, dhānya-hiraṇy-ādeya revenue in kind and in cash.

Dhānya-varga lit. 'the grain group', a class of taxes payable in grains.

Dhātuśila metallic ores.

Dhárekár (in Bombay and Konkan areas) a privileged tenant under *khot* proprietor; who paid no rent beyond the *dhára* or established rate of land revenue payment; 'quasi-*dhárekár*', term used in the Khot Act, 1880, for another kind of privileged tenant of a lower grade than the *dhárekár*, *i.e. dhárekárs* who had, in process of time lost something of their privileges.

Dhaḷa-vādi, dhala-vali (Telugu-Kannada), a tax connected with *dala-vṛtti* or with *dala* or the army.

Dhall, dholl red gram (*Cajanus indicus*) a very important food for vegetarians adopting rice diet as it would remedy the deficiency of rice in protieid.

Dhaṁñikas, dhannikas corn-dealers.

Dhanyadhikari superintendent of granaries.

Dharm-ādhyakṣa lit. 'a judge,' superintendent of charities; chief of the department of charity and justice.

Dharma-āsanam, durmasanam durmasenum, dharmāsana, dharmasanam places where water and rice are distributed gratis to travellers. Religious establishments. Lands granted for religious institutions at a low rent, during the Hindu rule, at Tinnevelly.

'Village court'; it was consisted of the chief men of the village and the twelve village servants known as *āyagār*.

A village held by Brahmans for personal benefit.

Dharma-chatra one of the various terms used for alm houses.

Dharma-dāna a religious gift; a gift for religious merit; grant of tax-free land.

Dharma-deya a religious grant in general.

Dharma-dána-patram a deed of gift for charitable purposes.

Dharma-hala a revenue-free holding.

Dharma-śāsana a document recording a gift made for charitable purposes.

Dharma-vṛtti-iṟaiyili (Sanskrit-Tamil), tax free land for the maintenance of some charity.

Dharmadayam, dharma-déya A general term used to denote *in'ams* granted for charitable purposes. Secular *in'ams*.

Dharmakaarta trustee; an office of temple management; it was one of their duties to distribute and redistribute periodically the cultivation of temple lands.

Dharmaraja mānyam the *mānyams* granted for charitable purposes.

Dharmikaḷ a body or commission managing endowments.

Dharwiyan *dharwai*, a village officer, the accountant who weighs grain.

Dhed, dherd, daird agricultural labour caste, usually found in the deccan and North Canara.

Dher a man of low caste, employed as watchman and messenger in the village establishments.

Dhobi washerman.

Dhobi in'am for the service of village washerman.

Dholl, redgram *cajanus cajan.*

Dhúli-battá a cess on rice lands (in Coorg); lit; 'dust of the threshing-floor;' the refuse of the paddy which was accepted as voluntary offering by the first Haléri chief, when warily assuming the dominion over Coorg. In due course of time it became a regular tax, and no refuse paddy. In 1868-69 it was commuted into a money-payment.

Dhurya in'am held by a servant employed under the *monigar* of a village in collecting government revenue; same as *tandal in'am.*

Dīnāra a gold coin, the name being derived from the Roman *denarius*; sometime called *kāśu* in Tamil records.

Dīrgha-mānya land set apart for the supply of water for the holy bath of idols.

Dih, deh a village.

Dih-dár, dehdar village keeper. An inferior officer of police in village, one of whose duties was to distrain the crop, when necessary to secure the rent.

Dih-kharch or *ráj-kharch*, an impost or cess to meet (real and supposed) 'expenses' of the village, the kingdom, etc.

Dih-kharchah, deh-khurcha village expense. Contributions for defraying certain expenses incurred in the villages for public purposes. Same as *Dih-kharch* above.

Dikshadar one to whom land had been granted on specially favourable terms on account of sanctity or learning. There was a settlement of some 3,000 Brahman *dikshadars* at Chidamaram, South Arcot, who owned the temple and were considered specially favoured of the gods.

Dikshatar in'am for the support of a Brahman who has performed the *yagnyam* sacrifice of a goat.

Dirhem one of the currencies of foreign countries in circulation; the *dirhem* vaguely represented the *drachma*, or rather the Roman (silver) *denarius*, to which the former name was applied in Greek provinces.

Dirroas in the Ceded Districts, wells or embankments for irrigation. Mounds raised on the banks of rivers for drawing up water in buckets.

Dittam a preliminary forecaste or estimate of the year's cultivation; an estimate was made at the beginning of the season-a kind of forecaste of what each *rayat* would hold and cultivate, and what crop he would sow. At first great importance was attached to this proceeding even by the English, but later it was abolished; estimated aggregate of the revenue of a village from investigation of each several holding; an arrangement; settlement.

Dittam in'am an *in'am* having no locality but consisting of a deduction of a fixed extent of land from the annual cultivation of the village, the proportionate revenue demand on which is paid to the *in'amdar*.

Ditya 'to be given'; 'an object that has been given away'; 'customary presents'.

Divākaram Tamil lexicon.

Divanottar, divánattár, dívánam the revenue or financial authority of government/state; a derivation from *diwán/diván* with the dialectic termination; the use of this term is found only in the 18th century deeds not in older ones.

Diwan, Dewan (P) native minister of the revenue department, and judge in civil causes within his jurisdiction; receiver-general of a province.

Ḍoms a low caste people.

Dóni, doony a large boat, or coasting vessel, used by the local persons.

Dolabehara in'am for the support of the headman of a village.

Domala assigned lands.

Dombariapaṇṇu a social tax collected for the benefit of *dommaras*.

Dommara in'am granted to persons of the *dommara* caste who gain their livelihood by performing as tumblers and ropedancers.

Dommaras a tribe of tumblers and mountebanks, some of whom wandered the country while others had become agricultural labourers, and others again made wooden combs. A community of jugglers, gypsies who wandered in the country.

Dommaripannu a tax collected either by or for *dommaras*, a community generally of acrobats. Same as *Dombariapaṇṇu* above.

Donthi a wooden harrow, with about 20 teeth, about 5 inches long, drawn by hand; used in paddy cultivation.

Dora 'lord' (Telugu); honourific for holder of power; landlord.

Dorasthanam seat; residence of Northern Circars hill chief.

Doratanam a class of Sirdars, known as 'Doras' in the district of Ganjam, enjoyed *in'ams* for maintaining the security of the country and preventing the incursions of hill tribes.

Doratanam in'am enjoyed by *doras* or Sirdars in the district of Ganjam for maintaining the security of the country and preventing the incursions of hill tribes.

Doruvu a kind of well; wells are sometimes made near the beds of rivers and are fed by small channels which lead water into them - are called *doruvu* or *sultán*; lands watered by these were treated as if directly watered by the river.

Dowles estimates of yield at harvest time.

Drávid'am the south-west division of India.

Dracham one of the currencies of foreign countries in circulation in many parts of south India and even Gujarat; it was a silver coin weighing in an average about 60 grains though coins weighing from 56 to 65 grains have been found.

Dramma name of a coin; originally derived from Greek *drachma*; a currency of foreign origin in circulation in the areas that extended from Gujarat to Tinnevelly; a silver coin weighing 11.2 grains; it can be thought of representing about 9 ¾ d.

Drōhin traitor.

Dubas iron shells.

Dubash one who speaks two languages; an interpreter; an Indian who, at Madras, managed the money concerns of the European and served him as a confidential agent in his private and public transactions with the other natives; (*dwi-bhashi*) lit. interpreter. As regards the *dubashes*, it is true that they stood, as the Tamil proverb goes, "with a foot in the river and the other in the mud."

Dudha milk.

Dugalam one sixteenth (or one anna) of the coin termed a pagoda.

Dumbālah-dharná, dumbalah deron taking a seizing by the tail (as a cow to urge her along, a common practice in India). An ultimate and positive order to the *rayats* for reaping the harvest in the Northern Circars, when the season is far advanced.

Dumbálah, Dumbala an order for giving up the government share of the produce to the cultivators; an *in'am* held free of quit-rent.

Durga-daṇḍanāyaka the ruler of a fort.

Duswanah a tenth. The name of an addition made to the standard rent in Bednore, in the year 1723.

Dvādaśaka partnership in a land.

Dvijas a term applied to those who carried on the occupation of cowherds, traders and mechanics.

Dwadasi kaṭtalai in'am for feeding Brahmans on the twelfth day of each lunar fortnight.

Dwitiya chokada in'am *in'am* scattered through several villages granted as supplementary to a whole village *in'am*, all the *in'ams*, including the whole village, being subject to a lump jodi; same as *paitari in'am*.

Dyūta gambling.

Dzamilika in'am for playing on a drum called *dzamilika* during the festivals of the village deity.

E

Ēkabhōgum, yekhabhogum, Ekabhoga, eka-bhogya a tenure indicating exclusive ownership of a property invested in a single individual; sole possession and enjoyment of a village by a single person (without any joint owner); *ekabhogairaiyili*, revenue-free land or village in the sole enjoyment of a single owner. Also see, *gaṇa-bhoga*; a village in which no other distribution has been made and no shares arranged, besides those of the original *gramuttan manium*.

In some villages the *manium* remained in the hands of the direct descendants of the original *gramuttan*, in others a division of it has taken place among branches of the same family, and from the poverty of some of the branches, at some time or other, individuals of other families, and other castes even, have occasionally been admitted to a participation of the *gramuttan manium* and privileges; but as long as the division is confined to the *gramuttan manimum* and *sosuntrum*, either according to the Hindu laws of relationship, or under the urgent necessity from poverty, or other strong cause of admitting individuals of a different caste, the village seems to retain its appellation of *ekabhogum*, which in its literal sense is supposed to imply possession or enjoyment by a single person.

When, however, a *sarvamānya* village held under such *ēkabhōgam* tenure was distributed among a number of persons, it simply meant that they were granted the right of enjoyment of the income from the village unless it was clearly stated by the donor that he was making a *sarvamānya* grant of the lands in question. In the absence of such a specific statement, it has to be understood that the donor reserved the right over the property to himself, but granted only the right of enjoyment to the persons in question.

A plot of land granted to a single brahman for his sole enjoyment and having on it his house and the houses of his dependents and farmers; a variation may also be noticed in the *ēkabhōga* tenure, as the study of the epigraphs show, that it often happened, that the individual to whom a plot of land was granted reserved for himself a portion of such land, and bestowed the remainder on others; in all such cases, however, it is not clear whether the sub-donees were allowed full rights over the land, or the rights of ownership were in part reserved for the second donor.

Ēr plough; the term was used to indicate the extent of land that could be turned with a given number of ploughs, e.g. grant of two *ēr* of lands, meaning that could be turned with two ploughs. Here it may be pointed out that per plough of land would be equal to an area of land that could be cultivated in one day by one plough and a pair of bullocks.

Ēr-kācu a term used to denote tax collected on dry land meaning a *kācu* on a plough. The tax was actually assessed on the area of land normally cultivated by a single plough a day.

Ērāl-oru-kācu a term used to denote tax collected on dry land, meaning a *kācu* on a plough.

Ēreḻupadu lit. 'seventy stanzas in praise of the plough'; a literary production written by Kambar, which may reasonably be assigned to the 10th century A.D., it is an account of the implements used in tillage and the processes of agriculture.

Ēri-āyam (Tamil-Sanskrit), amount payable by the owners of the fields irrigated by the tank for its upkeep; also income from fishing in the tank; cess on using water from tank.

Ērimīn-kāśu, ēri-mīṇ-kācu, ēri-mīṇ-pāṭṭam terms used to denote a kind of duty levied on fishermen.

Ērippaṭṭi, goḍage, kulappaṭṭi several terms used in the epigraphs to denote gifts of land provided for the maintenance of irrigation works.

Ētta, ēttam a pulley wheel used for lifting up the water from a well.

Ēttamaram water lift.

Ēva orders.

Eccōṟu a kind of present which was a very popular item from early Chola days. It was an obligation of providing food to public servants, who visited the villages on official business. Some inscriptions, especially of Kulottunga I and his successors refer to *eccōṟu* and *Kurrarici; eccōṟu* and *kūṟṟunel*. It could be surmised that with *eccōṟu* paddy and rice were demanded as presents on occasions; it was a kind of small contribution of cooked food provided to the visiting officers of state or to the local officials.

Edangali, edangari, edangazhi one *edangali* = 4 *nalis*, one Madras measure = 7 *nalis*. One Madras measure = 108 cubic inches or 62.5 fluid ounces. Hence one *edangali* on the West Coast may be said to be nearly a pint and three quarters. But like all other Indian weights and measures it varied from village to village.

Edigi-Gandlas (Ganigas) the oil pressers of the Telugu and Kanarese regions.

Edroo pramânum it was a deed supplemental to deed called *swamy bhogium chitta* earlier granted to the same grantee; from the land assigned on *swamy bhogium* the grantee was to pay a specified sum for a specified period to the owner; under the new arrangement another piece of land, earlier given to someone else, was to be redeemed and given to the *swamy bhogium* grantee along with the land granted earlier; the condition was that the specified amount earlier payable to the owner was to be deducted from the *swamy bhogium* rent, and the amount payable by the owner to the one from whom the new piece of land had been redeemed was to be paid by the new grantee; the owner would pay in ready cash the balance amount due to the new grantee on a specified date and would receive back the land earlier granted on *swamy bhogium*; meanwhile the grantee would enjoy the products of the field and every other profit whatever.

Ejoo tree it in its shape much resembles the beetle tree, *i.e.*, arecanut palm though somewhat larger.

Ekabamhaṇasa 'the unique Brāhmaṇa'; 'the only protector of Brāhmaṇs'.

Ekkatlu (singular *ekkati*) 'heroes of single combat' in Kakatiya period; they were hereditary group of warriors renowned for their skill in hand-to-hand fighting who formed a reserve force in Telugu armies. When not on campaign the *ekkatlu* dispersed to their homes where they held grants of land 'in every important town and village in the kingdom'.

Ĕḻuttu-viniyogam (Tamil-Sanskrit), dues payable as *ĕḻuttu* for the village accountant to be apportioned among the villagers.

Elā cardmom.

Elavai, ĕlavai (Tamil), death duty; fee

for crematorium.

Ella in'am granted to a person who settles boundary disputes by treading the boundary line in solemn manner with a pot of fire on his head, a wet cloth round his waist, and a garland of flowers round his neck.

Ellu, gingelly, gingelli *sesamum orientala; sesamum* cult (in Malabar); one of the 'miscellaneous' cultivations undertaken on the bare uplands of Malabar where there was no forest; apart from *ellu* or *til* seed (*sesamum*). the other thing produced was *modan* or hill-rice.

Eluvas, Ezhuvans see *Tiyyas, Thiyyas*.

Eṇi-kkāṇam (Tamil), ladder tax levied on toddy-drawers.

Ĕṇṇĕy (Tamil), tax levied on the oil-trade; obligation for the supply of oil.

Er-kkaḍamai (Tamil), tax on ploughs.

Er-ppŏn (Tamil), tax to be paid in cash for each plough; also called *er-kkaṇikkai.*

Eraṇḍa castor

Eravari tribute due, and rent: the compound means all dues in money receivable by the *mírásidars* from *paracudis,* etc.

Eri tanks.

Eri-ivu (Tamil), share in the expenses of the maintenance of the tank.

Erikkāḍi tank cess of one *kāḍi* of paddy per field.

Erinīr-kōppu the high land, *i.e.*, catchment area for an *ēri* which will be covered with water in flood time but will be dry at other times and may be cultivated; also translated as 'collections of water below lake (*bunds*)'.

Erivirappatanas protected mercantile towns. *Erivirappattanas* were more in the nature of protected towns for stocking merchandise and could well have been distribution points protected collectively by the merchant body.

Erkádu a system of management of land practised in Kundahnad area of Niligiri; it consisted in levying a rate of tax for each plough (*er*). The cultivator cleared and sowed where he pleased. 'No restrictions even on the felling of forests were imposed, so that the hill-sides and valleys were cleared at will'.

Erukala in'am granted to persons of the *erukala* tribe for collecting medicinal drugs or plants for the use of the *zamindar.*

Erukalai *calotropis gigantea.*

Erumai-ppŏn (Tamil), tax payable on buffaloes.

Eruvaka in'am granted to the person who first ploughed the lands of a village.

Etchóru it is the same as the *nal'padi,* or daily batta paid to persons deputed on any account to the village by the officers of government except that *nal'padi* is given to peons or others of pure caste in money or raw grain, and *etchóru* is an allowance made to *talaiyáris,* or *tukiris,* who are generally pereiyer; a collection is often made on these accounts from the inhabitants, and if not disbursed is divided among the *mírásidars.*

Ettak-kaṭamai, eṭuttukkoṭṭi a term used to denote a fee levied on those lands irrigated by water drawn from common wells using water lifts; dues on water lift.

Ettugāṇa mills in which bullocks were used, e.g. oil mills; they were also used for lifting water from the wells.

F

Fanam English version of Tamil *paṇam*; see *paṇa*. It was sometimes regarded as a gold coin equal to 1/10 of a *partāb* and 1/20 of a *varāha*; 42 *fanams* made on one *Star Pagoda*; worth 2 d.; the 5-grain *fanam*, heavily alloyed, was one of the smallest gold coins known, and was in general use for the ordinary commercial transactions; one of the standard coins used by the indigenous pre-Muslim kingdoms; the Qutb Shahs continued to issue this coin from their mints with the Hindu types unaltered (along with the Muslim type coins); in 1687 the Mughals stopped its, along with other old type coins, including pagodas and half pagodas, production and issued gold *muhurs*, silver rupees, and copper coins in the usual imperial types.

Fanaos a standard coin equivalent to 30 *reis* (each equal to less than a penny).

Farash caretaker (of the mosque).

Farman (P) Imperial Order

Faṣl (Arabic), harvest; *fasl-jyástí* or *faṣl-kamí*, addition or reduction in the revenue on account of double crops, or the loss of one; land assessed as one-crop land but the second crop is also raised-would result addition in the revenue; crop deficiency was allowed when land assessed to two crops, and one fails.

Fasal Jāsti second crop on land assessed as one-crop land.

Faujdar An officer under the Mughals invested with the charge of police and had jurisdiction on all criminal matters charged with general maintenance of order; a fort commander in charge of the greatest stronghold; generally got salary assigments on lands.

'Field lake' its construction and utility has been described by Charles Harris in his report dated 15 June 1803 : "A field lake in good repair is a quantity of common *nunjah* land described by a bank four, five or six feet high and seven, eight or nine thousand feet in circumference... A field lake hold all freshes, rain, etc., received between May and September. Either at the end of September or at the latest by the middle of October, it is emptied and cultivated as a field with Sambha-Peshanum plants grown from the last seed sown in August. These crops grow well in the field lakes though sown late because they contain good nutrients. They even give double the yield of the neighbouring fields which were not field lakes."

Firka, Firqah a part, a sub-division, a division of a taluk in charge of a Revenue Inspector, comprising 15-25 villages; a party.

Florin English money in circulation in South India; *florin* (gold) mainly represented the Florentine currency and was with a value of 9s. 4.8516d.

Fulooce pice.

Fusgee a small duty levied at fairs and weekly markets on shroffs in money and on other dealers in kind.

Fusli, Fasli (from A. *fasl* or *fasal*) the harvest year. *Falsi* 1210 corresponds with 1800-1801, difference of 590 years. The Madras government fixed its commencement to the 12th July. A crop or harvest; the *fasli* year furnishes the official date, the revenue year.

G

Gāmuṇḍa, Gāmuṇḍa (Kannaḍa), same as *Gāvuṇḍa*; a village headman; *Nāḍa-gāmuṇḍa, Nām-gāmuṇḍa*, headman of a district (*nāḍu*); village officer (Chāḷukyan period); was the link between the villagers and the king's government, and seems to have been an official appointed from the centre.

Gāndharva art of music.

Gāndhika perfumers.

Gānuvuku-ari-suṅkamu annual or semi-annual tax payable on an oil mill as such.

Gānuvula oil-mills.

Gānuvula-mudra-suṅkamu duty on oil-mills paid as registration fee.

Gāvuṇḍas holders of the headship of the *maṭhas*.

Gángánah by village, a settlement by villages. A term, equivalent to *mouzhwar*, used to designate a village settlement.

Gáyál the land finally abandoned; see also '*gat-kul*'.

Gadaba in'am for the service of repairing irrigation channels.

Gadabalu in'am for the services of palanquin-bearers in *zamidaris*.

Gaddatiru in'am lands which were originally on a high level, and which were granted on a favourable assessment in consideration of the difficulty of bringing them under wet cultivation.

Gadya, gadyana, Gadyāṇa gold coin generally regarded as weighing 88 grains; an indigenous gold coin in circulation in south India; the *gadyāṇa*, which occurs in Kanarese inscriptions, has been referred to equate with the *pagoda*; it was perhaps the Kanarese name for the *kaḷañju*, a term likewise used in Telugu; the weight of the *gadyāṇa*, however, was a little more than the *kaḷañju*, ranging between 61.75 and 63 grains-obviously heavier than the *pagoda* or *varāha*; this was also in keeping with the grain-weight of the Kanarese *haṇa* which was approximately 6.2 grains, 10 *paṇam* or *haṇa* making one *gadyāṇa*; in calculating the value of a *gadyāṇa*, therefore, it should be approximately half a sovereign, while that of a *varāha* or *pagoda*, or *kaḷañju* or *hun* was 4.90 of a sovereign; a coin like a farthing equal to $^1/_4$ or $^1/_5$ of the *paikamu*; also a *dinār* or *varāha*; equal in some place to 20 *vals*, 8 *māṣas*, or half a *tola* in weight; a gold coin equal to a *varāha* or *pagoda*. However, sometimes its value/weight used to vary from area to area.

Gahapati appears to have been the designation of the head of certain number of households of cultivators.

Gal-puṭṭi (Telugu), a measure of land, a variation of a *puṭṭi*.

Gaṇa 'an aggregate of kulas'.

Gaṇa-bhoga, gaṇa-bhogya, gaṇa-bhojya, gaṇabhōgya, gaṇabhōgam a tenure in which land is held in common by a group of persons, joint ownership of a village or villages by a number of persons; system under which the lands were held jointly by the people, and hence under a joint tenure; no single individual had any absolute ownership of the soil, any sale or gift of lands under this system would be made jointly by the donees; lands held by a community of Brahmans.

Gaṇaka *Kaṇakka* in Tamil; a village accountant; also *vāśal-kanakka*, account of the *vāśal* (palace or palace-gate); *ūrkkaṇakkar-jīvitam*, land assigned in lieu of a salary to the village accountant or perquisites of the office of the village accountant; accountants (yādava kingdom); members of the inspecting staff with whose help the central secretariat controlled the provincial and district officers.

Gaṇapaṇa communal and professional guilds.

Gaṇḍā sort of coin prevalent in some areas, equal to four cowne-shells and 1/20 of a *paṇa*; also a small area of a land, twenty of which make one *kānī*.

Gaṇikā prostitute.

Gaṇin an astrologer.

Gaṇu (Kannaḍa), 'one span'; a unit of measurement.

Gaṅgaikoṇḍa title of a Coḷa king meaning 'the conqueror of the Gaṅgā'.

Ganachari in'am for the support of a servant of the *chaudhari*, his duty is to convene meetings for the settlement of caste disputes, and to report to the *chaudhari* all violations of caste.

Gandha sandal.

Gandha-Śāli a kind of rice or paddy.

Gandum, godhuma wheat.

Garaḍi umbaḷi a revenue free land granted for the maintenance of gymnasium.

Garadi in'am granted to persons skilled in legerdemain.

Garhí lit. a small fort; *patels* residence, or the centre of the village; it was the original founders of the village who built the '*garhí*' or mud-fort, which formed the centre of the residence, and while they alone were entitled to occupy that, all the other settlers would build round it for protection.

Garige in'am granted for dancing before the village deity bearing on the head a number of pots, filled some with water and some with fire.

Garise a measure called grace; a hamper or large basket for storing grain.

Garudakkal in'am granted for the service of making *puja* to the post with bells on the top which is erected before temples. This post also goes by the name of *garuda stambham*.

Garudan samba a type of paddy crop raised from seedlings transplanted about the beginning of October and reaped at beginning of March. It is generally grown on channel lands in clay regurs.

Gass a standard coin equal to 1 1/4 Dutch *ell*.

Gat-kul 'abandoned or lost', and *kul*, 'family'; one of the terms indicating the existence, (pre-British) of a land lord class in Dakhan villages; when the original holder had disappeared, the holding was known as 'gat-kul,' *i.e.* the family (*kula*) was lost or had disappeared (*gata*).

It should be noted that it was held in old times that the *mírásí* rights could never be lost. A *mirásídar* might return and reclaim his land within thirty years. The families were also held jointly responsible for the revenue. However, during the British period, it does not seem that people enjoyed the same rights, especially in *gat-kul* cases. One can draw inferences to that effect from the Bombay *Administration Report* for 1882-3 (p.36) where it is mentioned that the mirásí right could be acquired by a sort of purchase, and consenting to or taking the responsibility of the payment of the government revenue demand.

Gatkul-miras *in'am* on unclaimed lands.

Gauda, gavuḍa, goud, gauda chief farmer; "he received the whole dues of the government and he agreed to pay so much to the government, and made as much as he could consistently with the rules of the village.

Besides the income he got, which was the difference between the amount of revenue collected and the payment made to the government, he was entitled to a share of the wet crops in the village.

The *gauḍa* also performed the village sacrifices which were in the Canarese Districts made to the Cumba (pillar), the image of the village God." However, this description seems to refer to a very small renter, and there were bigger farmers who were incharge of the revenues of larger areas.

Same as *gāvuṇḍa*; a village headman; the chief farmer of a village.

Gauda in'am granted for the service of headman of a village.

Gauda manda in'am held by a shepherd for the service of supplying milk to the *zamindar* and for manuring the fields of the village with his sheep.

Gava in'am granted for the service of offering a sacrifice of a goat or fowl at the festivals of the village goddess.

Gavadhyaksha superintendent of cattle.

Gentoo Indian. One of the aborigines of India; the English used this term to designate the language and the people of Tellingana, *i.e.*, Telugu and Telugu-speaking people respectively.

Ghās-dān obligation of supplying grass from the pastures.

Ghát a hill range; a mountain pass; a ravine or passage leading into the country above or beyond.

Ghát-wál, gatwall who has a charge of a pass in the mountains, or a landing place on a river.

Gháts the (Eastern and Western). The Western Ghat range forms a continuous chain, tolerably equidistant from, but near, the coast line all along from north to south.

The Eastern coromandel Gháts are much farther inland; they only form a simple chain in their upper portion, *i.e.* from Krishna river to the North Arcot district, at which point the main chain seems to turn inland, and sweep across the continent. Following this line, the *gháts*, skirting the Karnataka state, form the hill taluks of Salem and Coimbatore district, and unite with the Málabár Gháts in the network of hills surmounted by a plateau, known as the Nílgirí (or Blue Mountains).

The Eastern coast, below the point of turning off above alluded to, is not altogether devoid of any hill barrier, for the place of the *ghát* line is still indicated by groups of hills rather than a chain line. Among these groups the Shevarái (Shevaroy) hills are well known.

The Western ghát line below the Níligirí group has several offshoots inland, of which the two most important are Áńamalai and the Palní hills.

Ghaḍa-puṭṭi a measure of land; a variation of *puṭṭi*; also *gāl-puṭṭi*.

Ghada-maṟuturu (Telugu), a measure of land; a variation of *maṟuturu*; also see *kālmaruturu*.

Ghair dakhala a term used to denote *in'am* which were not entered in the *inamati* register for *fasli* 1242 prepared under the administration of the Nawab of Kurrool.

Ghale (Kannaḍa), measuring rod; for example *Gańgana ghale*, 'the rod (measured by the length of the forearm) of a person named Gańga'; also see for example, *hasta* in *Śivacandra-hasta*, etc.

Ghaṭa earthen pots.

Ghaṭachakra a water lifting machine; see *araghāṭṭa* and *udghāṭana*.

Ghaṭi-yantra same as *ghaṭachakra* and *araghāṭṭa*.

Ghaṭī name of a measure of capacity.

Ghaṭikā an educational institution, same as *śālā* and *mahāśālā*; institution of higher learning; assembly hall.

Ghaṭikā-madhyastha an intermediary officer having the authority of *ghaṭikā* or recognised by the *ghaṭikā*.

Ghaṭikaiyār (Tamil) members of a *ghaṭikā* managing its affairs; officials who declare to the public, by beat of tomtom, the orders of the king and others.

Ghee clarified butter.

Ghora-kṣetra, gṛha-kṣhetra a building site.

Gírás lit. mouthful, originally applied to the provision in land or money made for the younger sons of noble houses, then a political allowance paid to certain families (esp. Bombay Presidency).

Gidagauvel forest lands on the plains; forested plains.

Gidda (Telugu-Kannada), a gill, or a liquid ounce; a quarter of *sola* weighing 16 *dubbus*.

Giñjaka tiles used for roofing the houses

Gingelly (*Sesamum indicum*); called *til* in north India; most highly esteemed vegetable oil in south India; used in cooking, for food and on the body and hair.

Gingille oil oil of the seeds of *sesamum orientale*.

Girásiyá properly a chief holding such a provision for life; applied generally in later times to land held by chiefs, as opposed to *khalsá*, that held by a chief ruler. Then applied to indicate that certain chiefs out of possession, were paid a kind of 'blackmail' to preserve the neighbouring lands from their depredations. During the English period applied to designate descendants of certain chiefs who received a cash (as political) allowance. (esp. in the Bombay Presidency).

Giraśal a variety of rice.

Giri-durga hill fort.

Girīndra 'a hill chief.'

Giridurga mountain-fort.

Go-gauḍa name of a tax levied on cowherds.

Go-pracāra-bhūmi grazing ground, same as Tamil *kanṟu-meypāḻ*.

Go-prachāra pasture land for cows.

Gō-saharra one of the various forms of gifts given to the brahmans.

Gōpracārabhūmi a piece of land intended as a cattle-stand; this was to be in addition to the grazing land; also called *triṇayūti*.

Godugu in'am for holding an umbrella over the *zamindar*.

Gocarman an area of land often regarded as equal to ten *nivartanas* although the exact area varied in different periods and areas.

Gola, Golla Supplier of milk or sheep; a cowherd.

Golakā, gulikā, goḷakkai, koḷakai, kuḻigai name of a coin, circular in shape.

Golawer a tribe of cowherds in Telinga and Orissa.

Golla in'am for supplying milk or sheep to the *zamindar*.

Golla-vāru (Telugu), a caste of watchmen (employed as treasure-guards), generally herdsmen.

Gomasta, Gōmāstāh, Gomashtah (P) an agent, steward, or representative.

Gonchee Pattahs *pattahs* granted where land was held in coparcenary.

Goortoo a land measure equal to $3\,^1/_8$ English acres.

Gooty a measure of weight.

Gopaully the name of a series of coins.

Gor in'am granted for the support of a tomb.

Gorru a seed drill; an agricultural implement.

Gośīrsha superior class of sandalwood.

Goṣṭhī an assembly; a corporate body; Tamil, *goṣṭhiśeydā*, convener of a *pariṣad*.

Gosayeen, Gosain follower of Shiva order, corresponding in many ways with the Bairagis among Vaishnavas, many of them officiate as priests in the temple of Shiva; one of the most respectable of the Hindu orders.

Gouḍ Anglicised form of *gauḍa* or *Gavuḍa*.

Govallabhas superintendents of cowherds.

Govallava a class of royal officers associated with the grazing of cattle and animals belonging to the king.

Gṛha-kara, ilvari, manai-iṛai, manaippaṇam house tax.

Gṛiha-sthāna a house site.

Grāma-bhogika one who enjoys a village as free-holding; village officers; sometimes looks identical with *gāmuṇḍa*.

Grāma-drohin traitor to a village.

Grāma-kārya 'village rites'; 'the various functions of the village'; village business; administration, committee of administration.

Grāma-kaṇṭaka a traitor to the village; enemy of the security of a village; annoyance to a village.

Grāmāgrāmabhojaka; Gramagrama-bhojaka one who enjoyed revenues of all the villages of a specified area; the free-holders of various villagers.

Grāmabhōjaka village headman.

Grāmakūṭakas village headman, the link between the government and the village (*Rāshṭrakūta* and *Chāḷukyas*).

Grāmapraverticam village senate; *panchayat*; by which all the affairs of the community, internal and external were conducted.

Though clause II Regulation XIV of 1816 provided for the appointment of *múnsífs* in all the villages through out the Tamil country, since it could not be expected that these newly created officers would or could depart so far from ancient custom and established usage, as to act in any instance, in which the interest of the community was concerned, without the consent of the whole body of the *mírásidars*.

Sometimes in villages, the proprietory of which was held by more than one caste, as where the Bráhmans had intruded on the Vellálers, or the Palli had contrived to possess themselves of part of the *swastyam* of the Bráhmans, there was a kind of double *praverticam*, each set deliberating apart, though mostly acting in concert.

Grāmas villages.

Grāmaṭikā a hamlet; a small village.

Grāsa-vāsas food and clothing.

Gráma-canaccu village accountant; as per certain recordes, as one of the *mírási* rights, the privileges of employing one were bestowed on Brahmans, on condition of their employing a person to discharge the duties of it.

Gráma-craya-sásanam deed of sale of a village; thin term, as contradistinguished from *nila* or *manei-craya-sásanam*, implies the transfer of the *mírási* right, and is implied to the sale of the whole or any part of a *gráamam* or township.

Gráma-otti-chittu deed of mortgage of a village.

Gráma-uzhavadei-otti-chittu mortgage deed of the proprietary of a village; the word *gráma* may mean here the whole or any part of the village.

Grámam a village; on the West Coast used for family settlements of Brahmans. In Malabár, amongst all the families who had formed their settlements, the Náyar groups were called *tara*, the Brahman *grámam*, the Tiyar and other foreigners *chérí*.

Grace a measure of weight; a grain measure, 3200 Madras Measures, equal to 7360 lb., or 400 maracals.

Grama kattubadi see *kattubadi.*

Grama kaval in'am granted for the service of a village watchman.

Grama kharchu chittah debit and credit account of current village expenses.

Grama piada the same as *grama-kattubadi.*

Grama silavoo the village fund; it could not be regarded as personal property of a *mirāsīdār*, it is an official fund and belongs to those who carry on the public concerns of the village; when a *mirāsīdār* therefore quits his land, he resigns his village duties, and can have no claim to privileges which belong exclusively to those who perform such duties.

Grama-maniyam, Grama-manyam, Grama maunium a certain extent of land enjoyed revenue-free by a hereditary proprietor of part of the village lands as a personal privilege attached to such a share; a term used to denote an *in'am* enjoyed by the whole community of *mirasidars*, hereditary functionaries-palegars, *zamindars, faujders, patels, karnams, kattubadis.* etc.; This tenure is peculiar to the Madras district.

Grama-shelevu the general purse of the village.

Grama-vicraya-chittu a deed of a sale of the whole or part of a village.

Gramabhagam in'am granted to the *mirāsīdārs* of a village in consideration of their having given up their *mirāsī* right to such lands as were granted as *in'am* in their villages.

Gramagarbha khandrika a term used to denote a large section of land granted as *in'am* on which a hamlet has been built, but which is not recorded in the revenue accounts separately from the village within the limits of which it is situated.

Gramakuta village headman.

Gramam a village-not connected etymologically with *agraharam.*

Gramanis toddy-tappers and arrack distillers.

Gramapanchaka a group of five villages.

Gramawari system village lease system.

Grammakantamu a term used for a glebe; a pasture pertaining to a village; the scite.

Grammu-in'am grants in support of village hereditary officers; *maniyam.*

Gramuttam manium assignment of certain tract of land of the headman of the settlers, on the first settlement of every village. He was also entitled to certain privileges or fees in kind, under the general denomination of *gramuttan sosuntrum*, bearing a certain proportion to the produce of the land of every cultivator within the extent of the village.

Both by the Hindu and the Muslim governments, their property of these descriptions would appear to have been much respected, and it was allowed to descend in hereditary succession, and even to have been left to their disposal to transfer temporarily or permanently to others.

Grámátan, grammatan, Gramuttan headman of the settlers, on the first settlement of every village; though enjoying hereditary position, was subject at all times to punishment, by fine or otherwise, for offences and misdemeanours, or by dispossession of his lands and privileges, the latter, however, being considered an extreme act of rigour, which it is pretended was seldom resorted to, except in very urgent cases, such as treason against the sovereign authority, or capital crimes.

Gramyakas inhabitants of the village.

Green gram, green pessaloo, pire *phaseolus aureus.*

Grīshmodaka summer.

Grihastha householder.

Ground-nut the 'monkey nut' of England, and 'pea-nut' of America. It is a leguminous plant, which requires little rain and is a profitable crop to combine or alternate with a cereal. It very seldom fails. Its cultivation was spreading very rapidly in the Madras Presidency, owing to the introduction of the Mauritius variety, up to the out break of the first world war. It was grown for export to Marseilles, where it was pressed in successive processes, first cold then with heat. The first pressing yielded an oil used as a substitute for olive oil, the second an oil used in the manufacture of margarine, the third one used in soap making; *arachis hypogaea.*

Gúntu or déna-guntu, gootoo lit. honey-comb. A license by custom paid for as much of honey and bees-wax as may be found by the renter in particular forests or mountains.

Guḍa-yantrika machine for extracting juice of sugarcane.

Guddad broken uneven land brought in to cultivation by the hand. A species of land holders in the Ceded Districts who held their lands at a reduced rent.

Gudikattu the round or total extent of land under a village; a district.

Gueny chalie in Kanara, a tenant at will. The same as *chalie gueny.*

Gueny nairmul in Kanara, a proprietor of land. The same as *nairmul gueny.*

Gueny shudmul in Kanara a tenant for ever. The same as *shudmul gueny.*

Guḷa sugar or molasses.

Gulies districts.

Gulikā, pudu-kkuḷigai name of a coin; vāḷāl-vāḷitirantā' *guḷikai*, a Pāndya coin issued by Jaṭā-varman Sundara-pāndya I who had the title *Vāḷāl-vali-tiṟantā.*

Gullige 'little balls' in old Canarese; the name used for the gold coins.

Gumastas lit. clerks, The advent of the *gumasta* system was an inevitable result of the Company's emergence as the ruler. For now the Company could dispense with the indigenous merchants who had hither to been indispensable middlemen in its trade in textiles. It was thought to be relatively uneconomical and uncertain, process of making advances to the merchant middlemen, and dependence on them for the timely supply of textiles of a standard quality. The Company could now directly deal with the weavers. In other words, the *gumasta* system was a classic manoeuvre in processual integration in the interest of economics of scale.

Gumika village headman.

Gunari in'am the same as *ganachari in'am* above.

Gundasala *haemorrhagic septieaemia*, otherwise called buffalo disease, and malignant sore throat. It would affect buffaloes more than cattle; 75 to 90 per cent affected animals would die, but that recovered would become immune for life.

Guñjās or *raktikās* or *ratis*, a small weight.

Guntaka, guntava a sort of a broad hoe, drawn by oxen; a sort of rake drawn by oxen.

Guṟṟamu horses.

Gurrapu in'am granted (i) for superintending and breaking in the horses of the *zamindar*; (ii) for the maintenance of a horse given as a present.

Gurukkal in'am for officiating as a priest in a Siva temple.

Guṭṭige almost same as *guttagai.*

Gutha a contract giving right to income, revenue, or perquisites in return for a fixed sum.

Guttagai, Guttige (Tamil), contract, lease, contract of lease; a deed of permanent lease; a contract or lease.

H

Hāda (Kannaḍa), same as Sanskrit *pāda*; a land measure equal to one-fourth of the standard measure-*mattaru* or *nivartana*.

Hāga (Kannaḍa), name of a coin.

Hakikat account, narration, events, explanation, affairs, statement.

Hajib (Mughal) 'resident' whose function it was to enforce the emperor's order; Mughal *hajib* was a prominent figure in Golconda's politics.

In Mughal and Qutb Shahi administration this word stood for an envoy; as the representative of the king he was deputed to settle political affairs and to promote freindly relations with foreign countries; *hajib* was either *muqimi* (residential) or *maslihati* (special) and the tenure of his office was fixed according to the needs of the situation; in the reign of Sultan Muhammad Tughlaq besides the *hajib*, there were also the *Amir-i-hajib*, *Naib-i-Amir-i-Hajib*, *Hajib-i-Buzurg* and *Hajib-i-Khas*; the *hajib's* function was to safeguard the dignity of the royal functions; he was incharge of the *darbar* arrangements and served as connecting link between the king and the *amirs* and the persons seeking royal audience.

Hajjam in'am granted for the service of village barber.

Hakikat-i-jama a statement or the particulars, of the *jama*, or the sum total of an account.

Hakim in'am granted for the service of physician.

Hala, hāla, hali lit. 'a plough,' a freeholding; an area of land; a land measure equal to 65856 square cubits-about 3.4 acres but varied in different periods and areas.

Halalkhor ina'm granted for the service of village sweeper.

Halu current.

Halut duties levied on cardamom, pepper and betel-nut.

Haṇa (Kannaḍa), name of a coin, same as Sanskrit *paṇa*; a gold coin; though generally considered to be same as *paṇam*, the weight of a *hana* was 6.2 grains as against that of a *paṇam* which weighed 5.2 grains.

Hangami jodi a quit-rent on an *in'am* fluctuating from year to year according to the produce or extent of cultivation.

Har-sal-makta tenure lands held on a perpetual and invariable rent, generally below the full rent.

Haridrā turmeric.

Haritaka myrobalan

Hasala Canarese caste.

Hásil produce, result, proceeds, revenue, duties; receipts (of the revenue).

In Hyderabad/Golconda records the *hasil* figures have generally been expressed in rupees and the *jama'* (assessment) in the units of account called *dams* (40 to the rupee); though, by and large, the *jama'* and *hasil* were virtually identical, in a number of cases the latter were of varying proportions to the former; the *hasil* figure was certainly the more significant of the two figures; in every case where the *hasil* figures differed from the *jama'*, the Hyderabad revenue officials used the *hasil* figures in preference; for instance, it were the *hasil* figures, not the *jama'*, which determined the allowances and appointment fees of the *deshmukhs* and *deshpandyas*; one of the important reasons for this was, the revenue office would simply raise the *jama'* to a fictitious level in order to make the *jagir* assigned conform to the month ratios of each *mansabdar*; there were instances, when the *diwan's* office agreed that the *jagirdar* could only expect to achieve between four-fifths and two-thirds the *jama'* figures.

Hasta a cubit (24 aṅgulas); sometime as 36 **aṅgulas**, 20 ¾ inches, 34 inches etc. in length; *Śivacandra-hasta*, 'the cubit measured according to the length of the forearm of Śivacandra'; a land measure. Cubit; equivalent to 18 inches.

Hattavally Register of actual crop yield.

Havili, havelly, haveli lit. a palace, mansion; 'haveli lands' (in Madras Presidency) crown lands, those reserved for the privy purse; reserved for the support of the royal family and its immediate dependants, and therefore 'crown' property.

House, habitation, domain. In Madras it designates such as are under the immediate management of government, without the intervention of zamindars or *jagirdars*.

Havir-bali *bali* offered with cooked food; same as Tamil ti-*yeṟiśoṟu*; tax payable for meeting the expenses of the same in a temple.

Hawaldars in Hyderabad, they were appointed as financial officers for the *mahal* (administrative subdivision) earlier managed by Golconda's central treasury, these appointees (though not necessarily new Mughal officials) alongwith the '*amils* were to collect the arrears of taxes accumulated as well as the revenue assessed for the current year.

Haweli pargana the area immediately surrounding the head-quarters of every district, meaning the *pargana* bearing the same name as the district, was called the *haweli pargana* and invariably classified as crown land; the *haweli parganas* were generally regarded as important sources of revenue which were customarily reserved for the support of the principal fort in the district, the district governors, etc.

Hēma-garbha one of the various forms of gifts given to the *brahmans*.

Hĕggaḍĕ (Kannaḍa), official designation indicating a chief.

Hĕjjuṅka, pĕrjuṅka (Kannada), name of a tax; a term denoting the duties on important articles of trade.

Heraṇika treasurer (Sātavāhana period).

Hingari 'Latter Crop'.

Hiraṇakāra the treasurer.

Hiraṇya tax payable to the king in cash; dues payable in coins; cash; could be in addition to the tax in grain or in lieu of; same as *hirany-āya*, *hiraṇya*-deya, also Tamil *kāś-āya*.

Hiraṇyasāmudāyika a collector of revenue in cash.

Hisa-i-zat personal salary.

Hissa Shortriyam a term given to villages the revenue of which was shared between the *in'amdar* and the Government, or the *in'amdar* and the zamindar, as the case might be.

Hissah, hissa share, portion, division, part. *Hissa* lands are such as are divided, with respect to the rent, into shares, payable to two or more *zamindars*, who are called *hissadars* or share holders.

Hobaḷi, hobḷi (Kannaḍa), small territorial unit; an administrative division made up of a few villages; it seems that at certain places this division had taken the place of the *sthala* and the *sammat*; a grouping of family holdings for land-revenue purposes, invented by the Mysore sultans where there were no 'villages'.

Holeya Canarese agricultural labour caste.

Hommai a kind of furnace or a large fire stand for smelting iron.

Hon a gold coin; the original name seems to be *pon,* which simply means gold in Tamil, becoming *hon* in Kanarese, and *hun* to Mohammedan authors; it may be useful to note that *pon* originally meant any metal, and later was restricted to gold.

Hona one of the subsidiary coins of south India; *hona* was equal to half pagoda and may be considered equal to 26 grains.

Honnu gold, the gold coin called a pagoda.

Hoolse nevise land valuer

Horsegram *dolichos biflorus.*

Hūn same as *varāha;* name of a gold coin of about 50 grains, called *pagoda* or 'star *pagoda* in English.

Huggi manyam granted to a person who settles boundary disputes by treading the boundary line in solemn manner with a pot of fire on his head; the same as *ella in'am.*

Hukámi revenue-free grants made by the '*hukám*' (of *hákim*) or state officers, as opposed to those formally made by royal order. The Regulations of 1793 called such grants 'Bádsháhi' (Royal) and '*non-bádasháhi*' respectively.

Hukumnamah a written order.

Hul koḍage a term used in the epigraphs probably to denote a land grant to be enjoyed by the whole body of villagers revenue free on condition that they would supply fodder to the army.

Hulu produce of the land.

Hundi bill of exchange; cheques for transfer of funds; in Hyderabad these were also used to pay the troops and were drawn on subordinate Mughal officials in the districts; a facility for transmission of currency.

Hunise-gadde the wet-land field of the tamarind tree.

Huttalu (Kanarese) serf; from *hutta*: birth; *alu*: servant; agricultural labourer.

Huzur, huzzoor the presence. The seat of government, or of European authority in a collectorship; 'supreme presence', honorific applied to people or places; 'head' or 'headquarter', head office; the presence, court, audience chamber.

Huzur sheristadar head clerk.

I

Īḍara-vāru, īḍige-vāḍu (Telugu); a toddyman or arrack-drawer; from *īḍa*, 'a date tree'.

Īḻam-puñjai, īḻam-puṭci (Tamil), tax for toddy-drawing.

Īḻavas toddy-drawers.

Iḍai-ppāṭṭam, iḍai-ppūṭci (Tamil), tax on herdsmen or cattle-breeders; a tax on shepherds.

Iḍaiyar-vari (Tamil), tax on shepherds.

Iḍaṅgai left-hand castes; broadly occupational groups associated with artisan and husbandry functions. Buchanan, who visited Mysore towards the close of the eighteenth century, found the following castes among those that constituted the *iḍangai* or left hand classes: (i) *Pancala* (ii) *Bericetty* merchants (iii) *Devanga*-class of weavers. (iv) *Heganigaru*-those who use two oxen in the mill. (v) Paliwanlu-two tribes of cultivators who are not of Karnataka origin. (vi) *Madigaru*-tanners or shoe makers. The *Pancalas* commanded the whole party; and the *Madigaru* were the most active combatants in all disputes among the *iḍaṅgai* and the *valangai* (the right hand group) divisions.

Iḍaṅgaivari a term used in the epigraphs to indicate a communal tax paid by *iḍaṅgai* class.

Iḍaṅgaḻi (Tamil), a measure of capacity.

Idatorai a type of tax accruing from the villages.

Idige in'am granted for having planted date-trees for the production of toddy.

Ijamana gramam (Tamil) same as Sanskrit *ekabhogam*.

Ijara-darkhast rental proposal.

Ijarah, ijara, ijāra the leasing of taxes to private entrepreneurs, who bid for the privilege and were allowed to retain all profits over the sum which they had agreed to pay; land leased at fixed rent, slightly taxed; a contract, a monopoly, a form of the revenue customs.

Ijaradhar the tax-farmer, who made predetermined payments on a regular basis.

Ikrar admission, acknowledgement, confession.

Ikshu sugarcane

Ilāqa, ilakh relation, jurisdiction, possession, a district, an estate, a property, an office.

Illadaarvar mel-saathanum chitta a deed of land tenure in Kanara according to which the land which had earlier been granted to some one from whom the owner had taken some money and could not return the same (see *illadaarvar saathanum*); in order to overcome his distress grants the same land to another individual in consideration of money taken from him; the new grantee also receives the original deed given by the original owner; neither the new would demand any interest nor the other party would demand any residue rent from the produce of the said grounds; should the original owner call upon the new grantee to resign the said ground, he was authorized to receive the full debt upon it according to the original deed, and there to resign it to him together with the original deed. However, a person transferring his *illadaarvar* tenure with the original deed in this manner, was to take a counterpart instrument from the transferee certifying the conditions on which the transfer was made. This instrument was called an *iqrarnamah* and was drawn on set specifications.

Illadaarvar saathanum a deed of land tenure in Kanara according to which the land is assigned to the grantee in lieu of the money taken; the grantee cultivate and enjoy the usufruct for a specified period by which the owner promises to pay back the money and get the land redeemed and receive back the deed granted; in case he fails to make such redemption within the specified time, the grantee was at liberty to possess the whole property of the said ground and register the same at the *sirkar kach'hari* by paying the full revenue and taking the receipt in his own name; ever after he would possess and enjoy all the benefits thereof himself and his heirs without any claim whatsoever by the previous owner.

Illam, illom house of a *nambudiri*; Brahmanical house.

Illuppai (Tamil), yilpah *madhuca longifolia*. It is least perishable. Timber is very hard and used generally for beams and other large articles. Fruit yields oil used for cooking and for burning in lamps in houses and temples. The oil cake is cure for itch.

Iman self-respect

In'am, Enam, Enaum (A) a grant of land in which the state has given up its rights to the land revenue, or a portion of it in favour of an individual or an institution in return for the performance of certain duties or as a charitable endowment; present, gift, gratuity, favour. Grants of land free of rent, or assigments of the government's share of the produce of a portion of land, for the support of religious establishments and priests, and for charitable purposes; also to revenue officers, and the public servants of a village.

In'am lands lands granted on specially favourable terms to particular individuals, or to persons holding particular offices or performing particular services.

Iṇavari a type of poll tax. However, the community on which it was levied is not known.

Iṇṇilattāl-vanta-nirk-kiṛai a phrase mentioned in the epigraphs by which it may be inferred that the cess was fixed on a unit of land which used the water for irrigation.

Ina-vari a type of tax accruing from the villages.

Inamati Patti a *jodi* (in Kurnool) imposed under the administration of the last Nawab for supposed defect of title.

Inamati mera same as '*Patti*', but in Udayagiri *jagir* in Nellore.

Inamati taffrik a tax (in Cuddapah and Bellary) nominally imposed on *rayats* with a view to restrain them, from the cultivation of *in'am* land in preference to government lands.

Inami, Inaumy Rupee one.

Inavari-kkāśu communal tax payable in cash.

Inqiyad-nama 'Document of submission'.

Iṛai, iṛai (Tamil), a general term used for revenue income and tax to be paid to government; land revenue.

This Tamil word is applied to God, king and taxes, a term connected with the land revenue during the Chola period, some epigraphs of the Pallava period also indicate its use as a tax item; in some cases the term *iṛai* is suffixed to other terms, e.g., *maṇai-iṛai*, *i.e.*, tax on house or house site, *kaṭai-iṛai*, *i.e.*, tax on shop, *taṟi-iṛai*, *i.e.* tax on loom, *ceṭṭiṛai* and *iṛai*, *i.e.* tax on Chetty merchant, etc. Some of the other terms are *aṭṭukkiṛai*, *cērippaṭuttum-varum-*

iṟai, ciṟṟiṟai, eṇṇai-iṟai, kāṇi-iṟai, māppaṭuttum-varum-iṟai, kiḻiṟai, maviṟai, nilai-iṟai, ninṟiṟai, palaviṟai, taṭṭiṟai, ūṟiṭu-varippāṭṭāl-vanta-iṟai, ūrkoṭuvanta-iṟai, ūrppaṭuttum-iṟai, alpamiṟai, aṇiyāyavāvataṇta-iṟai, ceṭṭikal-vāṇikar-maṇaiyiṟai, cilliṟai, kaṇṇāriṟai, kaṭaippāṭṭattālulla-iṟai, māviṟai, nakarañ-cuṭṭ, vanta-iṟai, nelliṟai, nirkkiṟai, paṟai-iṟai, paṭṭiṟai, pēr-iṟai, piṭākai-ōpāti-iṟai, poṇṇiṟai, taṟiyiṟai, uṟaviṟai, ūrcuṭṭivantaiṟai. However, *iṟai* was the land tax which probably went direct to the King.

Iṟai-dravyam (Tamil-Sanskrit), lumpsum paid in lieu of land revenue; amount payable in commutation of the taxes payable in landed property; a term used in the epigraphs to denote the lands which were exempted from taxes by the king on its authority generally on payment of capitalised money.

Iṟai-kāval (Tamil), tax for police duties; also amount of deposit yielding interest per annum equal to the tax due on the land.

Iṟai-kaṭamai land tax.

Iṟai-kaṭṭiṇa-kāṇík-kaṭaṇ same as *kāṇik-kaṭaṇ.*

Iṟai-vāri the term is used to designate not the dues and rents receivable by the *mírásidars*, but the taxes and rents payable to government.

Iṟaikāval a term used to indicate a lumpsum amount received by the local body e.g. *sabhā*; tax-vigil.

Iṟaikaṭṭiṇa-nellu, kaḷarnilam saline land.

Iṟaikūli cash wages for collection of taxes.

Iṟaiporuḷ money for paying taxes; the amount that is required to compound the tax for all time to come by one lump payment; also see *kāśu-kolla-iṟaiyili.*

Iṟaiyili tax-free land; the term used in the epigraphs denoting remission; it was generally granted on the lands gifted to temples.

Iṟaiyili-kkāśu (Tamil), amount paid for compounding taxes in order to make the land revenue- free; amount payable to meet the shortage in the revenue occasioned by the grant of exemption of revenue on certain lands. It may here be pointed but that there used to be parallel by putting the actual sale of landed property in the form of a sacred donation. Sometime the sale of the property was openly recorded and donation was proclaimed as the purpose of the sale. In such cases the vendor was the state and the donor was the individual who had purchased the land and had requested the government to make it revenue-free holding. While on certain other occasions the king himself was the donor and yet he appeared to have actually sold out the property to the person on whose request the grant had been made. The landed properties transferred, as such, were actually sold out to individuals, proposing to make a gift and conceding the position of the principal donor to the vendor - the king.

Irā madagu kāval śēri a term mentioned in an inscription to refer to settlement for guarding the sluice at night.

Irāca-niyōkam a term used to denote a type of payment demanded by the state for the despatch and delivery of the royal order to the party concerned.

Iraikudi in'am the same as *pedda kapu in'am.*

Irasam a measure of 24 seers.

Irsāl a remittance of money.

Irsalnamah a statement of money or goods remitted, an invoice; remittance roll.

Iruman a term generally used for the land which was mixture of clay and sand of light brown colour.

Irumbukatti in'am granted as an encouragement to manufacture iron.

Iruvataṭik-kōl a measuring rod prevalent in Karnataka, equal to approximately 20 *aṭi* = 17 feet 4 inches. It may be kept in mind that invariably the measuring rods were named after a king or god or village.

Iswaran mānyam the *mānyam* granted to a Siva temple.

Iṣṭāpūrtta a charitable deed; performance of charitable deed.

Iṭaip-pāṭṭam, iṭaivari the terms used to denote tax on shepherds.

Iṭaṅka-śālai a mint.

Ivu in'am an *in'am* consisting of a deduction of percentage from the extent of the annual cultivation of a village, the proportionate revenue demand on which is paid to the *in'amdar*.

Iwaz substitute, exchange, recompence, money, property, stock, principal, capital.

Iyenberiz actual or normal account of produce.

Izáfat (Arabic), a tenure in Konkán. It also applied to grants revenue-free as an extra allowance to hereditary village or district chiefs. In Northern Konkán the *izáfatdár* was a grantee or assignee, allowed to take the revenue as a personal benefit or increase to his income. It is also explained as applying to a *farmer*, appointed to realize an 'increased' revenue. During the British period he ceased to enjoy the right to increase the 'rent' of any cultivator, nor was he personally entitled to lands that lapsed or were abandoned.

The term, however, had variable usages-in some cases the *izáfatdár* paid a fixed sum and got the benefit of all actual revenue payments (by increased cultivation or otherwise) above that; in others, he simply got an allowance of 10 per cent on the revenue; in still others, he paid the revenue on rice-lands, and appropriated whatever rents he could get on dry lands for the year of cultivation (and on which no government rates were imposed).

J

Jāgīr, Jagir, Jaghire, a Persian word; a tenure in which the public revenue of a given tract of land were made over to a servant of the state together with the powers required to enable him to collect and appropriate such revenue, and administer the general government of the assigned territory. The assignment could be conditional or unconditional. During the early period of British rule it was also the practice to confer *jagir* as rewards for meritorious services to the state.

Jāti-siddha-āya communal tax payable in coin.

Jack a tree needing a wet climate, common on the west coast. It yields good timber and produces a green fruit about the size of a vegetable marrow, which grows on a thick stem from the trunk or large branches *artocarpus heterophyllus.*

Jadimadu highly bred ox.

Jagattumunūru village assembly.

Jaghire, The first acquisition by the East India Company, from the revenue point of view, was the area around Madras, -known as the *jághíre* because it was originally granted by the Nawab of the Karnátik as a *jágír*; the revenue thus assigned was intended as a contribution towards the expenses of the wars undertaken in aid of the Nawab. The final acquisition of the territory was piecemeal, and dated between 1750 and 1760 (being finally confirmed by the Emperor Sháh' Alam in 1763). Th revenues were collected on the existing plan, and it was not till 1780 that English offices took regular charge. The *Jaghire* later formed the Chingleput district, out of which a single taluk formed the separate district of Madras.

Jagīrdār holder of a *jāgīr.*

Jakarai, jaggery sugar, sugar in its unrefined state.

Jala water.

Jala-dvāra drains.

Jaladurga water-fort.

Jalaśāstra the science of hydraulics.

Jalasūtra the hydraulic engineer.

Jam'i-kamil 'perfect assessment', James Grant (in 'Political Survey of the Northern Circars' completed in 1786, *Fifth Report*, pp. 619-94) was of the opinion that even after a century this *jam'i kamil* was still essential for revenue collection in Andhra 'as exhibiting the only authoritative account extant in use, made from an actual survey of the local sub-divisions, number of villages, quantity of ground in or capable of cultivation, together with the estimated territorial produce in money, according to the established rule of Buttai into ½ share for the cultivator and ½ for the state's demand'.

Jamá, jama, jamma (Arabic), total sum; the total sum of land-revenue exclusive of any cesses or rates, as levied from the estate, *mahál,* or individual holding according to the settlement system in force; assessed revenue; total amount of rent or revenue payable by a cultivator or a *zamindar.* The whole, total, sum, amount, sum total, assembly, collection. The total of a territorial assessment.

Jama'bandí, jamabandi, jummabundy

a rent-roll; a roll showing both revenue and rent-dues in a village (meaning varied according to the system). In Bombay and Madras Presidencies applied to the annual account made out for each 'occupant' of his actual holding and payment due for the year; the annual settlement of revenue accounts in an estate, village, or district; settlement of the assessments; settlement of the amount of the revenue assessed upon an estate, a village or district. An annual statement of revenue due from any estate.

Jama-i-tumari, jamma tumary the total according to the tumar or rent-roll.

Jama-wasul-baki account of revenue settlements, receipts and disbursements.

Jamadar-khana, Toshe-khana Treasury.

Jambu rose-apple.

Jaṅgama, jangam a priest of the liṅgāyat or vīraśaiva sect.

Jana-pradhānin a minister governing a district.

Janma eternal, birth, birthright.

Janma-bhūmi gift of land, made for the lifetime of a person; called *janmakkāṇl* in Tamil; a term used to denote lands granted as life-time tenure.

Janmabhogam rights of *janmi*.

Janmam, jenmíkar, janmíkar (or *jemnum* as written in the *Fifth Report*), the right or tenure of the *janmí* landlord; according to *Fifth* Report - "... almost the whole of the land in Malabár, cultivated and uncultivated, is private property and held by "*jemnum*" *(janmam)* right, which conveys full absolute property in the soil... We find the land occupied by a set of men who have had possession time out of mind." The English administrators and revenue and legal experts were not sure about the origin of the term *'Janman'* and could not trace back its origin before the end of the sixteenth century, when Mohammedan institutions were already well known in Southern India. It is suggested that the people of Malabár only corrupted the common land-term of the Mohammedans - *zamin* (as in *zamíndár*). 'In Hindí dialect this would become *jamín*, and 'janmí' may be merely the same as 'zamíndár' = landholder. Quoting the example from Coorg, they have pointed out, the land rights were claimed exactly the same way, calling their tenures by the term '*jamma*'; literally birth-right, used in Malabár to denote a superior form of land tenure.

When a *jenmíkar* mortgages his *jenmi* to a mortgagee *i.e. kaanumkar*, it will be settled between themselves by mutual agreement as to who would cultivate the pledged land. All that the *kaanumkar* looks to is securing the interest of his money. He may, for example, be a trader, and totally ignorant of agriculture or farming. He will, thus circumstanced, agree to the *jenmíkar's* cultivating the pledged land by any means in his power. The *jenmíkar* might, or not possess such means. If he possesses them, he will most probably be his own farmer. If not, he will let out the land to others to cultivate on simple rent. In doing so he makes the best bargain he can; and the lessees being actuated by the same principle will strive to obtain it at the lowest rent. There is no such thing as an established division of the produce in shares whatever that might be, between *jenmíkar* and tenant. If the slave, cattle and seed belong to the *jenmíkar* and are hired by the tenants, the latter will pay the higher rent than if the stock were their own property, or if they were to obtain it on hire from others.

The tenants have to pay a certain rent to the *jenmíkar*, and above all it, which their industry can extract from the soil, is their own.

Out of his rent the *jenmíkar* has to discharge the interest of the *kaanum* on his land, and the government tax. The *kaanumgar* might engage to pay it on condition that the *jenmíkar* shall give him an equivalent in grain at a stated price. The residue, technically called the *shistum* or *parapaád*, remaining to the *jenmíkar*, will thus depend on what he has to pay as interest and government tax.

The *jenmíkar's* engagement with his *kaanumkar* binds him, on failure to discharge the *kaanum* interest, to put the *kaanumkar* on demand in possession of the pledged land. This conditional entry of possession forms the principal clause of all *kaanum* deeds.

The *jenmíkar's shistum* being entirely dependent on what might remain after discharging the paramount claims, he cannot insist on more. He must be contended with what the *kaanumkar* is pleased to give him as *shistum*, the latter being ever ready to resign the *seisin* of the land on his interest being insured to him, or his *kaanum* redeemed.

If the land, in the lapse of a few years, has been greatly improved, the *jenmíkar* seizes it, by demanding from the *kaanumkar* a larger *shistum*, or a further advance, under a threat of redeeming his *kaanum*. The *jenmíkar*, having already secured a person to advance him a larger sum than the original *kaanum*, cancels the latter and enters into a fresh engagement with the new *kaanumkar*, the conditions of which in regard to cultivating the pledged land shall be the same as the former one.

So that the *kaanum* tenure may be transferred in whole, or in part, and, again sub-divided into any number of portions, and transferred from one hand to another, with the *jenmíkar* being competent to inferfere. He cannot interfere. His rights, as *jenmíkar*, being totally suspended so long as the *kaanum* upon his land shall remain unredeemed.

It was, however, a prerogative inherent in the *jenmí* right, that the *kaanumkar* should renew his *kaanum* deed after the lapse of a certain number of years. The renewal entitled the *jenmikar* to a remission of a fixed per centage on his original debt. But such periodical renewals and concomitant deductions, the land in process of time became disencumbered of its *kaanum*; and the lease naturally fell in, unless the heirs in succession may have been satisfied with levying a fee in money instead of granting a renewed lease with a reduced *kaanum*.

In Major Walker's Treatise it is noticed that a lease in *every case must expire with the life of the jenmikar and that it must be renewed by the heir*. However, there were exceptions and the lease would run a specific duration of time before the heir can claim the right of renewing it.

Janmi, Jenmi a term used for a landlord in Malabár; also see *janmam*; holder of large landed property.

Janmí paimáish to get an enumeration of fields, and of garden trees, and to make a survey (in Malabár).

Janmis absolute owners of land or proprietors. See, *Janmam*, above.

Janmisabha organisation of *janmis* or land owners.

Jaram tomb.

Jareeb muktusser head surveyors.

Jareebdars, jereebdars surveyors.

Jari in'am a grant of land or other endowment still in force, not reserved.

Jaríbiyán, jarebian from *jaríb*, a certain land measure. Land measures in the Northern Circars.

Jarib the mensuration of land; a survey measurement.

Jase a kind of boat/ship.

Jatha procession; political procession.

Jati pasungarai village concentration of land within the *jati* group; also see *pasungarai.*

Jāti-siddha-āya communal tax payable in coin.

Jawabnavis clerks who conducted the collector's correspondence with all the Indian revenue servants.

Jayapāla a class of merchants.

Jena (Telugu), a span (about 7 inches).

Jetti in'am held by wrestlers in the service of *zamindars* or palegars.

Jīraka cumin seed; or any wild or cultivated crop of the cumin variety.

Jīvita, Jivita, Jivitam a revenue free grant of land for maintenance, or as a reward also; maintenance; income or wages. Also known by the terms, *jīvita-ppaṟṟu, jita* and *jīta.*

Jīvita-kkārar persons in enjoyment of lands in the *jīvita* tenure; a class of officials enjoying *jivita.*

Jīvita -ppaṟṟu service tenure lands.

Jinālayas Jina (Jain) temples.

Jirar in'am the same as *tambala in'am.*

Jital a copper coin; *jithala*, 1/48th of a silver *ṭaṅka* of the Delhi Sultans; sometimes, a copper coin equal to 1/3 of a silver *tār* which was equal to 1/6 of a gold *fanam*; also called *dehlīwāl.*

Jitavritti in'am held by a class of *kattubadi* peons known by this name who formerly used to draw pay without rendering any service. Service began to be demanded of them from *fasli* 1255.

Jitotra in'am the same as *jitavritti in'am.*

Jivisthanam land assignment for maintenance or subsistence.

Jivitam tenure these tenures were peculiar to the Madura district. They were of the same nature as the *mukhasa* in the Northern Circars/*zamindaris,* and were granted by the *zamindars* to their relatives or dependants either for subsistence or on the condition of performing 'feudal' service.

Joḍi, jore quit rent. It implies that *in'am* granted was not absolutely revenue-free but subject to the payment of a *jodi* or *salami.* Generally a half or quarter of the gross value of the produce was paid as *jodi.* In certain districts *jodi* charged on *in'am* lands was of a fluctuating character according to the terms of grants or established usage. The *jodi* consisted in some districts of a certain rate to be levied on quantity of grain grown on the *in'ams*; in others, though the *jodi* was fixed, only so much of it was collected as was in proportion to the extent of the *in'am* actually brought under cultivation during the year. Of this description were the *hangami jodi* in Cuddapah, the *putla kattubadi* of the Krishna district, the variable *jodi* of certain *in'ams* in Madura, and the *patam* and *poruppu* lands in Tinnevelly. They involved an annual scrutiny by the village and subordinate revenue officers into the produce or the cultivation of each *in'am*, and as a consequence were attended with many abuses. Moreover, a variable quit rent was incompatible with the conditions of the permanent title conferred on the recommendations of the In'am Commission. For these reasons, all such *jodi* was permanently commuted into fixed sums calculated on the average of the actual collections of past years or other equitable data.

Jodi in'am an *in'am* subject to a quit-rent.

Jogida a branch of revenue received in

money consisting of a quit-rent paid by brahmans for *in'am* lands held by them.

Josi in'am granted for the service of astrologer and astronomer to the village community.

Julah hatkar in'am granted to weavers to encourage them to settle in a village.

Jumla in'am *in'am* scattered through several villages granted as supplementary to a whole village *in'am*, all the *in'ams*, including the whole village, being subject to a lump *jodi*. The same as *paitari in'am*.

Jumta total.

Jyarum in the Karnataka, a register of lands.

K

Kācu-kaṭamai dues payable in gold.

Kāḍu-kāval (Tamil), tax for the presentation and maintenance of forests.

Kādi a grain measure.

Kākkunāyaka-viḷagam a term used in the Tamil epigraphs to denote the grant of service *in'ams* for the duty of policing or watching the standing crops; also called *kāval-kāṇi*.

Kāl-maṛuturu (Telugu), a measure of land.

Kāla dōṣam seasonal failure or drought conditions.

Kālu (Kannada), 'one foot'; a unit of measurement.

Kāma-dhēnu *kāma-dhēnu* made of gold was, as mentioned in the inscriptions, given as one of the gifts to the brahmans.

Kānuka (Telugu) an offering or courtesy made in homage to a superior or a god.

Kāṇam one of the indigenous gold coins in circulation in parts of south India; as a coin or weight of gold is mentioned in the Travancore inscriptions; it appears that *kāṇam* was less in value than a *kaḻañju*; according to some inscriptions, it appears to be equivalent to 1/10 *kaḻañju*, a little more than 5 grains, in fact, equivalent to a *paṇam* or *fanam*; name of a coin; a gold coin; a weight; a share.

Kāṇi (cawney), kāṇiyāṭchi (cawney autchi), Kāṇiyāṭchikārar (cawney qutchikar) (Tamil), a land measure equal to one-eightieth of a *veli*; a weight; a measure equivalent of 1.33 acres and land or domain, ancient form of land control, and land controllers respectively; in Tamil the term *kāṇi* has several connotations; in narrow sense, it is a measure of land, in its broader sense, the term meant land in general; in the broadest sense it meant territory; the term *āṭchie* connotes sovereignty, power, control and dominion; as much, *kāṇiyāṭchi* meant dominion over land or control over territory; each village was under the influence of one or more *kāṇiyāṭchikārar*, *i.e.* those who controlled the village domain; thus, *kāṇiyāṭchi*, in terms of its epistemological basis alone, implies a somewhat autonomous system of localised land control. *Kāṇiyāṭchi* was an ancient system of land control and *kāṇiyāṭchikārar* were land controllers in Tondaimandalam.

Kāṇiyāṭci, cāniyāṭci have frequently occurred in the Tamil inscriptions to indicate property; in Tamil lexicom it has been explained as property, dominion, power; *kāṇi/cāni* signifies literally that which is seen, marked, or recognised, and hereditary property, one who governs himself, self-rule, freedom from all restraint, independence, etc., *Kāṇiyāṭci*, as thus deduced, signifies, therefore, that which is held in free and hereditary property over which the holder possesses dominion or full power; it can be further explained as hereditary right to land, to offices, to fees, to an estate or to a kingdom, domain obtained by inheritance; that which is held as free and hereditary property; estate, one's own possession; the ideas implied in the world closely correspond to the Sanskrit word *kṣētrasvāmyam*.

Kāṇiyāṭchi was an inheritable privilege.

Under the Muslim rule, this inheritable, partially autonomous privilege was considered significant. Hence their revenue documents referred to *kāṇiyāṭchi* as *mirāsi, mirās* being the generic Persian term for inheritable rights. By the end of the 18th century, *kāṇiyāṭchi* was officially referred to only as *mirāsi*. However, such a reference understated many other facts constituting the complex phenomenon that *kāṇiyāṭchi* was.

The most clearly defined aspect of *kāṇiyāṭchi* was the control of resources and their distribution within the village, and, of course, the *kāṇiyāṭchi-kāras* were the major resource controllers. The entire village domain was controlled by them. The original *kāṇiyāṭchi-kārars* or the original colonists and their descendants acquired resource control in accordance with the prevalent criteria.

As regards the concept of 'ownership', the documents regarding transactions in *kāṇiyāṭchi* refer to *ashṭabhōgaswamitvam i.e.*, eightfold enjoyment. It clearly refers to the right of use and right of enjoyment of production and does not refer to the right of disposal or sale. The fact that an act of sale of *kāṇiyāṭchi* was often couched in the deed of sale as *dānam i.e.*, gift or charity, shows that at the time of its inception *kāṇiyāṭchi* was not saleable. As such, *kāṇiyāṭchikārars* were somewhat less than landed proprietors. On the other hand it can also be argued that the land classification under *kāṇiyāṭchi* included within it not merely cultivable land but also all the land in the village including grazing grounds, the village site, irrigation tanks, temples, cremation grounds, and roads. In this case the more appropriate term to describe their resource control would be dominion rather than *proprietas*. Moreover, the *kāṇiyāṭchikārars* were bound to the rest of the village through a series of privileges which varied from locality to locality, known as *swatantradiṭṭam i.e.*, scheme of privileges and freedoms, and a matching set of obligations. This shows that the *kāṇiyāṭchikārars* were a bit more than proprietors of land. As such, it would be proper to say that they were both less and more than proprietors.

In the later stages it can also be noticed that one of the crucial conditions of purchase or sale of *kāṇiyāṭchi* was the sanction of the fellow *kāṇiyātchikārars*. The dominance of *kāṇiyātchikārars* not only extended to the resources of temples but also stretched to the credit market. In the armoury of *kāṇiyāṭchikārars* the most potent weapon was the organisation of desertion, which could cripple the economy.

Lionel Place's 'Report' held *kāṇiyāṭchi* as a privilege held by the subject at the pleasure of the 'government', and that it could be sequestered if the *kāṇiyāṭchikārar* failed to till the land and raise the revenue demanded by the 'government.' Hence the dominon status of *kāṇiyāṭchi* was reduced to 'right of inheritance of property' in a village owned by the government. The Board of Revenue, however, developed an understanuing of *kāṇiyāṭchi* and advocated a settlement with individual *kāṇiyāṭchikārars*, but as the time passed, *kāṇiyāṭchi* could never regain its sway over the village.

Kāṇik kaḍan a term used in the epigraphs to denote having fixed the assessment; a charge on the land holding.

Kāṇik-kataṇ this term consists of two words-*kāṇi* and *kaṭaṇ*. The former means among other meanings, (i) property, (ii) possession, (iii) right of possession and (iv) hereditary right. The right of possession refers to that of land. The latter term-*kaṭaṇ* may be explained as a due payable by an individual. This term would ordinarily mean a debt or payment, easily compared with another term *kaṭamai*, a tax levy on land. Thus, *kāṇik-kaṭaṇ* may be explained as a tax, levied on the land or a tax paid by a land holder. Another contemporary term sometime used in place of *kāṇik-kaṭaṇ* was *iṛai-kaṭṭina-kāṇik-kaṭaṇ* and refers to the same item of tax, *i.e.*, land tax. As per one of the Thanjavur inscriptions of Rajaraja I, it has been mentioned equal to 100 *kalams* of paddy.

Kāṇikĕ, kāṇiki (Telugu-Kannaḍa), a land measure of 5700 sq. feet; sixty-fourth part of any coin; also 1/8 or 1/34 part; a visit; a present or gift.

Kāṇikuḍi see, *uzhavadai ulkuḍi.*

Kāṇippiḍipāḍu a lease under which the tenants could enjoy the land only after repairing the tanks in disuse and bringing under cultivation such of the lands as were covered with jungle, and it was stipulated that the lands were not to be kept without being cultivated and mounds and low grounds should be levelled and the jungle removed.

Kāṇiyāḷar, kārānmaiyāḷar another term used in the epigraphs to denote an occupant either under the king or under a grantee; he had an inextinguishable right over the land which was his holding (*kāṇi*) and had to bear the obligation fastened on the land (*kāṇikaḍam*); this term, as also *kuḍi;* also occurs in various other meanings, e.g., a service holder, service tenure holder, or having a right to any particular privilege, or franchise; occupants of lands; lords of the village domain; land controllers in the Chola mandalam; same as *kāṇiyāṭchi;* did not exist historically, there were other terms such as *kāṇiyāḷar*, which had the same meaning; term denoting sub-occupant; occupant, those having inextinguishable occupancy of land.

Kāṇiyāṭchi mānyam a collective *mānyam* held by *kāṇiyāṭchikārar*.

Kānchipuram (Conjevaram) a famous centre of weaving, trading and pilgrimage in Chengalpaṭṭu district.

Kānika offering (act of homage to the king).

Kānika Kārnika (Tamil), same as *kārṇika;* also *kārnikĕ* or *kānikĕ-kappa* or *Kāṇika-kānĕ* in Kannaḍa; 'presents from an inferior to a superior'; tolls.

Kāṇikkaṭaṇ a term connected with land revenue during Chola period in Cholamandalam.

Kār crop a short term crop; first crop.

Kār-varaku tax levied on dry land crop; it refers to levy in the land cultivating *varaku, i.e.* millet, a coarse grain in the *kār* season.

Kārāṇmai (Tamil), occupancy share; lands held free hold directly from the state; a tenure with the hereditary right of enjoyment; cultivation right; tax for the same. Also see *kāṇiyālar* above.

Kāraṇavan (Tamil), an accountant.

Kāriya-vārāycci, kārya-vārāycci (Tamil), tax paid for the superintendence of transaction also called *ārāycci.*

Kārpāśanam land wet land.

Kārpāsa cotton.

Kārtikai-arici same as *kārtikai-paccai.* However when these presents were made they were made in the months of *āḍi* (July-August) and *kārtikai* (November-December) they were known as *āḍi-kārtikai-paccai.*

Kārtikai-kāṇam, kārtikai-kācu types of presents paid by the cultivators in the month of *kārtikai* (November-December). These presents were paid in the form of money (*kāṇam* = gold coin, *kācu* = a coin).

Kārtikai-paccai a type of present paid by the cultivators in the month of *kārtikai* (Novermber-December) in kind in the form of grain or rice.

Kārttigai ariśi one of the taxes collected for maintenance of temples, brahmans, etc.

Kārttigai kāśu one of the taxes collected for the maintenance of temples, brahmans, etc.

Kāṛttigai-ṗpaccai tax on land for the maintenance of temples, brahmans, etc.

Kārttika crops reaped in the month of *kārttika*.

Kāś-āya, Kāś-āyam, kāśu-āyam (Tamil-Sanskrit), tax and dues payable in coin/cash; also, *kāś-āya-vargam, kāśu-vargam* and *kāśu-kadamai*.

Kāśāyam a term current during *Chōḷa* period used in the epigraphs to denote cash revenues of the state.

Kāśu (Tamil) *kāśu* in its general sense means coin or money in general; it is difficult to give any definite value to the *kāśu*; the attempt to give a uniform value would be clearly unscientific, due to the variety of meanings attached to the term; it is safe to say that *kāśu* was a general term applied to coins, the metallic content of which varied between 6 grains and 156 grains if gold; and if copper, the smallest copper coin, probably equivalent to a *pie*; money; a coin; 'a tax'; *kāśukaḍamai*, tax payable in cash; name of a copper coin believed to have been introduced by the Coḷas: *palaṅ-kāśu, natkāśa, nal-kāśu*, generally regarded as 1/100 of a *paṇam*.

Kāśu pottagam (land dues collected on the basis of) cash accounts.

Kāśu-kaḍamai (Tamil) tax payable in cash/coin.

Kāśukoḷḷa iṛaiyili, Kāśu-koḷḷā-iṛaiyili 'remission'; a term used in the epigraphs to denote 'in consideration of money received, the taxes were remitted'; often when lands were purchased from the village assembly by private individuals, they paid both purchase money and tax money-the' latter being the capital sum which would yield interest to enable the dues on the land to be paid year after year; the same thing is expressed in other terms in inscriptions-*vilai poruḷ* and *iṛai poruḷ*; the term used in the epigraphs to denote the township undertaking the obligation to pay the land dues themselves without any compensation or capitalisation, *i.e.* the land in question was rendered tax-free.

Kāsa stone-cutter or mason.

Kāsākāras braziers.

Kāshṭhakāri-karmāra carpenter and blacksmith.

Kāṭṭārampam the term used in Karnataka to denote forest tracts.

Kāṭṭu kōdage grant see *daśavanda* grant.

Kāval manyam the *mānyam* granted to the watchman; often these *mānyam* belonged to the *palayakkarar*.

Kāval-kāṇiyāḷar a term used to denote for men appointed for leasing out lands and realising the assessment.

Kāvalgār, kāval kāvalgār the village watchman, whose duty it was to watch the bounds of the village, crops, sticks, heaps of grain, hay, and other property of the inhabitants in the village; was held answerable for thefts committed on the heaps of the village and for such of the property of the inhabitants as was stolen by night; they were given additional grants of land inasmuch as they had to make good the loss of any property within the limits of the village boundary. *Kāval* = police duties, *kāvalkāras* = one who is appointed to attend to police duties.

According to T.V. Mahalingam, the origins of this system can be traced to the policy of setting a thief to catch a thief. These *kāvalkāras* belonged generally to the criminal tribes and they were required to prevent theft by their castemen and restore the property stolen within their locality. For this service they were paid by assignments of land for their maintenance. They themselves appointed a *talaiyāri* for each village under them. These local policemen were liable to be punished if they didnot discharge their duties properly.

In some places the *kāvalkāras* were responsible to villagers themselves. The villagers at times sold the right of policing, *pāḍikaval* as it was called. (*Ūrkāval* which was similar to *pāḍikāval* was the office or right of policing in an *ūr*). In such cases they were, as some inscriptions show, permitted to collect, at times, from each family one *panam* annually and one ring on the occasion of each marriage. It was not unusual for the village communities to sell away the *pādikāval* duty to some local chieftains or influential persons if conditions were insecure in the locality. In due course these persons, who came to hold the office by inheritance, began to collect the tax, for the police duties they discharged. The tax was called *arasu svatantaram* in some parts of Tamil areas, and *kāveli russom* in some parts of Telugu areas.

Sometimes the *kāval* rights were granted to people as a reward for certain services rendered, or to meet the expenditure for the services required of them.

Some records show the grant of *pāḍikāval* rights for repairing the tank in a village.

Most of the *kāvalkāras* of South India held their estates on *kāval* tenure. Francis (Bellary District Gazetteer) describing the method of their remuneration, writes, "The Kāvalgars were highly paid officials and granted payments as follows : (i) a village rent-free or at a very low quit rent, (ii) a certain portion of rent-free land in every village under their jurisdiction, (iii) an allowance in grain upon each plough or upon quantity of seed sown, (iv) an allowance in money paid by husbandmen or ploughs and by tradesmen on houses, shops and loomes, (v) a small duty levied or fairs and weekly markets, on shroffs paid in money and other dealers (paid in kind). Merchants who travelled on roads with merchandise had to make arrangements with the *kāvalgārs* that they would pay a particular share of their earnings if they were protected from robbers.

In some parts there was a system of chief *kāvalkāra* and was known as *arasu kāvalkāra*.

Kāvalgar in'am held for the service of a village watchman.

Kāvalpperu an additional demand on the land collected for payments to village officers.

Kāvērik-karai-viṇiyōkam the term used for the distribution of maintenance work among the villages situated on the banks of the river Kāveri.

Kāvērik kari-viṇiyōkam a phrase used in the epigraphs which may mean that for raising embankments, as a precautionary measure against floods and seepage of water, the services of the holders of land, who utilised the river water for cultivation were probably commanded.

Kāviri-kulai a special levy commanded for maintaining the banks of the river Kāveri.

Kāvitikāṇi a piece of land granted to the accountant as remuneration for his services.

Kábulait corrupted form of *qabúliyat*; an 'acceptance' form or transfer of land; 'where any land becomes available, application for a number is made by filing what is called a *Kábulait*, *i.e.* a document agreeing to take the number and pay the assessment.

Kála-vásam, Kála-vasam, callavassum from *kála* time and *vásam* residence. Temporary residence. A term applied to the *pariars* and others who in the Company's *jaghire* were employed as labouring servants, and cannot acquire property in the soil.

Kánam (Malayalam) the (so-called) mortgage tenure of Malabár. Despite a controversy over the origin and exact meaning of the term *kánam*, no reasonable doubt exists that it was wholly connected with the idea of property, and that at some time or other it became specialized to mean the sort of property, which the subordinate Náyar had when he took his lord's land against a money advance; literally property or possession, used to denote a quasi-mortgage form of land tenure in Malabar.'

Kánam pátam, kanum patum a mortgage deed. A form of conveying land in leasehold, and by which a mortgagee gets possession of land.

Káni (cawnie) a land measure of 1, 1/3 acres, but varied locally; the land was measured by a rod of 36 feet, 100 square rods being one *káni* or square feet 129, 600 equal to a *káni* 6 *manei*. See *Kāṇi*.

Káni-átachi kaurers, cawneyatchee caurers the hereditary possessors of the land.

Káni-átachi, kániádsi (Tamil), term used for '*mirási*' or hereditary (proprietary) right in village-lands etc; hereditary possession, whether of land or office. See, *Kāṇiyāṭchi*.

Káriya, kárya, carreah affair, business, employment.

Kárya-káram, kariakaram, kárya-kárah the performer of a business, an agent. The principal *mirāsdar* of a village appointed by the rest to act as their common agent.

Kával-désa, kával désha, cawel desha, cavel desha guarding the country. District watching fees, or perquisites collected from the inhabitants by the palegars for protecting those travelling on the roads, and making good, property stolen.

Kával-talam, caṿel tallum, cawel tallum watching the place. Village watching fees, or perquisites, formerly received from the inhabitants by the petty palegars; but which belonged to the *talliars*, or public officers, of each village.

Kávalkāni grant for the duty of policing.

Kabúliyat, cabooleat an agreement; particularly that entered into by the *zamindars* and farmers, with the government, for the management and renting of the land revenues. Also see, *Kábulait*.

Kach'hari court of Justice; also the public office where the revenues were paid, and other business, respective the revenue, transacted.

Kaḍai iṟai a tax on merchants.

Kaḍaippū lands lands on which only the last crop is raised; the third harvest raised on wet land.

Kaḍamai ūliyars a term appearing in the inscriptions to denote forced labourers or serfs; they were paid generally in kind at a monthly rate; besides they were allowed a piece of land to live on, and given small presents of cloth, paddy and cash on important religious and ceremonial occasions every year.

Kaḍamai, kuḍimai (Tamil), revenue, tax to be paid to the government in kind.

According to K.A. Nilkanta Sastri these terms mean 'duty' and 'tenancy dues'; he had further clarified that the term *kuḍimai* applied without distinction to the dues levied by the local assembly, the *ūr*, the *sabhā*, or the *nagaram* or in other words taxes levied by the town or the village; thus understood, *kuḍimai* stands for the duties of the *kudis* or the burdens of citizenship and is quite close in meaning also to *kaḍamai*.

T.N. Subrahmanyam renders '*kuḍimai*' as a general term denoting all taxes with the exception of land revenue payable to the state for the protection it offers to the civil rights, teñancy tax. However, the implications of both these terms can be made only with reference to the context, and the content of which they occur in the inscriptions. *Kaḍamai* is the land revenue fixed on the land, due from the occupant to the king or his assignee. It could be prefixed on it even prior to the induction of an occupant or when the lands were graded for assessment. The obligation to pay *kaḍamai* becomes effective only on the induction of an occupant. It is payable in kind or in cash or both, in the case of irrigated crops. It is a primary charge on the land and its occupant.

The usages of the term *kuḍimai* in the inscriptions that it can be distinguished from *kaḍāmai* taking into consideration the nature of the obligation as well as the persons on whom the incidence fell. It is evident from the epigraphs that *kuḍimai* was in the form of services to the king, or to the deity or to the *nāḍu*. It also included the communal obligation of raising, protecting and maintaining the river embankments (*kulai*), or cross-bunding the river for diverting water into the supply channels (*korombo*) and also for periodical silt clearance of field channels when the freshes arrived. Other services that could be added were the contingent services due, the attendance on the king and his entourage when on tour, or at the palace gate. Every village had to depute its quota of men for watch and ward at the palace. Instances in which the *kuḍimai* was payable in kind or in cash are also noticeable in the epigraphs but their quantum was far smaller than *kaḍamai*. The *kuḍimai* obligations could and did befall a person who was not necessarily an occupant. One inscription is quite explicit according to which "No part of the *kuḍimai* shall be collected from the brahmans and the *veḷḷāḷas*."

As such, it can be opined that the primary obligation of *kaḍamai* or land demand was that of the occupant. The primary obligation for the services and the miscellaneous levies (*kuḍimai*) was that of the tenants and the cultivator, under the occupants. *Kaḍamai* was essentially an obligation cast on land and the attribute of occupancy. *Kuḍimai* were the obligations varied in their nature, contingent, seasonal or communal in their character', and invariably borne by the tenants and the cultivators, especially in cases where the occupants or the landholders were not themselves the cultivators. Land revenue; taxes on land; terms current especially during the Chola period.

Kaḍhichakas bricklayers.

Kaḍit-āmātya, kaḍita-vĕrgaḍĕ (Kannada-Sanskrit), official designation; superintendent of accounts and records.

Kadaiyan in'am held for the service of supplying fish and cadjan leaves to the *zamindar*.

Kadambu the piratical rendezvous of the tribe who became later known as the *kadambas*.

Kadarambam 'land which was dry or chiefly watered by rains'; dry land, dependent on rain for cultivation; dry land, depending entirely upon rains for watering.

Kadeem see *qadim*.

Kadikaluthan a type of paddy crop raised from seedlings sown about the third week of July and transplanted a month later. The crop is reaped at the beginning of March. It is raised on one crop land, and is suited to grounds on river-banks and tank-beds liable to inundation. It is chiefly cultivated on the soil termed *'oouarkally'* or *'alal sherndakally,'* a saltish clay.

Kadir-kkāṇam (Tamil), tax paid in sheaves of corn.

Kaharan porters and labourers.

Kai a unit of measurement; same as *hasta*, 'cubit.'

Kai-kánam-pátam, kay-kanum-patum conveyance of a spot of land, in Malabar, to one who undertakes to fence it with mud walls, and plant it with trees, being insured in the possession of it for a specified period.

Kaigāṇa one of the three types of oil mills mentioned in inscriptions; a hand mill; as the process of extracting oil in this form of mill was slow, only half of the tax that on *ettugāna* was charged.

Kaikkōḷas one of the communities engaged in the textile industry; weavers; though there were other communities, like *śāliyas* and occasionally the *pariahs*, engaged in this profession, *kaikkōlas* were supposed to be an influential community who supplied the necessary clothing to the people.

Kaikkoḷar (Tamil); this word was used in two senses e.g. a soldier and a weaver.

Kaikolans an important Tamil caste of weavers, specially numerous in Kanjeevaram. According to tradition they are descended from nine heroes who assisted the God Subrahmaniam to destroy certain demons. One girl at least from each *kaikolan* family should be dedicated to temple service. Also see, *kaikkōḷas* above.

Kail experimental reapings (*kail*) conducted both by the revenue staff and by the settlement to test the rate of produce on different soils, and compared with opinions of the *rayats* and the *tahsíldárs* (a pre-British system).

Kailu heaping

Khairáti, Khairát (Arabic), alms; *In'ams* granted to Muslims for charitable purposes. Secular *in'ams*.

Kaittaḷaikai kūṭṭam royal servants or soḷidery.

Kaivarta-bhoga periodical supplies of fruits, firewood, flowers and the like which the villagers had to supply to the king; sometimes explained as 'tax in kind'; also used as, tax-free land set apart for the performance of specified services; same as *mānya.*

Kaiviṇaikkuḍi a term referred in a few inscriptions to denote a labourer hired daily as distinct from *puṛakkuḍi* or *piṛakkuḍi*, or simply *kuḍi*.

Kal-velai in'am granted for service as a sculptor in stone in a pagoda.

Kaḷañju, Kaḷañju a term which often occurs in Tamil is to be interpreted sometimes as gold weight, and sometimes as coins; as coin it weighed about 52 grains and evidently derived its name from the *kaḷañju* seeds; *kaḷañju* continues to be mentioned in inscriptions till the seventh and eighth centuries, and perhaps later, but probably as weight only. Name of gold coin; also of the equivalent weight; about 32 *ratis.*

Kaḷa punjey dry lands abutting threshing floors or bunds.

Kaḷam, kaḷaṭumēḍū a place or location of the office of village accountant; threshing floor, an invariably common place for the whole village; *kaḷam* is the Tamil form of the Sanskrit *khala*; threshing ground or threshing floor.

Kaḷani vāriyam 'wet fields committee'; its function was to see that proper cultivation of the lands was not neglected.

Kaḷanilam inherently infertile land.

Kaḷaṛu in the inscriptions, *kaḷaṛu* was probably intended to mean the barren land, not fit for cultivation; the expression *kaḷaṛu*, however, can mean barren or brackish land.

Kalagam chaos; it has been used in the epigraphs in the context that because of *kalagam* the occupants and the tenants left the particular area and migrated to some other area.

Kalai bull.

Kalali tax on sale of intoxicants, a tax on spirituous liquors, an excise.

Kalam, collum a measure in common use in the Tanjore delta and adjoining districts; varied from place to place; approximately equivalent to 1.5 kg. of paddy. In Madurai 1 *kalam* = 48 Madras measures (*a kalam* of paddy being therefore about 120 lb.), in South Arcot-equal to 24 Madras measures, near Palur 36. Also, store house of paddy.

Kalappai, alappadai the terms used for the plough axe-that which digs the earth and makes the furrows.

Kaliṅga-vāriyam (Tamil), committee looking after the sluice; the term is derived from the word *kaliṅgu*, 'a sluice.'

Kaliṅgam cloth

Kalinga manyam granted for having constructed a sluice or outlet for carrying off the surplus water of a tank.

Kalippanam money realized from peasants by landlords for staging plays like kathakali.

Kaliyuga the last and the worst of the four ages of human deterioration; iron age.

Kallāṇa kaṇikkai a term used in the epigraphs to denote tax on marriages; the rate of this tax probably differed with the kind of marriage. As a matter of fact taxes were levied on marriage processions, marriage pandals and marriage celebrations which included dusting of sandal powder and taking processions in palanquins.

Kallans a Tamil caste, traditionally thieves and cattle lifters or burglars, largely employed in Madurai district as watchmen-subsisting in many parts on blackmail and robbery, while in others agriculturists.

Kallasaris workers in stone, the occupational name in Malabar of a section of the great artisan caste of *kammalans*.

Kaliṅkattup-paraṇi, kulōttuṅika-choḻaṉ ula; vikarama-chōḻāṉ ula, maṉtalikaṉ, or maṉtalikar (plural form of *maṉṭalikaṉ*) different terms used in the epigraphs which means the ruler of a *manḍalam*.

Kalum crop the term refers to the first crop of paddy in some areas. It was raised when the north-east monsoon sets in August or September. The best variety was grown in this season.

Kāluve a tax on land for the maintenance or irrigation works.

Kalvay pannadi in'am granted for the service of opening and closing irrigation channels.

Kaṁsāli gold smith

Kamál, kámil (Arabic), perfect; the full assessment of land, consisting of the older rate ('<u>ain</u> and *tank<u>h</u>wá*) increased up to a higher standard; after the fall of the Vijayanagar empire, the Muslim rulers, who took possession of the empire, conducted a survey of the land and assessment made by them was known by the term 'Kamil Assessment.'

Kamanisu the business of collecting revenues; period of government; time of management.

Kamati in'am granted for the support of a bricklayer attached to a pagoda.

Kamba, kamma (Kannaḍa), a post or pillar; a land measure equal to one-hundredth of a *mattaru*; same as *stambha, skambha*.

Kambakkaran in'am the same as *nirganti in'am*.

Kambamkatti in'am the same as *nirganti in'am*.

Kambangatti mānyam the *mānyam* granted to the irrigation attendant.

Kambankatti the irrigation attendant; their number would vary from village to village and sometimes from time to time; an essential component of many a village; some of them had *mānyam* land, some would get fixed share of the village output, while some would get both for their maintenance.

Kambharti in'am *in'am* granted to village officers in the Ceded Districts to make up their *in'ams* to the standard scale of emolument adopted by Thomas Muuro.

Kambu spiked millet (*pennisetum typhoideum*); also *sazzulu*.

Kamil, Kamal (A. = perfect) the full assessment of land.

Kammāra, blacksmiths, the workers in iron and steel; also called *lohakāra, lohavaniya,* sometimes he is also referred as coppersmith.

Kammāṇa, kammāḷar, kaṇmāḷar (Tamil), the five artisan classes; also called *āju-pācālattār*; the artisan communities.

A term used for carpenters, masons; generally for five castes of skilled artificers; they trace their ancestry to the five sons of Viśvakarma, of whom the first-born, Manu, worked in iron; the second, Maya, in wood; the third, Tvastram, in brass, copper, and alloys; the fourth, Silpi, in stone; and the fifth, Viśvajña, was a gold and silversmith and jeweller.

Kammāra in'am held for the service of village blacksmith.

Kammaralas, kammalas, kammalans the great artisan caste of Tamil and Malayalam areas, divided in the five sections, *tattans* (goldsmiths), *kannans* (braziers), *tachans* (carpenters), *kaltachans* or *kallasaris* (stone masons), and *kollans* or *karumans* (blacksmiths). Also see, *kammāṇa* above.

Kammas originally a soldiers caste, then landowners and cultivators, and very industrious and intelligent agriculturists.

Kammayi vettu held for the service of collecting work-people to repair tanks; the same as *kulam vettu*.

Kampala, kampaṇa name of an administrative division.

Kamsala in'am held for the service of village goldsmith.

Kamukukku-kaṭamai a tax on the *kamuku i.e.* areca palm tree.

Kaṇakka-kkāṇi (Tamil), land set apart for the village accountant.

Kaṇakka-pperu (Tamil), tax, payable in grains, for the maintenance of the village accountant.

Kaṇakkavari one of the taxes collected on land to suport village officers.

Kaṇakku this term seems to have been used in the epigraphs in the sense of revenue accounts.

Kaṇḍuḷavu crown lands or the palace estate.

Kaṇikkai, kāṇikkai a voluntary offering; presents or customary payments to the king and other high officials.

Kaṇkāaṇi, kaṇkāṇik-kaṇakkar-mutal, kaṇkāṇyār-nellu, kaṇmi-pēṟu different terms used to denote payments as remuneration to servants of the king or local bodies.

Kaṇkāṇiccu officers of the temple appointed to supervise the harvesting.

Kaṇṇāla-kkāṇam (Tamil), the marriage fee; a tax on marriage; same as *vivāhappanam*.

Kaṇṇālak-kāṇam, kallāṇakkāṇam different terms used to denote marriage tax. At some places marriage fee was assessed on both the parties. The evidence clearly shows that it was a voluntary communal levy imposed by the community. Also see *kallāṇa, kaṇikkai* above.

Kaṇṇāṟu channel, a term used in the epigraphs to emphasize that the lands were localised and grouped under each channel; block of land.

Kanaga the bastard rose-wood (*dalbergia lanceolaria*). The oil extracted from the fruit-used as an illuminant and on the hair.

Kanakkan mānyam the mānyam granted to village acountant

Kanakkar (sl.), kanamdar, kanakkaram (pl.) one who holds hands on *kanam* tenure. A redeemable right; cultivating leaseholder or mortgagee.

Kanakupilai, conicopoly an accountant, writer, clerk.

Kanam mortgage or lease.

Kanam patom ola karunum deed of lease or mortgage on *patom*.

Kanamkar, kanamdar, kanakkar (Malayalam) mortgagee; one who has land pledged to him in security for the interest of money advanced to the *jenmikar*, which advance or debt is the *kanam* that is ever incumbent, or remain fastened on the land, until it be redeemed. Whether the *jenmikar* or *kanamkar* shall cultivate the pledged land is a point settled between themselves by mutual agreement. All that the *kanamkar* looks to is securing the interest of his money. He may, for example, be a trader, and totally ignorant of agriculture or farming. He will, thus circumstanced, agree to the *jenmikar's* cultivating the pledged land by any means in his power and discharge the interest of the *kanam* on his land, and the government tax. In case the *jenmi* fails to meet the requirement or can cultivate or get the land cultivated, he would put the *kanamkar* on demand in possession of the pledged land. This conditional entry of possession forms the principal clause of all *kanam* deeds.

The *kanamkar*, after entering into possession, is invested with every right of proprietorship excepting that of alienating the land by sale. He can only alienate the right he has purchased. The right of sale therefore he can only command after he has completed the *jenmi* purchase. But his *kanam* right, he can transfer in full, or parcel it out in sub-divisions on mortgage, or any other subordinate tenure.

It was a prerogative inherent in the *jenmi* right, that the *kanamkar* should renew his *kanam* deed after the lapse of a certain number of years. The renewal entitled the *jenmikar* to a remission of a fixed percentage on his original debt. But such periodical renewals and concomitant deductions, the land in process of time became disencumbered of its *kanam*; and the lease naturally fell in, unless the heirs in succession may have been satisfied with levying a fee in money instead of granting a renewed lease with a reduced *kanam*.

In Major Walker's Treatise it is noticed that a lease in *every case must expire with the life of the the jenmikar* and that it *must be renewed by the heir*. There were, however, some exceptions, and provided for the old lease running a specific duration of time before the heir can claim the right of renewing it.

Kanchani in'am *in'am* held by dancing girls.

Kañchara blacksmith

Kañchuki chamberlain.

Kāñji, kāñjika sour gruel

Kanda name of a metre common in Telugu and Kannaḍa.

Kandāyam, condoyam a fee which a *pāḷayakārar* was entitled to get from the territories under his jurisdiction.

Kandachar in'am held by *kattubadi* peons employed in the western taluks of Bellary who were remunerated by fixed remissions from the assessment of the lands held by them.

Kangani in'am held for the service of watching the crops.

Kani, Kani-atchi, Kaniadsi (T.) hereditary rights; Tamil term for *meeras*. Also a particular measure of land (fixed in 1800 at 1.32 acres), but varied locally. Also see, *Kāṇi*.

Kani manyam the same as *grama manyam*.

Kanians one of the castes mentioned by Barbosa, engaged in making umbrellas, bucklers, etc. from the leaves of the palms.

Kanjud oil seeds.

Kanjurnoi (Tamil), lit. 'dry disease'; a name given to various plant diseases.

Kankāṇi one of the taxes collected on land to support village officials.

Kanni month September-October.

Kanomdar holder of a privileged tenure from a *jenmi*.

Kanṟu mēyum pāḷu part of the cultivable land left uncultivated for the cattle to graze; it has also been translated as 'land lying as pasture for the calves'; also some good portion of the uncultivated land appropriated for the pasturage of the kine and the like.

Kappa (Tamil-Telugu-Kannaḍa) periodical and customary payments by persons engaged in some professions.

Kapu a cultivating class of sudras; they may even stand for leading agriculturists of the place if not village officials; enjoying considerable status in the society; or *reddis,* the largest caste in Madras Presidency, at one time numbering over two millions, though Telugus, quite numerous also in Tamil districts; almost invariably landowners or cultivators. The word *kapu* is said to mean watchman and Reddi king.

Kapu in'am the same as *pedda kapu in'am*.

Kaṛenāḍu black soil.

Kaṛkkiṭai stony waste land.

Kara 'the dues (bhāga) to be realised by the king for the enjoyment of royal land by using it for cultivation and for grazing cattle'; tax in general; a tax or impost; royal revenue; rent, dues; toll, tribute.

Kara-grāma a revenue paying village, could be a *rayatwari* village.

Kara-śāsana charter recording a grant of land for which the donee had to pay rent; a grant for which revenue, either in full or at concessional rate, was fixed; land granted in the said way.

Karāṇmaiyāḷar this term is almost similar to *vellān vagai* but had a little distinction; in this case, the land-obligations to pay *kaḍamai* (the principal levy on land) could be due to an assignee; the proceeds or yield of cultivation *minus* such obligations could be held by an occupant, who may himself cultivate or cause it to be cultivated for himself; briefly the present term denotes an occupant, having the right to enjoy the fruits of cultivation after paying the land-dues.

Karabādai tax-obligations.

Karagrāma revenue village.

Karai share of joint village or land; blocks; the term has been used in Tamil inscriptions to denote division of a village in to several *karai*.

Karai manyam the same as *kulam vettu*.

Karai-yidi a tenure under which the lands of a village are exchanged amongst the coparceners periodically.

Karaikaran headman of a *karai*.

Karaikkattu vaikkalkattu an account of the positions, variations and maintenance of bunds and irrigation channels.

Karaiyar share holding occupants.

Karaiyedu, Karaiyīd *mirasi* village shared by *sudras*; a variation on *pasungarai*, but was less ancient system; under it all land was held individually, but redistributed once in certain number of years; a village or a portion of a village held under joint ownership which consisted either of waste land or inferior fields of which the cultivation was precarious; these were therefore such lands as it was expedient not to divide or such as were not worth dividing; such a state of things might arise also by the terms of the original grant when land was granted to a group of colonists, the land itself being divided equally among them; such a village in Tamil areas was known by the name of 'Karaiyīd.'

A system of periodical redistribution of lands. "Under this system the community is the owner of all the lands in the village, but it does not cultivate the lands jointly or enjoy in common the fruits of the labour spent on them. The lands in the village are divided into three classes, good, middling and bad, and every individual member of the joint community is given a portion of each of these three classes; he is not to be in permanent possession of the allotted lands, but is required to part with them after a fixed time in return for other plots in each of these three classes." As such, there is a periodical redistribution of the lands held by the joint community among its members. Same as *Karaiyīḍu*.

Karaiyīḍu, Kareiyídú, Kareiyédú (Tamil) form of communal land holding with rotation of shares; one of the ancient methods of holding in the 'landlord villages' under which there was a periodical exchange of holdings; where the land was temporarily allotted, but the shares were periodically exchanged so as to give good and bad in turn to each; a system of periodical redistribution of lands; *mirasi* village shared by *sudras*; a variation on *pasungarai*, but was less ancient system; under it all land was held individually, but redistributed once in certain number of years. Also see *Karaiyedu* above.

Karanavan head of a matrilineal Hindu family in Kerala; an elder; head of the household.

Karaṇam, karṇam village accountant; a document; also *kaṇakkaṇ, karaṇikka.*

Karaṇas village-accountants (Chāḷukyas of Bādāmi).

Karaṇattān (village) accountant.

Karaṇike one of the taxes accruing from the villages.

Karaṇikka-joḍi the quit-rent of the *karaṇam* or *karṇam.*

Kaṟppūra-villai (Sanskrit-Tamil), this term has been generally explained by the scholars as a royalty derived on camphor.

Some of the records pertaining to the Pandya period have explained this tax in somewhat detailed manner. It can be understood from some epigraphs of the period that the *kāṇi* right of land was granted by the local chief to an individual after having received from the latter the *kaṟpūra-villai*, meaning thereby, that the right to the *kāṇi* land was purchased by the individual. The term would certainly indicate some kind of fee levied on the individual by the local chiefs for recognizing land right.

The *kaṟpūra, i.e.* camphor was used for various purposes, especially for performing worship in temples. As such, since the lands on which the said levy was collected were meant for temples, *kaṟpūra-villai* may be explained as nominal price of these lands. It also said to be a lumpsum payment in lieu of land dues; sale price paid for temple lands; price paid for cultivation rights of temple lands and in commutation of taxes thereon.

Kareekar lit. husbandman; a simple tenant of land who has no personal claim on the ground he cultivates.

Karisal, karasal a term generally used for a type of land of dark clay containing a small proportion of the sand; black soil, black muddy soil.

Karkoon a clerk acting as an assistant to *sheristadar* and *tehsildar.*

Karkunan clerks, writers, registrars, used also generally in financial and revenue collections.

Karnam, kurnam, curnam (K.) a village accountant, also *patwari, shenbogue, kulkarni, menon* etc.

Karnam in'am granted for the service of village accountant.

Karnika-mirasi *in'am* giving land and perquisites to village accountant.

Karpūra-mūlya, kappūra-vilai, Karpūravilai the sale-price paid for temple lands; the price paid for cultivation rights of temple lands and in commutation of the taxes thereon.

This term has been used in the epigraphs in the context that the kings dues could be purchased on payment of a capitalised amount in cash, capitalised levy.

Karpura-dipam in'am granted for the service of burning camphor in pagodas.

Karshaka sangham association of peasants; peasant union.

Karugal a plant disease, involving blackening of the tissues; not specifically identifiable.

Karumān field the field of the blacksmith.

Karuman blacksmith; their number may vary from village to village and from time to time; an essential component of most villages; got their remunerations in the shape of a *mānyam* land or a fixed share of the village output, or in some cases both.

Karuman mānyam the mānyam granted to the blacksmith.

Karuṇai tubers.

Karuppukittinoi (Tamil), *karuppu* back, *kitti* approaching, *noi* disease; a plant disease, not specifically identifiable.

Karuvans, karumans blacksmiths, a division of the *kammalan* caste. Also see, *karuman* above.

Karūvel (Tamil), cadvel a thorn tree; the *babul*; *acacia arabica*, wild. It consolidates and strengthens the banks of paddy fields. Timber used for making ploughs, carts and charcoal. Leaves are excellent manure and a nutritious for sheep.

Karyasthan manager of the property of a landlord.

Karzi in'am granted for the service of headman of a village.

Kasai in'am granted for the support of a butcher.

Kasalu (Telugu) personal servant.

Kasawurgum the derivation of the word does not seem to be wellknown; in some records hardly any distinction is made between *kasawurgum* and *purakudi* rayats; in some cases the court considered both as 'tenants at will'; in Kanara it certainly conveys the idea that the person to whom it is applied, held the land whether house site, or arable land, on his own private account under the *sirkar* and not as the sub-tenant of another landholder. *Wurgum* or *wurg* though from the permanence of tenure in Kanara it has there come to mean *on Estate*, signifies primarily *an account*, and hence the land included in a landholder's account and it stands in the village register and in the government revenue accounts.

Kasawurgum would then mean *private account*, and certainly if used in contradistinction to *parakudi* as distinguishing the respective rights of individuals would to any one convey the idea above mentioned.

It is perhaps not impossible that the use of the word in Tanjore indicates the former existence of separate rights which in the course of time have been absorbed by the *mirāṣīdārs*.

Kassa unstarched cloth; a type of calico cloth made especially in Vijayanagar empire.

Kaṭai-iṟai tax on shop.

Kaṭai-taram a term used to denote the lowest grade of land in South Arcot Ramanathapuram and Tiruchirappalli districts.

Kaṭaippāṭṭattāl-vanta-kaṭamai, kaṭaippāṭṭam, kaṭaiyāyam, kaṭai-yiṟa

different terms used in the inscriptions to denote tax on shop.

Kaṭaiyiṭu deed or execution.

Kaṭamai, kuṭiamai a common term used to indicate land dues, assessed on the basis of unit *mā* of land current especially during the Chola period; a term comparable with *iṟai*; it was also suffixed to other terms; to cite a few examples: *kācu-kaṭamai* - dues payable in gold, *tēvar-kaṭamai*-dues payable to the king, *peruṅ-kuṭikal-pēṟāl-kaṭamai* - dues on land owner/cultivator, *vāṇikkar-pērāṟ-kaṭamai* - dues on merchant, *cekkuk-kaṭamai* - dues on oil press, *ēttak-kaṭamai* - dues on water-lift. It shows that the term had a wider application and used to connote dues of other kind. It also seems that perhaps the term *kaṭamai* replaced *iṟai* during the later stages of the Chola period. Other terms with which *kaṭamai* was suffixed especially in Cholamandalam are : *iṟai, kumukukku, kāṇik, kār, kiḻiṟaik, māvinta, neṟ, nilak, pañcavārak, peruṅkuṭikaḷ-pērāl, pirāmaṇaṟ-pēṟ, poliyūṭṭuk, puṇcey, toṇik, taṇpaṭu, tēvar, tiruvācalil-pōnta, ūrmāvīnta.* During Tondaimandalam *kaṭamai*-suffixed terms included: *ācivak, ācivikaḷ-pērk, ācuvikaḷ-potumakkal-peral-vanta, cālikar-vāṇkar-pērāṟ, cekkuk, ēttak, kācu, kamukukku, kaṭaip-pāṭṭattāl-vanta, makkal, maṉṟātikaḷ-pērk, naṇcey-puṇcey-nilam, neṟk, nilak, oṭṭumpaṭiyāl-vanta, poṟ, purakkalaṇaik vāṇikar-pēr, vāṇiyar-perālum-maṉṟātikaḷ-pērālum-vanta.*

Kaṭikai-kōl a measuring rod used in the revenue surveys; equal to 16 *cāṇ* = approximately 12 feet in length.

Kaṭṭārampam a term used to denote tax collected on dry land in Karnataka.

Kaṭṭaṇa periodical presents made to superiors by their subordinates.

Kaṭṭe, kāluve, keṟe several terms appearing in the epigraphs to denote taxes, the proceeds of which were used for repairing tanks; an additional tax on land for maintenance of irrigation works.

Kaṭṭē custom house.

Kaṭṭha wood.

Kaṭṭigevarttanai a term used in the inscriptions of the first half of the fifteenth century to denote a tax that accrued from the villages.

Kaṭṭilērap-pōm-pōtu a term used in the epigraphs which denotes that outside settlers would provide one sheep each whenever any one among them consummated a marriage.

Kaṭṭilērutal a term which denotes that the shepherds agreed to pay a sheep to the temple on the occasion of marriage of their sons and of their daughters setting up of separate families.

Kaṭṭu bundles (of betel).

Kaṭṭu-kkuttagai, Kaṭṭugutagai, kaṭṭukkuttagai, Kaṭṭu-guttagai, Kattukuttagai (Tamil), *kattu* tie, *kuttagai* rent; a defined fixed rent; the letting of land for a defined rent; a contract; revenue fixed at the time of farming out of the land; payment of consolidated revenue; farming system of land; land given on contract or lease; payment of a fixed rent to the landlord; it seems that this system was generally prevalent in dry lands.

Kaṭṭumukkai (Tamil), a contribution of three handfuls for every bundle of paddy stalks harvested-payable to the temples.

Katai-āyam cess on shop.

Katti (catty) a measure of land, which differs in various districts; in government accounts a *'cutty'* is rated at 40 acres and 14 *guntas*; it is considered to be as much as a man can reap in one day; a certain weight in Kánara; the *katti* was 3200 rupees in weight.

Katti-kkāṇam (Tamil), tax on weapons like swords etc; tax in manufacture of swords or arms.

Kattiyam in'am granted for the service of proclaiming the praises of an idol when carried in procession.

Kattu kodige in'am the same as *dasabhandam in'am.*

Kattubadi in'am *in'am* held by the *kattubadis*, a class of peons who discharged police, military and not unfrequently, revenue duties. They were called into existence by the palegars who remunerated them by assignments of land and paid them *batta* besides while on actual service, and were chiefly employed in the hilly and inaccessible parts of the country. On the introduction of the British rule, they were generally left in the quiet possession of their *in'am* and but seldom called out for duty. The Inam Commission enfranchised all their *in'ams*, but the issue of title-deeds was suspended pending the completion of the new police arrangements which were to altogether relieve the *kattubadis* of their police duties; were found in the greatest numbers in the Ceded Districts and North Arcot; *in'ams* were subject to quit-rent, but hereditary in nature.

Kattubadis, Cuttobuddies peons or militia men employed by the palegars for military service, performed police and revenue duties, *grama kattubadis*, village servants and peons, performed service throughout the year; *jangi kattubadis*, called for service on emergent occasions. In practice both the classes performed revenue and police duties indiscriminately, as occasion required.

Kattugutta in'am *in'am* lands held on a fixed rent less than the full assessment. They have been treated as *jodi in'ams.*

Kattuva a dam, mole or bank.

Kaul (Hindustani) agreement; contract; negotiated revenue engagement.

Kaulika-nikāya the weaver's guild.

Kaval protection money.

Kavale, kavaleḍu, kavaligĕ Telugu-Kannaḍa, a pack of written leaves; palm leaves prepared for writing accounts.

Kavalgar, Kavalkaran (Tamil) watchman, police incharge for the protection of the village. Same as *kāvalgār* discussed above.

Kaveli russom protection money; fee or perquisite of a *kavalgar.*

Kaviraya in'am held by Tamil poets, generally in the service of *zamindars* or palegars.

Kavitai patam in'am held by a Brahman poet attached to the court of a palegar.

Kavu shrine.

Kawali (in the Karnatik) a chief appointed by the king to maintain a force for policing the roads and keeping order over a number of *parganas* or even a full district; same as in Telugu *mannevadu* and *kavali*, also *muniwar* in northern Golconda.

Kayam jodi in'am an *in'am* held on a fixed quit-rent not subject to variation with reference to cultivation or produce.

Kayam Pattah *Pattah* granted to substantial *rayats.*

Kazi in'am held for service as *kazi*, a Muhammadan judicial officer who administered both civil and criminal law, chiefly in towns, according to the principles of the Koran. During the British period their duties were mainly confined to the general superintendence and legalization of the ceremonies of marriage, funerals, and other domestic occurrences among the Muhammadans.

Kēḻdavadhārisi complaints.

Kelẏarku, Kēḻvaragu *rāgi.*

Kedāra wet land; also a measure of land; equal to 7/8 *bigha*; 12 *kedāras* equal to one *hala.*

Kedaranarthy *citrus medica.*

Keppai *tenai*, Italian millet.

Kere an additional demand on the

land collected for the maintenance of irrigation works.

Ket-punjai, kate punjah land which from situation cannot be irrigated, and which, strictly speaking, depends upon the falling rains.

Keyār a measure of land and another name of *kedāra*.

Khādaka, khanaka, khātaka digging; the terms may be also taken to stand for the abrogation of royal right of digging pits for extracting salt.

Khās lands lands held privately for his (king's) own personal use and benefit, as distinct from the lands held under him by others; lands held by a prince; the revenue of which ought to go to the public purse; king/prince was at liberty to alienate such lands.

Khāvandu lord, master.

Khátedár the term used for 'registered occupant' of land in Bombay and Berar.

Khadim (Hindustani) servant

Khajan, khājan, khajjana, khajjaṇa, khajjāna, khajjaṇaka different meanings have been attributed to this term —' a specific area of cultivable land or locality'; 'marshy land'; 'a salt-marsh or meadow'; land lying along the shore of the sea or of inlets, and exposed to be flooded; 'ground recovered by embankment from sea'; 'the area (near the sea-shore) on which a thin layer of sand and mud accumulates after the ebbtide coming through inlets'; 'a rice-field created out such an area near a hillock by erecting embankments on the three other sides'; 'a field created by reclamation of the river bed'; cultivable land created from a bed of river which carries the flood water from the sea; a salty marsh or meadow; a rice field created near the bed of a nullah on the sea shore by putting embankment.

Kham hissab general statement.

Kham wasual revenue statement of exact conditions in each village.

Khaṇḍī, khaṇḍi a land measure; spelt in English as *candy*; also a measure of capacity.

Khaṇḍa subdivision of a province or district.

Khaṇḍaka a land measure; also in Tamil *Kaṇḍakam*.

Khaṇḍuka, khaṇḍuga, khaṇḍika, khaṇḍikā khandi, Khaṇḍika Khaṇḍikā (Telugu-Kannaḍa) measure of capacity; same as *khaṇḍi* or *candy*; often equal to between 800 to 1000 seers; a weight of about 60 maunds for silk, sugar, drugs and cotton; a land measure-64,000 square yards of dry and 10,000 square yards of wet land (in Mysore); varied in different areas; a term used in the epigraphs to indicate the sowing capacity of a particular piece of land *i.e.* a unit of land requiring a *khaṇḍuga* of seed to be sown.

Khanduka vāpa an area of land requiring one *khaṇḍuka* measure of seed grains for sowing.

Khanah zadan (long-established) official families.

Khandi a certain measure of grain; a measure of weight equal to 20 *maunds* (pukhta). Same as *khaṇḍī* above.

Khandrika a small hamlet.

Khandrika in'am a large block of land granted as *in'am*, less than a village but much larger than an ordinary *in'am*.

Khandriká one of the three categories of lands in the Telingana viz., the *māniyám* revenue-free land, the *khandrikā* subject to a quit-rent, and the revenue-paying land.

Kharvaḍa, kharvata, kharvaṭa, kharvaṭam an administrative unit; according to some name of a market town.

Khas own, private, personal.

Khas khail élite royal house guard.

Khas lands royal estates. Same as *khās lands*, above.

Khasa in'am held for domestic service in the house hold of a *zamindar* in the Northern Circars.

Khassgut private revenue records maintained by the *subedar*.

Khaṭā cot; the term is used to indicate the obligation of the villagers to arrange for the amenities for touring state officers.

Khatib in'am granted for the service of reading the Koran in a mosque.

Kheḍa same as *khaṇḍa*.

Khetwar field assessment.

Khichádi a 'mixed' village under the *khot* landlord in Konkán area especially Ratanagiri district. The villages under *khots* were either (i) entirely held by peasant proprietors or '*dhárekár*' or (ii) entirely held by common tenantry, or (iii) by '*khichádi*' or mixed *i.e.* partly held by *dhárekárs*, partly by common tenants.

Khoobash one who lives at his ease; a description of inhabitants in the Ceded Districts.

Khot in Konkan districts, originally a revenue-farmer; whether as a former landowner or local land officer with an ancient hereditary title, or otherwise; later proprietor; the terms *khot, khotí, khotgí* or *khotkí* (for the office or grade), are given as Maráthí by Wilson.

Khulga in'am granted to tank-diggers for the service of executing petty repairs to tanks and channels; the same as *potula in'am*.

Kīḻ kārāṇmai tenants deriving cultivation rights (from the holder of land).

Kīḻ kuḍigaḷitār, kīḻ kāraṇmai uḍaya kuḍigaḷ this term relates to the land rights; K.A. Nilakant Sastri, explaining this term, has observed, "As the landlord might himself be the actual cultivator, the class of occupant cultivators was sometimes distinguished by the name *kīḻ kuḍigalitār*, that is, the occupants with subordinate cultivation rights." However, this term needs further clarification and revision. If this term denotes occupant cultivators, then the term '*kārāṇmai uḍaiya kuḍigal*' should suffice. The better interpretation of the term, if the inscription in which it occurs is given a further probing could be 'the tenants having sub-occupancy rights' as distinct and separate from the 'main occupant' (the *kuḍi*) under the *dēvadāna* tenure of lands. Alternatively, as per the inscription, the temple itself could be the *kārāṇmai* holder, and *kīḻ kārāṇmai udaya kuḍigal* should then refer to the tenants under or deriving their cultivation rights (*kīḻ kārāṇmai*) from the *kārāṇmai*, the temple. The prefix '*kīḻ*' in '*kiḻkārāṇmai*' denotes the subordinate interest of this category of tenants as distinguished from the principal interest of the occupant from whom the former interest is derived.

Kiatu a kind of indigenous boat built like grain measures.

Kiḍangu ditches; some epigraphists have translated this term as 'tanks', but at the same time the word *kuḷam* has also been given to mean tanks; the term should be taken in its more common sense, a ditch or a small pit.

Kiḻān village headman.

Kiḻiṟaip-pāṭṭam a type of taxes.

Kiladar, Qiladar fort commandant.

Killar-ulai-pāṭṭam the term used to denote tax on backsmith. It may be understood that the tax was levied on the furnace, which was the unit of assessment.

Kin gold.

Kinaru small wells either of brick or earthen rings burnt in the kiln, commonly called 'pot-wells.' Wells are sometimes enumerated distinct from the public waters in which the whole village has a joint property, as they are usually constructed by individuals, therefore, as an individual property.

Kindi a vessel

Kiṟṟu vari tax for re-roofing

Kiramam revenue village.

Kirana spices and condiments

Kirrit palm-leaves.

Kiru-kuḷa-viśeṣam one of the various terms used in the inscriptions of the first half of the fifteenth century to denote the tax that accrued from the villages.

Kirukula (Tamil), tolls or commercial tax on retail articles.

Kirukulaśunka type of duties on miscellaneous articles in which the transactions were small.

Kisan rayat; cultivator, tenant.

Kisan sangham peasants union.

Kist, Qist, Kisht stated payment, instalment of land revenue; ordinarily used to denote the land revenue payable to government, but sometime used also for the rent paid to the land-holder under government.

Kistabandi list specifying instalments paid on *kaul-namas* issued to each cultivator or cultivating community and containing the *kabuliyats* signed by the same.

Kistu zabitas statements of assessment classified by crops, by productivity factors, and by exemptions (e.g. *in'am, agraharam, shrotriam, maniyam, vandra, pagoda, chaultry*, and other lands).

Kḷipta-śulka fixed duty.

Klinna, klinnakreni moist substances like sugar obtained by boring certain trees like palmyra palm.

Knḍinīngakkārāṇmai a term denoting the sub-tenure under which reclaimable temple lands were taken up for occupancy.

Knots a term used in reference to node *i.e.*, the place on the stem of a paddy plant from which each leaf grows.

Ko-muṟai, ko-pada-vāram (Tamil), (Tamil-Sanskrit), revenue/tax due to the King.

Kōcceytu the term used in the epigraphs to indicate 'bed treatment' used in order to realize taxes.

Kōiltamarppēṟu a cess for the king's servant; this cess was sometimes collected even on the *dēvadāna* lands.

Kōl, kol a term used to denote a measuring unit/rod used in the revenue surveys. As the rods were usually named after a king or god or village, that name was prefixed to *kōl*; they would be of varying different sizes, of different names, and used at different places. Sometimes, the same named rod also used to have different length at different areas or at different periods; a measuring rod; for example the references like, *śrīpāda-kkol*, 'rod measured according to the length of the king's foot'; *māliga-kkol*, 'the measuring rod of the palace'; etc.

Kōḷvari (Tamil) tax in kind.

Kōt-toṭṭuṇṇappālatevvakaip-paṭṭatum 'all that is due to the king;' this expression in the inscriptions denotes mostly in respect of land grants, and may also mean that the king demanded taxes from his subjects.

Kōṭṭai magamai contribution for the fort; a tax collected for the maintenance of the forts.

Kōṭṭaipaṇam probably the same as *kōṭṭai magamai*, but according to some an unusal tax at the rate of some *paṇams* for lands having a sowing capacity of a *kōṭṭai* of paddy.

Kōṭṭakam vast expanses of water; the epigraphists have translated this term as 'cowpens' and have connected the word with the Sanskrit '*gōsthaka*'; *kōṭṭakam* is commonly used in the Thanjavur and Chingleput districts presently in the sense of a large sheet of water, and a proverb says: 'a man who has not seen the ocean, let him at least see a *kōṭṭakam*'; the word, moreover, occurs in close proximity to the tank.

Kōṭṭam a division of the *rājya*; as per some inscriptions a *kōṭṭam* was divided in several *nāḍus*; an administrative sub division.

Kōyil temple or palace.

Kōyil-vācalaṟ-pōnta-kuṭimaikaḷ 'the services rendered at the sacred gate of the king'; such expression in the inscriptions was used mostly in respect of land grants, and may also denote that the king demanded taxes from his subjects.

Kōyilkaṇkku the temple accountant; also called *ōlai eḻttu*.

Kōyiṟṟamap-pēṟu the payment demanded by the officers of the king; the payment for the officers of the king.

Kōyiṟṟamar king's agents.

Kōḍi-kkaḍami (Tamil), tax for the cultivation of medicinal plant *kōḍi-veli*.

Kōḷmuṟai-ppāḍu (Tamil), customary dues

Kósham, kásha, koshan case, repository, treasury, register. A village register in which are entered the lands held by the brahmans in the southern palegar district.

Koḍagu the proper form which 'Coorg' is anglicized.

Koḍaga the Coorg caste, former ruling race in Coorg.

Koḍe (Telugu), a measure of capacity.

Koḍige cultivated land.

Koda-visa an allowance of a *visa* of grain, etc., for every bullock-load that came into a town, paid to a person employed to check the demands of the toll-collector.

Kodai vritti in'am held for the service of holding an umbrella over the village deity during festivals.

Kodali a type of axe.

Koday crop the term refers to the second paddy crop in some areas. It was raised when the south-west monsoon sets in May. In this season the inferior varieties were said to be grown.

Kodungone a term used for a harsh king or ruler.

Kol fields lands on the west coast partially reclaimed from backwaters or paddy cultivation; during and after the rains under water; in the hot dry season kept partially dry by pumping.

Koḷaga, Kolaga (Telugu-Kannada) a land measuṟe; measure of capacity equal to 4 *baḷas*; a dry measure of 768 or 384 or 72 *tolas* in different places.

Koḷar-nilam saline land; it may be considered as uncultivated waste or inferior kind of land.

Koḷu the pointed or sharp iron at the end of the plough-axe, which digs the earth and causes the furrow.

Koḷuvāṇi the nail that joins the pointed iron (*koḷu*) to the plough-axe.

Kola payko in'am held for the maintenance of armed retainers in *zamindaris* in the district of Ganjam.

Kola-bhanḍālu, kolla-banḍi (Telugu), a bullock-cart load.

Kolakāndru salt officials; also called *tirparulu*.

Kolam kaval in'am granted for guarding tanks and seeing that the *rayats* do not waste the water.

Kolīkanikāya weavers' guilds.

Kolika 'weavers'; may also refer to the well-known tribe of the *kolis* who were slaves.

Kolinji, kollingy *tephrosia purpurea.*

Kollai outer backyard of house; whereas during the pre-British rule this was held separately by a *kāṇiyāchikārar*,

Lionel Place levied cash imposition on this place also.

Kollaip-puṇcey levy on crops raised on dry land. (*kollai* = dry land)

Kollan in'am held for the service of a village blacksmith.

Komaṭi, Komatis (Telugu-Kannaḍa), a Vaiśya shopkeeper; a member of the mercantile caste; merchant midlemen; trading class of the Telugu country; were a flourishing community whose benefactions to temples and other religious and charitable foundations often figure in the inscriptions; their organisation in to a powerful guild (*nakara*) which at one time had its headquarters in Penugoṇda (West Godavari) and branches in seventeen other centres had its beginning in the Eastern Chālukyas period; the great Telugu trading caste of the Madras Presidency, corresponding to the Tamil *chettis*.

Kombú in Coorg and west coast, the district or area earlier under a 'Náyak' or chief.

Kommu in'am granted for the service of blowing a horn before the *tahsildar*.

Kommu-maṟturu (Telugu) a land measure; also see *maṟuturu*.

Komutty the name of the caste in south India who considered themselves to be a branch of the pure *vaisya* caste; they followed trade as shopkeepers and merchants and assumed the denomination of *chetty*. Same as *komaṭi* above.

Kon in'am held for the service of supplying milk, ghee, etc., to the *zamindar* or his servants when they halt in the village.

Konda-kavali in'am granted for watching hills and jungles.

Kondapurirogam (Telugu), *kondapuri* a variety of paddy cultivated on high lands, *rogam* disease.

Kondikar in'am held by a servant of the Sri-Vaishnava priest of Sudras. He carries a *kondi* or stick as a badge of office.

Kootshee a sort of pulse.

Koṟṟa king.

Korja a *corge* or 20 pieces of cloth.

Korra Italian millet.

Kośa treasury; one of the elements of the state.

Kosham register.

Koss, Kaus, Coss (P. Karoh, S. Karosa) a term used to denote measure of distance about one-and-a half to two miles; varying in different parts of India.

Koṭṭagāram, Koṭṭāram (Tamil), treasury, store-house; stables.

Koṭṭakāram the granary of the village; it has also been translated as 'stables'. Same as *koṭṭagāram* above.

Koṭṭam (Tamil), a district; a district within a *maṇḍala* or province; a division of rājya; sometime sub-divided into *nāḍus*. Same as *kōṭṭam* above.

Kota in'am the same as *buruj in'am*.

Kota kodige in'am granted as a reward for building a fort.

Kota, kotah, kotai, kottai the measure of grain commonly used in the extreme south, the districts of Rāmnād and Tinnevelly. Its measurement varied generally 90, 97, 112 or 120 Madras measures.

Kota; Kotadi in'am lit. 'wall of the compound.' *Kottai* is 'a fort'. (D.C. Sircar, *Indian Epigraphical Glossary*, Delhi, 1966) *Kota in'am* — may also mean an *in'am* for protecting a fort or tomb or its walls (?). *Kota*, also mean — A measure of grain used in Ramnad and Tinnevelly districts varying from 96 to 112 Madras measures. (P.J. Thomas and K.C. Ramakrishnan (ed.), *Some South Indian Villages*: *A Resurvey*, Madras, 1940).

Kottaḍimai see, *aḍimai.*

Kottam in'am the same as *kamati in'am* above.

Kottam-vakai in some of the epigraphs this officer is seen bringing a settlement on the lands, while in others makes a grant of provisions for performing festivals in the local temple. His functions seem to be similar to *kōṭṭam-vakai.*

Kotwal chief officer of police

Kotwal in'am held for the service of *kotwal* who was the chief police officer of a town.

Kovai (Tamil), name of a gold coin.

Kovil, cóvil see *chauri, chávaḍi.*

Kovil-antarāyam small cess for temple or palace.

Kovil gurukkal mānyam the *mānyam* granted for brahman temple priest.

Kovil kanakku in'am granted for the service of keeping the accounts in a pagoda.

Kovilakam in'am the term *kovilakam* applied to the place of residence of a Raja or of Brahmans. The sites on ancient palaces and *agraharams,* exempted from assessment by long prescription, consequently the *in'am* were known by this name in the district of Malabar.

Kovilakan palace.

Kozhu plough share; a type of mortgage in which the possession of land is transferred to the mortgagee.

Kramavittam a brahman who knows the proper performance of the rituals and rites in sacrifices.

Kshetram temple.

Kūḍai a basket.

Kūla tax on grains and pulses; *Kirūkulam* in Tamil.

Kūlam (Tamil), a market; tax on grains and pulses.

Kūli (Tamil), hire.

Kūlikku paid labourers or agents.

Kūṟṟams same as *kōṭṭam.*

Kūra boiled rice.

Kūrait-taraku-āyam cess on the sale of roofing materials like coconut or bamboo plaits.

Kūrma elevation; a term used in the epigraphs to denote *kūrma* in the middle of the tank bed as one of the defects in the tanks.

Kūṭṭum-vargattukku additional varieties of crops.

Kúḷikánam, kuyyikanam in Malabar, a form of tenure which combined the mortgage with a waste reclamation tenure; *kuḷi* is also a pit in which young coco-nuts are planted.

Kúnbhává a Maráthí term for the hereditary rights in land (in Tanjore).

Kucak-kāṇam, Kumāra-kaccaṇam terms used to denote tax on potters.

Kucakkāṇam lit. a *kāṇam* = a coin, in several revenue terms the amount of tax to be realized was indicated in money; this coin was payable by the *kucava* or potters.

Kucava potters.

Kuchal a measure of land equal to 20 acres.

Kuchela land measure; about twenty five acres.

Kuḍaimānyam revenue free land granted to persons who had to hold the umbrella over the king.

Kuḍi, kudi this term is used in variety of meanings; it has to be understood only with reference to the context in which it occurs; the term, in its generic sense, could mean a tenant and more particularly, an occupant; it is also used to denote a cultivating tenant, a service holders or a tenant-at-will or a mere cultivator hired for labour; the specific sense of the term could be ascertained only from the context in which it occurs; it is not necessary that the *kuḍi* should himself be the 'actual' cultivator of the land; in fact, the epigraphs apply this term to a brahman (*Sarvakṛatukka*) and to a chieftain from afar, who could not be the actual cultivators themselves; it will be more appropriate to interpret the term '*kuḍi*' as an 'occupant'; it should, however, be added it occurs also elsewhere in the sense of a sub-tenure holder, a cultivating tenant or a cultivator-at-will; citizen, resident; generically, people.

A term used in the epigraphs to denote persons connected with lands as servants and they were in the nature of serfs on the soil; they generally belonged to the place being attached to and possessing an interest in the land; they had a permanent and inalienable right (*kuḍikkāṇi*) to cultivate the land. "In some cases they were residents of antoher village who were induced to settle in the village and cultivate the lands therein by the concession of permanent rights therein and who were given free rights in the village for building houses thereon; in some cases they were residents of the village, to whom a similar right had been given in respect of the hitherto uncultivated lands as an encouragement to bring them into cultivation and a recompense for the trouble and expense involved in rendering them such; and in some cases a similar right had been purchased by tenants on payment of a consideration." The landlord usually enjoyed only an over lordship (*mēlvāram*) right over land, and shared the income from it with the tenant in a proportion based on an agreement arrived at after having duly considered the nature of the soil and the kind of crop raised on it. The share of the *kuḍi* was known as the *kuḍivāram*. Whenever a piece of land passed from the hands from one person to another either as the result of a gift or sale usually the *kuḍi* or tenant in it also passed hands; and there was specific mention made of it so that he may not be dispossessed of his right on the specified land.

Kuḍi marāmattu, coody maramat ancient system of collective maintenance of irrigation system by villagers.

Kuḍi nīkki, kuḍi nīkkā the expressions like "*kuḍi nīkki*" should not be taken to mean that there was an area-wise exclusion from the grant-deed; nor can it mean physical eviction of tenants from the area concerned; what was intended was to extinguish the subsisting terms of occupancy so that new grantee could enter into mutually acceptable terms afresh with the occupants; in consistence with the terms of grant; in actual practice, too, their residential attribute conferred a preferential claim on them; it acted both ways - the occupant's choice was restricted, so too was the tenants.'

Some of the tenures during *Cōla* period were named like this; these terms have been interpreted to mean "evicting the earlier occupants" or "without evicting the earlier occupants"; they have been rendered differently as "transferring the labour employed therein" respectively.

Kuḍi niṅga dēvadāna, kuḍi niṅgiya dēvadāna, Kuḍiniṅgādēvadāna, kuḍiniṅgādēva-dānam, kuḍnīkkā dēvadānam the expression used in the epigraphs to denote a *devadāna* grant to a temple along with the *kudis* on the land; it shows that whenever a piece of land passed from the hands of one person to another either as a result of gift or sale usually the *kuḍi* or tenant in it also passed hands, and there was specific mention made of it so that he may not be dispossessed of his right on the specific land; a type of land grant granted to *tapasvi*; according to some epigraphs it could also be in the form of grant of tanks; in general these lands had variable demand, usually referable to the crop-yields actually estimated or assessed; the grant of the land with permanent occupancy for the tenure and his descendents, with assignment of land-demand to the temple; "endowment to a temple of lands already in the occupation of the cultivating tenants, *i.e.* only the *mēlvāram* share alone was granted to the temple.

Endowment to a temple of lands already in the occupation of the cultivating tenants, *i.e.*, only the *mēlvāram* share alone was granted to the temple.

Land or village endowed to a temple, after removing the previous tenants, thus making the temple enjoy both the proprietary and cultivating rights, as such, grantee could stipulate revised terms for occupancy.

Kuḍi nīṅga iṟaiyili tax-free land or village without evicting the existing tenants, thus making the grantee only enjoy the proprietary right or the *mēlvāram* as such, grantee could only demand the subsisting rate of land-dues from the occupants; a term used in the epigraphs to denote tax-free grant along with the *kuḍis*; also see *kuḍis* and *kuḍinīga dēvadāna*.

However, in some of the epigraphs both the terms i.e., *kuḍi nīṅga dēvadāna* and *kuḍi nīṅga iṟaiyili* have been used to give the expression that the transfer of land from one owner to another very often stipulated also the transfer of the labourers employed therein.

Kuḍigal the tenants and the cultivating tenants.

Kuḍikalyānam a term used for the procession of a nupital party after the marriage to the bridegroom's house; a tax was also levied on it.

Kuḍikkāṇi a permanent and inalienable right of *kuḍis* to cultivate the land.

Kuḍimai (Tamil), taxes in general (with the exception of land revenue) payable to the state for the protection of civil rights it offers; tenancy tax. See also, *kaḍamai* above.

Kuḍimaippāḍu service, common work of the village; the uses of word *pāḍu* would connote the distribution of the share of obligation among every one of the tenants and the cultivators.

Kuḍimakan cultivating tenants.

Kuḍimakkaḷ tenants and cultivators.

Kuḍinīngākārāṇmai a term used in the epigraphs to denote the grant of occupancy rights in the lands.

Kuḍipaṟṟu lands held by tenants-at-will.

Kuḍiwāram (coody waurum) Kuḍivāram share of the *kuḍi* in the income from the land; villager's or cultivator's share of farm output; the resident's share, which was the residual share of the resident. In most cases, the *kuḍiwāram* went to the *kāṇiyāṭchikārar*. If, however, the cultivation was done by *payirkārar*, the *kuḍiwāram* went to him. The *payirkārar* paid the *swāmibhōgam* or *tuṇḍuwāram* to the *kāṇiyāṭchikārar* out of their *kuḍiwāram*. In general, it was a system of distribution of gross village output following customary practice under different heads, and *kuḍiwāram* being one of the major ones; villager's or cultivator's share of farm output.

Kuḍiyiruppu kāniyākṣim the right of living on a piece of land belonging to the landlord.

Kuḍuppōlai lands granted on occupancy.

Kuḍuppukūli wages paid by the cultivators to tenants.

Kudi, Kudí, coody, agricultural labourer; *rayat*, inhabitants, tenants, cultivators. Also see, *kuḍi* above.

Kudian, kudiyan rayat, cultivator, tenant.

Kudikidappukars small plot-holders without rental arrangements with a landlord.

Kudirai kāśu payment in cash for the king's cavalry.

Kudirai-val horse gram (*dolichos bifiorus*), a small grained pulse grown over a large area in Madras Presidency, the regular feeding stuff for horses, also used for cattle food and for human consumption.

Kudivāṛatāṭkūli wages of the ploughmen engaged by the *kuḍivāram* holder.

Kudiyan sangham tenant's organization.

Kudiyirippu renters of tiny hut sites or small houses and lands plus garden plots; compound; right for dwelling in a property by constructing one's own hut.

Kudukuduppai in'am held by fortune-tellers who beat a kind of clapper called *Kudukuduppai*.

Kudumban in'am held by a village servant, whose duty it was to measure the grain previous to its division between the *zamindar* and the cultivator.

Kudy (kury) irippa kury kanum ola karunum lease for bringing in to cultivation and residence on the ground.

Kul'am, cul'am ponds.

Kul-bab all the items of statements or accounts.

Kul-qanum all laws and regulations in force.

Kuḻavaḍai tax for the enjoyment of the tank and its income; one of the terms appearing in the inscription of the first half of the fifteenth century to denote the tax that accrued from the villages.

Kuḷam tanks.

Kulai small embankment put across a canal to divert water.

Kulai-veṭṭi, kulai-vaṭai, kurai-vauppu, kurappu-vetti different types of taxes demanded for maintaning the bunds of an irrigation tank or a river.

Kulam members of the lineage group.

Kulam vettu in'am held for the service of collecting work-people to repair tanks.

Kulargi, kularg in Konkán village under a *khot* entirely held by *dhárekar* tenants at fixed rents.

Kularika śreṇī potters' guild.

Kularikas potters.

Kulavalay a paddy crop raised from seedlings sown about the third week of July and transplanted a month later. The crop is reaped at the beginning of March. This crop is raised on one crop land and is suited to the grounds on river-banks and tank-beds liable to inundation. It is chiefly cultivated on the soil termed '*oouarkally*' or 'alal sherndakally', a saltish clay. The rain is required in July and August and again in October and November.

Kulgootason in Tinnavelly, a fixed sum so called for which the *punjai* land was given up.

Kuli (Tamil), a small land measure.

Kulika 'the chief or head of a guild'.

Kullar, Kuller in the Ceded Districts, barren land; barren soil.

Kultai field

Kulwár to settle a village '*kulwár*', or according to (*wár*) the holding of each and every individual (*kul*), was Thomas Monro's term for the *rayatwari* settlement.

Kumāra-kaccānam, Kumara-kaccāṇam (Tamil), a tax payable in cash for the maintenance of the temple of Kumāra of Subrahmaṇya; a term used to denote dues payable by potters, one gathers from the epigraphs that it was collected in most of the instances on lands granted as *dēvadana*. It may also be inferred that a *kaccānam* (=*gadhyāṇa* = a gold coin) was assessed for tax.

Kumāra-vrtti tax for the upkeep of the order of *kumras i.e.* princes.

Kumbharti in'am held by dancing girls for the service of carrying a light placed at the top of a water-jar, round the principal idol during the performance of *puja* in a pagoda.

Kummara in'am granted for the service of village potter.

Kummaras the Telugu and Kanarese caste of potters.

Kummarik-kaṭamai tax assessed on the products of forest and hilly regions occupied by the hunters; a term used in the epigraphs of the Karnataka area.

Kumpini a term generally appearing in Telugu records denoting either a company of sepoys or the East India Company.

Kumpli a draw-well in the Ceded Districts.

Kuṇḍigai collection pot; a term used in the epigraphs to denote that the payment of the land dues on authorization or deposited in to the collection pot (*kundigai*) against signed receipts.

Kuṇṭalu, kuccelu a measure of land.

Kunbhava Marathi term for the hereditary right in land.

Kunbi the name of chief agricultural caste in southern India.

Kunchamu a measure of grain, varying in different areas; generally equal to four *manikas* or one quarter of *toom*.

Kunda the rolling grassy downs or low hills on the Nílgirí plateau.

Kunds holy pools much used in ceremonial ablutions, cannot be termed as lakes.

Kunnal the term used for ordinary fever in cattle, and in some places for black quarter.

Kunparars same as *kummaras* above.

Kunta a land measure.

Kupadarśaka 'an inspector of wells'.

Kupadarśakar 'water-diviners'; 'inspectors of wells.'

Kuṟṟam (Tamil), a district or its subdivision; at times the same as *nāḍu*, and could be only a part of a *nāḍu*.

Kuṟṟu-nĕl, Kūṟṟu-nĕllu (Tamil), tax for husking paddy payable to king.

Kuṟangaṟu canals.

Kuṟṟat-taṇṭam, taṇṭak-kuṟṟam terms used to denote fines levied on those who had committed a crime; judicial fines and was current during the Chola period.

Kuṟṟattaṇḍam a term used in the epigraphs to denote one of the fines imposed.

Kura 'boiled rice'; may also mean 'unboiled rice'.

Kurama disease of sheep and cattle, transmissible to people; anthrax.

Kurinji tinai hilly areas.

Kuruba in'am held for providing sheep for the sacrifices to the village deities.

Kuruvaikalayn a type of usual paddy crop for purely rained tanks, and is sown in November and reaped in March. It depends on there being a good rainfall in October and November. The soil is generally clay regur.

Kuśa, Kuśa–kkāṇam (Tamil), tax on the potters.

Kusa caste name.

Kushavan in'am the same as *kummara in'am* above.

Kushem in the Ceded Districts, a streamlet or water–course from a spring.

Kusīda lending of money; investment

of wealth for the sake of increment; it was one of the legitimate occupations of the *vaiśyas*, along with trade, looking after cattle and agriculture; even brahmans were permitted to live by lending money at interest while in distress.

Kuṭi household; cultivator.

Kuṭi–kāṇam, kuṭumpak–kācu the terms used to refer to poll tax in general levied on the individual cultivators or the agricultural labourers. (*Kuṭi* = cultivator)

Kuṭumbha–vṛtti gift of land for the maintenance of the donee's family; also see *kutumbiti.*

Kuṭumbin a cultivator, an agriculturist householder; a householder or *rayat.*

Kutchala a heap of cut corn; a land measure which in the Guntur district is 29 acres or 33, 3/16 *guntas.*

Kuthakai, kuttakai a lease of land.

Kuthugai (Tamil) rent fixed in cash.

Kutimai a tax on cultivator.

Kutlai in the Ceded Districts, a field.

Kutta Towcoof Sum held in suspense.

Kuttadi in'am held for the service of dancing before the village deity.

Kuttam assembly.

Kuttikkanam fee claimable by the owner for every tree cut down by the tenant.

Kuttumbitti (Kannada), a grant of certain towns; grant made for the maintenance of the donee's family; also see *kuṭumba–vṛtta.*

Kuyavan mānyam the mānyam granted to the potter.

Kuzhi a land measure which was equal to 1147 1/64 square feet i.e.one square rod; 100 *kuzhis* make one *mow or mha* which was equal to 14701 9/16 square feet; 20 *mows or mhas* make 1 *valley* which was equal to 294031 1/4 square feet or 6 3/4 English acres. However, according to W.H. Bayley (*Memorandum* on Land Measures and on Weights and Measures in the Madras Presidency, 1856) one *valley* was equal to 6.6157 acres or 6.62 acres roundly.

Kuzhikanakkar holder of *kuzhikanam* deed.

Kuzhikanakkaran tenants on improvement leases.

Kuzhikaṇam (Malayalam) form of *kanam* tenure; a deed of mortgage for the improvement of cultivated land; a deed acknowledging the rights of the *janmi* given by the mortgagee.

Kyvedooth a form of mortgage and transfer of landed property in Malabar.

L

Lābhālābhau a term used in the records to denote profit or loss, or an increase or decrease.

Lá–khiráj, lakeraje compounded of the private particle *lá* and *khiráj* rent. Rentfree. Lands rent-free; or lands the government dues from which area assigned to any person for his own benefit, or are appropriated to any public purpose.

Láni a small percentage on the revenue collected.

Lagayat since, for a long while, from the commencement or beginning.

Laick daub a report in which the fields fit for harvest were mentioned with other necessary particulars.

Lakṣana a document or deed; an inscription.

Lambadies, lumbadies a caste of itinerant traders.

Langarkhana in'am *in'am* for the support of an alms–house, a place where food and alms were distributed to the poor under the Muhammadan government.

Lankas low alluvial islands.

Larin or laris a foreign currency in circulation in south India; named from Lar, their place of origin, was Persian currency; it was not a coin in the ordinary sense of the word, but a bent rod or bar of silver stamped at the end; worth 1s. 5d. Being 1/7 of the gold *cruzado*.

Lavaṅga clove.

League equal to 3 miles.

Lella a term used for the broker.

Leṅka, Leṅkā a servant; a Sūdra servant; a writer; 'hereditary military slaves; they followed stringent military ethic under which their loyalties were given first to their immediate masters who need not necessarily be the king. 'The *leṅkas* were slaves who had entered into a covenant with their lord to devote themselves exclusively to his service. They took an oath (*basa*) to look on their lord as their *guru* and deity in this world and the next, to have no regard either for their own property or for their lives in furtherance of his interests, to stand by him in the hour of danger,... either to perish with him in the clash of arms or to kill themselves if they should chance to survive him.' See, Venkataramanayya, N.and Sarma, S.'Kakatiyas of Warangal' in *The Early History of the Deccan*. Edited by G.Yazdani,2 vols.(London 1960, New Delhi 1982), ii,p. 670.

Lenas caves.

Ling Buljewars people who kept bullocks for hire. Also engaged as agents for merchants.

Lópala–bhávalu a kind of well; one which is near the water source, be supposed to derive their supply for percolation.The existence of such wells generally implies that the tank supply is uncertain as to its duration: in that case the land was not to be registered as certain to bear two crops.

Loha–charmakāra metal-workers (smiths) and leather workers.

Loha–charmakār–āpaṇa shops of metal–workers (smiths) and leather workers.

Lohakāra, lohavaniya blacksmiths, the workers in iron and steel.

Lohar in'am same as *kummara in'am*.

M

Ma'mūl the government land-revenue assessment, the 'custom' due to the state.

Mā (Tamil), a land measure equal to 1/20 of a *veli*; also the name of a weight.

Māḍa (Telugu); Tamil *māḍai*; a coin of gold and silver; 40 *ratis* in weight; half a *pagoda*, half of a *dīnār* or the tenth of a *paṇa*; half or 50 per cent of revenue; a weight of gold; money in general. Four *māḍas* were equal to one *carṣam*. A coin named *kulottuṅga–māḍa* was issued by the Doḷa king *Kulottuṅga*; an indigenous gold coin in circulation in south India.

The Telugu *māḍa* and the Tamil *māḍai* form part of the names of various gold coins;their relations to other gold coins is one about which, in the face of the varied, and sometimes conflicting, evidence, it is difficult to make a general statement; from the inscriptional evidence available it is only safe to say that it was either half a *pagoda* or a *pagoda*, according to the particular context in which it finds mention.

Māḍa-baḍi-pātuka (Telugu) coin with a fraction of the value of a *māḍa*. *Baḍi* means petty and *pātika* 'a quarter'.

Māḍai (Tamil), same as *māḍa;* a gold coin; a weight same as *māṣā* or Sanskrit *māṣaka;* a half *pagoda*;coin issued from Nellore; also known as *nellūr-ppudu-maḍai*. Also see, *Māḍa*.

Māḍalu same as *māḍa*; a levy; 'payment of 50 per cent'; also see Kannaḍa *pannasa* or *pannāsa*.

Mādārikkai one of the terms appearing in the inscription of the first half of the fifteenth century to denote a type of tax that accrued from the villages.

Māgāṇam, magam a revenue sub division under the Muslim rule during the 18th century.

Māgāṇi an administrative unit.

Māgāni wet crop lands in Telingana.

Mañjāḍi (Tamil), a weight for measuring gold and silver; about 2 or 3 *ratis* or 4 or 5 grains; a weight equal to two *kunṛi=mani* used in weighing gold; 1/10 of a *kaḷañju* and 1/100 of a *śatamāna*.

Mālākāras florists.

Mālāris those who sold flowers to the public.

Māmadi a leveller of floor.

Māmūl-ādāya customary payments.

Māmūlādāyam a term used for the duties taken from goods exported to foreign countries.

Māṇikya-bhāṇḍāra 'keeper of the treasury, of precious stones, in the temple or palaces'.

Māna (Telugu-Kannaḍa), 1/16th part of the measure called *tūmu*; one which can hold rice of the weight of 4 *taṅkalamulu*, though varying in different areas; a particular measure or weight often regarded as half a *seru*; a measuring rod; also *mānaka*: name of a measure; a liquid measure.

Māna-pautava a storehouse where grains were measured and stored.

Mānadanda one the various types of units of length for measuring lands; its length varied from place to place and period to period, e.g. equal to 18 spans (*kōlār*, 1072 A.D.), 20 feet (1447 A.D.)

and 34 feet (S.Arcot 1504 A.D.).

Mānasāra a work on the science of the essence of measurements and held by the south Indians as a standard work to which they invariably referred when problems connected with the subjects came up for solution. The word *Māna-sāra* comes from the words *māna* or measurement and *sāra* or essence,thus meaning a science of the essence of measurements. It is also believed by some that it may also refer to the name of the author as there is clear verse at the close of the first chapter which signifies that the name of the author who composed the verses was *Mānasāra*.

Mānika (Telugu), a measure; 1/4 of *kuñcamu* and 1/16 of a *tūmu*.

Mānya a revenue-free holding; tax-free land; same as *sarva-mānya*.

Mānyam tax-free land grant to the servants of government granted as remuneration; the *ayagārs* were also granted *mānyams* which they were to enjoy in perpetuity for their services; it could be granted with or without any other source of income; there are instances when in addition to *mānyam* the donee was also granted the right of collecting certain dues on lands; areca nut gardens, irrigation wells, etc; grant of sustenance, granted by the king and sometimes by the *kaniyāṭchikarar*.

Usually a certain area of land was earmarked for this purpose and recognised as *mānyam* land. *Mānyam* was awarded to an individual, who need not always have been a *kāṇiyāṭchikārar*, as a token of appreciation, regard or respect by a ruler.

Mānyam was also granted to village functionaries and artisans (over and above their share of *mereis*), to temples, other religious institutions, and *chattirams* (hospices).

When an entire village was granted as *mānyam*, it came to be known as *shrōtrium* villages. All forms of *mānyams* were totally exempted from *mēlwaram*, *Shrōtrium* villages, however, paid a token *mēlwaram*, which was usually fixed, irrespective of output levels. There were two kinds of *mānyam* lands in the eighteenth century: *tarappadi, mānyam* ancient *mānyam* and *sannad mānyam* (those granted by Muslim and European rulers).

Mānyas lands free of taxes.

Māppaṇam (Tamil), name of a coin; a tax payable at the rate of one *panam* for every *mā;* cash levy per *mā* on land.

Mārg–ādāya levy for passage of articles of merchandise through the gift village by the village road; tolls on the articles on transit.

Mārgādāyam the term used to denote the duty levied on goods in transit through a district; type of local dues levied on articles of trade.

Mārjavāḍa an abridged form of *mahārājavāḍ* a district comprising the whole of the present *Rāyalasima*. The name of the district survived. In Vijayanagar times the territory included in the old *Mahārājavāḍi* fell under two *rājyas*, Penugoṇḍa and Udayagiri; hence they were occasionally referred to a Penugoṇḍa marjavaḍa and Udayagiri mārjavāḍa.

Māshaka one–sixteenth of any standard weight and seems to be identical with the south Indian *fanam*.

Māttu yēr, māttu yer, maththu–yer lit. exchange of ploughs; a traditional system of labour exchange for ploughing among kinsfolk in Chengalpaṭṭu district. However, this system prevailed only within kin and *jati* circle. A traditional system of labour exchange for ploughing among kinsfolk in Chengalpaṭṭu district.

Māttu–āḷ, maththu–aal a traditional system of labour exchange among kingsfolk in Chengalpaṭṭu district. However this pattern seems to be prevalent in single *jati pasumgarai* villages and land holdings, beyond a certain size were likely to render such system non–viable. Moreover, it was possible if labour supply could be guaranteed only by retention of a certain section of the population exclusively for this purpose. This system prevailed only within kin *and jati circle*. Also, *Māttu yer*.

Magane, mágánam, magamy maganny, magaum a district; a term used in Kánara for an administrative subdivision of a district; a group of landholdings; for administrative purposes a number of hamlets or holdings were united under one local accountant; also called *tarf*; also see *ámisham*.

Mángan, magun begging; request; one of the cesses or *abwab*. A tax or imposition formerly levied by the officers stationed at the *chokies* and *ghauts*.

Mávadei, maravadei to obtain,possess game of all sorts; mean all kinds of game and woodlands, being always found together in some of the deeds, the scribes frequently transferred to the former the meaning of the latter, and considered it a kind of plantation; a term used in the inscriptions to denote a tax that accured from the villages.

Mávina care tamarind trees.

Mávu *má* and *māvu*, twentieth part of anything; villages were frequently divided in twentieths and the extent of each person's share was expressed by saying it was such a part of a *mādvu*, or it contained so many *mávus*. For instance one record shows that, as half of a *cáni* was 2 1/2 *mávu*, the whole cultivable lands of the village was only 4 *cāni*.

Macchino one of the varieties of ginger and is named after the place where it was produced.

Machir an aromatic and medicinal bark.

Maḍakku assessment classification as contrasted with area measurement.

Madakkuma, Maḍakku mā standard *mā* or conversion–factor based on assessment and land–classification; standard conversion unit or scale; lands of various *terams* or asssessment-classification fastened on them were folded in to a *maḍakkumā* and total assessment in terms of paddy and *kāśu* were given at the rate applicable to *maḍakkumā*. It was the constructive unit of assessment computed on the basis of the assessment–classification–wise distributed area, and the total area, by measurement, was reduced in terms of such unit of assessment–area. It has also been suggested by some writers that the assessment based upon *maḍakku mā* rates was unusually excessive. Also it is noticed in some inscriptions that the occupants, the tenants and the cultivators were deliberately preferring the *maḍakku mā* as the basis for calculating some of their obligations, in their attempt to contain the higher demands made on them. However, one cannot be dogmatic on the qualitiative excess of the rate under the *maḍakku mā* computation.

Maḍappuṛam a tenure denoting land endowed to the *maṭhas*.

Maḍippu a term used for the second crop especially in Chengalpaṭṭu district (February–May).

Madad–i ma'ash tax–free grants.

Madadgar clerk.

Madaivetti in'am granted for the service of opening and shutting the sluices of a tank and distributing water to the fields.

Madam in'am granted for the support of a covered place where refreshments are given gratuitously, a halting place for the accommodation of travellers;

the same as *chattram in'am.*

Madavadiyal in'am granted for the service of sweeper in a temple.

Madham house of an upper caste Hindu.

Madhūka *bassia latifolia*, popularly called *mahua.*

Madhyastam a term used in epigraphs to denote the accountants.

Madhyastha a neutral person generally a village headman.

Madiga Telugu caste.

Madiga in'am granted for the one who works in hides and leather; the same as *chamare in'am.*

Madigaru tanners or shoemakers.

Madiyastam, madhyastham, madestrum standing between, mediation. The mediation of a palegar to protect a *circar* village from any breach of faith on the part of government or its officers. Also see, *madhyastam* and *madhyastha* above.

Madras Candy used for gruff goods-equal to 500 Ibs. (Fixed in 1802).

Madras Grace used for measuring grains. Equal to 9256 ½ lbs. (Fixed in 1802).

Madras ***Marcal*** a grain measure 8 Madras measures equal to 18.4 lb.

Madras Measure a grain measure, equal to 2.3 lb = 108 cubic inches = 8 ollocks; 8 Madras measures = 1 marakkal =500 fluid ounces.

Magama the duty collected on sales effected in the *pēta* on articles of trade; also called *pēmṭa-śuṅkamu.*

Magamai maganmai, magaṇamai (Tamil), a tax; as per one inscription it was levied at the rate of one *nāli* on every *kalam* of produce; an administrative unit; name of a tax; an additional tax charged apart from the usual land revenue for the maintenance of temples, brahmans, etc; small portion of the income or of the value of articles of merchandise collected as voluntary contribution by the merchants from among themselves for the maintenance of temples, etc.

Magamey, magarry wet lands.

Magani wet lands irrigated for cultivation.

Maganmai voluntary contribution.

Maggadere a professional tax collected from the weavers.

Mahāmaṇḍaleśvara as per the lexicons–a sovereign ruler who is the lord of 40 *yojanas* of land and a lakh of villages; generally, the governor of a district or province; title of a feudatory ruler or governor; the status seems to have been superior to that of *mandaleśvara,* while *Mahāmandaleśvarādhipati* apparently enjoyed still higher status and rank.

Mahā–nāḍu general assembly of the mercantile community of a district.

Mahā–nagara merchants' guild of a city.

Mahā–sabhā 'the great assembly'; meeting of the general assembly of the *sabhā;* meeting of the *mahājanas;* body of the *mahājanas.*

Mahā–vyavasthā the regulations framed by the *mahā–sabhā.*

Mahābhārata–vṛtti land endowed to persons for expounding *Mahābhārata.*

Mahābhojas feudatory chieftains; held their lands as hereditary possessions; could make similar donations by their own authority; they exercised power in the northern Konkan.

Mahābhūmi public land; the term occurs in the context that the *mahābhūmi* was the common property of all the living beings and the king had no right to give it away.

Mahābhūta–ghaṭa one of the various forms of gifts recommended for the brahmans.

Mahābhūtagahṭa-dāna a great gift; name of a *Mahādāna*.

Mahāgrahara see *agrahāra*.

Mahājana Brahman residents of the entire village; all the members of a village assembly; general body of the *sabhā* or village assembly; in charge of the local administration.

Mahāmātra 'a senior minister'.

Mahāmaṇḍaleśvar-ādhipati title of a feudatory higher in rank than *Mahāmaṇḍaleśwara*; one who had some subordinate chiefs under him.

Mahānāḍ-prabhu, Mahānāḍprabhu head of an organisation or guild in a city; chief or leader of the mercantila community; sometime same as *Paṭṭana-svāmin*,
The *prabhu* or a local dignitary of a *nāḍu*; it seems that at times he was the headman of some village; these offices were generally granted by the king, and generally remunerated in the form of the grant of a field.

Mahānāḍu (a local) general assembly.

Mahānāvika master mariner.

Mahāpaṇa name of coin; could also be 'tax of one *paṇa* per *mā* measure of grains'; also *māppaṇam*.

Mahāprabhu 'the great banker'; the senior merchant; the title enjoyed by the leader of the *nānādési* merchant community.

Mahāpradhānas highest rank officials; served the state in different capacities, as the members of the king's ministerial council, as heads of departments, and as governors of provinces.

Mahāpradhāni; Mahá Pradána Prime Minister; the chief minister or administrator; the high executive officer.

Mahārāja-prayojana same as Tamil *araśu-ppeṟu*; fees collected for the performance of police duties.

Mahāsāmanta the vassal chief, may be holding the position of a minister or governor.

Mahāvaṇḍavyavahārin the great banker or chief merchant; head of a mercantile guild; also *mahāvaddavyavahārin*.

Mahá-janam, mahajanum, maha-jana a great person; a merchant.Proprietor of land equivalent to *mirasdar*.

Mahájenam it often signifies the whole of the principal inhabitants of a place; sometime, used in a restricted sense, e.g. applying to the Brahmans only.

Mahal (A) administrative subdivisions; place, house, revenue district sub-division, places, districts or sources of, or yielding revenue, particularly of a territorial nature, sometimes encompassed the entire *pargana*.

'Maharatta carnatic' the territory south of Gingee (in South Arcot district) was called the 'Maharattara Carnatic' as this was intimately connected with the Maharattas.

Mahattaras elders; *vishaya-mahattaras*-elders of the district; *rāshṭra-mahattaras* -elders of the province; *grāma-mahattars* village elders (*Rāshṭrakūṭa* period); suggests the existence of popular bodies at the district and provincial headquarters and at the village level; though no formal elections were held, but the *grāma-mahattaras* used informally to appoint sub-committees to manage local schools, tanks, temples, and roads; would also receive trust properties and administer them according to the conditions laid down by the donor; these sub-committees worked in close cooperation with the village headman and received a fair percentage of the village revenue for financing the various public welfare schemes; civil suits were also decided by the village council and its decisions were enforced by the government.

Mahimai (Urdu), a tax for religious or charitable purposes; village octroi.

Mahiṣa-kara tax on buffaloes; also Tamil *erumai-ppon*.

Mahōksa sprinkling of seed; sometimes a bull was specially reared for impregnation; the bull thus reared was exempted from punishment even if he trespassed in to others' fields.

Mahrattah tallabund Marathi account exhibiting the receipts and disbursements of the preceding month and the balance at its close.

Mahsuldar in'am granted for the service of preventing the clandestine removal of the produce of a field before the revenue has been paid.

Maikuruvay it is a usual paddy crop for purely rainfed tanks, and is sown in November and reaped in March. It depends on there being a good rainfall in October and November. The soil is generally clay regur.

Majal in South Kanara, an irrigated land yielding two crops; the land in Kanara is undulating, composed of laterite ridges intersected by the deep-soiled valleys of the streams coming down from the hills, and by estuaries running in from the sea; making very rich cultivation; the land has three categories-land is known as *'bail'* when irrigated or yielding three crops; *'majal'* is irrigated land bearing two crops; *'bettu'* is land dependent on the abundant rainfall only and yielding one crop.

Majmu'-dar accountant; a head accountant in the taluk *kach'hari*.

Majhumu'-dar in'am held for the service of district revenue accountant under the native governments.

Makkaḷ-cēvakap-pēṟu a payment demanded for the service rendered by the local officials who were in the service of the people.

Makta fixed field assessment.

Mal the land revenue.

Maḻu lit. red hot iron; its reference in the epigraphs attains importance as it has been used to denote that the accountant while presenting the accounts had to undergo the ordeal of *maḻu*.

Maḻabraya a term used in the epigraphs to denote a tax on dry crops and edible vegetables.

Mala Telugu caste; traditionally weavers and agricultural workers.

Malai-yidu in'am held for the service of keeping in good order burial or burning places.

Malakaran in'am granted for the service of performing music in a pagoda-also see *chinna melam in'am.*

Malavadu in'am the same as *vetti in'am*.

Maldar flag-bearer.

Maliahs, the name by which the hill tracts in Ganjam are known; during the British period they were the 'Scheduled districts'; having been removed from the ordinary jurisdiction according to the Act xxiv in 1839.

Malikana an allowance to an ex-proprietor (Bengal N.W.P.); who was kept out of his estate (South etc.), or who had lost it all but this vestige (Bihar).

Malkiyat, Milkiyat the usual term for property in land; ownership.

Mallāyi-maghami one of the taxes, as per an inscription of the first half of the fifteenth century, accruing from the villages.

Malli cariander; grown chiefly in Tinnevelly for its seeds, but the leaves also used as a vegetable.

Malvandloo; Malvadu holder of a low office in a village, as that of a porter, grain watcher, scavenger, etc.- Remunerated with a land grant-*Malvadu in'am*. Same as *vetti.*

Malzamin bondsman of the discharge of a debt or payment of revenue.

Mamool-warum the former standards according to the soil of the respective districts and places.

Mamoti a short handled broad bladed hoe, used instead of a spade, or shovel, and for a great variety of purposes.

Mamul practised, established, usual customary; custom, hence a customary payment as to a village blacksmith; a bribe or illicit fee extorted by a village official, minor government officials, etc.

Mamutties spades.

Maṇai–iṛai, manaiyiṛai terms used to denote levy on house. (*mana* = house); tax on house or house site.

Maṉṟuppāṭu a term which generally conveys–what accrues by way of fines or confiscation etc. The term *maṉṟu* is understood to mean, a place of justice. This word is also used as a verb in many an instance to denote 'to collect'. Sometimes it is also used in the sense 'collection of fines'. Some epigraphs show that even the *dēvakaṉmis* i.e. the temple servants also collected *maṉṟupātu*. The inscriptions hardly show much difference between the two terms *maṉṟupātu* and *taṇtam*.

Maṇḍal–ādhipati the ruler of a *maṇḍala*.

Maṇḍala an administrative unit; a district or province; a province consisting of several *koṭṭams* or *valanāḍus*; sometimes used in a wider sense to indicate a country.

Maṇḍala-mudanmai (Sanskrit–Tamil), leadership or governorship of a province, governor or chief known as *Manḍal-mudaliyār*.

Maṇḍala–mutali (*mutali* =chief), chief officer of a *maṇḍalam*; sometimes also called *mahā-mandalēśvara*; the names *maṇḍali; maṇḍalikan* and *maṇḍalamuṭaiyāṉ* i.e. the posssessor/ ruler of a *maṇḍalam* are other variants of this name. The *maṇḍalaṇ-mutali* seems to be the authorized officer in the *maṇḍalam* to make entries in the *puravu–vari* register.

Maṇḍalam a term designating regions in pre–British Tamil regions; a very broad zonal concept; however, it is difficult to identify the precise connotation of the term *mandalam*; it certainly did not signify a socio–ecological unit for which Tamil word was *tinai*; some *mandalams* were certainly ecologically heterogeneous areas; it is difficult to think of *maṇḍalam* as a political unit, since the actual political boundaries of Tamil kingdoms rarely conformed to the known *maṇḍalam* boundaries; originally an important political divisions under the *Cōlas*, they continued to be so called in later times though they no longer constituted any accepted political division. From the point of view of size, the *maṇḍalam* was bigger than a *rājya*, the regular largest administrative division in the Vijayanagar empire.

Though there are inscriptions which mention governors over the *rajyas* there is none which specifically mentions a ruler or governor who was incharge of a *maṇḍalam*. Reference to a particular district or place as situated in a particular *maṇḍalam* was too conventional and old to have had any political significance in the Vijayanagar days; and in this connection it may be remarked that even in the modern day South India, these *maṇḍalams* are mentioned though they have absolutely no connection with the administrative divisions of the day.

Maṇḍaleśvara title of a feudatory or governor lower in rank than *Mahāmanḍaleśvara*.

Maṇḍalika, Māṇḍalika, Maṇḍalīka ruler of a *maṇḍala* or district.

Maṇi–grāma a mercantile guild.

Maṇiam a village headman.

Maṇikāra jewellers.

Maṇṇāḷar land controllers; fellow *kāṇiyāṭchikārar;* also see *kāṇiyāḷar and kāṇiyāṭchikārar*.

Maṅgala a Brahman village; shortened form of *caturvedi–maṅgala*; a small administrative unit.

Man–pan herediatry rights or privileges attached to respectability of station or official rank; the honours and presents due to the *man–kari*, the rights of the village hereditary officer, etc.

Mana house of a nambudiri.

Mann–varei rent of plots of ground occupied by persons not *mírsidars* in the *nattam*.

Manai–kávali, munny cavelly a term used in Mysore for village watching fees.

Manaikkaḍaiyār a term mentioned in the epigraphs to denote the shopkeepers or merchants who opened the shops in their own houses and tax levied on them.

Manaippaṇam levy for house–site.

Manalvary a type of paddy crop of short growth sown when there is not a full supply of water under rainfed tanks. It is sown in December and January and reaped in March, red sandy soil being considered the best.

Manavāri lands the rain–fed lands; also *accukkaṭṭu* lands.

Manavary rain irrigated rice lands.

Manda varisei the right to have the flocks of the village folded on the lands of every proprietor in turn.

Mandai–kaṇḍēṟṟam one of the taxes, as per an inscription of the first half of the fiteenth century, that accured from the villages.

Mandai–ppaṇam (Tamil). tax on cattle grazing in the village common.

Mandei varisei, mandei morei 'the turn in folding flocks' and 'the custom respecting flocks'; in some of the deeds both these terms have been used, they designate the same thing, namely, the right of the *mírásidar* to have the flocks of the village folded in turn on his lands for the sake of the manure.

Manei, maṇei, ground as divided or divisible in to lots for building, or small enclosures, or the ground forming the site of the *nattam*, contradistinguished from the rest of the village; as a term of land measurement; it is implied at Madras to an oblong space 60 feet by 40 equalling a twenty–fourth part of a *káni*, this being the extent considered sufficient for a single house.

Manen a caste of people,who, according to Barbosa, was engaged in making mats from the leaves of the palms.

Mangalams small administrative units.

Mania sunkam, and mania ravesh Hindu religious taxes.

Maniac *manihot utilissima.*

Manikkattal in'am granted to a dancing girl for attending as a mourner in the funeral processions of persons of the Mudaliyar caste in the Madras district.

Manivar the revenue account of a district; a superintendent of police.

Manjanathi, *morinda tinctoria*, a common shrub, used for green manure; the bark of the root yields a yellow dye.

Manmaari a deluge of sand.

Mannalu (Kanarese) serf, from *mannu*: earth; *alu*: labourer; agricultural labourer.

Mannans Vannans a caste of washermen in Tamil and Malayalam areas; on the west coast they also act as priests of Bhagvati, a goddess of the Gangamma type, and as devil dancers.

Mannawurty revenue-premium.

Manneya, manniḍu, Manniya (Telugu),a respectable man; a chieftain; ruler of a group of villages; over lordship or seigniory of a village which carried certain fiscal rights with it, and that the total sum of these rights; together with the *manneya* itself, was transferable and could become the subject of charitable gift; whether such assignments could be made permanent or were valid for the period during which the *manneya* vested in the donor? Though some inscriptions say 'for all time', it is, however, possible that the provincial governors had the power to dispose permanently of the *manneya* of particular places in this manner.

Manneya–svamya tenure held by a *manneya*.

Mano–vritti, munnoverty *manah* the mind and *vritti* profession, livelihood, maintenance. A class of military tenants of a higher order, in the Northern Circars, who were bound to bring their adherents with them in to the fields.

Manotti in'am held for the service of driving away deer from the crops.

Manṟāḍi this word generally occurs in inscriptions in the sense of a '*shepherd*'.

Manṟam the open platform under a tree where all people of a village meet together.

Manṟu "Common meeting place" in a village, it was originally translated by the epigraphists as 'openfield' and was connected with *manṟādi* which generally occurs in inscriptions in the sense of a 'shepherd'; the sense 'open field' does not seem to be correct as there is separate reference to the wet lands and dry lands, the phrase 'open field' does not cannote any distinctive sense; the word *manṟu*, therefore, should not be connected with *manṟādi*; it, however, can be connected with *manṟam* which is explained as 'the open platform under a tree where all people of a village meet together'.

Mantrin recognised from very ancient times onwards as one of the seven constituent ministers (*saptāngas*) of the body politic.

Manvarti stipend, pension, allowance.

Mānyam (*mauniam, manniyam*) revenue exempt land granted for the maintenance and services of different functionaries and temples etc. Also see, *maunium*.

Mauzawar used of a survey or other proceeding taking the area of the '*mauza*' as the local unit, as opposed to *mahālwār* or *rayatwar*.

Manzur approval

Mappilas, Moplahs the Muhammadans of West Coast, originally the descendents of Arab traders and native women, but with their numbers swollen by accession of converts from depressed castes of Hindus, who by conversion escaped from slavery and degradation; physically vigorous, but turbulent and disorderly; adopted usages and in Malabar became '*kanam*' landholders.

Maqta a term is a used to denote a land or village granted at a fixed rent without liability to enhancement, usually the rent fixed below the actual revenue to the profit holder; rent, tenure; usually a contract.

Maṟutu, maṟuturu, mattaru (Telugu), a certain land measure generally used as an equivalent of *nivartana;* different kinds–*kāl–maṟuturu, ghaḍa - maṟuturu, kommu maṟutu*, etc.; in Kannaḍa *mattar* or *mattaru*.

Maṟumanna local dues; sort of tolls.

Marah perquisites from the crop, fees in kind, so called in the Northern Circars, the same as *russoom*.

Marakkaḍamai a term used for one of the taxes accruing from the villages, as per an inscription of the first half of the fifteenth century.

Marakkal, Mercal a measure of volume equivalent to four *paḍis* and one–twelfth of a *kalam*; usually 8 Madras measures, but 2 in Tanjore and Trichinopoly, 4 in Tinnevelly, and 3 in parts of Rāmnād; equal to around 6.5 Kg; equal to 27 lb.

Maramut, Marammat repairs; ordinary maintenance.

Maravaḍai one of the taxes that accrued from the villages, as per the inscriptional evidence of the first half of the fifteenth century.

Maravadei woods of all kinds; woodlands.

Maravalli *manihot utilissima.*

Maravars a numerous caste in the southern districts of Madras Presidency, originally robbers, cattle thieves, village watchmen, and blackmailers, then partially converted to agricultural pursuits.

Marah An allowance in grain upon each plough or upon the quantity of seed sown.

Margosa also called *neem, asadirachta indica*, a very common tree yielding hard, durable timber; the seeds yield oil, the leaves and bark yield a febrifuge.

Mari sub-group of the Holeyas

Mark one of the foreign currencies in circulation in south India; a Venetian currency, information mainly gathered from the pages of Marco Polo; it was a silver coin, may be taken fairly at £2-4s. of English money.

Marumakkattayam, Marumakkathayam the matrilineal system of inheritance practised in Kerala; matriliny; the custom of inheritance through the female line, from mother to daughter, that prevails among the Naris, Bants, Billavas, Tiyyas and other castes on West Coast. As the property is usually held by large undivided families, and administered by the eldest male who is succeeded in the management by a brother or nephew, it is called in North Malabar *Aliyana Santana*, or sister's son inheritance.

Maruthu *streculia villosa.*

Maryādā customary dues; manners; ways; extent; limit; in Tamil *mriyādi, marjādi, mariśādi, maruśādi.*

Masab mixed soil.

Masala a type of boat in the coromandel coast which is in use even now; it is admirably contrived to resist the impetus of the surf; built of planks of wood sewed together with jute twine and caulked with coarse grass not a particle of iron used in the entire construction.

Masalia, musala the name used for Masulipatnam, which was the chief port of entry for the Deccan.

Mashrut 'conditional'.

Masjid in'am granted for the support of a mosque.

Maṭhāpura lands the lands which were granted to the *maṭhas* for their maintenance, promotion of study and spread of their respective theologies; grants were subject to the payment of a small quit rent unless otherwise specified in the grant.

Maṭṭu (Telugu), a measure of land.

Matapati endowment for cooks or butter milk suppliers of village officials.

Matapati in'am for the service of supplying butter–milk to public officers and cooking food for the *reddis* when they left the village on public duty.

Matham In'am for the support of a building where Hindu religious mendicants used to reside under a superior, or where they halted when travelling. The term (*Matham*) was also applied to the spiritual headships of three leading sects of Brahmins; the valuable endowments attached to the different *mathams* or spiritual headships of the three leading sects of Brahmans were also included under this head during British rule.

Mathas monasteries.

Mattah, metta high and dry land, not capable of irrigation and so unfit for paddy.

Mattar (Kannaḍa) land measure; same as *maṛuturu* or *nivartana.*

Mattaru same as *mattar.*

Maund a variable weight; a railway *maund* was 82.28 lb., a Madras *maund* about 25 lb,

Maunium a grant of land, or assignment

of the government share of the produce therefrom to the revenue officers and the public servants of the villages; land of which the public revenue has been transferred by the government to certain individuals, with a right to receive it from whoever cultivates the land. Also see, *mānyam* above.

Mauqub abolishment.

Mawās recalcitrant areas or villages which refused to pay taxes unless forced to do so, same as *zor–talab*.

Mawashigiri rebellion, plunder of the country, outrage.

Mayadis originally a hunting tribe living on the forest–covered hills of the West Coast; lowest of the untouchable castes, would pollute a Brahman at a distance of 300 feet; would often serve as watchmen, guarding crops from wild beasts at night sometime do agriculture work.

Mazkur aforesaid; above mentioned; vulgarly this means the said village.

Mazra, muzera a hamlet; a cultivated field sown or ready for sowing in the Northern Circars the term implies a component part of a *mouza* or village.

Mēḻi a handle which the peasants press in order to adjust the plough and make the plough axe run deep in to the earth and make deep furrows.

Mēlātcuiḍayār the principal grantee.

Melkuḍi occupants of lands; *kaḍamai* was the land–dues obligations payable by them; also *perumgudimakkal*.

Mēlwaram (mel warum), Mēlvāram lit. over lordship; the right enjoyed by the landlord over land; occupants' share; the upper share; share of village output appertaining to the ruler. It normally averaged from 33 per cent to 40 per cent. However, there was no *mēlwaram* paid from *mānyam* lands. It was a system of distribution of gross village output following customary practice. *Mēlwaram* was one of the major heads under which it was disbursed.

Médipālu in Telingana, 'share of the plough handle' – share of the produce left with the cultivator after paying the revenue on *māgāni*, the wet crop lands (share taken as revenue used to be in kind, called *koru*).

Mél–udenpadicai–olei a supplementary agreement written on the palm leaf.

Mérá, merái fees and shares in grain, allotted for remuneration of the village officials and functionaries. Also see, *meirei* and *mere*.

Meeras; Miras (A.) 'permanent hereditary property'; 'heritage, succession, patrimony'; hereditary right whether to land, office, or other resource. According to one of the judgments, 'without the consent of the proprietors of the soil, the collector has no authority to deliver any part of these lands to other persons'. Also see, *mirās*.

Meirei, merah, murah, marrah, murai tradition, practice or custom. Also see, *mere*.

Mel–vĕṭṭa–pperu land set apart for meeting expenses of publilc works.

Melaḍi (Tamil), taxes paid in kind.

Melagy a type of paddy crop raised from seedlings transplanted about the beginning of October and reaped at the beginning of March.It is generally grown on channel lands in clay regurs.

Melam in'am granted for the support of a musical band employed in pagodas.

Melcharth the eviction of a tenant in favour of a new one; overlease.

Melcharthdar holder of a *melcharth*.

Meli the Tamil word for plough.

Melkāṇam, Melkanam, an additional advance to be taken on *janmi* rights in *Malabār;* over lease of *kanam* tenure; the payment and receipt of an extra *kanam*,or fine on renewing a lease, in excess of that paid by the actual *kanamdar* or leaseholder, to secure a transfer of the lease. Also see, *melcharth.*

Melkanamdar holder of an over lease of *kanam* tenure.

Melkoyma right of suzerainty of kings/ chieftains over religious institutions.

Melviṭṭiya–vaaḍḍāravauḷa (Kannada), name of a tax.

Menewar in Malabar, a person who keeps the district accounts called *hobly.*

Menkaval in'am held for the service of the superior or district watcher under the old native police system.

Menon an accountant (like *patel, patwārī* etc.) of the *amisham* or *amshom* in Malabār.

Mera (Telugu), a fee.

Meralu customary fees in money or in goods or grain to which the government servants and their menials were entitled, and which was collected periodically or seasonally.

Mere, mureh, merah, marrah, merai (Tamil) portion of crop given at the threshing floor to certain village officers and servants as perquisites; a corruption of the Tamil word *murai,* meaning tradition, practice or custom, customary or traditional practice, which consisted of payments to village functionaries (apart from what they received through the *swatantraditam*).These averaged around 12 per cent. It was a system of distribution of gross village output and disbursed under major heads, *merei* being one of them. Also see, *merá* and *meirei* above.

Merei sundantira padam a schedule of *mereis* and *swatantrams.*

Meri sub–group of the Holeyas

Meru name of a gift.

Meṭṭugana a term used in the epigraphs to denote one of the oil mills.

Mete lit. death; the name given to a harbour.

Meti in'am granted to the head *rayat* for encouraging the settlement of *rayats* in the village.

Mey–kaval in'am granted for the service of guarding the idol in a temple.

Meykāval a term used to denote a watchman in a temple; temple watchman; also called *tiru mēni kāval;* remunerated in the form of land grants or cash.

Mīṇ–pāṭṭam a kind of duty levied on fishermen.

Mikarp–pāṭṭam a tax levied on boatmen.

Minha substraction, deduction,

Minnai oil, commonly called *pinnai* or *punnai* oil, extracted from the fruit of the common poon (*calophyllum inophyllum,* Linn), which is also called Dilo oil tree or Domba oil nut tree.

Mirās (meeras, meerassy), a Persian word; hereditary landed rights; also included *mānyam* of artisans and village functionaries; *mīrasidār* (*meerassydar, mirrassydar*) holder of hereditary landed rights; prior to the establishment of Muslim rule in different parts of south India, the term in vogue for inheritable privilege used to be *kāṇiyāṭchi,* and as partially autonomous privilege was considered significant, the Muslim revenue documents, referred to *kāṇiyāṭchi* as *mirāsi, mirās* being the generic persian term for inheritable rights; by the end of the 18th century, *kāṇiyāṭchi* was officially referred to only as *mirāsi;* however, such a reference understated many other facts constituting the complex phenomenon that *kāṇiyāṭchi* was; some historians have given numerous illustrations of distinction between *mirāsi* and *kāṇiyāṭchi,* but though the latter was subsumed under the former, the converse was not true; also the argument that although the term *mirasi* is of Persian origin, the practices denoted by the term originated in the older practices of land grant to brahmins or to the institution of *brahmadeya* villages, does not as per the sources prove that *brahmadeya* was an earlier form of *mirāsi;* for instance as in the case of 18th century *kāṇiyāṭchi,* so also in the case of the early Chola *brahmadeya* there was a lot more than merely inheritable rights in land; also see, *kāṇi, kāṇyāṭchi, kāṇiyāṭchikārar.*

Mirāsī, (Perso–Arabic). The hereditary right to a share in the estate; in Tamil areas the right was called *kānī–ātchī* (inheritance in land); Brahman owners spoke of their 'Swāstiyam', *kūnbhāvā* was the (Marāthī) term used in Tanjore. The Perso–Arabic term '*mirāsī*', however, gradually came in to use, and was so generally understood, that '*mirāsi* right' was used to indicate the remains of any kind of right (of the landlord type) wherever found. It may also be pointed out that the term *mirāsī* came to be used of any hereditary right, e.g. the *karnam* or even that of the village watchman or the temple dancing girl, all of whom might have a *mirāsi* right to fees or perquisites or even bits of land held as remunerations for service. It may here be pointed out that in mortgaging or selling the whole or any part of the *mírási,* he mortgages or sells a proportionate part of his share in these; but he cannot divide and dispose any particular spot of land in the *perumboc,* the *tarisee,* or *mírási maunium.* No particular spot in any of these belongs to him; he possesses a *share* in all not a *part* of each, and the whole must remain entire.

The Tamil *mirāsī* never appears to have been of equal value to the *jenm* of Malabar, or the *wurgha* of Kanara, and the *mirāsīdārs* seem to have united in their own persons the character of farmer with that of landlord, much more universally than the *jenmakars* or *mulees* of the western coast. The difference in the value of these properties is distinctly traceable to the larger portion of the produce taken as public revenue, the less productive nature of the soil, and less favourable, climate on the eastern side of the peninsula, compared with the advantages enjoyed by the occupiers of land in Malabar and Kanara; but, from the numerous deeds of sale, there is no doubt that at one time *mirāsī* was universally a saleable and transferable property, and that the *mirāsīdārs* every where enjoyed a *toondoo warum,* or clear landlord's rent, from all the lands cultivated by their *paycarry* tenants, and both as landlord's rent and a farmer's profit from the lands which were cultivated by their own labourers and slaves.

It is by no means, however, to be understood, that this was the state generally of *mirāsī* property during the English rule. The policy of the Muslim princes, which, notwithstanding their short and unstable authority on the other coast of the peninsula, so, materially affected the interests of the landlords both in Kanara and Malabar, proved much more deterimental to the *mirāsidārs* of the Tamil areas, where their authority was of considerable duration, and their dominion was firmly established under the commanding influence of European power. It is well known that, by successive augmentations, the demand on the *mirāsīdārs* of the Carnatic was gradually raised, so as at last very generally to absorb not only the whole of the landlords rent, but in many places a portion of the farmer's profit also. Most of the *mirāsīdārs* in that part of the country were thus reduced to a situation which, except in name, differed little from that of the *ulkudy paycarries* or permanent farmers. (There was some difference. The *mirāsīdār* besides his right in the cultivated lands, whence he derived his landlord's rent and farmer's profit, possessed other privileges in the *perumboc, tarisee, mirāsy maunmim, marahs,* etc., and these privileges continued to be enjoyed, and sometimes to be sold, though his landlord's rent was gone). The Muslim government, by absorbing the whole landlord's rent, became not only the sovereigns but the landlords of the areas, enforcing thier favourite maxiim, that the state is the exclusive proprietor of the soil. Accordingly of the Tamil provinces, Tanjore, which was transferred to the English directly from the Hindu government, and was scarcely ever under the Muslim power, was the only one in which on the English acquisition, *mirāsī* right was found nearly unimpaired. In the Chingleput district, also which was ceded to the Caompany as a *jaghire* before the full extent of the Muslim government had begun to be felt, as well as in Dindigul, Madura, Trichinapaly, and Tinnevelly, the latest of their southern conquests, *mirāsī,* though greatly reduced in value, was found in a tolerably perfect state; but throughout the *subah* of Arcot, and very generally in Salem, Baramahal, and Coimbatore, the successive augmentaion made to the land tax, or the excessive demands made by the Muslim government in other shapes, had left of *mirāsī* little else than the name.

In Malabar and Kanara, where the land tax was a portion of the landlord's rent, fixed on the land, and collected from the landlord, or those in possession of his rights, whether the fields were cultivated or fallow, the government did not interfere in any respect with the cultivation of the soil; but from the greater part of the land in the Tamil areas consisting of *nanjei/nunjah*, and the land-tax thereon being a portion of the produce, any failure of the *mirāsīdārs* to cultivate their lands directly affected the public finances. Hence it became an established principle of *mirāsī* tenure, and it was incumbent on the *mirāsidārs* to cultivate all the *waraput* and *teerwaput* lands attached to their village, either by means of their own servants or slaves, or by renting them out to *paycarries* or tenants. Due to the loss arising from compulsory contracts, or forcible impositions at arbitrary prices of the government portion of the produce, the *land-tax* was converted into a *land-rent*, the *landlords* sunk into *land-occupiers* or *holders*, and restricted to the profits of mere farmers in the land cultivated by their own labourers or slaves, they ceased to employ *paycarry* tenants in those other lands, from which they no longer derived any advantage. To prevent the public revenue suffering from arable land thus left vacant, the government resorted to the expedient of transferring it temporarily to *paycarries* or tenants of their own selection. The employment of *paycarries* by the government itself, the natural result of over-assessment, greatly contributed to the level the earlier distinctions between the *misāsī* landlords and their *paycarry* tenants. Under these circumstances, the *paycarry*, or tenants, in many instances, from the secession, emigration, or removal of the *mirāsīdār* or landlords, became possessed of a great portion of the cultivated lands in the village. Where the *mirāsī* was not yet destroyed, the *misāsidārs* still possessed a saleable property in the land.

The *mirāsī* of the village officer is hereditary and saleable property as well as the land, but in like manners as *manium* and *coopatum* cannot be sold without the duty attached to it. If the *karnam* sells his *mirāsī* the person purchasing it must write the village accountants either himself or by a substitute. So a *taliary* may give away a part of his *mirāsī,* but he must perform the duty of watching upon the remainder.

It appears from the reports that the *mirāsīdārs* of the Deccan where *mirās* existed, was answerable for the revenue whether the land be cultivated or fallow. That if he declines to cultivate or pay his rent, he may be compelled to give in a written deed of renunciation.That the right of government to dispose of the land after the long absence of the *mirāsīdār* is not disputed. That the *mirāsīdār* gets back his land when his absence has not been long, and when it has been given in temporary lease to another person, but not after a long absence, and its having been granted in *mirās* to another; and that though he is supposed to have a right, even for a century, to reclaim his land, usage does not allow so long a period.

In the opinion of Ellis," The *mirāsī* right is not forfeited by the discontinuance of cultivation for a single year or a longer period during the life of the *mirāsīdār*, his son or his grandson. It would become forfeitable, that is, the claimant could not regain it if it had passed into the possession of another, by the Hindu law after the third generation or after the lapse of the period of memory determined to be one hundred years. It, however, by the word forefeited, it be intended to ask whether by omitting to cultivate, the *mirāsīdār* render his lands liable to confiscation by government, it may be answered that by the implied compact under which these lands and the various *mirāsī* privileges are held, he is bound to cultivate his full proportion of the *varapet* lands according to the general practice of the country, the permanent forfeiture of *mirāsī* would ensue from discontinuing merely the cultivation either for one or any determinate number of years. If a *mirāsīdār* be so reduced in circumstances as not to be able to bring under cultivation his share of the *varapet*, or, if he should have abandoned agriculture for other pursuits, it is incumbent on him to provide for its culture by granting to *payacaries* such term as will induce them to bestow on it the advantage of their stock and labour. If he does not do so, the state has then a right to employ *payacaries* either for the current year or for a fixed, not an indefinite number of years."

The Indian view on the subject was, "The *mirāsī* right is not forfeited to the *sirkar* from the circumstances of the *mirāsīdār* having failed to cultivate for a year, but in case the inhabitant absents himself from his *mirāsī* lands for a long period, neither cultivates nor rents them, and in other respects, acts with determined opposition to the interests of the state, it has become customary for the *sirkar* to select a person to enjoy the *mirāsī* and confirm him in possession by *cowle*". Frequent instances of this took place during Mr. Place's time in Chingleput, and in Tanjore the Rajah has transferred by *sasamum*, villages to others not *mirāsīdaṛs*.

The purchaser of *mirāsī* right may remove the former *paikaris*, or tenants, labourers and slaves. But the slaves are seldom removed from the estate on which they were born. It is contrary to the interest of the owner to detach them. He only disposes of the increasing stock for which he might have no immediate use on his own lands.

Mirāsīdār though "they possess the exclusive right of cutting firewood, working quarries, etc., they have no right of cultivation, much less can they claim any to break up common used for pasturage or to cut down productive trees, as plamira, cocoanut, etc" It is also stated that "the consent of the circar" is necessary towards any beneficial change being made with the appropriation of the lands.

Commenting on the rights of *mirāsīdārs*, Thomas Murro wrote, "The right of the Meerāsīdār to derive a rent from land for which he neither pays the public revenue nor finds a tenant is certainly not acknowledged now and probably never was so at any former time." Again with respect to the waste he wrote, "The waste in Meerass villages in Arcot is supposed by Mr Ellis to belong to the Meeraṣidars jointly, and supports his opinion by documents shewing that when a Meerasidar sells his cultivated lands, he transfers by the same deed to the pruchaser his right in the produce of the waste, the quarries, mines, fisheries, etc., within the limits of the village. But this appears to be a mere technical form, which can give no actual proprietory right in the waste. It confers a right but not the right of ownership, to the pasture of the waste lands and the fishery of the tanks and nullahs, in common with the other Meerasidars of the village."

In Tanjore, Trichinopoly and North Acrot districts, where the *rayatwari* lands were generally held by Brahmans, the *pattadar* who held direct from government was frequently termed a *mirasidar;* an honorific title, and the *mirasdar* would usually be unwilling to do the actual work of cultivation. Also see, *mirāsī* above.

Miśradurga mixed fort.

Misal it is a letter written by the princess or *wazirs* and nobles and sometimes it is also applied to *farmans.*

Mittadar holder of a small property under permanent settlement.

Mocassa revenue free. Also see, *Mokāsā.*

Mochai, Mochay *dolichos lab-lab; lignosus;* the country bean.

Modala-vāḍa (Kannaḍa), the chief village in district consisting of villages; i.e. headquarters; also called *rājadhānī.*

Modan hill rice, grown on the uplands (in Malabār).

Mogeru fisherman caste in Kanara.

'Moghul Carnatic' the tract north of Gingee was the 'Moghul Carnatic' as this was under the Nawab of Arcot.

Mohtad, Mohatadi a village peon employed to watch crops; village revenue peons; remunerated with land grant-*mohtad in'am.*

Mohtad in'am held for performing the service of village revenue peon.

Mohtarfa the *mohtarfa* tax levied on merchants and artisans; in Ganjam it is a tax on houses.

Mohtasib in'am granted for the service of inspector of weights and measures.

Mokāsā, Mokasa (Arabic-*mukhāsa*), the portion of the land-revenue under the Marāthās, devoted to some special purpose or person; *Mokāsadār,* a grantee of the whole or a part of the local revenue on specified terms; granted; a *mokasa* village is one that is granted either free or on a light rent. Also see, *mukhasa.*

Moliko in'am for the support of the headman of the village; the same as *dolabehara in'am.*

Momins Muslim weavers.

Monigār, Monigar māniyakāran a village headman (holding the revenue-free grant of land (*grāma-māniyam*) for his services; *munsif.*

Monigar in'am *monigar* corruption for *maniyakaran; in'am* land granted for the service of headman of a village.

Moolumunishers slaves.

Moolvies a small duty on goods passing through the areas concerned.

Moot dal; peas.

Mootahadar a person on whom the *zamindari* rights of a *mootah* are conferred by the government, under the condition of a perpetual settlement; the holder of a mootah.

Mootahdary what relates to a *mootahdar.*

Mora equal to 28-29 *seers.*

Morah in Kanara, rent in kind. A field let to a tenant at will, is reckoned and called a field of so many *morahs.*

Morei-nir, moranír waters, the supply of which is governed by fixed rules; the supply from large reservoirs is governed according to time and season by fixed rules; water allowed to flow in turn and for a fixed period every day to the fields of each cultivator, from the beginning of April to the end of May; the beginning and ending of these periods are stated generally; they depend actually on the forwardness or backwardness of the season.

Motapati in'am granted for the service of supplying butter-milk to public officers and cooking food for the *reddis* when they leave the village on public duty.

Motarpah, Moturfa taxes, personal and professional, on artificers merchants, also on houses, implements of agriculture, looms etc. Basically meant a levy on non agricultural activities or establishments. Also see, *muhtarafah.*

Mouza hamlet; a dependancy of a village.

Mu'afi (lit. expempted from the payment of revenue) Revenue-free holdings; any revenue-free grant may be called *mu'afi;* no condition of military service was attached.

Mu'azzan public crier.

Mu-ayyan zabitah, moyenzabitah established custom. Charges, collections so called in the Ceded Districts.

Mūḍai-kkūli (Tamil) tax for minting gold into coins.

Mūla original; a document regarding a title to the property or right.

Mūla-sadhana or *mūla-olai* in Tamil; the original deed.

Mūla-ratna-panṭārattār the term used in the epigraphs to denote the treasuries of the central ornaments; treasury.

Mūla-vīsa (Telugu-Kannada) *vīsa* 1/16 of a *haṇa (paṇa);* name of a tax or levy.

Mūlāwargdār an ancestral estate *(warg)* holder (in Kánara).

Mūladhana, mūladravya the capital or principal in sale and purchase and such other transactions.

Mūlgénī a hereditary tenant (in Kánara).

Mūrdh-ādhikāra supreme authority; in Tamil *mūtt-ādikārama.*

Mūsara-vāru (Telugu), goldsmiths or manufacturers of metallic objects.

Mubbottu the fraction called three annas 3/16.

Muchaaram residue rent.

Muchalka bond; a 'recognizance', bond for responsibility formerly executed by zamindars.

Muchalkah in dárad, muchelka in darud "The engagement contains this". The title of a written declaration, which, under the Muhammadan administration of the Northern Circars was produced by the *amildar* signed jointly by the *deshmukhs* and *deshpandyas,* purporting that they had not in the way of bribery or otherwise, paid anything to the agent of government, except what is specified in the public accounts of receipts.

Muctah a fixed rent.

Mudal (Tamil), cost.

Mudali, Mudaliyār (Tamil), a chief.

Mudam in'am the same as *mohtad in'am* above.

Mudavan in'am granted for the support of a cripple.

Mudavandi palayam village of disabled destitutes. In certain regions of south India there prevailed the practice of setting up and maintaining villages for the disabled and destitutes. Such villages were maintained through annual contributions by the *kāniyātchikārar* of a group of villages. It is difficult to know whether *mudavandi palayam* was a single *jati* village or not. However, in Kongumandlam it appears to have catered to Yellala Gounder *jati* members.

Mudde in'am held for the service of carrying balls of rice while trading the boundary line of a village during the festivals of the village goddess and depositing the balls at different points of the line.

Mudur a term used to denote 'old settlement'.

Mug Tiragee loom tax.

Muggaḍu (Telugu), 'a junction of three or more villages'.

Muhtarafah, moheterefa, Muhtrfa an artificer. Taxes, personal and professional, on artificers, merchants and others; also on houses, implements of agriculture, looms, etc, a branch of the *sayer*; a tax or taxes levied on trades and professions on artificers of a village or their implements as upon the weaver's loom, upon tradesmen and their shops and stalls. Also see, *motarpah*, above.

Mujera a cultivated field sown or ready for sowing.

Mujra allowance, substraction, reduction, remission.

Mujudat present.

Mukarrar certain, fixed, appointed.

Mukaveṭṭi an officer who may be considered as the affixer of royal seal as *mukam* = seal; and *veṭṭi* = to cut or fix.

Mukhadharakas mask–actors.

Mukhasa a term used in the Northern Circars to denote those grants of land which were made by the zamindars for the support of their relatives, followers and dependants, or for military service. Also see, *mokāsā*, above.

Mukhasa, mokassa in'am a term used in the Northern Circars to denote those grants of land which were made by the *zamindars* for the support of their relatives, followers and dependants, or for military service; land assignment at nominal assessment conditional on service.

Mukhyasthan a village chief.

Mukkal a cash payment to the landlord.

Mukri a general functionary in a mosque whose special task is to give the call to prayer.

Mulada, muladalu (kanarese) serfs; agricultural labourers; traditionally hereditary serfs attached to the *mulawargas;* they were paid in grain.

Mulaguena chitta a deed of land tenure in Kanara according to which a specified amount of land was transferred to another for a specified amount in cash and rice every crop; out of the said cash amount the grantee was to discharge the *sirkar's* revenue and the remainder was to be paid to the owner; in the case waste ground was planted, the grantee was to pay specified amount after the expiry of ten years. The grantee was at liberty to plant in the said ground cocoanut and other trees including plaintain trees, and he and his heirs were to enjoy the products; the owners would not be concerned with any thing except the said amount nor would they ask the grantee to quit. However, the tank which was situated within the ground kept by the owner, the owner would draw water for two days for their plantation, and on the third day,the grantee would be allowed to draw water for his plantation.

Mulawarga (Kanarese) ancestral estate.

Mulawargadar (Kanarese) holder of *mulawarga*–an ancestral estate.

Mulgar the proprietary right in Kanara is termed *mula* (lit., a root) and the *mulgar* is in many respects identical with the *jenmika* of Malabar and *mirāsidār* of Karnatic.

Mulgeni (Kanarese) permanent lease; hereditary occupancy right.

Mulk–i–jadid 'new lands'.

Mulk–i–qadim old country (land).

Muluḍa, Muḻuḍa villagae headman.

Mummeyvaydoo holds a share of a village, is entitled to share in every part of it.

Munneyvaydoo, manavadoo inhabited by *sudras*; this term when applied to a whole village, appears to be generally used as signifying that it is the *mirāsī* of *sudras*; but when casually used in reference to a dependent hamlet, it must be obvious that nothing more was meant than to say that such hamlet was *inhabited* by *sudras*, although dependent on and part of an *agraharam;* for it is notorious and beyond doubt that dependent hamlets always follow the main village of which they form a part, and that a person who holds a share of village is entitled to share in every part of it.

Muṅgari 'Early Crop' –sown at the commencement of south–west monsoon towards the end of May or beginning of June.

Mundala sub–group of the Holeyas.

Mundu waist cloth.

Munevet village village possessed by *shudras;* all such villages of the districts may be said to be under different tenures of *yekkabhogam* or *pushoonkary*, or *urdakarry*. The *munevet* villages have no regular grants, that is *danapattrams* or *dana shasanums, or tambur shasanums*; that they originally had certain portions of the land of the village, called *gramuttan manium*, and certain privileges, tythes, or fees in kind, under the general denomination of *sosuntrum*; that neither a single *gramuttan* where one headman possesses the *manium*, nor a number where they are several *mirāsīdārs* enjoying the *manium*, can dispose of any thing but the *gramuttan manium* and the *sosuntrum* fees, all the other lands of the villages being considered out of the power of his disposal, and exclusively belonging to government, that no permanent rent was ever settled either by grant or custom for the village, but that the annual rent depended upon the actual state of cultivation, the proportion only being fixed by general usage.

Except that the proportion of *mailwarum* which the sirkar received, was smaller from the *agraharums* than from the *munevet* villages, it does not appear that the *sirkar* exercised any greater degree of control over the *koodeewarum* of the one or other, that is as far as regarded those *agraharums*, which were at first or afterwards became liable to a certain payment to the *sirkar*. Occasional agents were appointed for the proper security of the *mailwarum* in both, but the management of the *koodeewarum* seems to have been left as equally to the *gramuttan* of the *munevet*, as to the *mahajanum* of the *agraharum* village.

Muniwar see *kawali*; some of *muniwars* also served as *nayaks*.

Munnims jungles, possessions in the Northern Circars.

Munshee, Moonshi clerk conducting the collector's correspondence with Indian revenue servants.

Muppatika–badi tenure lands held on three–fourth assessment.

Muqaddam (A.) head rayat or principal man of a village, looked after the affairs of it and collected the revenues within his jurisdiction, same as *patel*.

Muqarrar hasil 'established receipts.'

Muqasa (mukasa) military fief; a land assigned to an individual either revenue free or at low quit–rent on condition of service.

Muqasadar holder of *muqasa*.

Muqiman petty officials posted to each *mahal*.

Muṟṟṭṭu for the appropriation of the full yield.

Mura a cubit; the lower arm.

Murattu mānyam the *mānyam* granted to the lame and disabled.

Murei custom of giving labour in rotation; they worked for the *mirāsidārs* in rotation (*murei*); got a house and yard free, also certain dues in grain and presents in clothes, grain, and money, at stated festivals.

Mureicáren persoṉ entitled to pre–emption; the way it has been used in some deeds means, 'the right of pre–emption is reserved to the seller.'

Mureicárs possessing the right of pre–emption.

Murtuzanagar the Persian name of Guntur.

Musaliar a subordinate religious functionary and teacher.

Musaris (Malayalam), brass and coppersmiths, a division of *kammalans*.

Musáharah–i–kulkaranán, mushaira koolkernain monthly allowance to brahmin accountants, in the Northern Circars.

Mushrif auditor.

Muster sample; this term is used even by cultivators.

Musud mixed land.

Muṭṭhai–āḷ a term connected with land revenue current during *Chola* period in Cholamandalam.

Mutah, Muṭṭhā, mootah, mittah, mótai artificial estates or parcels put of for sale during the attempt to make zamindari, settlement; applied also to a sub–division of a zamindari estate; a sub–division; a portion of a district.

Lit. a heap of parcel. In the Northern Circars, a small district or subdivision of a country, consisting of a certain number of villages more or less. A farm of several villages.

Mutal revenue income.

Mutalikan in'am granted for the support of the dependants and servants of a great man.

Mutasaddi a clerk, accountant, writer or scribe.

Mutawattinin important notables officials.

Muthalali term of deference, used while addressing land lords.

Muthuvelly a type of paddy crop raised from seedlings sown about the third week of July and transplanted a month later. This crop is reaped at the beginning of March. It is raised on one crop land, and is suited to grounds on river–banks and tank–beds liable to inundation. It is raised in clay rugur and is seldom cultivated in channel lands.

Mutirigai (Tamil), a small land measure equal to 1/320 of a *veli*.

Muttaratsa in'am granted to a man of the *muttaratsa* caste for the service as a *kattubadi* peon.

Mutuda village headman.

Myrobalan a kind of dried fruit used for dyeing purposes.

Mysore breed of cattle well–bred Mysore ox, good sized, strong and active animal, allowed to run wild when young, and very hardy. Great attention was paid to the improvement of cattle for draught by Hyder Ali and Tipu Sultan, and they established systematic cattle breeding, using the best of the animals they captured. To their success was due the rapidity of their marches.

N

Nāḍu, Nāḍ a country; a territorial division; a district or a subdivision; the local assembly to govern the civic affairs of the division called *nāḍu*; a district; the assembly of a district; the professional association or guild of a district; local union of villages or family settlements in South India; this term was applied to the larger territorial divisions with numbers attached to their names.

Apart from the village, which was the primary basis of the territorial organisation, the administrative divisions (esp. during *kāktīyas)* fell in to two main classes the *sthala* and the *nāḍu*; the former being smaller of the two, and several combined to form a *nāḍu*; a number of *nāḍus* formed a *vaḷanāḍu*.

Basic territorial unit found throughout the Chola, Pandya and Tondai-mandalams; a revenue unit; also known as *kūṟṟam*.

An administrative division; also the assembly of a larger rural division, obviously larger than the village sabhā; many Vijayanagar inscriptions show that the *nāḍu* and the *sabhā,* the local assemblies, were incharge of collection of the revenues of the government in the areas under their jurisdiction; the government dealt only with these bodies in places where they existed; remission of taxes by the government or by high local officials had to be made only with the consent of the local bodies which carefully guarded the interests of the community.

An ancient territorial unit; a certain social space encompassing varying numbers of villages; regional council; more generally, nation; territory or country. A certain social space encompassing varying numbers of villages governed by *jati* leadership; *jati* council of the *nāḍu*.

Nāḍ-sēnabōva, Nāḍa-senbova incharge of the *nād* revenue accounts; officer incharge of the accounts of a *nāḍu* or district.

Nāḍa-gauḍa the head of an organisation relating to a district; also *nāḍu-gauḍa, nār, gāvuṇḍa,* etc.

Nāḍarasa head of the general administrations of a *nāḍu*; his duties were entirely general and all-embracing; also called *nāḷ prabhu*.

Nāḍu vagaiseydal land settlement after survey.

Nāḍu-cey, nāḍu-vakai-cey the settlement officer of *Nāḍu*, the officer who actually conducted the revenue survey.

Nāḍu-kāval (Tamil), 'policing duty of the *nāḍu*'; tax payable by the residents for the same; also called *nāḍu-talaiyārikkam*.

Nāḍu-kaṇkāṇi-nāyakam a term used in the epigraphs to indicate an officer of *nāḍu* engaged in auditing accounts of temples; there were instances when one officer was holding the office for more than one *nāḍu;* in some instances he would be auditing the articles of the local temple treasury; while in some instances he would be engaged in the distribution of temple cows to various functionaries.

Nāḍu-kūṟu-ceykiṟa-atikari the term used in the epigraphs to denote the *atikari* who is doing the work of *nāḍu-kūṟu;* the term *nāḍu-kūṟu literally means settlement of a nāḍu, (kūṟu* = to settle or divide); in some epigraphs the *nāḍu-kūṟu* officer fixed the boundary of lands of a newly constituted *dēvadāna,* acting on the authority of a *tirumukam* i.e. royal order, conveyed in the *kaṭaiyīṭu* (deed or execution).

Nāḍukas, nāḍuka same as *nāḍu;* administrative divisions; subdivision of a *sthala.*

Nāgarika the chief bailiff or prefect at Vijayanagar.

Nāhala barbarians and outcasts.

Nāḻi, nāḻi a grain measure.

Nāḷgāvunḍa an official in a *nāḍu;* his duties related to the collection of revenue, particularly land revenue.

Nāla cultivated land; same as *nāla-bhūmi.*

Nāla-bhūmi 'cultivated land'.

Nālān-taram a land of the fourth grade.

Nānādeśi guild of merchants coming from outside.

Nāndu one of the minor administrative subdivisions (post-Sātavāhana period).

Nār-gāvunda village headman; also *Nada-gauḍa.*

Nāttukkōn chief executive official of the assembly of elders.

Nāṭṭāmai arbitration and adjudication by *nāṭṭar.*

Nāṭṭār, nāṭṭavar, nautaur, nattaru, nattvar the members/inhabitants of the *nāḍu;* gifts; was entitled to receive all the taxes (specified); in perpetuity; *jati* leaders of the *nādu,* or locality, leading *kāṇiyāṭchikārar;* representatives of the *jati* from the villages of the *nādu.* It is also possible that the *nāṭṭār* were 'elders' of the *jati* within the region. However, they were usually men of great wealth, influence and authority. The crucial roles that they performed in the 18th century society included; they adjudicated over disputes among villages concerning boundaries and water management, and this role assumed greater significance in case of villages sharing the water of a single tank; the *nāṭṭārs* adjudicated over those issues which could not be settled locally and relied far more on arbitration and compromise than did the later day English courts; the *nāṭṭārs* based themselves on custom and tradition and tried to function as conscientious insiders on their own social milieu; the *nāṭṭārs* were responsible for the establishment and maintenance of *chattrams* in various religious centres, catering to the members of their respective *jatis;* as such, performed crucial roles of ensuring stability on a range of fronts from water management to pilgrimage.

Nāṭṭamai arbitration and adjudication of *nāṭṭār.* Same as *nāṭṭāmai* above.

Nāṭṭavar a variation of the term *nāṭṭār;* residents (of the village).

Nāṭṭu viniyōgam, ūriniyōgam, Nāṭṭu-viniyogam (Tamil-Sanskrit), individual share payable to make up the shortage in the total revenue by the grant of exemption by the assembly of the nādu; the *nādu* and township obligations; one of the variety of obligations that came to be fastened on land severally and progressively.

Nāṭṭu-kāṇikkai a term denoting a tax that accrued from the villages; this term appears in an inscription pertaining to the first half of the fifteenth century, but no other details are available.

Nāṭṭu-kkaṇakku-vari, Nāṭṭukaṇakku-vari (Tamil), one of the terms appearing in the epigraphs to denote a tax accruing from the villages; tax for the maintenance of revenue accounts of the nāḍu or the country as a whole.

Nāṭṭunāyagam seyvār, nāṭṭunāyakam

śeyvār, nāṭṭunāyakar superintendent of a *nāḍu;* a person of some consequence; though he is referred to in inscriptions as an important officer in the *nāḍu*, it is difficult to make out his exact functions, or even whether he was a royal officer in *nāḍu*, or simply an influential person in the locality vested with certain honorary powers by the government. According to some epigraphs he was granted land grants exempt from taxes; was allowed to grow any crop he pleased on all the dry and wet lands of the village excluding former gifts; was entitled to receive all the taxes (specified) in perpetuity.

Nāṭṭupati, nāḍu–upādi the obligations to be met and taxes payable to the local assembly of the *nāḍu*.

Nāṭṭusammadam levies by sanctions of the *nāḍu*.

Nātamkār headman of a *nāḍ* or a village group.

Nāvalō–nāval the labourers who come first to work in the fields call their comrades to work, with these words.

Nāyak, Nāyaka one who held lands from the Vijayanagar kings on condition of offering military service; the Vijayanagar empire was divided in to the chieftainships who acknowledged the suzerainty of Vijayanagar, the chiefs were called or entitled *Nāyaka*; this could perhaps be identified with the *'Nāik'* of the Marāthā territories of southern India; in caste they were of a proud military order, probably Dravidian or mixed origin. It seems possible that they might have been connected with–at any rate they resembled closely-the Nāyak of Canara and the Nāyar of Malabar. In the earliest form of government established in Coorg, the country was formed in to twelve *'kombu'*, or 'districts', each under a *'Nāyaka'*. In south Canara, the *Nāyaks*, as also other colonists of the military castes, had obtained the petty chiefships by conquest. Also see, *nāyaṅkara* system.

Nāyaka–wár, nāyakwár, naikwar a village under the management of a *naik*.

Nāyakavāḍis (Sanskrit–Tamil), watchmen stationed by the state or landlord to keep watch over the crops before or after harvest time; *in'am* granted to such persons; persons appointed for the purpose of watching the standing crops; peons stationed in the villages by the collector or landholder specially to superintend the villages in their cultivation and see that the produce was not misappopriated or stolen; performed also on occasions the duties of a watchman and a policeman; they were remunerated by the grant of service *in'ams* which were apparently called in the Tamil inscriptions *kākkunāyaka*.

Nāyaṅkara system an important feature of Vijayanagar provincial organisation whereby lands were granted to certain persons against annual tributes and military service. As in other parts of India during medieval period, the service to the ruler in this part also were rewarded by the grant of lands. Those who held lands, on the above conditions from the king were called *nāyakas,* though the term was later used to denote a variety of offices and communities. They ruled over the areas granted with great freedom. It was the king that fixed the number of troops and the amount of money each of these *nāyakas* was to keep, and they were generally in proportion to the revenue each derived. The estates of these *nāyakas* were liable to be confiscated if they did not maintain the full number of soldiers or pay tribute according to their obligations. A *nāyaka*, it seems, was a military vassal and enjoyed comparatively greater freedom in his territory than a governor. The *nāyakship* which was in the initial stages personal became hereditary in course of time when the kings at the centre became weak and effeminate; the 'feudal' system prevalent in the Vijayanagar empire, in which *Nāyakas* enjoyed royal land on condition of offering miliary service: also see *Nāyaka, Amara-nāyaka*.

Nálá, nulla a streamlet, rivulet, watercourse.

Nár-pángellei this word, which means the limits on four sides, describes, of course, the whole property sold.

Nátam, nátha, naut, nautum lord, master, headman.

Nátam-kár, nautam kar headman or cultivator of a village.

Nátawár, náthawár, nautawar having a lord or master. Certain villages superintended by headmen called *nauts* or *nautams,* on the part of government. The term is also used for headman.

Náyak-wárí, náyakawárí, naikwarry anything connected with a village, etc. under a *naik;* establishment of village peons.

Naḍuvazhi ruler of a *nāḍu*, region, chieftain.

Naḍavumunai a small wooden peg used by the peasant in order to make the small pits when the seedlings are transplanted.

Naḍu-vakai lit. settlement of a *naḍu (vakai* = to settle or organise); the term has been used in the epigraphs to indicate revenue settlement officer of a *naḍu*; in some of the epigraphs he has figured in a number of other allied activities also, e.g. he commanded a defaulting person to pay the dues to the temple; he brought about a grant of tax free *dēvadāna* acting under the authority of an *atikāri;* he assisted an *atikāri* while the latter was inspecting the temple affairs; he along with other officers received the order to the effect that the accumulated gold in the temple should be converted in to jewels for the deity; he punished the temple priest by levying a fine, because the latter failed to turn-up at the instance of the queen on the occasion of a solar eclipse; sometimes he is also mentioned as a *paṇimakan* (lit. a servant) of *ciṟcutaṇam* grade (i.e. a lower grade).

Nadam or nadum purthy (lit. a triennial shrub) biennial cotton-sown in the month of August, September and October with gram and the inferior late grains. It occasionally bears in August and September, twelve months after sowing, but is scarcely ever gathered until the month of October. This is the first gathering. The second gathering is during March and April and the third in the following October. The plant then drops and is plucked up in January and the ground prepared with manure etc., for the next sowing. *gossypium arboreum.*

Nadar the term used for indigent community; poorer people.

Nadavar a military caste (South Kánara).

Naday olungu an account of the measurement and extent of fields composing a village.

Naḋ talari in'am granted for the service of a district watchman under the pre-British police system.

Naduwari, naduvazhi chief of a *nadu*.

Nagadali *opuntia dillenii.*

Nagara larger centres of population; the towns; large mercantile settlements; in Tamil country, the term *nagara* was reserved exclusively for mercantile centres; we hear casually of *nagara seṭṭis,* but get little information on even the outlines of the constitutions under which the administration of the cities was carried out in general; a commercial guild; guild of merchants; a mercantile town; sometimes it has also been used-in the sense of the *sabhā* and *ūr*; the merchant community in general or the organisation of the merchant community of a town; at times the *nagara* and *ūr* carried on their functions side by side; a township where *par excellence* the merchants had occupancy rights in the land.

Nagara–svāmin headman of the merchants.

Nagaram village assembly; market or commercial centres. The *nagaram* represents the first 'secular' element in society in so far as the membership of the *nagaram*, unlike that of the *sabha* and *ūr* was determined by a common profession.

The *nagaram* organisation assumed the character of a local body maintaining local markets, supervising the flow of goods, providing a regular link between *nadus* and itinerant traders, thus breaking the insularity of the *nadu* and its ties of kinship.

Nagarattār a guild of the town; members of a guild of a town; members of a merchantile guild.

Nagasarm in'am granted for the service of playing in pagodas on a musical instrument called *nagasaram,* a kind of clarionet.

Naidu a village headman. Also spelled as *nayudu.*

Naikvariyan a petty officer in forts or police stations having authority over some ten or fifteen men.

Nair gueny probably from *nair* chief, head, and *gueny* a tenant. Or it may be from *nair*, a plough, and *gueny* a tenant; a plough tenant. A kind of soccage tenure in some parts of Kanara.

Nakara guild.

Nakara in'am held for the service of beating a drum at mosque or at the gates of *nawabs* or men of rank.

Nakara parivāras an organization empowered to issue coins; these coins were local currencies which were in use only in the localities concerned; the members of this organisation also enjoyed the right to confer honours on some highly placed officials.

Nakarak–kaṇakku an official mentioned in the epigraphs who seems to be an accountant of the *nakaram.*

Nakharadavāru merchants.

Nal'padi it is the same as *etchóru* or daily *batta* paid to persons deputed on any account to the village by the officers of government, except that the former is given to *peons* or others of pure caste in money or raw grain, and the latter is an allowance made to *talaiyāris,* or *tukiris,* who are generally *pareiyer,* a collection is often made on these accounts from the inhabitants, and if not disbursed is divided among the *mirásidars.*

Nal–kiḍa a term denoting a tax that accrued from the villages as indicated in the inscription pertaining to the first half of the fifteenth century.

Nal–paśu one of the taxes accruing from the villages.

Nala measuring rod equal to 7 *cubits*; same as *daṇḍa*; varied in sizes like 12 cubits; 22 cubits, 56 cubits etc.in length.

Nali, nari, nazhi a west coast measure, one–fourth of an *edangali.*

Nalinavāru assembly.

Nall–ĕrudu (Tamil) cess for the maintenance of a model bull, also used for breeding purposes.

Nallāvu a professional tax collected from the shepherds.

Nallerudu a professional tax that accrued from the shepherds as per the inscription of the first half of the fifteenth century.

Namaud shown, mentioned, specified, exhibited.

Nambi in'am held for the service of performing *puja* in Vishnu pagodas.

Nambiyars a section of *Nayars* or *Nairs.*

Nambudri, Nambudiri the Brahmans of the Malabar coast; having highest reputation of all Brahmans for piety and Sanskritic learning.

Naṇcey, nīrnilam, nīrārampam a term used to denote the wet land tax. Different terms used to denote wet land; all paddy fields were classified as wet land.

Naṇcey-kaṭamai: land tax on wet land.

Naṇcey–puṇcey–Pottaka(m) the register of wet and dry lands; probably whole land revenue transactions pertaining to these lands were recorded in this register.

Nanadesi 'merchants of many countries', an itinerant guild.

Nanal in'am held for the service of planting needs for the protection of anicuts and irrigation channels.

Nanawutta monetary allowances for depreciated currency.

Nandavanam garden attached to the temple.

Nandavanam in'am granted for the maintenance of a garden, the flowers of which are appropriated to the use of a pagoda or of the village community; revenue–free grant of land consisting of topes of groves, flower gardens for temple–service.

Nanjai taram–punjai, nunjah taum punjah wet land like dry. The least valuable of *nanjai* land, from the uncertainty as to water for irrigation.

Nanjal–mel, nunjahmel probably a contraction of *nanja–mel–punjai.*

Nanjai–mel–punjai, nunjay mail punjah dry land cultivation upon wet. In Tinnevelly, when, from an accidental deficiency of water, land, which is usually cultivated with rice, happens to be unfit for that grain they plough up the stubble, sow it with the best sort of dry grain.

Nanjei, nunjiah wet lands. See also *Nunjei.*

Nankar revenue free grant of land; the assignment of *nankar* was made within the jurisdiction of a *zamindari;* in various parts of India, the *nankar* instead of being given as land grant assumed the shape of payment in kind (grain) or cash known as the *rasum–i–zamindari.*

Nantangauls beds where paddy seed is sown.

Nāpita barbers.

Naqal a copy or transcript.

Nar pangellie within the four boundaries of the village.

Nar–samatu district governors in Andhra.

Nari–vetti in'am granted as a reward for having killed a fox during a chase.

Nashta, nesht, nisht lost, deficient, extra assessment in Kanara for deficiencies of rent.

Nat ambalam in'am granted for the service of head *rayat* of more than one village.

Naṭṭiṛaiyili (*nāḍu+iraiyili*) the term used to indicate the remission granted by *nāṭṭār* or *nāḍu.*

Naṭṭupāḷ (lands) that died in planting.

Nata–silavu, nautsellavoo expenses or charges account of headman.

Natcheny *spermacoce hispida.*

Nattamai in'am held for the service of headman of a village.

Nattangcál small plots of wet land highly manured in which the rice–plants are raised for transplantation.

Nattar district revenue office whose duty it was under the pre–British administration to superintend cultivation. *In'am* land grant for the above service. Also see, *nattvar.*

Nattar in'am granted for the service of

a district revenue officer whose duty it was under the pre-British administration to superintend cultivation.

Nattvar, Nāṭṭavar, nāṭṭār, nattaur, nautaur (Tamil), members of an organisation relating to a *nādu* or district; *jati* leaders of the *nāḍu; nāṭṭr* (as a body) seems to have played an important role in deciding the revenue matters of the *nāḍu*. Also see, *nattar*, above.

Naut karnam head village accountant.

Navarai summer crop.

Navidan in'am granted for the service of village barber.

Nayadis originally a hunting tribe living in the forest-covered hills of the West Coast; lowest of the untouchable castes, would pollute a Brahman at a distance of 300 feet; would often serve as watchmen, guarding crops from beasts at night; sometime do agriculture work.

Nayadu in'am held for the service of head *rayat* of a village.

Nayak-wadi in'am the same as *mohtad in'am*.

Nayakars a Telugu-speaking caste of agriculturists, numerous in the Rāmnād, Tinnevelly and Madura districts, closely akin to the *Nayudus* of Tanjore, and to the *Kapus* or *Reddis*.

Nayakwarian-i azam 'great *nayaks*'.

Nayars, Nairs the military and once ruling caste in Malabār; the name means a leader or soldier. The military skill and valour of the *Nayars* was highly praised by various travellers of the seventeenth and eighteenth centuries, and by Camoens. It was the ancient custom for their chieftain the Zamorin, to cut his own throat after reigning 12 years. This was modified at an unknown date, and during the seventeenth century the Zamorin instead held a great 12 days feast every twelfth year, at the close of which young men were invited to fight their way through the Zamorin's guards, and kill him, with the prospect of succeeding to the throne if successful.

Nayel kaveli, nayel cavelly see *desha kavel*.

Nayudu a title assumed by certain Telugu castes; according to some writers same as *Kapus* or *Reddis*. Also spelled as *naidu*

Nazar, Nazrāna (Persian), customary presents; a fee, offering, tribute, a fine on transfer of land; the sum paid down to secure a grant of a revenue-lease of a village.

Nazūl (Arabic), property escheated or lapsed to the state; commonly applied to any land or house property belonging to government either as an escheat or as having belonged to a former government.

Nĕy (Tamil), tax on the traders in ghee.

Neer moodut, ner moodut a contract by which a mortgagee in Malabar advances a further sum on a landed estate at the expiration of the former term.

Neergaṇṭee, nirgranthi distributor of water for irrigation in the peninsula; distributor of water of the streams or reservoirs in just proportion to several fields. Also see, *nirguṇṭi*.

Neernally the offering to the deity upon commencing the measurement.

Negamā, naigamāḥ the word inscribed on the coins; it lit. means 'trade' or 'members of an administrative board pertaining to a town'; these coins were issued privately.

Neguadee, nikuti a tax.

Nelevīḍu permanent camp.

Nelgutta in'am villages held on *in'am* tenure on payment of a certain quantity of grain per annum.

Nell-āyam, Nellāyam, Nĕll-āyam

(Tamil–Sanskrit), tax payable in paddy; tax in grains. Revenue in paddy; a term used in the inscriptions to denote the collection of land revenue in kind or grain; this term indicates that the payment of the government share in the revenue could, as a general rule, be made in cash or kind; same is indicated in other terms used in various other epigraphs, e.g. *pon–mudal, nel–mudal, kāśāyam,* etc.

Nella yendagha chitto a deed of land tenure in Tanjore given by mortgaging a portion or the whole land after getting a loan of money. The interest (specified percentage) on the money loaned was to be paid per month and the principle on the specified date; failing which the other party was at liberty to possess and enjoy the produce pledged on *yendaga* as if it had been transferred on sale by *shûtta kreya shâasanum.*

Nellicoy *emblica officinalis;* yields a wood useful only for the foundation of wells. Fruit held in esteem and preserved the whole year.

Nellore breed of cattle more correctly called 'the Ongole breed'; largest and heaviest breed in south India, the oxen though slow, very suitable for heavy work; cows the best milkers of the native breeds; bred in the Guntur district and adjoining parts of the Nellore district, Ongole being about the centre of the area; the soil in the locality rich in lime, favours the growth of bones; fed on private pastures; certain bulls dedicated to the gods and set aside for breeding.

Nelmudai a term used in the epigraphs of Pudukōṭṭai region to denote the collection of land revenue in the form of grain.

Nesara koḍage, nettra koḍage, nettaru–paḍi mānyam ,ratta–kuḍangai terms used in the epigraphs to denote a piece of revenue–free land granted for service rendered in the battle field at the cost of life; it was granted usually to the close relations of those who fell in the battle; in the Kannada districts grants of land made for a particular purpose were known as *koḍage,* or at times as *kuḍangai.*

Neṭṭāl superintending manager (who was entitled to get share in the residual paddy).

Neṭṭāl kūḷi superintending fee.

Nettara gōḍage, Nettara–goḍaga a term used in the epigraphs to denote a type of land grant given to the aggrieved party. This grant was given to compensate the remaining members of a family whose other members have been killed by some professional killer. In such cases the loss of the aggrieved party was sought to be compensated by the state; a kind of compensation.

Netti–velai in'am granted for the service of making artificial birds, flowers and toys in pith work for the use of pagodas.

Netturu–kattu in'am granted to the family of a person killed in battle, or as a compensation to a person who has been wounded in the public service.

Netturu–veṭṭu in'am corruption for *netturottu in'am* which is same as *nestturu–kattu in'am.*

Nharel *cocos mucifera.*

Nīr vilai, Nīr–kkāṇam, nir–vilai (Tamil), water–cess; sale of water. A term connected with the land revenue current during Chola period; it was a tax levied on a unit of land as a fee for using water for irrigation.

Nīr–nilak–kācu tax on wet land.

Nīr–vilaik–kācu same as *nīr–vilai.*

Nīra–gṛha 'a water house'.

Nīrānivari one of the terms used in the inscriptions, especially of the first half of the fifteenth century, denoting a tax accruing from the villages.

Nīrguṇṭi a village functionary for

upkeep of irrigation channels, regulation of sluices and water distribution. Also see, *neergaṇṭee*, above.

Nīrk–kūli nīrkūli, nīrvilaikūli tax levied on a unit of land as a fee for using water for irrigation; irrigation tax; it was one of the additional charges over and above the land revenue for the maintenance of irrigation works.

Nīrkkīya–vilai same as *nīṛ-vilai.*

Nīrkkiṛai a term connected with the tax levied during *Chola* period on a unit of land as fee for using water for irrigation. Same as *nīr vilai,* above.

Nīrkūli sarvamānyam grant for maintaining the supply of water to the villages.

Nīrnilakkāśu same as *nīrkūli.*

Nīru–nela, nīr–nela (Telugu), low lying land irrigated by water from a tank, canal, well, etc.; usually called 'wet land' and considered the most valuable; as against this type of land–*veli–volamu veli–cenu,* land on comparatively higher level and depends solely on rain, called 'dry land'.

Nīvī a permanent endowment.

Nīr, nir water in general; tanks, large and small watercourses, etc., also used to mean, a share in public ...

Nibarava (Telugu), weight used in the case of salt and paddy (unhusked rice).

Nidāna (Telugu), a treasure; a hoard or fund; store, wealth or property; same as Sanskrit *nidhāna.*

Nidhi–nikṣepa treasure trove; a treasure hoard; hidden treasure under the ground; one of the eight kinds of enjoyments allowed to the donees of revenue–free land.

Nidī, nidhi buried treasure; treasure or wealth; treasure trove.

Nigama central town in a bigger administrative division; some towns also had *nigamasabhā,* an assembly of the cities.

Nikshépam deposits.

Nilai–iṛai, vāḍākkaḍan a term used in the epigraphs to denote state demand fixed on immutable basis especially in lands newly reclaimed.

Nilak–kaṭamai land tax.

Nilam land, earth; land in general; the whole soil of the village; or that part under tillage in particular years.

Nilam aḷarpōr perumakkal the land survey committee.

Nilamaḷavu–kōl, tiruvulakaḷanta–kōl names of measuring rods gathered from epigraphs; the only way to know the exact length of these rods used in the survey could be known from the markings engraved on the temple walls. Moreover, the length of *nilamaḷavu–kōl* varied at different places. Its length was 12 feet 9 inches at Siyamaṅgalam in North Arcot district in 1004 A.D., 12 feet at *Iḍaiyāḷam* in South Arcot district in 1063 A.D., and 16 feet at *Kōṭṭūr* in South Arcot district.

Nilam kalandapadi lands not divided by metes and bounds.

Nilams the name given to paddy lands in the Malayalam areas.

Nilamutal–pottakam a register of land revenue; it seems that whole land revenue transactions were recorded in this register.

Nilavari, Nilaviṛai land rent.

Nillāyam a term used in the epigraphs denoting the fact that the payment of the goverment share in the revenue could, as a general rule, could be made in cash or in kind; same is indicated in other terms used in various other epigraphs, e.g. *pon–mudal, nel–mudal, kāśāyam,* etc. Same as *nĕl-āyam,* above.

Nilōpādi demand due on the extent of land (based on area–measurement).

Nimme badi tenure lands held on half assessment.

Niṉraiṛai, Niṉrirai (Tamil), permament

tax; (land given) on permanent assessment.

Nir sarihadd in'am an *in'am* granted to the *rayats* of a village as a compensation for allowing a channel to be dug through their lands for the benefit of another village.

Nir–attipper free–hold property transacted with the sprinkling of water.

Nirārampam tax on wet land; a term used in Karnataka.

Nirarambam wet land, fit for rice cultivation, irrigated for cultivation.

Nirganti in'am granted for superintending the distribution of water for irrigation.

Nirmunaka in'am granted for the service of diving in to the water and opening or shutting the sluice of a tank.

Nirnilam wet land.

Nirpoku, nilam field through which a rivulet flows.

Nirrlu–pandal water hut; refreshment station same as *'Tannir Pandal'*.

Nirūpa written order; communication from the superiors or the king; the carrier of a royal order.

Nirūpachchambaḍam one of the additional taxes charged over and above the usual land revenue for the support and payments to village officers.

Nirvana manyam an *in'am* granted for the support of a Hindu ascetic who goes about naked.

Nirvṛtti an administrative division; same as *viṣaya* or *koṭṭam*; an important administrative division; according to some sources this division was perhaps larger than a *kōṭṭam*.

Niṣka one of the indigenous gold coins in circulation in south India; this coin occurs in the south Indian inscriptions, though not very frequently; the weight and denomination of *niṣka* cannot be accurately determined; there is only one inscription which gives us some guidance and according to which it corresponds to the *kalañju,* it would be approximately equal to 52 grains and may be taken to correspond to the *kaḷañju, pagoda* and *varāha*.

Nivāra a kind of wild rice.

Nivanda, nimanda (Tamil), the fixed requirements of a temple; expenses or arrangements; arrangement for the conduct of affairs in a temple.

Niyāyattār (Tamil), a judge; same as Sanskrit *Nyāyastha.*

Niyogas offices: *niyogādhikṛta* – superintendent of the *niyogas.*

Niyogi a class of Brahmans in Telugu speaking land.

Nizám, nizam order arrangement, an arranger. *Nizámul Mulk* the administrator of the empire.

Nizámat, nizamat arrangement, government. The office of the *Nazim* or *Nizám*. The administration of criminal justice.

Nizámat–adálat, nizamat adawlat the court of criminal justice.

Nokkan in'am granted to persons of the *nokkan* caste in the south, who correspond to the *dommaras* in the Ceded Districts; see *dommara in'am.*

Nondā–viḷakku a gift for maintaining an ever burning lamp in the temple.

Nottan in'am granted for the service of village shroff, whose duty it is to examine the coin received in payment of the government revenue.

Nūl–āyam (Tamil–Sanskrit), tax on cotton thread for weaving.

Nuckhood small grain used for making bread.

Nukattāṇi the iron or wooden rod at the centre of the yoke which holds it in position.

Nukattaḍi the yoke

Nukkattoṭai the holes on either side of the yoke in which two iron or wooden rods are thrust so that the yoke may rest on the neck of the bulls and not slip from position.

Nunjei, nunjiah wet land.

The great distinction between the wet lands of Malabar and Arcot is, that in Malabar the cultivation of them depends entirely on the falling rains, while in Arcot it depends chiefly on tanks and other artificial sources of irrigation, constructed at the expense of government.

In Malabar the cultivator of wet lands is not at all dependent on the aid of government, in Arcot he can do nothing without it. In Malabar, therefore, the cultivator trusts to the seasons and to his own industry for success, and he can with confidence venture to employ all his savings in the improvement of his land. As government furnishes him with no water and bears no share of the expense of the improvements, it had no fair claim to any additional rent on account of it, and has in fact not made it to any great extent, and hence he has been enabled to render his land a valuable private property saleable at all times and transferable at will.

In Arcot the nature of *mirāsī* or hereditary landed property is very different, and is much less perfect; because being dependent on government for its supply of water, and being, in fact, held in partnership with the government it does not hold out the same inducement to undertake improvements; and hence the land in general is but indiferently cultivated, and though it is nominally saleable it will seldom fetch any price in the market.

In Malabar, where the falling rain during five or six months supplies all the water of cultivation, the proprietor can lay out his money with safety on his land, for he knows that he cannot be disappointed while the order of the seasons continues as it is. But in Arcot the proprietor has no such certainty, he is not even sure that he can keep his lands in their present condition; for unless government keep the tanks in repair this cannot be done; or it may sometimes happen that the bursting of the tank may render his land for ever unfit for cultivation, because the tank may be allowed to go to decay, from its being found that the revenue of all the land watered by it would not defray the expense of repairing it; the land formerly watered by tanks was necessarily either left waste or cultivated with dry grain.

The cultivator in Arcot can never have the same share of the produce as the owner of rice land in Malabar. From these causes it happens that in Arcot, the most substantial *rayats* are found engaged, not in cultivation of wet land, where government supplies the water, but in that of the dry, where they can improve without the aid of government and drive the exclusive benefit of every improvement.

Nuri when paddy rent is being measured, a handful of paddy is put on one side to denote the number of measures which added to the share of the landlord in addition to the rent.

Nyāsa mortagaged property.

O

Ōḍakkūli a professional tax charged as tax on ferry; fee.

Ōlai (Tamil), 'palmyra–leaf; an order from the king or person in authority; written order.

Ōlai–eḻuttu the temple accountant; same as *kōyilkaṇakku*.

Ōṭak–kācu,ōṭak–kūli the terms used to denote tax levied on ferries. Same as *Ōḍakkūli* above.

Obolus one of the Greek coins in circulation in south India; it was equal to *boddika* and one–sixth of a dramma; can be thought of as representing 1.625d.

Oḍaya (Telugu–Kannaḍa), a king, ruler, master or leader.

Odayaṁtrikas hydraulic engines; the use of this mechanised device for irrigation purpose was so popular that there developed in the Deccan many guilds of people working in *odayaṁtrikas*.

Oddars Telugu–speaking caste of navvies and earth workers, originally came from Orissa.

Odukkam in'am the same as *chatram in'am*.

Oduvan in'am granted for the support of a sudra attached to Siva pagoda, whose duty it is to recite *tevaram* or Tamil divine hymns during the perfomance of *puja*.

Oḻugu, Ooloogo register of occupancy and enjoyment; also see, *ulūngu*.

Oḻugu–nīrpāṭṭam one of the taxes accruing from the villages.

Olai–ccādanam (Tamil), a document written on palm–leaf.

Olai–ccampadam, olai–ccambaḷam, olaiccammādam (Tamil), wages paid to the one who brings the *olai* to meet the expenses on the way.

Olai–nāyaka senior officer looking after correspondence.

Om ! this word occurs in some of the deeds on the conclusions of the bargain, between the parties,. Whenever it occurs, it implies solemn consent; but it is disputed, whether it ought to be considered the mystic triliteral monosyllable of the Brahmans, or merely the third person to 'adhere, agree, ratify'; the latter seems better interpretation.

Oṇtudāru (Telugu), a revenue officer.

Onam harvest festival; a festival of Vishnu in the form of Vamana.

Oolcoodie, oolcoody, ooloocody see *ulkūdi*.

Oolky *amildar's* messenger

Ooppers salt makers.

Oouarkally a saltish clay land.

Opādi (Tamil), lit. Obstruction; dues; anything payable as debt or obligation. Also see *upāti*.

Oṟṟi making a usufructary mortgage of land.

Oranglaut a term used for sea–gipsies.

Oṭṭi (Malayalam), a king of 'mortgage' in Malabār; when the advance was considerable that the interest swallowed up the whole of the *janmi's* produce•share, the transaction was called *oṭṭi*; usufructuary mortgage.

Ottakaran in'am granted for the service of tappal runner.

Otty moory (Tanjore) deed granted in lieu of the sum advanced; the land under consideration had earlier been cultivated by some one else; the condition attached with the deed was the grantee had been authorised to cultivate the said ground as *ottykar* for a specified period; the sum of money was to be returned only in the shape of giving the cultivation rights.

P

Pāñcālas artisans; any decent village had its complement of artisans, known generally as the *pāñcālas*, divided into five groups namely, black–smiths, gold–smiths, brass–smiths, carpenters, and idol makers; craftsmanship was usually hereditary; an inscription of the time of Dēva Rāyal states that there were seventy four divisions among the *pāñcālas*.

Pañca–karmara the five castes of artizans, viz. goldsmith, blacksmith, brassmith, carpenter and stone–mason; also called *pañca–kammāḷar*.

Pañca–māśattam grant of 40 *mattars* of land to a piper for arranging to play the fine musical instruments.

Pañca–vāram one–fifth of the produce due to the government as land revenue; five branches in the administration of big villages, each looked after by a committee called *pañcavāra vāriyam*.

Pañcāla an artizan; members of the artizan classes; also called *pañcāhaṇa, pāñcāhaṇaṁvāru, pāñcāḷaṁvāru*. Same as *pāñcālas*, above.

Pañcāḷattār an organisation of the artizans.

Pañcamṛta lit. nectar of five ingredients; fruit salad; some famous shrines specialize in this variety of the deity's *prasāda*.

Pacahānamvāru or **pāñcālamvāru (in Telugu) and pāñcāḷattār** (in Tamil) the terms in the epigraphs to denote the artisans; these artisan classes seem to have had a corporate existence in the early period as they were taxed collectively and made grants under the direction of the rulers in their corporate capacity.

Pāñcavāram a term used to denote land tax.

Pāñchāṇaṁvāru the artisans who use the five kinds of tools.

Pācip–pāṭṭam a kind of duty levied on fishermen.

'Pāḍi' one of the classes of territorial units (Kākatīya period).

Pāḍi–kāppān village watchman.

Pāḍikāval, padikavaḷ the right of policing, which was sometime leased to people on payment in cash or share in produce, etc.

Pāda 'one fourth'; a measure equal to one–fourth of the standard land measure.

Pāda–padam–opajīvin, pāda–piṇḍ–opajīvin 'subsisting (like a bee) on the lotuses that are the feet of..'; 'subsisting on the food supplied by the feet of..'; technical expressions in medieval south India to denote the relationship of subordinates to their master.

Pādar 'common land adjacent to a village left uncultivated',

Pāḍava–kkāṇi (Tamil), land given as wage for temple service.

Pādika, pātika (Telugu–Kannaḍa), a share; one fourth of anything; 1/64th part of the coin *pagoda*.

Pāga same as Kannaḍa hāga; name of a coin, one fourth share of the revenue collected.

Pāga or hāga a subdivision of a coin called Paṇa–one fourth of a *paṇa or paṇam or fanam*.

Pāḻ destroyed plants.

Pālaiyàkkārar (Tamil), pālegāra (Canarese), Pālegādu (Telugu) Poligar (Anglacized) a chief; a revenue agent; could be easily compared with the different categories of zamindars during the Mughal rule; territorial chieftain who either governed the territory or undertook police duties of a territory.

Pālaiyam, Palaiyam, pollam (T.)–An estate, district, village or villages, war camp, fotress held by a palegar. Estate or zamindari of a *palegar*.

Pānbuḍit, pāimāli, pāmālī lit. Inundated; 'crops destroyed by flood'; one of the remissions regularly allowed in Madras.

Pāra ferrying across rivers.

Pārasi, pārasī, pārasika a Persian

Pāṣāṇa one of the eight kinds of enjoyment of landed property; rocky soil and its produce; mineral products; could be, stony and hilly land referring to the right of quarrying, etc.

Pāśippāttạm, mīnpāttạm terms used n the epigraphs to technically mean ncome derived from the rents for the ight of fishing in the tank; the income ealised was utilised for deepening the ank, for removing silt from the tank or or the repair of the tank.

Pāsārī general grazing land (in Coorg).

Pāṭaka 'part of a village', a quarter; he outlying part of a village; a hamlet; portion of a field.

Pāṭikāval the *kāval* (village police) luties were entrusted to a group or an ndividual and for the service a payment n kind or cash or land grant or any wo or all the three were demanded. It s referred to in the inscriptions as *āṭikāval*; also *pādikāval*.

āṭṭa–nēl (Tamil), paddy to be paid by he tenant to the landlord as per terms f lease.

āṭṭam an occupational due or a levy nposed on profession. Though it was used as an independent term, it also appeared as a suffix to other terms. e.g. *taṭṭārap–pāṭṭam* due on gold smith.

Pāṭṭamkār in Malabār, a tenant, person holding a *pāttam* or lease; simple tenants-at-will or under contract, are called *pāṭṭamkār*.

Pātāsthal land irrigated by a small channel (*pāt*), from a tank etc.

Pāvu ceydu distribution of dues.

Pāvai similar to persian *nazarāna*.

Pālyapati, pooliaput head of the *pálaiyam*. Lands in hands of *palegaras* or *zamindars*, and not under the immediate management of government.

Pán–málá, paunmala betel–leaf garden. Ground suitable to the culture of the *piper betel* plant. *Nunjai* garden lands.

Pátam, patam a Tamil word for Sanskrit *patram* a leaf. A lease or simple lease, in Malabar.

Paccar a kind of rice.

Pachalai the green plant bug *Nesara viridula*.

Padāgai, pidāgai hamlet; to each of a smaller administrative unit, like *agarams* or *maṅgalams*, or *ūrs*, were attached a few villages which were called *piḍāgai* in the Tamil areas; in some cases the village was smaller than the average type, such one being generally denoted in insriptions by the term *paḍāgai or piḍāgai*, i.e., hamlet.

Paḍaga, pādaga (Tamil), name of a measure of land; a land measure which was equal to 240 *kulis*, and 6, 1/4 of which made one *veli*.

Paḍaipāṟṟu the area in which the land holders had the obligation to render military service when required by the king or their chieftain; military tenure;in such cases the granatee had the right to levy taxes at certain fixed rates on the lands held by him; the term is almost similar to *nāyankara* tenure during Vijayanagar period.

Paḍaiparṟu garrison township.

Paḍalikai name of a measure of quantity.

Paḍayli-ānavaḻi a term used in the epigraphs to denote billeting or feeding of the soldiers on the move (and it was not be borne by the cultivators.).

Paḍugaitākku banks of rivers.

Pada śēṣa lit. quarter of the surplus or ¼ reserved quantum; its use in the epigraphs indicates that if the accountant could pass the ordeal of presenting the accounts successfully he was awarded *pada śēṣa* as bonus.

Padakku 1/6 of a *kalam* (of paddy).

Padar village.

Padavāra, paduvāra, padavāram fee payable for exchanging landed property; transfer fee.

Padi a local measure.

Padi (Tamil) fixed daily allowance of food.

Padia waste land; land immemorially waste.

Padikkaval manyam the same as *grama kaval*.

Paditaram order, general rule; allowance at a pagoda, annual grant or income stipend.

Padiyal (Tamil) from *padi* a measure; one who receives a defined quantity of grain from his master; hired farm servant receiving wages in kind; *padi*, a fixed allowance of food; a labourer; the Malayalam equivalent of *padiyal* is *vallial*. The *padiyals* were hired for a very long periods, and they could be enchained by debt to one master.

Padugai alluvium.

Pagalve-shakarar men wearing disguise during day time; they were the alm-seekers.

Pagod, pagoda English name of the gold coin called *hūn* or *varāha*; probably so called because the coins often bore the representation of a temple called *pagod* or *pagoda* by the early European travellers; a coin = 3½ rupees; the subordinate coins were *fanam* and *cash* (*kās*) 80 *cash* = 1 *fanam*, 42 *fanams* = 1 *pagoda*; currency in which accounts were usually maintained in most parts of south India. The most prevalen pagodas were Star Pagoda and Cantaro pagoda. The former was usuall understood to be equal to 3½ rupee and latter equal to 3 rupees. Also a idol temple.

Paiiki-guntaka more correctly, *palik guntava*, twelve-toothed rake, draw by oxen.

Paik in'am held by military peons i the district of Ganjam on condition c service.

Paikārar, pāikārī, parakūdī, poycarry paicari, payeecari non-resider cultivator; this term, observes Ellis, "i said to be derived from the Persia words *paye*, the foot, and *kurdun* t labour, or *kisht carkurdun* to cultivat The proper Tamil word is *payer-cudi* c *payercaren*, from *payer*, cultivatio and *cudi* or *caren*, an inhabitant, person, from the latter of which it probably corrupted."

Mírásidars occasionally rented out the lands to under-tenants, name *paycarries*. The *paycarries*, on conditic of paying to the *mírásidars* a certa share of the produce or sometimes c *punjah* land a certain *teerwa* in mone but rarely a fixed sum of money for given extent of land, rent from t lands of a greater or less extent, f one, two, or more years.

In *pasang-carei* villages they hold of the *mírásidars* collectively, in t *arudi-carei* villages from ea individually, and in the *eka-bhogu* villages from the sole *mírásidar*.

In *Tondei Mandalm*, in addition their stipulated rents in kind or mone they pay the established *marahs* of the mirásidars, known by the denomination of *cooputtum, cawnyatchey,* or *grama marah* etc.

In no case have they any concern whetever with the *perumboc, tarisee,* or in *Tondei Mandalam* with *mírási manium*; and of the rents paid by the *paycarries,* what remains to the *mírásidars,* after the liquidation of the land–tax, is called *toondoo–warum,* or *swam–bhogum*, the clear net landlord's rent.

The *paycarries* or tenants are divided into two distinct classes, named *oolcoody paycarries* or permanent tenants, and *paracoody paycarries* or temporary tenants. One of the judgments says, "Unless Payacaree ryots become issueless, the Meerassidars should not take possession of their kyput lands. The Payacaree Ryot is considered to possess equal right with the Meerassidar except the former has no power to dispose of their kyput lands."

Strangers admitted into the village as tenants from year to year, or for some other limited period. The terms on which the rent are settled between themselves and the *mírásidar;* and on the expiration of their leases their rents may be raised, or they may be altogether ousted from their farms. A *mírásidar* of one village could at the same be a *paracoody paycarry* in other village, and of course, vice–versa. If the tank of a *mírási* village is burst by too great a flow of water in a storm, and the water runs off, the *mírásidars* of the village visited with so great a calamity would carry their labour to the neighbouring village and cultivate as *paycarries,* but must pay the fees of superiority to prevent their laying any claim, at a future period, to a share of the *mírási* of the village in which they have been admitted as temporary cultivators.

A tenant at will; casual tenants; outside tenants; as opposed to *'ūlkudi'*; non–hereditary casual tenant; possessing only cultivating rights;cultivators possessing only cultivating rights over land; persons of this category had no privilege other than that of tilling the land, in return for which they paid a part of their produce as *swāmibōgam* (master's enjoyment) to the *kāṇiyāt chikārar* under whose share their lands fell; the *payirkārar* could be either *ulkudi* (resident of the village) or *purakudi* (resident outside the village).

Some historians have tended to classify people of the *payirkārar* status as 'tenants'. This is a misconception. In the first place the concept of tenancy derives from the concept of proprietorship. In as much as *kāṇiyāṭchikārars* were not proprietors proper, their dependents in the forms of *payirkārar* could not be considered their tenants. The possibility of transition of a *payirkārar* from the status of *purukudi* to that of *uzhavadi ulkudi* suggests that the *payirkārars* were both less and more than tenants.

Paikamu (Telugu), name of a coin.

Paili a measure of capacity/weight varied from area to area–12 or 10 or 8 or 6 or 5 1/2 or 3 seers.

Painers slaves employed for field work; however, were held in higher estimation than some other slaves; they were admitted to the threshold of their masters, houses, and even employed in grinding rice for the use of the temples.

Painth market of a town.

Paisārī general grazing land (in Coorg).

Paitari in'am *in'am* scattered through several villages granted as supplementary to a whole villlage *in'am*, all the *in'ams*, including the whole village being subject to a lump *jodi*.

Pakka ripe, perfect; of standard weights as opposed to the local *'kachchā'* or rough weights; also of masonry finished with mortar; wells lined with masonry, etc.

Paḷampuḷḷi-māḍai (Tamil), name of coin; see *māḍai.*

Paḷḷi-ccanda, paḷḷi-grāma, palli-cchanda (Tamil), temple land; a village belonging to a temple; land granted to Jain or Buddhist temple-*paḷḷi* being shrine of non-Hindu shrines like the Jains and Buddhists; mentioned along with *devadāna* and *brahmadeya*.

Paḷḷavāy the land used as a pit (*paḷḷavāy*) which is dug for the water from the tank of the village; or the land which had become a pit owing to the accumulation of the water from the tank of the village.

Paḷḷiccandam grant a term used in an inscription to denote a grant of village endowed as a *Paḷḷiccandam* to a Buddha image.

Pala name of a weight; a weight equal to that of 10 *pagodas*; four *karṣas* or 1/100 of a *tula*; the 8th part of a seer, or 3 tolas or rupees; 4 tolas or 320 *guñjās*.

Pala-kāya sundry spices as pepper, etc., used in preparing curry.

Pala-rājākkaḷukku-iṟai-iṟuttu 'revenue assessed by various kings'; the expression in the inscriptions suggests the assessment of taxes by the kings.

Palabhōgam, pulbhhog, palabhógam, palabhogum severally controlled villages; from Tamil *pala* many, several and Sanskrit *bhógam* enjoyment. In the possession of several villages the landed property of which is held in common by all the hereditary proprietors, or *mirāsidārs*. Also *pashengary;* in such villages different families spring from the first settlers, or in some other way; their successors and representatives have found it expedient to divide the lands of the village in to separate shares. *Sumohi* or joint villages sometimes become *pulbhog* villages when the copartners in the *sumohi* village quarrel; and in the same way *pulbhog* may again become *sumohi* when they are again reconciled; this makes a *rayatwary* system, and even a survey, necessary, or at least proper, in the *sumohi* as well as the *pulbhog* villages. Also see *arudicarei.*

Palaki umbaḷi a term used in the epigraphs to denote a grant of revenue-free land for the upkeep of a palanquin or for making arrangements for carrying the kings palanquin; also *dandege umbali.*

Palalu, paleru (Telugu) 'hired labourer'; they were not saleable, but when the land was sold they went with it. They might not desert their master,or if they did, he could claim them back. To these persons, however, although they live in a state of perpetual servitude to their masters, the term of "hereditary servants" might be more properly applied, as they are neither saleable nor is the authority of the master legally recognized. (*Report on Slavery, 1841*, Appendix IX, pp. 444–5).

Palampat or ghargaon: these are *maqtas* granted to the *zamindars.*

Palapati in'am granted for the service of performing the ceremony of pouring milk at particular places on the boundary line of a village on the last day of the procession of the village deity.

Palataḷi a term used in the early fifteenth century inscription to denote a tax accruing from the villages.

Palaveli in'am held for performing all the minor duties in a pagoda.

Pali bund (of the tank)

Palkalaykkundu in'am held by shepherds for the service of supplying milk to the *zamindar.*

Palkavadi in'am granted for carrying milk to the pagoda at Pulney.

Pallan Tamil agricultural labour caste; the great caste of agricultural labourers of the south of the peninsula, almost entirely engaged in the cultivation of wet lands; once slaves; also went to Sri Lanka as labourers on tea and rubber estates.

Pallan in'am granted for the service of measuring lands and the *melvaram* grain.

Palle kattu in'am *in'am* granted for founding a village.

Pallevadi in'am *in'am* land granted for the service of ferryman.

Palli Tamil caste; most likely agricultural labour caste or labourers for hire.

Pallivasal in'am granted for the maintenance of mosques and tombs of Muhammadans.

Palliyal paddy field which could be cultivated without much water.

Palmyrah, palmira *borassus flabellifer.*

Pambakkaran in'am held for the service of beating a drum called *pambam* at the festivals of the village deity.

Pambala in'am granted for the service of beating a drum during the festivals of the village deity.

Pambatti pambu pamula in'ams *in'ams* held by snake charmers.

Pangu share.

Paṇṇiratik-kōl a measuring rod used in the revenue surveys of 1112 A.D. at Tiruvidaimarudur (Thanjavur district, Tamil Nadu) and of 1156 A.D. at Māgaral in Chingleput district, Tamil Nadu; its approximate length was 12 *aṭi* =10 feet 4 inches approx.

Paṇa Tamil *paṇam*, spelt in English as *fanam*; name of a coin issued by the *Yādavrāyas* as is indicated by *Yādavarāyanpaṇam;* 80 rattis in weight. In Tamil, *paṇam* means a particular coin, usually, a small gold coin or money in general, or taxes; for instance *paṇa-vargam,* a class of taxes payable in cash, like *kāśāi-vargam;* also *paṇa-vāśai* 'discount payable for the exchange of coins', 'amount payable to make up the wear in the coin'. Also *vil-paṇam,* sale-tax; a tax on bows and archery; *vāśal-paṇam,* door-tax or periodical payment due to the palace. See also, *paṅa.*

Paṇavattam levy for any currency variation.

Paṇḍāravāḍai lands belonging to the state; crown lands.

Paṇi-kkŏttu (Tamil), cess collected for the maintenance of the village servants.

Paṇimakaṇ an officer who checked the accounts of the temple.

Paṇṇai a system of cultivation in which the landlord carried on cultivation with the farm servants; the servants were/are paid generally in kind at a monthly rate; also allowed a piece of land to live on, and given small presents of cloth, paddy and cash on important religious and ceremonial occasions every year.

Paṇṭāram (Tamil), bhaṇḍāra (Sanskrit) the place where the taxes collected in kind and money were deposited for safety; the temples had their treasuries which were variously named, e;g, *tēvar-paṇṭāram, chaṇḍēsvara-tēvar-paṇṭāram, Śribhaṇḍāram,* and *Uṭaiyār (perum) paṇṭāram;* the epigraphs also mention about *ūr-paṇṭaram* or *uḷṭūrup-paṇṭāram* which denote a local treasury or treasury of the village; inscriptions also mention *nāṭṭup-paṇṭāram* or the treasury of the *nāḍu,* the term tālam can be explained as king's treasury; a treasury could also be named after a state e.g. *Thāñjāvūr-perum-paṇṭāram;* also *maḷikaimūla paṇṭāram* i.e. the central treasury of the place and in this context sometimes the term *rājabhaṇḍāram* is also mentioned in the epigraphs.

Paṅa, paṇam or fanam one of the chief coins in circulation in south

India; the gold *fanam* was 1/10 of the *kaḷāñju;* the chinese evidence says; "In trading they use gold and silver coins. The gold coin with nine-tenths fine is called *fanam*; it is reckoned (in weight) one candareen." one *candareen* was about 5 grains. See also *paṇa* above.

Paṅga, pāṅga (Telugu. Kannada), one-fourth of the produce sometimes collected from revenue-free holdings granted for temples, gods and brahmans; a kind of tax; the term is also used to indicate 'taxes in general'.

Pañca-gavya the five products of cow, viz., milk, butter, curd, urine and dung; same as Tamil *ān-añju*.

Panāḍi canal.

Panam a gold coin (equal to 100 *kasu*, copper coins). Also see *paṇa* and *paṅa* above.

Panayam an ordinary mortgage (in Malabār); the simple pledge of the *janman* or any other right was called '*panyam*', the general term for which had practically become a mortgage.

Panchángen astronomer of the village.

Panchams lit. The fifth caste; a general name of all untouchables as *pallams, paraiyam cherumas*,etc.

Panchanam workmen, mechanics or handicraftsmen; the united five castes of the carpenter, blacksmith, brazier, gold smith and stone cutter.

Panchangi in'am granted for the service of calender Brahman, whose duty it is to announce to the villagers lucky days for commencing to plough or reap, for celebrating marriages or festivals, or engaging in any business. He is also the village priest and as such performs certain ceremonies connected with births, marriages, and deaths.

Panchayats lit. The assembly of five men; actually a small committee of five or more or fewer men, either elected or nominated, to attend to the common affairs of a village, or caste or other small aggregations of people,

Pandárattar from *pandáram* a treasure;the treasury; the officers of the tresury or of the revenue.

Pandaram ascetic mendicant of south India; a non-brahmin temple attendant; a Saiva mendicant or priestly class among Hindus. Also, a treasury.

Pandery a tax on shops and retail merchants in town in the Northern Circars.

Pandluminu a wooden harrow, with about 24 wooden teeth about 5 inches long, drawn by hand.

Pandum the dry measure of 'ten tooms'.

Pangali Tamil term for a male agnatic kin who sub-divided an original share according to the customary law; all the *pangalis* together represented resource control on lineage unit, and as such, it rendered kinship into an all important instrument of land control.

Pangu shres; share in village; Tamil term for share. Also see *paṅga,* above.

Pangu mālai (pangoo melah) an account of *kāṇiyāṭchi* shares, detailed data on all aspects of agriculture were to be found in the *pangu mālai;* all the transactions with respect to *kāniyāṭchi* shares (*pangu)* were carefully entered in the *pangu mālai.*

Panguvali in'am granted for the encouragement of cultivation to a body of co-parceners holding a village in common.

Pani seivan mānyam the *mānyam* granted to the trumpet blower, carrier of dead bodies and village lamp lighter.

Panika-seni, pārṇika-śreṇi the guild of the sellers and growers of betel-leaves.

Paniar slaves

Panikkan mānyam the *mānyam* granted to the well-digger.

Panikkans term is variously applied in Malayalam country-teachers, workers, barbers, fencing masters and craftsmen.

Panipan in'am granted for performance in a *pagoda* of *kumbharti* service, q.v.

Panisavan in'am the same as *toti in'am*.

Panivaragu *panicum miliaceum.*

Panjanga mānyam the *mānyam* granted to the almanac reader.

Panji karnam in'am held by certain servants of the *karnam* class who do duty in the *huzur* office of the *zamindars* in the district of Ganjam.

Pannāya (Kannada), name of a tax; see for example *pannasa.*

Pannai (Tamil) field, farm.

Pannaiyal (Tamil) *pannai* labourer; *al* land; farm labourer; *serf*; permanent farm servant; in 1836 some of the *pannaiyals* had purchased their liberty (e.g. Tinnevelly) although they had to pay double the market price for slaves to do so. (*Report on Slavery*, 1841, pp. 457–9). Even when they were freed by the extinction of their master's family, they were so poor that they had frequently to sell themselves into bondage again in return for a small loan. In Madura they had the right to own property, but after their death that reverted to their respective masters, whether they had heirs or not. (*Report on slavery*, 1841, pp. 455-7); the term *pannai* is also understood as cultivated field or home farm and *pannaiyal* as men who worked the *pannai*; also agricultural labourer tied to a patron by herediatry *jajmani* relationship.

Pannasa, pannāsa, pannāsu (Kannada), the term is used in the sense of a tenure in which the donee enjoyed fifty per cent of the revenue of the donated land.

Panniya in Coorg, 'Royal farm' land allotted to the king and worked by 'slaves'; the Raja there not only took the revenue from the territory directly under his rule–as distinct from that held by his chiefs–but also had special allotments of land called *'panniya'* consisted of farms and estates, scattered over the domain, the produce of which went entirely to the king. The lands were ordinarily cultivated by a large body of 'slaves'. The Raja generally took care to secure the best lands. The farms were exceedingly well cared for and highly cultivated.

Pantoji in'am, pantulu in'am, granted for the service of village school master.

Paoni an advnce of money.

Paṛait–taṛi, paṛaiyar–taṛip terms used to denote tax levied on looms owned by *paṛaiyar* weavers.

Paṛaiya cultivators.

Paṛṛadai a term used in the epigraphs to denote taxes on the workshops.

Paṛṛu, Paṛṛu (Tamil), a small terriorial unit; an administrative division; according to one inscription it was below a *nāḍu*, a division of a *kōṭṭam*, while according to another the *paṛṛu* was a division bigger than a *nādu* and smaller than a *kōṭṭam;* the inconsistency in the order of these divisions makes one doubt if by the term *paṛṛu* any political division was meant; as such, *paṛṛu* may simply mean a rural area or a portion of a particular area which might have been made up of many villages.

Para a local measure of quantity.

Para–deśin an outsider; an emigrant; the term is used along with *sva–deśin*–native, while mentioning two classes of merchants or their representative guilds.

Para–manei, pira–manei outlands; lands without the site of the village.

Para–tider see *paracheri.*

Parachéri, tider pareiyer *tider* signifies 'an open barren space', and the whole means the *pareiyer* who resides in the regular *parachéri,* or suburb set apart for them, and those whose habitations are scattered over the wastes. These terms are intended to comprehend generally the whole of the pareiyar 'slaves' attached to the soil of the village, and to express especially that a right to a participation in their labour inherently attached to the one-third share of the *cániyátchi* transferred.

Paracheri suburbs of the village, occupied by the huts of *pareiyer* slaves and other outcasts. Same as Parachéri above.

Paraḍai, Paraḍatti (Tamil), an assembly.

Paradavar a community earlier engaged in trade, fishing and manufacturing of salt, gradually diversified their interest to become pearl fishers; engaged in coastal trade dealing in expensive items like pearls, gems and horses.

Paraga nagaram a group representing sea faring merchants who were seen only in areas making the trans-peninsular routes.

Paraikkauḷak-kuri separate ponds and wells for the *pariahs*; it may here be mentioned that in villages the low class people were not permitted to draw water from tanks or wells used by caste people.

Paraittaṛi one of the professional taxes charged from the weavers.

Paraiyans (Tamil) agricultural labour caste; commonly termed *pariahs*, a large untouchable caste, mostly living in areas immediately to the south of Madras; like the *pallams* largely agricultural labourers on wet lands, and practically in 'serfdom'; the domestic servants employed by Europeans in Madras were mostly of this caste. Also see, *pareiyar*.

Parakesari-kāl, Parakesari-kkal (Tamil), name of a land measure; name of a weight.

Parakesari-nāḷi (Tamil), name of a land measure.

Parakesari-uḷakku (Tamil), name of a land measure.

Parambas (Malayalam), cultivated lands under any crop other than paddy.

Parambu, paramba garden land.

Parameśvara-hasta the royal cubit; cubit measured according to the length of the king's forearm.

Parado (partab) one of gold coins in circulation in south India; according to 'Abdu-r Razzāk' (1443 A.D.), a *pardao* contained 10 *fanam* and was half a *varāha*, while according to Varthema (1504 A.D.) it contained 20 *fanam*; according to Barbosa, it was 320 *reis*; Paes would have it at 360 *reis*; however, it appears fair to say that 'Abdu-r-Razzāk's *pardao* was the *pagoda* of 10 *paṇam*, containing 52 grains of gold.

Parao a term used for rowing vessel; 'boat of ten paces each, and all of one piece, and goes with oars made of cane, and the mast also is made of cane'.

Parasangs equal to 3½ miles.

Pareiyar a '*pariah*' slave or outcaste; Brahman and also other proprietors largely employed 'slaves' (*pareiyar*) to cultivate for them. Also see, *paraiyans*, above.

Pargana, parganah an administrative and revenue sub-division under the Muslim rule'; administrative division or subdivision of a *sarkar*, a tract of country consisting of varying number of *tappas* or villages; a fiscal district usually comprising many villages; a group of villages.

Pariar a man of low caste performing the lowest menial services often as serfs or slaves of agriculturists. Also see, *paraiyans* and *pareiyar* above.

Paricharaka in'am granted for the

support of the servants of a pagoda with the exception of the *archaka* or chief priest.

Parihāra, maryādā–parihāra exemption from taxes and obligations granted to the donees of revenue–free land; privileges of the donee of revenue–free holdings; certain privileges in respect of number of taxes and obligations are enumerated in Tamil records, which are; *vaṭṭi–nāli*–payment of one *nāḷi* per *vaṭṭi; pudā–nāli*–cess on each door or tax for the maintenance of sluices; *manṛupādu*–fine imposed by a court of law; *ūrāṭci*–tax for running the village administration; *taragu*–tax on brokers; *kūlam*–tax on grains; *ilam–puti*–tax on toddy–drawers; *nāḍu–kāval*–tax on policing of a district; *ūdupokk*–its meaning is not certain; *uppu–kocceyagai*–tax for the manufacture of salt; *nall–ā*–tax for maintaining specimen cows; *nallerudu*–tax for maintaining specimen buffaloes; *nerv āypuvun*–its meaning is not certain, etc.

Parihara in'am granted for the service of a physician; the same as *vaidya in'am*.

Pariharas privileges.

Parikāra a servant.

Parikara requisites of a village.

Parikraya an exchange.

Parinki; a term used for the Portuguese.

Parintiriss a term used for the French.

Pariśu boat made of wicker and leather; this type of boat was used in Tamil areas.

Parisūtra 'an establishment'.

Parittivari term used in the epigraphs to denote a tax on cotton; however, the epigraphs have made only a mention of such tax but not the rate.

Parivarthanai (Sanskrit) exchange or barter.

Parivṛitta income accruing in the gift village (?).

Parpattegār the term used in Coorg for the headman of each *nād;* the Coorg province was divided in to six taluks comprising twenty–four *nāds*, the *nād* consisted of a group of *grāmas*, or hamlets, there being no villages, the headman, by and large, had both civil and criminal jurisdiction.

Partāb a half *pagoda*.

Partab an indigenous gold coin in circulation in south India; for details see, *pardao*.

Paruḍal kuḍigal the tenants with subordinate rights under the principal occupants; also see *kīḷ kārāṇmai uḍaya kuḍigal*.

Parutti in'am granted for the service of weighing cotton when the *melvaram* of the *zamindar* on this crop used to be received in kind.

Parwāna (Persian), any official order in writing; a warrant, license.

Pasāitā of certain lands in villages held wholly revenue–free.

Pasang–carei, Pasangkareī (Tamil), term used in the old joint village for the tenure undivided; cultivated and held entirely in common and their produce distributed, after defraying the revenue charges and village expenses.

Pasang-carei and *samadayem* in Sanskrit, are terms both implying collective proprietary right, used to denote that particular joint tenure of the cultivated lands which was anciently universal through out the Tamil areas, and prevailed in early British period in many villages in every part of it, but especially in that known by the name *Tondei Mandalam*. Under this system, the *mírási* right to any particular spot of cultivated land in the village is not vested in any individual. The *mírási* of the entire cultivated lands attached to it, like that of the *perumboc, tarisee*, etc., belongs to the whole body of the *mirásidars;* each, in proportion to the shares or parts of share he holds, being entitled to participate in the common property. The number of shares belonging to each *mírásidar* being known the lands are either cultivated by them in common, and the net produce, after payment of tax, divided according to the share of each in the *mírási*, or the land itself is thus divided, either annually, or every five, or six, or ten years, the fields of which the *mírási* to be held by each for that period being fixed by drawing lots.

In many villages, however, especially in those of Tanjore, Tinnevelly, Madura, Dindigul, etc., the *mírásidars*, instead of dividing the cultivated lands of the village periodically, according to the shares or parts of a share held by each, appear, after having once divided them in that manner, to have declared the division permanent, and thus to have converted the ancient collective tenure of the cultivated land in to one in severalty, which is distinguished by the Tamil denomination *arudi–carei*, or by the corresponding Sanskrit word *pala–bhogam;* no village could be partly *pasang-carei*, partly *arudi–carei*, and partly *eka–bhgam*, it must be one only of the three.

Pasankarei (Tamil) earliest and strongest form of communal land holding. Same as Pasang-carei above.

Pashánam rocks.

Pashungherry villages there were two sorts of such villages, one where lots were drawn, and other where there were none; and although the cultivators may not have hitherto received annually their puttahs from the *sirkar*, yet from their having once obtained them, they consider themselves the sole proprietors of the lands they cultivate, and at full liberty to dispose of them.

Pasungarai (pashoonkarah), Pasungcarie the joint proprietary of the lands of a village by a number of coparteners who had no power to sell any actual piece of the village land but could sell their shares with the consent of the other coparteners; a form of joint land control by *kāṇiyāṭchikārar*, whereby all lands and privileges were held jointly; the most ancient variety of *kāṇiyāṭchi*. Same as, *pasang-carei* above.

Paṭai–mutalis army officers.

Paṭaiyilār lit. military; it has been used in the epigraphs to denote that it subjected the members of the *sabhā* to torture while collecting the fine.

Paṭel, pāṭel, pāṭil village headman.

Paṭṭa a royal charter.

Paṭṭāḍai–ayam (Tamil–Sanskrit), tax on silk cloth.

Paṭṭāḍai–nūl–ayam (Tamil–Sanskrit), tax on silk thread used for weaving cloth.

Paṭṭāṁśuka a kind of silk cloth.

Paṭṭaka an administrative division.

Paṭṭakara 'silk–weaver'; also used in the sense of the writer of official documents.

Paṭṭalekhin writer of official documents.

Paṭṭaṇa seaport.

Paṭṭaṇasvāmin a term by which the president of local–merchant guild was known. Same as *paṭṭana-svāmin*.

Pṭṭaṇiga merchants.

Paṭṭana–svāmin head of an organisation or a guild in a city; chief or leader of the mercantile community of a town. Same as *paṭṭaṇasvāmin*.

Paṭṭasāhiṇi an officer attached to the royal establishment.

Paṭṭavaṭṭam a kind of tax.

Paṭṭayam grant inscribed on copper–plates.

Paṭṭe account books; these books contained the names of the tenants and the amount of assessment they had to pay.

Paṭṭi–kkāḍi (Tamil), tax payable at the rate of one *kāḍi* of grain for each *paṭṭi* of land.

Paṭṭi–ppŏn (Tamil), tax payable in cash.

Paṭṭit–taṇṭam, paṭṭik–kācu the fines levied on stray cattle.

Paṭṭōlai, paṭṭlā, paṭṭolai, pāṭṭai (Tamil), a document; official designation; lit. palm–leaf; the term has been used in the epigraphs to indicate the keeper of palm–leaf records.

Paṭṭōlai–kacu, paṭṭōlaik–kacu a term used to denote a type of payment demanded by the state for the despatch and delivery of the royal order to the party concerned. (*Paṭṭōlai* = royal writ); a variant of the term *irāca–niyōkam.*

Paṭṭōlakāsu a term used for an additional demand over and above the usual land revenue for the support and payment to the village officers.

Paṭṭolī 'a deed of purchase'; 'land purchased by means of a *paṭṭolī*'.

Patakdár, puttuckdar lit. Book–keeper, accountant. A species of *zamindar* or collector in Tanjore, who had the charge of a greater or less number of villages.

Patam tenure wet lands held on a favourable assessment paid in gram.

Patasala in'am *in'am* held for the support of schools where the Vedas were taught.

Patchei–vadam lit. 'a green thong'; signifies a long web of cloth consisting of four or five pieces of lower garment given in presents on festivals and other similar occasions to the inhabitants by the officers of government or of their representatives.

Patel (k.) headman, *munsif* of a village, titled variously in local usage in south India (*pedda rayat, reddi, kapu, dora, kadim, mirasdar, naidu, nattamkar, monigar, maniakkaren,* etc. The adjective *pedda* was often prefixed there to). The British Board of Revenue recorded (22 August 1816), that the *patel*, and the office, as described by Col. Munro and Wilkes, did not exist in Tondei Mandalam, or as they believed anywhere east of the *Payenghat.*

Patel in'am granted for the service of headman of a village.

Patha it is a suffix as there are a group of administrative units whose names end *in patha.*

Patika-badi tenure lands held on one fourth assessment.

Patikaval the levy for guarding duties; it was collected from individual land holders; the unit of land formed the basis of this tax assessment.

Patinaṛucāṇ–kōl a rod for linear measurement equal to 16 *cān*, approximately equal to 12 feet.

Patiṇen–cāṇ–kōl a measuring rod of 18 cāṇ approximately equal to 13 feet 5 inches. The epigraphs show that this rod was in vogue during the revenue surveys conducted during 1003 and 1014 A.D. at Mēlsēvūr (in South Arcot district) and Mēlpādi in Chittoor district respectively.

Patiperaḍu term used to denote a piece of ground within or on the outskirts of the village site and held free of assessment. The term is also sometimes applied to large tracts of land granted by *zamindars* subsequently to the permanent settlement.

Patna setti in'am granted for settling caste disputes among the *lingaits* in the Bellary district.

Patomkar lit. a renter; a simple tenant of land who has no personal claim on the ground he cultivates; same as *paragoody.*

Patra a letter or document; a note; a written paper or deed.

Patta monigar the principal or managing holder of land held by several persons under a *patta* granted in the name of the principal.

Pattā, patta, pattah a lease, deed contract, receipt, or official document of certification; specifically, a document specifying, the land revenue due from a piece of land or a person; terms and conditions on which the lands were held. Lands which were thus granted were called *patta* lands; the title-deed to rayatwari land ganted to the peasant individually by the revenue officer; a sheet or leaf; a written lease or document given to tenants, or other landholders showing terms of payment, area held, period of lease, etc.

Pattadar the holder of a *patta*. His tenure was for life, on his death to be divided among the heirs according to the customs of his community, i.e. if a Hindu, equally among his sons, if Muhammadan, two-thirds of it between the sons, one-third between the daughters; could mortagage or sell his rights.

Pattagar traditional leader of Gounder Vellala community.

Pattam rent, share of the produce of land due to officials and princes; rent fixed in kind; during certain periods it indicates an occupational due.

Pattanappagudi tolls or shares of the town (on merchandise).

Patti in'am held for the service of preventing cattle from trespassing and destroying the crops.

Pattī cesses levied by Marāthās, both on village and for district and general purposes (largely for private official levy or 'extortion' in addition to the land-revenue). The chief were the *sādir wārid*. It had different meaning in N.W.P., Oudh, Punjab, etc.

Pattinams a term used to denote commercially active and organised towns located on coast.

Pattivali in'am the same as *panguvali inam*.

Pattiwaris keepers of pay lists.

Pattunūlkārar a term used in the epigraphs to denote the silk weavers.

Pattupadi additional levies.

Pazhikkani in'am granted as a compensation to a person who has been wounded in the public service; the same as *netturu kattu in'am*.

Pēmṭa-śuṅkamu the duty collected on sales effected in the *pēṭa* on articles of trade; also called *magama*.

Pēr, pērāl, pēril different terms which may be taken to represent a tax on individual.

Pēr-kaḍamai a term used in the inscription of the first half of the fifteenth century to denote a type of taxes accruing from the villages.

Pēṭe, santhe, santepēṭe, pēṭa, pettah market-town or market place; the suburbs of a fortified town. Different terms used in the epigraphs to denote the market place; the mention of *santhe* and the establishment of a watershed in the market place (in the epigraphs) shows that the place was set apart for the fair and intended to be permanent; it is also clear from the epigraphs that occasionally a piece of land was given to the head of the guild that he might establish a place for the market.

Pĕdda-gaḍyamu (Telugu), unit of measurement.

Pērjuṅka (Kannaḍa), name of a tax or toll.

Peddā kāpu in'am granted for the service of the headman of a village.

Peddā-kāpu one of the various titles for a village headman.

Pellettu in'am granted to the person who dug the first clod of earth in constructing a new tank.

Peon a footman, a foot soldier, an inferior officer or servant employed in revenue, police, or judicial duties, sometimes armed with a sword and shield.

Perike–eḍla–suṅkamu tax on pack oxen (perike–eḍlu) laden with sacks containing articles of trade.

Perike–eḍlu pack oxen.

Peṛu–vartam a kind of mortgage in Malabār; it was a very stiff type of nortgage. In it right of redemption was not lost, but could only be had by paying the market value of the estate at the time of redemption.

Perāṟu river channel.

Periḷamayār assembly of cultivator–elders.

Periya aramanai in'am granted for watching the *zamindar's* palace.

Periyanāṭṭān–śandi a kind of service offered in the temples for which an assignment of the taxes was also nade.

Periyanadu 'Sat–Sudra–controlled xtended locality'. The *periyandu* nstitution encompassed a much larger rea than the *brahmadeya*, the latter eing included in the former, or 'great ountry' assembly. In function the *eriyanadu* assembly was most likely a egislative body for the entire nuclear rea. It was dominated and directed by he dominant, respectable, agricultural astes of the Sat–Sudras. The style of hese assemblies was very nearly the ame as that of the Brahman settlements nd itinerant merchant associations. he composition of the *periyanadu* aried according to the problem with hich the asssembly dealt. In some ases it comprised only of agriculturists; others, it included members of local nd itinerant merchant associations. n certain occasions these assemblies cluded even the Brahmans. However, is not clear whether they formallly cluded members of all castes, including rahmans,or they were comprised cclusively of agriculturists of Sudra rank whose protection and jurisdiction extended over the institutions of merchants and Brahmans. Moreover, the right of the assemblies to adjudicate and punish was recognised by the rulers of the country.

Perjjunka or peruśunka two different terms used in the epigraphs to denote duties on important articles of trade.

Peru–nilac–celviyuṉ–taṉakke–urimaipūṇṭo the term used for the king who was conceptualized as the rightful owner of the great earh.

Perūṅguḍi makkal collective deliberations of the occupants.

Perukuli in'am granted (i) for the benefit of persons who gave to their children the name of the reigning *zamindar* in Sivaganga; (ii) for giving names to the children of the *zamindar*.

Perum–pāḍi–kāval (Tamil), police duties of larger area, as distinct from the *śiṟupādi–kāval* for the village.

Peruṇguḍi–makkal the share of the *mēlātci* or the *mēlvāram* belonging to the occupancy holders.

Perumāṇaṭigal 'a great person'; an appellation used in Chola inscriptions to denote king and god.

Perumál the title of a ruler or viceroy in Malabār and Cochin; the viceroys were mostly members of the family of the paramount prince and frequently bore his title with some distinguishing epithet, as Tondira Shozhen: they sometimes had the title of *perumál* Lord, as Shéramán Perumál, the vicegerent of Shéren in Malayálam; sometimes *Rájen* or *Arasu*.

Perumakkal the elders among the occupanṭ holders.

Perumboc, peramboke land incapable of cultivation consists of rocks, public roads, the bed of river, tanks and water–courses, the public ground in which the bodies of dead are burnt or interred; the *mirasidars* had the privilege to appropriate the produce of quarries, mines, or fisheries in the *perumboc*, which, being incapable of being cultivated, was not liable to any tax.

Sometimes some portions of these divisions of land might be found to be cultivable; the English Board of Revenue was aware that portions of *peramboke* were sometimes cultivated. When given by the *sirkar* for cultivation, the *mirasidars* would then receive their customary *swatuntrums* from them, in common with the other cultivated lands; when *peramboke* land ceased to be required for the assigned purpose, would cease also to be *peramboke*, and became liable to the usual laws of waste.

Peruñ–kuṭikal–pēral–katamai dues on landowner/cultivator.

Peruṅkuṭikaḷ–pēr–kaṭamai a type of tax to which land owners or big cultivators were subjected to.

Perunguḍi occupant land holders.

Perunír water allowed to flow without limitation during the heavy rains of the north–east monsoon and for sometime afterwards from the beginning of September to the end of March.

Peruvaḷi a term used in the Tamil inscriptions to denote a road; the term for minor roads used is *vaḷi*.

Peruvari a term connecterd with land revenue current during the Chola period in Cholamandalam.

Peshkar a government official.

Peshkash, peshkush (p)–offering or tribute paid to a superior or the government. The payment of the *peshkash* was a mark of subordination to the superior; a fixed tribute or offering; in Madras, the land–revenue paid by the permanent–settlement *zamindars* and the *palegars* of their *palaiyams* were also given the name *peshkash*.

Pessaloo, green or black *phaseolus mungo*.

Peta gadu in'am granted to the headman of a *peta* or suburb of a town for encouraging the settlement of weavers.

Pettah, petha, pettai, Peṭha a small territorial unit; a group of villages; a fortified market town; the suburbs of a fortified town.

Pettendar a village official.

Phaiṇdi–āyāyi, phaiṇdivāya–maṟuturu (Telugu), a *maṟuturu* measure of land which brought an income in cash and not kind; in Telugu, *paiḍi* means gold and *āyam* income.

Phala–sthirā fruit giving land.

Phalabhogam (Sanskrit) same as *arudikarei*.

Phalia cotton.

Phuṭṭaka probably a variety of printed calico.

Pīṭalikai–vari, piṭakai–ōpāti–iṟai terms used in the inscriptions to denote tax on shop.

Piccottas a term used in the epigraphs to denote to bale out water in baskets.

Piḍāgai a hamlet.

Piḍāri, piḍāri–paṭṭi, ellai–amman 'the goddess of boundary'; it may here be pointed out that undue expansion of the boundary of the village or land was considered an evil and method adopted to prevent such expansion was to set up stone slabs on the outskirts of the villages; some of them bore the rude outline of a deity and were accordingly given such names as *piḍāri* or *ellai–amman*, the goddess of boundary and even lands were sometimes allotted for the proper maintenance of worship for such deities.

Piḍārivari a tax charged for the maintenance and upkeep of the temple of the village goddess.

Piḍaligai low bushes and plants intertwined; the meaning is, however a tentative one, and has been suggested by the contrast with forest land.

Pidara vaidyan in'am granted for the support of a native doctor who cures the bites of snakes.

Pidari kovil, perumal kovil, amman kovil mānyam the *mānyams* granted to temples for various female deities and for Vishnu.

Piḷḷai kaṇakkanār kings's or the chief's head accountant.

Pillai in'am granted for the support of the headman of a village in some part of the Salem district. No service was attached to the office during the British period.

Pilwări, pulwări, pillwany a tax on grass or pasture; grass land.

Pippali (Sanskrit) *piper longum* or *officinarum* of the Botanists ; the long pepper.

Pirāmaṇar–pēr–kaṭamai a kind of poll tax the Brahmanas were subjected to pay. (*Pirāmaṇar* is the Tamil form of Brahmana).

Pirlu in'am granted for the maintenance of the *panjas* or insignia used during the celebration of the Muharram.

Piṣāraḍi (Malayāḷam), the manager of a temple.

Piśānam crop second crop.

Pisanam, peshanum a species of fine rice; the *pisanam* harvest begins about the later end of January, and ends about the beginning of June.

Piṭi a handful.

Pizhacadei, puzhacadei backyard; the difference between this term and *collei* is that the former immediately adjoins the dwelling, where as the latter may be at some distance from it; this and the *collei* are considered as included in the *nattam* and are held free of rent; though sometimes of considerable extent. As such enclosures are always highly manured. They afford valuable produce, tabacco, sugar, plantains, etc.; if they are extensive, therefore, and the proprietor industrious, they often constitute a considerable proportion of the value of the whole proprietary. The *pizhacadei* is held, not only by the *cániyáchicár*, but by all the *Maneiollaver*, all those having habitations within the village.

Plantain *musa paradisiaca.*

Poā a land measure, 4 poā = 7/8 bighā.

Poduvāḷ (Tamil–Malayalam), the officer supervising charitable endowments.

Pohal shrotriyam the same as *khandrika in'am.*

Polichezhuthu renewal of tenancy right; a fine or fee paid to the proprietor by the morgagee on the periodical renewal of the mortgage; a new deed or bond.

Polikōl a stick steeped in dung water or *chunam*,or some coloured water, – which is used to make some mark on the heap of corn covered with hay.

Polimera in'am granted to a person who settles boundary disputes by treading the boundary live in solemn manner; the same as *ella in'am.*

Politūṟṟun kūḍai a winnow (a fan like basket) which is used to sweep off the dust and the bits of hay that are mixed with the paddy and make it clean.

Pon, poṇ probably a coined gold of the full weight of one kaḷañcu; name of a gold coin also called *mādai.* The uses of this term–*pon–bhandāram,* 'gold-treasury'; *pon-pandāra-vāśal,* 'the gate of the gold treasury;' 'royal gold–treasury'; *ponvari,* 'tax payable in gold (cash)'; also the fee for minting gold in to coins'.

Pon–mudal tax payable in paddy; tax in grains; see, *nellāyam.*

Poṉmudal a term used in the Vijayanagar inscriptions in the *Pudukōṭṭai* region to indicate the revenues collected in cash.

Poṇ paṇḍāram temple treasurer.

Pongal harvest festival held early in January, the first three days of the Tamil month *Tai*.

Ponvari a tax which was imposed uniformly on all the lands in the country, without exempting, as usual, the uncultivated waste in villages; this tax was imposed to discourage wilful neglect of land by cultivators and to induce the cultivators to keep the lands under tillage; it is believed that such an imposition of tax had the desired effect at least in some instances.

Pooleyars slaves (Malabar)

Poonas fussil, poonass fussil cotton harvest. Small grain harvest in the Northern Circars.

Pooragoodies newly established *rayats*; if by death or emigration any of the *puttookaut* lands, should fall to their occupancy they paid the *teerwai* of the *puttookauts*.

Pooroopa *in'ams* or grants of land paying a fixed money rent or tribute in the Dindigul and Trinnevelly provinces.

Poramboke land in a village reserved for purposes other than cultivation. Same as *perumboc* above.

Porruppu in'am wet or dry lands held on a favourable assessment paid in money.

Portia *thespesia populnea.*

Porutpuṇai a term used in the epigraphs to denote surety for the cash dues.

Potaraz in'am granted for performing *puja* to a village deity named *potaraz.*

Pottakam, Pottagam (Tamil), register, as of land and revenue; a term mentioned in the epigraphs whose full form is *nilamutal-pottakam*, which means a land revenue register.

Potula in'am garnted to tank-diggers for the service of executing petty repairs to tanks and channels.

Prāṇāntika 'till the close of one's life'.

Prāpti benefit; revenue; enjoyment; what is obtained from someone.

Prativyañjana articles other than rice for the preparation of food-offerings in a temple; etc. Tamil *paḍi-viñjanam.*

Prabhu-svāmya a tenure held by a *prabhu* a village official.

Pradhāna an official designation sometimes indicate the chief minister or administrator; officials, in general mere administrative officers; *mahāpradhānas*- highest rank officials.

Pradhāni-joḍi (Sanskrit-Tamil), an *in'am* held on a fixed quit-rent; the chief-minister's quit-rent.

Pradhānin; Pradhani a governor, minister or president; noble or courtier, etc; a high executive officer, a village headman; technically the finance minister, principally engaged in directing the collection of revenue and its expediture.

Pramāṇa a document; a title deed; *mūla-pramāṇa*, original order.

Prapā water houses (constructed by the side of the roads for the travellers).

Praśasti formal preamble in the inscriptions.

Prasāda kāṇikkai a tax collected for the temple.

Pratigraha acceptance of gifts.

Pratyāya rent or taxes.

Praverticam a joint management of the village; general managment of the affairs of the village.

Praveśa, prāveśa 'small territorial unit', also refers to the assessment of the revenue of a locality along with another; for example, *Siviḍi-praveśa-kandalivāḍa-grāma* interpreted as '*Kandalivāḍa-grāma* having its revenue assessed along with Sividi.

Prayāṇa-daṇḍa a small tax levied for providing means of transport for the touring of royal officers.

Pricchanda a vessel.

Pūgāḥ corporations, generally of men though belonging to different castes and following different occupations, but residents of the same place e.g. of a city, town etc., they also acted as courts of comparatively higher grade.

Pūjā–vṛtti revenue–free land endowed to a temple for conducting worship.

Pūrv–ācāra an ancient custom; an old usage.

Pūrv–āgrahārika the former holder of an *agrahāra*.

Pūrv–maryādā ancient constitutional usage.

Pūṭṭānkayiṟu the rope that binds the yoke on the neck of the bull.

Pú kizhar possessors of land.

Puddee equal to ½ Madras Measure.

Pugdi an extra assessment imposed in 1711 in Kanara.

Pujari in'am granted for the service of the priest in a pagoda who conducts public worship.

Puḷudi a method of preparation of the field for sowing when water is scarce.

Puḷudi lands lands producing gram (*kāṇam*), paddy and large number of other crops.

Puḷuku–vari duty levied on incense articles sold in shops. This duty could have been levied like sales tax.

Puḻḻipārta assessed estimates in field.

Pulam a field of corn.

Pulattil–kuḷangal ponds in fields.

Pulavar in'am granted for composing verses in honour of the *zamindar*.

Pulavri a term used in the inscriptions to denote a tax accruing from the villages. See, *Pullari*.

Pulikattu in'am granted under the native government to persons for stopping tigers' mouths by enchanting and rendering them harmless.

Puliyamarum, paleamunaum tamarind tree.

Pullari, poolary, pullavari lit: grass tax; revenue by a tax on the pasture land; grazing tax; tax on pasture lands (*pullu* = grass and *ari*=tax); it was collected on cattle grazing on the government pastures attached to each village or in the adjacent forest areas; tax payable for grazing cattle.

Pulleas slaves (Tanjore)

Puller the name of a low caste people who tilled the land in the southern districts and were considered the slaves of the soil.

Pullu grass.

Pully the name of the caste that had a hereditary right of service under the *mirasidars* and were entitled to one–third of the share which the latter received of the crops.

Puṇcey, pūñcey, kollai–nilam different terms used to denote dry land; all non-paddy fields were included in this type of land.

Puṇcey–kaṭamai a term used to denote tax collected on dry land esp. during Chola period.

Puṇcey–puravu a term used to denote tax collected on dry land.

Puṇpayir lands lands producing dry crops.

Punam in Malabār, jungle–rice grown in *kumeri* clearings, in Malabār, forest–clearing for temporary cultivation (*kumeri* or *kumri* in Canara) was quite common, and in those clearings, *punam* or jungle–rice was the chief product; waste land cultivation of the forest region; shifting cultivation.

Pundarah vadiky, pundarah vandiky, pundary vadiky villages in the southern *palaiyams* of which the absolute proprietary right is chiefly held by the inhabitants of *sudras*.

Pundarah–vadiky mirási villages of *shudras* (esp., in Tinneveḷly).

Punganur breed of cattle a breed of cattle peculiar to the *zamindari* village of Punganūr, of short stature not over 36 inches in height, but esteemed for the milking qualities of the cows and the excellence of the oxen for drought; the pure breed extinct.

Pungoo bhogium muree (Tanjore) deed for the mortgage of ones share in property; the conditions being–to allow the grantee to enjoy the products of the field as also the *vāram* (rent) remitted by the *sirkar;* together with the members of the *grahmam* he was to pay the share which would fall on him of any general extra taxation and such expense as may be incurred in supplying the public exigency in sheep and coolies and subsisting people sent by the *sirkar,* and should the *sirkar* levy either a grain or money assessment, he would equally with the body of the *gramakars* bear his portion thereof. The agreement would last for a specified number of years beyond which in whatever year at the close of the specified month when the full amount of loan is paid back; the privileges mortgaged would be taken back, clear of every debt or balance either to the *grahmam* or the *sirkar.*

Pungs the share of each individual *mirāsīdār.*

Punjah, punjei, punjah dry lands. In Tanjore there were usuallly three kinds of *punjah* land, namely-(i) *tuddel punjah,* (ii) *varasha putcut* and (iii) *punjah putcut.* The first alone, as it yielded grain and not vegetables, was properly called *punjah.* "It either lies close by the side or is slightly raised in the middle of the paddy fields from which and the adjacent channels it receives water by buckets. The *varasha putcut* yielded dry grain, fruits and vegetables and therefore had both topes and spots of land either enclosed or open and situated between the houses and fields where water could be drawn by buckets from channels, tanks and hollows. The *punjah putcut* also yielded dry grains, fruits and vegetables. It was different from *varasha putcut* as it consisted of the 'topes' growing with *tuddel punjah,* of 'house gardens' watered by wells and the lands lying under the banks of rivers and water by picottah, so as it induce the inhabitants to cultivate on it likewise a small quantity of paddy.

Punjei otty muree (Tanjore) deed for the mortgage of a portion of ones *punjei* land, for the interest of which the mortgagee would enjoy the usufruct of the said portion of land specifying no period; whenever the full amount of loan was paid back, the grantee would resign it to the original owner.

Puntottam in'am granted for the maintenance of a garden-flower gardens for temple service; the same as *nandavanam in'am.*

Punyam–patam, paunyam patram, poonyum patam lit. a fair or equitable *pattah,* or written engagement. A lease where the rent and interest of the sum advanced by the tenant to the landlord seem security for each other.

Puppotti in'am held for the service of supplying the *zamindar* with flowers.

Puṟa–kkaḍamai (Tamil), taxes and fees payable to the state.

Puṟāpaṟṟu land held by occupants from outside.

Puṟakkalaṇai–kaṭamai a type of tax to which agricultural labourers or cultivators were subjected to. (*Puṟakkalaṇai* = agricultural labourer).

Puṟakkuḍi farm servants; occupants of land from outside. Also see, *paikārar.*

Puṟav–āyam (Tamil), revenue from external sources collected mainly in cash.

Puṟvari cash levy.

Puṟamāgaṇi an administrative division

Pura the name/term *pura* signified a

definite constitutional status, with certain specific privileges; that the *puras* had to be particularly recognised as such; and that it was within the competence of the heads of the executive government in the province to grant such recognition; such a grant or charter certainly implied the enjoyment of much more extensive autonomy than was general.

Purakalam gleanings.

Purakkadai, puzhakkadai inner backyard of house; whereas earlier this place was held separately by *kāṇiyāṭchikarar*, Lionel Place levied cash imposition on this place also.

Purana in'am granted for the service of reading the *puranas* in pagodas.

Purav–āyam cess on land; land tax.

Puravari superintendent of revenue.

Puravu (Tamil), land revenue; this term is used in the early Chola epigraphs in the sense of land tax. However, the term *iṟai* to denote land tax was most frequently used and probably from the time of Rajendra I; *kaṭamai* was substituted and became a popular term; also land–register showing lands assessed to full demands.

Puravu–vari a department in a *maṇḍalam* dealing with revenue accounts; also land–register; *puravu* and *vari* used separately in the epigraphs denote revenue; also head of the land revenue department.

Puravu–vari–śrikaraṇam the land revenue department.

Puravu–vari–tiṇaik–kaḷam a term used to denote the revenue department; the head of this office was also known by the same name.

Puravu–vari–tiṇaik–kaḷak–kaṇkāṇi the head of the land revenue department. As a matter of fact the epigraphs of Chola period refer to different terms who headed the land revenue department, e.g. *puravu–vari–tiṇaik–kaḷa–nāyakam, puravu–vari– tiṇaik–kaḷa–kūṟu, puravu–vari–tiṇaik- kaḷattu–kaṇkāṇi.*

Purbatty village revenue offical.

Purkudy (poorah coody) non–resident cultivators. Also see, *paikārar.*

Purmbōkku, poramboke, purambok, puramboku, uncultivated common lands, uncultivated land in a village reserved for certain purposes; according to Wilson it means 'excluded place'. Its cultivation was strictly prohibited, and if it was broken up a high revenue–rate was enforced as a sort of penalty; claimed as government property during British rule. Also see, *perumboc.*

Puro–nāyak, poṟṟu–nayak the chief *Nāyaka.*

Purohit in'am the same as *panchangi in'am* above.

Purohita principal priest; supposed to possess all the learning and statesmanship of a minister in addition to being an adept in matters of religion; village purohit was supposed to conduct religious rites in the houses of the villagers and to fix auspicious days for ploughing the fields and harvesting the crops.

Purohita mānyam the *mānyam* granted to the brahmin who officiated in rituals.

Pushoonkarry seems to have been an association of partners subsequent to the original institution of the village. When the population and cultivation increased, it became necessary to add some new respectable inhabitants to the original proprietor, to assist in repairs of tanks, in the distribution and settlement of the different lands, and to regulate the irrigation. But these new partners were not participators in the original *gramuttan manium* lands, or any of the *sosuntrum,* but were partners in the profit and loss of the cultivation of all the lands. Where shares are liable to a periodical interchange among the partners, the village is called *pushoonkarry;* where the shares remain as at first fixed, *urdakarry*.

Puṭavai lit. cloth; on lands cultivating *kummari* crop, tax was collected in the form of *putavai*.

Puṭṭi (Telugu) a measure of the sowing capacity of lands; the inscriptions refer to certain measures of capacity in which *putti* is one of them which means that the sowing capacity of a piece of land was so many *puṭṭis* of some seeds; a land and grain measure; a measure equal to twenty *tūmus*; also called *khanḍi* (spelt *candy* in English and *khanḍika* in Sanskrit) and regarded as equal to between 800 to 1000 seers. *Khandi* at Masulipattam had three weights, viz., 488 pounds for tobacco, 500 pounds for metals, hardware etc., and 560 ponds for sugar, dates and other soft articles. The *puṭṭi* and its fractions also denote the area of land that is supposed to produce the particular quantities of grain. Also it is a land measure equal to 8 acres being presumably the area which could be sown with a *putti* of grain. There were different kinds ofd *puṭṭis*, e.g. *gā1–puṭṭi*. Also *pelle–puṭṭi* equal to 80 *kuñcas* and *Malaca–puṭṭi* or Malacca ton equal to 240 to 300 *kuñcas*.

Puṭṭi–dosillu (Telugu), 'a fee of two handfuls from each *putti* of grain paid to the village servants'.

Putcut assessment on the *rayat's* farm as a whole.

Putla kattubdi in'am *in'am* held subject to a quit–rent payable at a certain rate per *putti* of rice.

Putti an extra assessment made in addition to the standard rent in Bednore in the years 1718 and 1758.

Putti, pukti the enjoyment of a property.

Puttiam a written engagement.

Puttookaut rayats those who having an hereditary interest in the village were considered the owners of the land and responsible for the payment of the revenue. They paid the highest land tax under the denomination of *kuttoogoottaga* or fixed rent, without reference to the extent of cultivation.

Puty an extra assessment, a measure of capacity.

Puvika confectioners.

Puvika–seni guild of confectioners.

Pykes, paykan, paikan foot messengers; village guards. Allowance for increased establishment of the *pykes*, or village guards.

Q

Qabūlityat (Arabic), (i) a document signed by *zamindar* (and *ta'aluqdār*) 'agreeing' to certain terms for payment on their estates; (ii) commonly, a counterpart to a lease, agreeing to terms, revenue, etc., corrupted to *kābuláit* in south and west India.

Qadīm, cadeem, kadeem old; old resident cultivators; on the cession of the Telinga provinces to the British government, the *qadīms* whatever their former situation may have been, were possessed of no rights than those of the *ūlcūdy paycarries* in the Tamil areas; if they at any time enjoyed a *toondoo warum* or clear landlord's rent, had long before that period been universally deprived of it. Their landlord's rent, if it ever existed, with all power of selling or disposing of the land, was universally gone; but they continued to be hereditary permanent farmers of their villages, and so long as they paid the public dues, they could not be ousted from their lands which, though not then saleable, had descended from father to son, from generation to generation. This hereditary right to their land seems indeed, to have been the only distinction between them and *paycarry rayet*.

In medieval India there were 'two categories of villages i.e., *zamindari* villages (*dehat-e-taaluqa*) and *raiyati* villages (*dehat-e-raiyati*).... The lands in the *zamindari* village may be divided into two categories i.e., *kadeemi* or *khudkashta* and *raiyati*. During the medieval ages, the primary *zamindars, muqaddams* as well as other *riaya* of different categories in a village constituted the cultivating classes. In the old settled villages, the ancestors of the *zamindari* families belonged to the conquering clans or were introduced by the state for revenue collection and the maintenance of law and order, or were the pioneer colonizers of the settlements'. They all had *kadeemi* or *khudkashta* land (owned personal lands for cultivation). Thus the *kadeemi* or *khudkashta* lands were 'owned by the *zamindari* and *muqaddami* families and peasant proprietor or *riaya* who usually belonged to the dominant and privileged groups of the agricultural community of the village. The peasant proprietor or *kadeem* or *khudkashta riaya* in stock belonged to the original *zamindari* families and would trace their descend to the ancestral *zamindars, muqaddams* or *choudaries*, etc., but of their own did not enjoy any such official status. They were the kith and kin of the *zamindari* and *muqaddami* families and owned ancestral self-developed lands....the lands in possession of the above categories were named as *kadeemi* lands. Such lands may be reserved by the pioneering families even in the newly developed villages. Under the revenue regulations they were assessed on fixed or concessional rates of assessment'. (B.R. Grover).

Qaul, Quoul, cowle an agreement (for favourable terms).

Qaul-nāma a proclamation of published offer of terms; a writing of assurance, agreement or engagement as granted by government to the cultivator of the soil.

Qist (pl.aqsāt), commonly written *'kist'*, the installments fixed for convenience in paying land-revenue.

R

Rāja–Vibhāṭan–kōl a unit of length for measuring lands; its length varied in different localities–18 spans, 20 feet, 34 feet etc

Rāja–kārya duties of the state; official work.

Rāja–kara, rāja–garam taxes in general.

Raja–karam, Rājakaram king's taxes; palace, or government; officers or authorities; taxes due to the same.

Rāja–māna royal measure; the standard measure fixed or accepted by the king or government.

Rāja–pradeya taxes.

Rājadrōhins a traitor to the king or state; the term appears in the context that their properties were confiscated by the state; and sometimes the proceeds were granted to the local temple for food offerings to brahmanas.

Rājakārya–bhāṇḍāra a treasury related to state business; an official committee of management.

Rājakara–upādi 'tax payable to the palace or to the government officer.'

Rājakāraṅ–kāṃikkai 'customary presents to be made to the palace'.

Rājakīyabhūmi crown lands; property of the crown; king's land; there are quite a few references to such lands in the inscriptions.

Rājakulaṅ–kaṇi–ppaṟṟu 'land or village in the enjoyment of the royal family'.

Rājanya officers of the king.

Rājarājap–peruvilai, Rājarājapperuvilai public auction; a term used to denote confiscation and auction of property.

Rājasva property belonging to the king or state (by confisaction etc.)

Rājikā a variety of mustard.

Rājya district or a province of a kingdom; the biggest administrative unit of the Vijayanagar empire.

Rāmānuja kūṭa a term denoting an almshouse, one of the important institutions of poor relief; a rest house for Vaiṣṇava travellers.

Rāśi–paṇa, rāśi–ppon 'current good coins'.

Rāshṭra, raṭṭha some of the Pallava monarchs showed a preference for the term *rāshtra* or *raṭṭha* as the most common designation of the districts. We have reference in their records to the *Sātāhaniraṭṭtha* (Bellary district), *Kămakă–raṭta* (Karmānka–*rāshṭra*, parts of Guntur and Nellore*)*, *Veṅgo–rāshṭra* (between the Godāvarī and the Krishṇā). Like the *āharas*, the *rāshṭras* too are in several cases transformed in to *vishayas.*

Rāshṭrakūṭa provincial or district governor.

Rāshṭrapati head of the administration of the rāshṭra (one of the administrative divisions), which was usually equal to four or five modern districts, he was incharge of both military and civil adminstration; had to maintain peace and order to keep a watchful eye on lesser feudatories and officers; was responsible for dealing refractory feudatories with immediate punitive expedition which accounted for his keeping a sufficient military force under his command and as such was usually himself a military officer; very often used to enjoy the status and titles of a vassal; was incharge of the fiscal administration and responsible for the prompt collection of the land revenue; had to keep careful records of local rights and privileges and to note the villages whose revenue had been granted to temples and Brahmans; could not alienate any revenue without royal permission, nor had the power of appointing district and sub-divisional officers.

Rāshṭrika rulers of districts.

Rāyabhaṇḍāri royal treasurer.

Rāyasa (Kannaḍa), a secretary; an officer in the Vijayanagar administration; royal order; office of a writer; clerkship; order of the king; written orders.

Rāyasa–svāmin 'the head of the *rāyasa'*; the chief secretary.

Rāyasam an office during Vijayanagar days; this ofice and its head along with its subordinate personnel have frequently occurred in the Vijayanagar inscriptions; this term, which is a popular form of the term, *vrāyasam,* means literally the profession of writing; there appears to have been an office of that name in Vijayanagar; people who held that office generally prefixed its name to their personal names, and in course of time was transformed in to their surname, e.g. *Rāyasm* Koṇḍamarasayya adopted in this manner the term *rāyasam* as a family name; the department to which he and his successors belonged was itself very probably known as *rāyasam* and the officer called *rāyasasvāmi*, mentioned in a Mysore inscription, was apparently its head; it is not possible to fix any definite position of the *rāyasam* in the administrative machinery of the Empire; persons belonging to it rose to high positions, and became ministers of state.

Rāyasavarttanai as per an inscription of the first half of the fifteenth century term denoting a type of tax accruing from the villages.

Rāj–wár, rachewar related to kings or nobles. A warlike tribe, from which a part of the *zamindars* of the Northern Circars are descended.

Ráya–récha register of assessments.

Ra'iyati peasant–held villages or lands as against *zamindar* villages or lands. The term should not be confused with *rayatwari* villages.

Ragi (*Eleusine coracana*), an important crop, usually a dry crop, but sometimes irrigated; a coarse millet.

Rahaṭṭa–ghaḍiya same as *araghāṭṭa.*

Rahdari transit duties, tolls and duties collected at inland stations upon grain and other articles levied by the government or sometimes by the *zamindars* on their own authority.

Raja king, prince, chieftain, noblesman.

Rajabandhu in'am *in'ams* held by the relatives of *rajas* or *zamindars*.

Rajjuka probably an officer in charge of the revenue administration and of the measurement of lands in the kingdom; sometimes entrusted with the task of executing charters alienating land revenue (*Vākāṭaka* period).

Rajjupratihāra rope–jugglers or dancers.

Rakṣā– bhoga a fee or a share in the produce given to the village watchman.

Rakta kodiga in'am granted as a compensation to a person who has been wounded in the public service; the same as *netturu kattu in'am.*

Rakta–koḍage, ratta–kuḍangai lit. a grant for the deceased in the battles; this type of grant was bestowed on the next of the one who had been in the battles; a piece of revenue–free land given to the family of those who were unjustly killed in the battle.

Rakta–mānya also Tamil *irratta–māṇya, iratta–kkāṇikkai*; 'blood present'; endowment of revenue–free land for the support of the descendants of warriors killed in battle.

Raktakanikai in'am granted for the support of the heirs of persons who were killed while treading boundaries on oath.

Raṅga–bhoga amusement to be arranged for a deity and land granted for it; enjoyment of splendour other than *aṅgabhoga* or personal decoration; gift land received for *raṅga–bhoga*.

Rangrizan dyers.

Ranuva kattubaḍi in'am the same as *jangi kattubadi*–see *kattubadi in'am*.

Rathākārs artisans.

Rayaji cáni or *'Saint Thome cáni'*, it is measured by a rod of 24 *Adi* or feet, the square of which is one *cól* or *cuzhi*, and 100 *cól* or 57,600 square feet is one *cáni*.

Rayalaseema the word in Telugu means the 'seema' or the country of the *Rayalu*, the title assumed by the Vijayanager rulers especially belonging to Aravidu dynasty.

Rayalu the leaders of the village; high caste elite.

Ryat, ryot, raiyat (or exactly, *ra'iyat*, Arabic) a term familiar to all acquainted with Indian finance, as applied to designate the cultivators of the soil in general, also employed by them to distinguish that particular class only among them who employ, superintend, and sometimes assist the labourer, and who are everywhere the farmers of the country, the creators and *payers* of the land revenue. In many parts of the Tamil areas, but especially in the province of Tanjore, the privileges of many of this class had been purchased, usurped, or acquired, by Brahmans, and in Malabar by Moplahs, who had started representing the original *rayats*; but in general like the Nairs of Malabar, the vellalers of the Tamil areas, the *kunbis* of the Ceded Districts, and the *Reddis* and Naidus of the Northern Circars, the *rayats* were principal among the *shudras*, the lowest of the pure Hindu tribes, who appeared originally to have possessed the occupancy of the land throughout Hindustan; a subject, but especially denotes a cultivtor, farmer or peasant, whether under a zamindar, or, as in Bombay and most of Madras, independant in his relation to the revenue authority. It is in the latter capacity that he is usually referred to here; a 'land–holder' or 'occupant' not under any landlord or middleman.

Rayatulu 'cultivators'.

Rayatwari, ryotwari, raiyetwar a settlement made by government immediately with the *rayats*, without intermediary renters or *zamindars*–also *kulwar* settlement; 'according to individual holdings'; the system of settlements and land–revenue administration generally, in which there is no middleman or landlord over the individual *rayats*, who are severally (and not jointly) liable for the land–revenue assessment on the holding.

Razeram government's share of revenue produce.

Razīnāma (i) any writing agreeing to terms, a compromise: (ii) in *rayatwari* provinces the written application resigning a holding either absolutely or on transfer.

Razu warriors.

Rēkai a type of tax generally paid to the palace.

Récha–sidd'hāyam commonly called *roy-rec'ha* from *réc'ha, a line,* and *siddhāyam* settled income; the fixed assessment; it is so named from the form in which the account of it was drawn out, which was so arranged in the village *cadattams*, that the assessment on every spot of land was shown in a separate *line;* the *réc'ha–siddha'yam* was established or more probably, completed during the reign of Krishnadeva Raya; it extended to the whole of the Kanarese provinces of the empire, but does not appear to have been introduced in to the Tamil areas, nor in to the part of Telingana and the Northern Sirkars.

Reals a coin (less than a penny).

Reḍḍi one of the titles for a village headman.

Reddi in'am the same as *pedda kapu in'am*.

Reddy manium the *manium* in the occupation of the head *mirāsīdār* or manager of the village by whatever term designated. In certain districts, especially the North Arcot, during the Muslim government, this was the only *mirāsī* privilege which was in some instances very extensive. The person holding it, though sometimes not actually the renter, had the collection of the revenue and it was his duty to see that the lands were properly cultivated; on being removed from the situation for any cause, the said *manium* was occupied by the person appointed to succeed him in his duties, and although the *maniums* in other places were accorded to the several *mirāsīdārs* agreeably to their shares, it is not unreasonable to conceive that such were originally granted in order that those holding them should provide for the cultivation of the lands, and consequent revenue to government.

Reddy, reddi see *patel*, also, agriculturist, chief; usually a rich man; warrior, *zamindar*. Also see, *reddi*.

Redgram *cajanus cajan*.

Regar pure black cotton soil; black soil.

Regar banjar kayem cowle black and waste lands on fixed *cowle*.

Rekhā, reka a standard assessment (in Kānara); the original assessment, with certain rates on cocoanut, and fruit trees (added upto 1660 A.D.) was called the *rekhā* or standard assessment.

Rekai, rekai–ppon, irekai name of a gold coin; revenue income in cash.

Reveg jasti extra rent on betel nut plantations.

Riaya, ri'aya All cultivating families paying revenues to the state.

Riayat remission, indulgence, favour.

Riayat mukhasa tenure *mukhasa* villages held on a favourable assessment fluctuating with the cultivation of each year–see *mukhasa*.

Roap–nuts (concinna), a species of bean. The outer cover of the seed is boiled or pounded in to powder, and used to rub over the skin and hair after taking an oil bath to remove the greasiness.

Roghan–i–zard ghee.

Rokka gutta in'am villages held on a fixed money–rent the amount of which is some what lower than the standard assessment of government lands.

Rozina pension, daily allowance.

Rusūm, Russom, russoom, rusum (A.) customs, customary, commissions, gratuities, fees, perquisites. Shares of the crops and ready–money payments received by public officers, as perquisites attached to their situations; a term used for fees, perquisites allowed especiallly to the officers such as *deshmukhs, deshpandias*, palegars, etc., dues, custom bribe, commission.

S

S-odraṅga a gift of land or village together with the tax called *udraṅga,* Tamil *uttāra,* fixed taxes.

Śālābhōga land grants enjoyed by the śāla i.e. feeding house; it has also been interpreted as 'land enjoyed by the royal palace', but the former translation seems to be more correct.

Śrībhandāram trustees of a temple.

Sāsan-ārdhika half of the cultivator's share of the produce of the land in the gift villages; name of a levy.

Śālā-bhoga land granted in favour of a feeding house; a revenue free holding in the possession of a *sālā* i.e. an almhouse or a school; this land grant was in the same category as *devadāna* and *brahmadeya.* Same as Tamil *arac-cālā bhogam.*

Śālāvaṇam a sale deed.

Śālai, Śalai an alms house; a feeding house, also see *śālā-bhoga.* A term denoting an almshouse, an important institution of poor relief.

Śālikattaṛi a term used in the epigraphs to denote a professional tax charged from a kind of weavers.

Śānabhoga village account; same as *senabova,* etc.

Śāsana-baddha original grantees of a charter; people bound by a royal charter.

Śāśvatīya eternity; perpetuity.

Śāttvika-dana not expecting in return for the donation; gift without the pouring of water.

Śāvi land the land that yielded only blighted grains.

Śaḍa-kkaḍamai (Tamil), tax on shepherds.

Śadiram block or square; a term used in the epigraphs to emphasize that the lands were localised and grouped under each block or square; a square field.

Saivācārya-kṣetra, Śaivācārya kṣetras revenue-free land endowed to a *Śaivācārya*-an ascetice of the saiva sect. Lands granted to *śaivācārya maṭhas.*

Śakkara-kāṇikkai, tirigai-āyam (Sanskrit-Tamil), tax paid by potters.

Śalāgai a term used to denote a metallic rod or silver or gold which served as money.

Śalāgai, śalākā name of a coin.

Śaṇa hemp.

Śaṭṭu-vari (Tamil), grazing tax.

Śattige umbaḷi a term appearing in the epigraphs which appears to denote a grant or revenue-free land for. the maintenance of an umbrella, apparently for the king.

Śēṇians a term used to denote Telugu weavers.

Śēṇigaru guildsmen of the town.

Śēru method of preparation of the field for sowing according to which land is prepared by ploughing after being flooded with water from a tank.

Śērvai service *in'am* lands.

Śekk-āyam (Tamil -Sanskrit), tax on oil-presses; also called *sekk-iṛai* and *śekku-kkaḍamai.*

Śekku-kaḍamai, śekkukkaḍamai a tax levied on oil industry. A term used for the professional tax charged from the oilmongers.

Śekku oil mill or press; it was usually made of stone or wood and was worked with two bulls.

Śelavaḍhaki stone masons.

Śennel the paddy in the main crop.

Serī (Marāṭhi), 'arable land originally excluded from the village assessment'.

Śeṭṭi the leading member of a guild.

Śeṭṭi paṭṭaṇasvāmis, Śeṭṭi paṭṭaṇasvāmin a term that occurred in some of the inscriptions and denotes presiding merchants; designation of the president of a merchant guild.

Śeṭṭi–iṟai, śeṭṭ–iṟai tax on merchants.

Śeṭṭiyār–magamai (Tamil), voluntary conribution (*magamai*) of the merchants.

Śeviḍu (Tamil), a small grain measure, 1/5 of an *āḻākku*.

Śīmai–vivādam (Tamil), a boundry dispute.

Sirmai, Śīmai (Tamil), a territorial division.

Sikhai dues or arrears

Silā–lekha writing on stone; an inscription on stone.

Śilliṟai a term used in the epigraphs to denote dues, payments or obligations and services due to the township; miscellaneous or subsidiary levies.

Śimĕhabbaruva an official associated with the administration of *śīmai.*

Śiṟṟāyam type of fines imposed.

Śoḍaśī, śoḍaśika a coin, 1/16 of the standard coin in weight and value.

Śoḍi see *jodi.*

Śoḻaga (Kannada), name of a land measure,

Śrāvaṇa sale deed; a document.

Śrēṇayaḥ guilds of persons earning their livelihood by the same kind of labour though belonging to diferent castes or to the same caste, e.g. of the dealers in cattle, betel, and weaver and the currier; the bond of union in the guild was the fact that members followed the same occupation.

Śrēṇi the vocational guild; the distinctive feature of the *śrēṇi* was the sameness of vocation of its members.

Śreṇi–bala members of the guilds probably joined the army in times of need to form a distinctive component part–*śreṇi–bala*–force, one of the six divisions of the royal army.

Śreṇi–dharma the rules and regulations of the guilds, the usage of the guild's had the force of the law. They served trade or craft interests in various ways. A special feature of these associations was the banking facilities provided by them. They received cash deposits and endowments of property, and undertook to spend the income from them in a specified manner.

Śreṇīs guilds. Same as *śrēṇi* above.

Śresṭhin a banker; merchant, head of a guild.

Śri–bali–bhoga land set apart to meet the expenses of the *śri–bali* (offering of *bali* in temple) service in a temple.

Śrī–mukha royal order or charter; a letter from the king or a chief.

Śrīballi–paṭṭi a piece of land the produce of which was intended for offerings to god.

Śrīy–ājñai (Tamil), royal order.

Śrotra a tax collected from the cultivators by a lessee of a state land.

Śrotriya land or village granted to a Brāhman learned in the vedas.

Sūlavari (Tamil), name of a tax; a term used in the inscriptions to denote a tax generally paid to the palace; it could sometimes be remitted by the local officers in order to make way for the rehabilitation of the villages, reconstruction of the temples and repair of breached lakes.

Śuḍ–kāṭṭu–ppāṭṭam (Tamil), fee payable by prostitutes, especially those accompanying the army.

Śulka tolls; custom duties; taxes particularly levied at ferries and passes and roads, etc.

Śulka–śālā, śuṅga–śālā custom house; place where tolls were collected.

Śuṅgam, śuṅkam customs, tolls.

Śuṅkada–adhikāri the customs officer.

Śunka–karaṇālu accountants of the *śunka* i.e. tax collectors.

Śunkarulu collectors of *suṅkamu (*taxes etc).

Śuvāstiyam (Tamil), hereditary rights; right of hereditary enjoyment.

Sa'ir *'sair* was a revenue category comparable to *mal* the tax on agricultural production, *peshkash,* i.e.. tribute, and *jiziya,* the capitation tax on non–Muslims. However, *sa'ir,* unlike the other major categories, was vitually a residual classification into which fell the multitude of specialized taxes common to pre–modern Indian states: road and ferry tolls, octroi, excise tax on merchandise, shop and house taxes etc.' see, Richards, J.F., *Mughal Administration in Golconda,* Oxford, 1975 p. 185.

Sa–bhoga a privilege of the donee of rent free land.

Sa–pānīyam the use of this term in any gift of land gives the expression that the donee was allowed to utilize the water in the gift land, it also indirectly indicates that ordinarily a person was not allowed to be benefited from the water resources.

Sa–tālaka an epithet of a gift–village referring to the right of enjoying the trees by privileged tenants in some areas.

Sa–toṭṭam 'inclusive of garden cultivation'; it indicates the transfer of the royal right of enjoying above produce to the donee.

Sādhya one of the eight kinds of enjoyment of property–see *aṣṭa–bhoga;* income from land that may be brought under cultivation in future; a type of income.

Sāgu in Coorg, the ordinary (unprivileged) tenure of all land that was not *jamma;* it was an occupant's or *rayatwari* tenure, with no condition of service, paid revenue at the rate of R.10 per 100 *battis;* remission of revenue was allowed for failure of crops; partition of jointly–held *sāgu* land was not objected to; the holder of *sāgu* land received a *sāgavali–chitu;* or lease from government, signed by the *sūbadār.*

Sāhaṇkāṭi name of coin.

Sālas feeding houses.

Sāliyas a community engaged in textile industry.

Sāndhi–vigrahika lit. 'maker of peace and war'; employed in the conduct of diplomatic negotiations; primarily connected with the relations of the state to foreign and subordinate powers; was supposed to have a competent acquaintance with many languages and scripts and outstanding tact and skill in dealing with *sāmantas,* etc., besides be an expert in diplomacy and finance; his duties were certainly of the highest political importance and they spread over the whole range of imperial relations, internal as well as external.

Sārthavāha a class of traders who carried on trade with distant lands; an experienced caravan merchant.

Sádir–wārid, saderwared ready money collection made in each village from the *rayats* for supplying the *kach'hari,* or office of public business, with lamps oil and stationary.

Sávarah, sávaram, saverum an allotment of land, or of the government's revenue thereof, held by *zamindars,* and other principal revenue officers, rent free, as part of the emoluments of their offices.

Sabhā the body of the Mahājanas; the assembly of a Brahman village of the Tamil speaking area–as against the assembly of non–Brahman village called Ūr; local assembly of a Brahman village–same as Tamil *kuṛi;* also see *mahāsabhā.*

Sabhā–madhyama common or waste land in the village belonging to the *sabhā;* also called in Tamil *sabhai–ppodu, ūr–ppodu; ūr–mañjikkam, sabhā–māñjikkam.*

Sabhā–viniyoga contribution payable to make up the expenses of the *sabhā.*

Sabhaik–kaṇakku an accountant who functioned in the *sabhā*-administered villages; he collected revenue dues and maintained accounts.

Sachimattam bribe.

Saḍbhāgin 'one who owns the sixth part'. Generally the land revenue demand of the south Indian state constituted a sixth of the produce. The rate seems to be so popular that the king was often known by this apellative. In his commentary to two verses of *Tirukuṛal,* Parimēlaḻagar, a 12th century commentator in the commentary on verses 43, 755, also verse 756 indicates the householder's duty with regard to making provisions for five persons (i) ancestor (ii) god (iii) guest (iv) relative (v) self, and the sixth part was the tax demand (*iraipporuḷ*) due to the king. In verse 755 the commentator refers that the income of the king if it is not on proper grounds shoud not be collected. He further adds that the proper form of income to the king is the sixth share.

Sadā–servai, sadā–sevai (Tamil), permanent service; constant service.

Sadar head of the Muslim judiciary and religious patronage.

Sadavritti in'am granted for the daily distribution of uncooked rice to poor travellers.

Saderwared ready money collection made in each village from the *rayats* for supporting the *kach'hari* with lamps, oil and stationery.

Sadwániyán, sadwannian a company of pikemen consisting of one hundred men. The expense of an establishment of pikemen of different tribes, stationed in different areas, and employed under *deshmukhs* and zamindars, in the Northern Circars.

Saggio one of the coins of foreign origin in circulation in south India.

Sagnally in the Dindigul province, means cultivated lands.

Sagoobady daub record of cultivation with fields arranged as per survey.

Sagoobady keyfeut a compilation relating to accounts of the village as a whole.

Sagoovaly annual cultivation.

Sagubadi in'am granted to head *rayats* with a view to their encouraging the cultivation of government lands.

Sagupadi kanakku an account of output in the different seasons.

Sagvaly register of ploughs employed in tilling.

Sagwan teak.

Sahib–i'iyar head of the assayers and money changers.

Sahukar, sowkar, soukar, savukar (H.) merchant, banker, a moneylender.

Saikalgar in'am granted for the service of polishing arms for a *zamindar.*

Sain year.

Saint Thome cáni see *Rayaji cáni.*

Sair different sources of revenue accruing to the government in addition to the land revenue, from customs, transit duties, license fees, house–tax and market tax, etc. Same as *sa'ir,* above.

Sakkath religious charity.

Salabhoga a kind of eleemosynary

tenure.

Salada (Kanarese) from *sala*, debt; debt slave; agricultural labourer; those working off a debt.

Saliya nagaram a *nagaram* trading in textile.

Saliyana annual, yearly.

Saṁvatsara-vāriya also called *āṭṭivāriyam* in Tamil; annual committee for supervising the management of village affairs; annual committee appointed by the *sabhā*.

Samāñjita accountant of a village or a village assembly.

Samaba a type of paddy crop sown in May and reaped in September; it is dependent on the river freshes occasioned by the South-West monsoon during June and July. A slight rainfall is requisite in the end of April to admit of the ploughing of the land; but after sowing, the ground is left perfectly dry for three weeks, and it is considered that rain during that time is injurious.

Samai *panicum miliase.*

Sāmantas feudatories .

Samasta-sippiga-gottali a term appearing in the epigraphs to denote 'all the headmen of the tailors'.

Samastanam peons in'am granted for the service of revenue peons in *zamindaris*.

Samatdar revenue officer.

Samavāsa 'dwelling'; this term is used to indicate the responsibility of the villagers to arrange for the shelter for the touring state officials.

Samavāyah partnership; a term used in the records to denote an agreement by which several persons agree to do any business together.

Samay-ācāra religious usage; established custom; supervision of the religious and social life of the people ; censoring of public morals.

Samaya cakravarti the king/emperor of the trading organisation.

Samaya-dharma expression generally used in relation to the organisation of merchants and agriculturist known respectively as nānādesin and *citrameḻi*; law of the *samaya* or agreement.

Samaya-patra a deed of agreement; a document containing an agreement; an agreement.,

Samayakar in'am held by a servant under the *Sri-vaishnava* priest of sudras. His duty is to report to the people the movement of the priest.

Samba-kattalai in'am granted for making an oblation in a pagoda with kind of rice called *samba*.

Samba-peshanum a large *nunjah* paddy crop which 'must be sown and transplanted with the freshes of August and September and nourished until its January, February and March harvest by the fall and not the preserved waters of the great monsoon and supplied by a reservation of part of this water in tanks and lakes until its March-April and May harvest'. (Report by Charles Harris dated June 15 1803, *Tanjore Collectorate Volume, General* No. 21494, pp. 304-342).

Sambandham loose or informal marriage.

Samjhaish making understand, explaining, warning, inducing the defendant to admit the justice of a plaint.

Sammat an administrative unit; same as *samuta*.

Samprati a public accountant; the register of the district; a head accountant; the manager of a temple; senior accountant.

Samprati in'am granted for service as the accountant of a taluk in a *palaiyam* or *zamindari* or of the whole estate when of small extent.

Samudāya a tenure in which land is enjoyed by a group of people; a village under the *gaṇa-bhoga* tenure; village common; managing committee of a temple. See also, *samudāyam.*

Samudāya-prāpti, samudāya-ppirātti any acquisition from the village to be enjoyed in common by the villagers.

Samudāyam, Samudāyanilam, Samudayam (Tamil), somadayem villages; villages belonging to the village community as a whole; same as *gaṇabhōgam* villages.

The most ancient variey of *kāṇiyātchi;* common holdings of the village; earliest and strongest form of communal land holding; same as *pasamkarei*; joint in tenure; by which the *mirāsīdārs* hold all the lands of the village in common; interchangeable at stated periods, probably arose out of the same view of keeping up the cultivation; for as in favourable seasons a portion of the lands could not be fully watered, it is evident that the *mirāsīdārs* who held this lands unless there were a periodical interchange, would be worse of and less able than the others to pay their rent regularly.

Samudrāntā a variety of cultivated cotton plant.

Samudragāh lit. 'seafaring men',

Samuta an adminstrative unit; same as *sammat.*

Sanad, sunnud (A.) a patent, charter, or written authority for holding either land or office; a title-deed; a patent of appointment to a grant, title, dignity or office.

Sanad-i-milkiyat-i-istimrar title-deed of perpetual ownership.

Sandai, shandy a village fair or market.

Sandhi special worship offered in the names of persons who arrange for it by creating endowment etc. 'service in the temple in the morning and evening' daily worship in the temple; but lit. 'twilight'.

Sandhivigraha-ppeṛu, sandhivigrahi-paṇṇu (Sanskrit-Tamil) a fee payable to document writers; a fee payable to the village *madhyastha.*

Sang tarash in'am granted for service as a stone mason.

Sangitam in'am granted for service of singing in pagodas or in zamindars' palaces.

Sangu-kulikaran in'am held for the service of diving for chank shells.

Sanguical a type of boat, called so from being built at Cinguicar,.

Sankarappadi nagaram the *nagaram* whose activities were the supplies of oil and ghee.

Sankhanadam in'am granted for the service of blowing a conch shell in a pagoda.

Sannad mānyam, sunned maunaim revenue free land granted under Muslim rule; generally not saleable, but mortgageable.

Sannad manyakkanakku an account of *mānyams* granted through the *sannads* of the Muslim rulers.

Sannad manyam (sunned maunaim) revenue free land granted by the Muslim and European rulers.

Santa (Telugu-Kannaḍa), a fair or market day.,

Santa basivi in'am held by a female servant of the *setti* caste who is employed in sweeping, lighting lamps, etc. She is also required to perform similar services for travellers when they halt in the village.

Santai weakly fair; during the Vijayanagar days almost every town had generally a weekly fair (*śantai*) while that was not the mark of all villages.

Santaka seems to denote officers in general, or perhaps district officers.

Santati–praveśam 'from generation to generation'.

Santheya–śunka a term used in the eigraphs to denote a small duty imposed in kind or cash on goods entering or in some cases only on goods sold and bought to facilitate the arrangements for holding weekly fairs for the wandering merchants to sell their goods.

Sappan *caesalpinia sappan*.

Sappani in'am granted for the support of a cripple.

Sapt–āṅga seven constituent parts of a kingdom–king, ministers, allies, treasury, territory, forts and forces.

Sapta–santāna, sapta–santati seven kinds of great deeds by the performance of which merit equal to was obtainable through progeny, those deeds were–digging of tanks, hoarding of treasure, founding of *agrahāras*, erection of temples, creation of flower gardens, getting literary works written by poets, and establishment of choultries.

Sar tiram, ser terrim *sar* head and *tiram* value or rate. Head assessor of land in the Ceded Districts. *Sar tiramdar* head assessor.

Sar–i–lashkar, seir lascar the Golconda term for governor.

Saralai white and grey calcareous soil.

Sararashtah the accounts.

Sarbasta tashkhis customary assessment.

Sardar commander.

Sarishtadār an office–superintendent who 'holds the files' of cases pending.

Sarkạr marammat, circar maramut repairs by government. Repairs performed at the expense of government to the rivers, and great water–courses.

Sarkar, sirkar, circar part of a *suba*; the government.

Sarkhel a general, a commander of a regiment, a troop or a body of men, a minister, a chamberlain.

Sarraf (corruptly shroff) in'am the same as *nottam in'am*.

Sarshapa mustard.

Sarv–ābhyantara–siddhi a fiscal term denoting full and complete right of enjoyment of agricultural income or internal revenue or taxes to be paid to the village authorities.

Sar–samatu: district governors in Andhra.

Sarva manyam, Semman in'am an *in'am* held free of quit rent; held for the service of supplying the *zamindar* with chunam. Same as *sarvamānya*.

Sarva–jātakam 'inclusive of all the produce'; the term used in any grant would mean that the king had transferred the royal right of enjoying produce of the gift land in favour of the donee; another version is that it actually referred to the grain–share to be given by the inhabitants of the gift land to the king or any authorized person.

Sarva–namasya same as *sarva–mānya*; a revenue–free holding.

Sarvābhyantara siddhi a grant with full and complete rights of enjoyment made only to one class of grantees.

Sarvādhyaksha prime–minister (Vākāṭaka period).

Sarvajāta–bhoga–nirasta 'the renunciation of all kinds of royal right'.

Sarvamānya, Sarvamanayam Sarva–mānya a revenue–free holding; a free tenure; lands and village fully exempt from all taxes; land exempted from taxes; same as *iraiyili* class of land during *Cola* period, it is also associated with *aṣṭa–bhoga*–the eight forms of enjoying the land. It however, does not completely rule out the possibility of payment of certain dues of the nature of taxes; (Sanskrit), *sarva* entire and *manayam* gift; a gift of land free of revenue; revenue –free village or lands granted to brahmans; complete enjoyment of land did not in all cases mean exemption from land revenues. Lands granted could be free from land revenues, if they were specifically exempted from such payment; *Sarvamānya (namasya)*, does not always have its exact literal meaning, and sometimes implies, not total exemption from all dues, but exemption from all dues other than those named in the charter itself.

Such grant by the *mírásidars* could be an encroachment on the right of the sovereign; may also apply to the whole of the inhabitant's interest in the land only, the consent of the king, or of those acting in his name, may have been actually obtained previously to making the grant; the same thing could apply to the *agraháram* grants; this term cannot be applied to any transfer by the people it is appropriate only to rent-free lands conferred by government.

Sarvamānyam villages, the villages where no *mēlwaram* at all could be levied.

Sarvasva-haraṇa forefeiture of one's entire property.

Sasanam, patram, chittu the two former being Sanskrit, and the, latter Tamil, are the same in meaning, though somewhat varied in use, and may be rendered, 'deed, instrument, writing, document.'

Sathāna-āchāryas the priest of the temple.

Satra-śāla a term used to denote a type of almshouse, an important institution of poor relief.

Sattra an alms-house; 'a charitable feeding house'; institutions for making provision for lodging, feeding, clothing, or nursing of the needy.

Sattum parisatta nagaram a *nagaram* specialising in textile trade.

Satyamkāra a term denoting earnest money.

Savaram a measure of land, nominally containing thirty catties (some contain only ten), each catti being about 14 acres and 14 kuntas, i.e. acres 14 7/20

Savarṇa-vṛtti profession of writing documents.

Sayer or sair the transit duty, variable imposts customs, duties, tolls,.

Sazzulu (Telugu), spiked millet, *pennisetum typhoideum* called *kambu* in Tamil and *bajra* in Hindustani.

Sēnāpatya kaṇakku a term used in the epigraphs to denote military accounts.

Sētu a water-embankment or a dam to a flow of water.

Seemai agathi *cassia alata.*

Seemai pala *artocarpus communis.*

Seer a variable weight; on the railways 80 *tolas* (=2.05 Ib), a *tola* being the weight of a rupee, in Anantapur 21 *tolas*, in many parts of the Madras Presidency 24 *tolas* (about 10 oz)

Seh-bandi, sebundy an irregular native soldier employed in the service of the revenue and police.

Sehbandi fasli, sebundy fusly irregular force employed at harvest time, or in collecting the revenues.

Seih tin.

Sekhā a standard assessment (in Kānara); the original assessment, with certain rates on cocoa-nut, and fruit-trees (added up to 1660 A.D.) was called the *sekhā* or standard assessment.

Sena-bhoga, Śeṇai-bhogam, senabova an accountant, a clerk; a village accountant; same as *Śānabhoga.*

Senaiy-alṅgāḍika a class of merchants who followed the army with their merchandise; a class of cloth merchants.

Sendal, sendalai lit. 'red leaf', a reddening of the *cholam* leaf through the attack of mites; sometime very destructive.

Sendi in'am held by toddy drawers for

service as bearers etc.

Seni, śreṇi guild, they were corporate bodies, wielding great influence in the state.

Senkarisel black soil mixed with red.

Seriyat tax-free lands; a grant of land to *zamindars* as a compensation for their duties.

Seruvelly a type of paddy crop raised from seedlings transplanted about the beginning of October and reaped at the beginning of March. It is generally grown on channel lands in clay regurs.

Servai (Tamil) a service *in'am;* revenue-free land given to servants for enjoyment in lieu of salary.

Servaikkaram in'am held for the service of village peon.

Seth chief merchants.

Setti in'am, patna setti in'am *in'am* granted for setting caste disputes among the Lingaits, esp. in the Bellary district.

Sevak-ttevai expenses in connection with the supply and maintenance of retainers of chiefs and officers during their visit to a place.

Sevvel, seval a term generally used for the red alluvial soil mixed with a small proportion of sand; red soil.

Seykāl karamb, Seykāl karambu, (sheycaul curramb) temporarily fallow land.

Shāmil (Arabic), 'added to'; 'together with'; increment on the old or standard assessment (*shist*); the term specifically comes in connection with south *Kānara;* the Bednūr rulers and the subsequent Mysore governments largely increased the existing assessment; the money-rate was called *'shist'*, and the increments the *'shamil'*.

Shāvī withered; remission granted for crops withered by failure of water, or blight.

Shánabhog, Shānabhogam local name of the accountant or *karnam* in Kānara; the situation of *shānabhog* is hereditary, and it appears to be his duty derived from ancient custom to be the writer of every deed connected with the transfer of land within the *maâgani* to which he is attached. Unless he draw out, transcribe, and authenticate it with his signature, the document is not considered valid.

The *shánabhog's* accounts having fallen in to the possessions of the Muslim government, no survey or inspection appears to have been necessary to ascertain the resources of the area concerned. Those accounts formed the basis of the annual *jammabandi;* in framing which all that seems to have been required was to put on such additional percentage on the original shist as the necessities of the government demanded, and so remarkably particular do the *shánabhogs* appear to have been in preserving the record of the earlier *shist*, that in the Deeds it is distinctly specified and separated from the subsequent additions put thereon called the *shaâmillut*.

Shahganj central grain market.

Shanan in'am granted for supplying cadjan leaves to the zamindar and the village accountants.

Shanars toddy drawing caste of the Tamil country, specially numerous in the extreme south of the peninsula, having considerable area where the palmyra being the sole means of subsistence; would call themselves Nadars, and claim to be by origin a landowing and soldier caste but worsted in war by the Madura monarchs.

Sharogar in the southern *palaiyams*, an officer of peons, or militia generally; but also an officer of any kind.

Shava in'am granted for permitting the dead bodies of persons dying in a village to be burnt within the limits of the village.

Shecal-carambu lands which have

been cultivated laying waste.

Sheccodu dues from oil presses.

Sheckizhar possessors of bulloks.

Shem purthee, sarum purtee a variety of cotton; it takes its name from its red flower; grows to a large plant and produces not very inferior cotton, which however is not cultivated but in gardens and is used only for spinning of Brahman's thread. Also called, triennial cotton and was grown on a 'dry firm soil'. It was always sown along the other grains so as to secure some margin of profit. The land was prepared early in June, seed was sown in August or September and cotton pickings were done in succeeding April–May; *gossypium barbadense var. brasiliense*.

Sheri or seri free land, which, though not *in'am*, pays no direct tax to government, land rented by a cultivator from a zamindar or a possessor of a *maniam* and free of tax to government.

Sheristadar the head accountant or manager in a revenue office or court; keeper of records, revenue accountant of a district who checked the accounts of the regular village accountants. Head ministerial officer of a court, hence a head native officer in district headquarters.

Shevul, shewul a description of land so called in Tanjore.

Sheycal carambu cultivable waste; cutivable land may be improductive at a particular time, but that will not make it *anadi carambu* or immemorial waste.

Sheykal fallow land.

Shikekayi a plant that is used for inclosures, being covered with strong prickles; the seed and leaves of the plant produce a sweet scent when crushed.

Shilotri term used in north Konkān for the plots reclaimed from the sea.

Shist, shistu derived from *sishta* i.e., remainder; an original assessment in money (in lieu of grain) by early Muslim and later Mysore rulers in South India; in Coorg, the term was used for the 'assessment under native rule' and was continued to be maintained by the English; the *shist* accounts give the particulars of every '*warga*' or holding, and of the position of lands attached to each; estate.

The term shist may bear the same signification as the *shistam* in Malabar. In Kanara it may have been 'residue' 'belonging to the state', after deducting the share of the rent allowed to the proprietor; as in Malabar, it is applicable to the 'residue' 'owing to the *jenmikar*', after providing for the encumbrances or his estate; a land tax, assessment, favourable assessment.

Shoru boiled rice allowed for the subsistence of the officers of government of low caste while on duty; almost same as *etcharu/etchoru*.

Shotriyam, shrotriyam Shrōtrium (shotrum) a general term for all favourably assessed villages held by Brahmans, a favourable assessment; an entire village held on concessional revenue assessment; *shrōtrium* villages, however, paid a token *mēlwaram*, which was usually fixed, irrespective of output level; such villages were granted to the brahmins.

It is evident that by the end of the 18th century *shrōtriums* were awarded to Muslims and revenue officials, it, as such, negated the very meaning of *shrōtriums* as it obtained earlier under *kāṇiyāṭchi*. During the English period these villages "appertained to meerasaydars".

Shroff a banker or money–lender.

Shûtta kreya shâasanum shûtta, meaning complete, entire, effectual, clear; *kreya*, sale; *shaasanum*, a written deed or document; together meaning deed of entire sale. After receiving the specified sum of money in cash, the land sold together with the dwelling house, relinquishing the rights to the *nunjei* and *punjei* land contained in the specified lot, its trees and woods and whatever may grow upon it, its hills and their contents, as well as its every property, whether arising from the discovery of concealed treasure, springs, quarries, good or evil, the dominion over it of gift and sale, and every possible claim of ownership thereto, and hereditary. Such deeds in Tanjore correspond with the *attypper* of Malabar and *kreya sâathanum* of Kanara.

Shuhur san (Arabic) the Bahmani, Qutb–Shahi, and Adil Shahi *farmans* as well as the orders issued by the Maratha rulers bear an era called *Shuhur San*, which was noted in Arabic. It commences from the month of June when the monsoon breaks and the cultivators spread seeds in the fields; almost same as *fasli*.

Sīman the subdivision of a district; a small territorial unit; also used to indicate 'a province'.

Sīmé (kannada), same as *śirmai, śimai* and *sīman*.

Sīrā a land measure equal to four *halas*.

Sibbandi rangers, militia, armed peons; irregular infantry; an establishment of clerks, peons.

Sibbandy fusly irregular military employed at harvest time or in collecting the revenues.

Sibbendy police, sebundy (p.seh–bandi) irregular native soldiers employed in the service of the revenue and police.

Siddh–āya, Siddhāya, Siddháya fixed income; regular income; also explained as a tax; agricultural income; minor taxes; minor taxes payable in cash during the Vijayanagar rule same as Tamil *sidd–āyam, sitt–āyam;* a term used to denote the taxes and revenue let out on contract on a cash basis; fixed rent; fixed assessment; it appears that fixed assessment in money existed long before the completion of the *ráya–réc'ha* (see in R.), but whether they were paid for dry field only, or both for wet land and dry–field, is not clear.

Siddhi one of the eight kinds of enjoying landed property; the right of cultivating land.

Sidi in'am granted for performing the swinging festival in honour of the village goddess.

Sih bandi temporary troops. Same as *Sibbendy*.

Sikasth broken, ruined, burst.

Silakasu a cash payment to the landlord.

Silvari ancilliary levies.

Sima basic territorial unit both in Andhra and Tellengana.

Simt a sub division of a taluk.

Simt bandi arranging villages in to a subdivision of a taluk.

Sippashari in'am held for the service of architect to a pagoda.

Siragu a field located on the side of the channel.

Sirkār the government ; *sirkārī* that which is public or crown property, etc.

Sirna gour, surnar gour the head *patel* or farmer of a district, in the Ceded Districts.

Siwar fields and meadows lying around and appertaining to a village.

Siyahiwala in'am granted for the service of supplying ink to public offices.

Soap–nuts (*concinna*), a species of bean. The outer cover of the seed is boiled or pounded into powder and used to rub over the skin and hair after taking an oil bath to remove the greasiness.

Sotical garden land cultivation.

Sournadayam taxes received in money, like taxes on the *rayats'* cattle and sheep.

Sripandáram the royal treasure or the revenue department.

Sthāna–āchāryas; the priests of the temple.

Srimukha a royal order.

St'hanicas ministers.

Sthāṁkas same as *sthānattār*.

Sthānattār the managers of the temple; they were authorized to collect the stipulated amount from each family of the area and were also authorized to grant remission, of course, in consultation with the revenue authorities.

Sthān–ādhipati a local governor; a police–officer; also called *sthānika-dharma-kartṛ*.

Sthāna–bhūmi land belonging to a temple.

Sthāna–mānya, Sthānamanyas an honour or land granted by the ruler on quit rent or on favourable tenures; land granted to the officials for the maintenance of *sthāna* in lieu of cash salary; lands free of taxes and earmarked for the priests.

Sthānapati a civil agent kept by the *Nāyakas* at the imperial court at Vijayanagar.

Sthalādāyam a term used in the epigraphs to denote duties on goods imported to be sold at one place.

Sthala an administrative division; smaller than a *nāḍu;* consisted of a group of villages ranging perhaps from ten to sixty in number; several *sthalas* were combined to form a *nāḍu;* not much is known about the government of the *sthala*, but the terms–*sthala-karnam, sthala–gaud* and *sthalam kaval,* would seem to indicate that the *sthala* had its own office and staff of officials. An administrative division that came after the *sīma* and was made up of a few villages; there does not seem to have been any definite rule regarding the number of villages that a *sthala* should comprise.

Some inscriptions mention *sthala* and *śīme* at the same time, however, it may mean that a bigger and a smaller administrative divisions might have been known by the same name, as in the modern day; it seems that at some later period the term *hobali* took the place of *sthala*, and in Karnāṭaka districts a division called *kampaṇa* took the place of *sthala*. A small territorial unit; a district or its subdivision; also, *deśa, maṇḍala, sīma,* etc., also a place, habitation; a holy place.

Sthala gaud in'am granted for the service of headman of a village. He differs from the ordinary *gaud* by always remaining in the village while the other leaves the village on public duty, when required.

Sthala–gauḍa official associated with the administration of *sthala*.

Sthala in'am in the district of North Arcot it is synonymous with a *pallekattu in'am*. In Trichinopoly and some other southern districts a certain proportion of the cultivated lands of a village was set apart as *sthala in'am* for the villagers, who appropriated to it various purposes common to the village.

Sthala–kkāval (Tamil), village watch.

Sthala-karnam an accountant associated with the administration of *sthala*.

Sthala–vṛitti free land for the maintenance of services in the *sthala* shrine to which the gift is made; also *tala–vṛitti;* 'a tenure in which payment of tax was made in kind from the produce'.

Sthalādāyam a term appearing in the epigraphs to denote the customs on goods imported to be sold at one place.

Sthalagaudika the headman of a *sthala* and naturally enjoyed higher status than a *gauḍda* whose functions were confined to the village over which he was appointed.

Sthalam a mound or a raised portion of ground.

Sthalam kaval in'am held by the village *kavalgar* who performs general duties, such as collecting revenue, watching produce, etc.

Sthanikam in'am held by the director of the ceremonies in a pagoda.

Sthanam a dignity; property holding agency.

Sthanapati in'am held by an officer who acts as the general *vakil* or agent of a pagoda.

Sthulwār the watchman of the village and of the crops; same as *taliary* or *tōṭi*.

Strīdhana though it simply means dowry, it attains importance in the agrarian system because one inscription shows that the land owners were debarred from giving as *strīdhana* lands in the village to an outsider.

Stullawari chittah a sort of census register giving the details of the economic condition of each *rayat* and the details of his holdings.

Suba, subah (A.) a province.

Sūbadār, sūbedār, Subedar (p.) the viceroy or governor of a province. In 18th century this office had become hereditary. The title also used to designate a military officer.

The term used in Coorg for the incharge of each taluk (the Coorg province consisted of six taluks).

Sudantram entitlement of the slaves to a share in the produce of every crop, which they receive at various rates and in various modes; also called *calvásám*.

Suddha-bhógyam the word *suddha* means clear, entire, prefixed to *bhógyam*, 'that which is enjoyed', the proper term for this species of mortgage bond, indicates that the entire enjoyment of the land and that the whole produce of it is given up for the consideration stated–in one of such deeds no time for redemption is fixed and it may, therefore, take place whenever the mortgager can repay the sum advanced, saying that according to one of the provisions of deed, it must be at a period when there is no crop upon the ground. Such a mortgage cannot be foreclosed.

Suddha-craya-patram final deed of sale.

Suddha-crayam the deed of final sale.

Suddha-vicraya-chittu a deed of complete and entire sale.

Suddula in'am granted for singing hymns in praise of the village deity.

Sukhavasi a person who is not bound to any particular spot by possession of house or land, but lives comfortably by trade or industry.

Sultān a kind of well; wells made near the beds of rivers and fed by small channels which led water in to them were called *dorovu* or *sultān*; lands watered by these wells were also treated as if directly watered by the river.

Summádu perquisites in grain.

Suṅkamu a term of broad import, used to denote taxes on garden lands, duties on exports and imports, custom duties collected on articles of merchandise brought to and taken from the *pēṭas* or market towns and places, and excise duties.

Suṅkapannāyadadhiṣ ṭhāyaka (Kannada–Sanskrit), superintendent of income from tolls; also *suṅka-vĕrgaḍĕ* in Kannaḍa.

Sunijaish see *samjhaish* above.

Sunkarulu the tax-farmers who gathered revenues which were collectively termed *sunkam*.

Surchasum head duffedar, head peon.

Suvarṇ–ādāya, Svarṇ–ādāya taxes payable in cash; 'revenue in gold; land revenue paid in cash.

Suvarṇ–āya land revenue paid in cash; same as *suvarṇ–ādāya* above.

Suvarṇa–daṇḍa tax on goldsmiths.

Svāmi–bhoga the land–lord's share; 'the master's share'.

Svāmi–vāram land–lord's share; also *melvāram* in Tamil.

Svāmin a proprietor, owner.

Svāmya right to property; proprietarship; ownership. Same as *manneya–svāmya* i.e. tenure held by a *manneya*.

Svāmyam ownership, right to property.

Svadśin two main classes of traders–*para deśin* and *nānādeśin*.

Svarṇakṣma lit. earth of gold; a term used to denote a gift.

Svarṇa–vari, śoṇa–vari 'tax payable in gold'; also, see *suvarṇa–daṇḍa*–profession–tax payable by goldsmiths; also *pŏn–vari* in Tamil.

Svarūpa an estate of the Nambūdris, royal personages, etc. of Malai–nāḍu.

Swāmibhōgam, Swāmi–bhōgam owner's share, or *mālikāna,* a fee paid by *payirkārar* to *kāṇiyāṭchikārar,* master enjoyment; however, it varied from a fair proportion of the output to a mere fistful of paddy.

Swāstiyam, Swāstyam term for ownership right among Brahmans; same as *manyam.*

Swámi–sudantram the landlord's right.

Swástyacraya–patram a deed of sale of landed property; *swa'astíti swástyam,* that which is his own is called *swastyam;* according to this derivation this Sanskrit word would mean property in general and be synonimous with *swatwam*; the word *kshétram* is however, understood, and it signifies, therefore, landed property. It is used only by Brahmans and is equivalent to *káníyátchicániyátchi* or *mirási.*

Swamy bhogium chitta a deed of land tenure granting *swamy bhogium* land to another for a specified period; the conditions were that (i) the grantee was to pay in kind a specified amount of paddy in a particular month (ii) the full amount of *jammmabandy kists* and take receipt in the name of the original assignee,(iii) to give a specified amount of jingely seed if grown; and (iv) other things to be furnished according to the custom.

Swatantra diṭṭam (swatantra dittam) a scheme of shares of village output appertaining to different individuals or groups; scheme of privileges and freedoms through which a *kāṇiyāṭchikārar* was bound to the rest of the village; it also consisted of shares belonging to village servants and functionaries, and a token share for the *kāṇiyāṭchikārar,* usually averaged around 13.

Swatantram, sotunterum, svatantra emoluments; a customary fee; a share; literally hereditary right, is the general name for the village privileges whether received by (i) the land owners, (ii) the village officers, or (iii) the husbandman. Whoever received it, possessed it in a *mirāsī* or *káni–átachí* tenure. (i) The land owners enjoyed village *maniums* which were lands free of rent, and *coopatum,* fees in kind. (ii) The village officers received *maniums,* and *sūdū, salegay, arg, pitchay, marah,* the fees in kind. (iii) The inhabitants, whether they were the cultivating *mirāsīdārs* or the labourers received fees in kind called *cullavausum* or *tauril,* and *poorakullum.* They were the wages of husbandary, and given to those who actually were engaged in it.

There however, were some exceptions. In some villages there was a *reddy manium* enjoyed by the head *mirāsīdār* who conducted the general affairs of the village at the collector's *kach'hari*, and in the taluk with the *tehsildar*. This existed only in a few villages in the *Jaghire*, and was evidently not the custom of the country as the name would denote. It may rather be considered a private arrangement of the *mirāsīdārs*, than a *manium* strictly separate from the village *manium*. Secondly, in some villages, there was a *marah* received by the *mirāsīdars*. There was no difference between this and their *coopatum*, and was nothing more or less than an excess of *coopatum*. With regard to exceptions of village officers' fees, it must be observed that in a few villages the *karnams* did not receive *salegay*, but in lieu of it that which was called *ary*. The difference, however, existed only in name, for they were essentially the same.

The *swatantram* enjoyed by the village officers were very different in one village from another. In every village there was a *manium* and fees in kind allotted for–the *karnam*, the *taliary*, the astronomer, the carpenter, the potmaker, the blacksmith, the *puneseven* or village servant, the *vuttyan* or measuring man, and the barber.

In some villages the servants who enjoyed the *maniums* and fees were–the *tuttan* goldsmith and shroff, the washerman, the *cumboocutty* the waterer of the fields, the cowkeeper, the temple officers and servants, the snake catcher, the schoolmaster (in *agraharums* and Jain villages only), the *vulloovun* or tailor the water pandal man, the *topookauren* who watches and waters the topes, the chuckler, the *puttikauren* who watches the crops and the water woman.

The three officers were commonly found with *mirāsī* but the others only enjoyed in a few villages, and generally only *pitchay* without *manium*.

Swayampakam in'am granted for the service of cooking in a pagoda.

T

Ta'tifawali in'am held by dancing girls.

Ta-ahhud, toorhadi an agreement, contract. A species of mortgage in Kanara which does not give the mortagagee any right of interference in the management of the estate; but entitles him to a quantity of rice equal to the interest due on his loan.

Tāla a palmyra palm; in Tamil-a dish; treasury.

Tāla-patra lit. palmyra-leaf'; an order from the king or person in authority; also see Tamil *olai*.

Tāmra-śāsanas charters recording revenue-free gifts of land.

Tāṉ-vēṇṭu-kōvinukku 'to the king'; this expression in the inscriptions was used in respect of imposition of fines on individuals and also indicates that fines, etc. on individuals were also payable to the king.

Tāniya-varakkam, dhānya-varga (Sanskrit), class of taxes payable in grains or kind.

Tāqavi, Taccavi, tackavi, takavi advance of money to tenants for cultivation when necessary means are wanting; money advanced to a cultivator for the purchase of seed.

Tār a silver coin, equal to 1/6 of a gold *fanam*.

Tārṟukkōl the whip in the hands of the peasant while ploughing the field.

Taaddi trouble, disturbance, affair, extortion, wrong, violence.

Taajkaurs collectors of customs duties.

Tabela in'am granted for superintending the stables of a *zamindar*.

Tacc-ācāriya-kkāṇi (Tamil), the right of officiating as the chief carpenter, as also the stone-mason of a temple; the land set apart for the enjoyment of the holder of that office.

Tacc-ācāriyam (Tamil) chief of the carpenters; status of the master carpenter.

Taccācārīyakkāṇi land set apart exclusively for the architects who were to look after the repairs in the temple.

Tachchan carpenter; their number could vary from village to village and from time to time; essential component of most villages; were remunerated either in the shape of a *mānyam* land or fixed share of the village output or in some cases both.

Taḍāga tanks.

Tael a chinese coin in circulation in South India made of both gold and silver; a gold *tael* was roughly equal to £3.5s. 10d. and silver one 6s. 7d.

Tafsil detail, particulars, analysis.

Taherior writing; fee for writing.

Tahwildar treasurer; part of *sa'ir* collection machinery.

Taiyalkaran in'ams the same as *darzi in'am*.

Takesim extra exactions.

Takhfif abatement.

Takid a written order by authority, a precept.

Takkā the term used in Coorg for the leading men in each *nād* (there being two or three in each *nād*) representing the old resident families; they also held certain lands by virtue of their headship.

Takya, takia in'am for the support of a *fakir*, whose duty was to supply Muhammadan pilgrims with water and shelter. *Takya*–also a residence of a *fakir*.

Taḻai–kkāṇam (Tamil), fee or tax on the *taḻai* or foot–binding used by toddy–trappers.

Taḻarndu impoverished.

Taḻavārikā (Kannaḍa), the village watchman's quit–rent.

Taḷavṛtitti a tenure denoting land endowed to the temples.

Taḷmāri–kār stubble or second crop.

Tala–bhoga 'land granted for the maintenance of a temple at the time its consecration'; 'the enjoyment of sites of land'.

Tala–dvṛitti same as *sthala–vṛitti.*

Tala–vāṭaka, tala–pāṭaka, tala–vṛtti same as *tala–bhoga.*

Tala–vāṭaka–vāstunā saha kṣetram a piece of land together with suburbs, gardens and homestead land granted for the maintenance of a temple at the time of its consecration.

Talāri, talaiyāri Talaiyari, talliari, tallari, (Tam), the village policeman; his duty was to protect the life and property of the villagers; had to watch the movements of vagabonds; wandering bands of players, dancers, etc., was held responsible for any property that might be stolen from the villagers and he had to make good all losses sustained by them if he failed to catch the thieves and regain the stolen goods; (Telugu–Kannaḍa), a village a watchman; a watchmen; *talāri* in kannaḍa; the village peon; their number would vary from village to village and from time to time; they were an essential components of most villages; they either got *mānyam* land or fixed share of the village output or in some cases both for their maintenance; the village watchman, guard, messenger etc.. Also called *totie.*

Talāri–pannu tribute collected from the public for the maintenance of a *talāri* or watchman.

Talārika the ofice of the *Talārī.*

Talāṭi a stipendiar, not hereditary, village accountant in the Kannaḍa and Marāṭhi speaking area.

Talab–diwani tenure this term is applied to a class of villages in the Vizagapatam district granted on quit–rent for general service to the *zamindar.*

Talai ahappaḍi prevailing rate.

Talai taram a term used to denote supreme or first grade of land.

Talai variśai highest grade or rate.

Talaivayccēri the *cēri* or quarter, or street near the entrance to the village.

Talaiyārikkam, Talaiyārikkam (Tamil) one of the additional taxes charged over and above the usual land revenue for the support of and payment to village officers; tax for the maintenance of the village oficers; tax for the maintenacne of the vilage watchmen.

Talaiyari in'am granted for the service of village watchman.

Taliccēru the 'temple quarter', generally inhabited by dancing girls.

Taliqa when the *yaddasht* was completed, it was abridged property and was signed and sealed by the *waq–ia navis* and the *risaldar* and later by the *mir arz* and the *darōgha*; the abridgement thus completed was called *Taliqa* which was signed and sealed by the Minister of State. (*Ain–i–Akbari*, Blochman p.269).

Tallabund account showing the receipts and disbursements.

Tallagi low marshy tract.

Talluqa belonging to; pertaining to.

Taluk, talook, taluq (A) an administrative subdivision of a district comprising 3 to 5 *firkas;* usually 8 to 10 *taluks* in a district.

Taluqḍaar holder of a *taluq.*

Tamalapakula in'am granted for supplying betel-leaf to the *zamindar.*

Tamarind a large evergreen tree, the heart wood of which is very durable and used for the mortars oil mills, shafts, axles etc. The fruit is sour and laxative and is regarded as a necessary article of food.

Tambala tanure in'am granted for the service of providing leaves, flowers, etc., for the ceremonies in honour of the village goddess.

Tamidelu natcheny; cynosurus coracanus.

Taṇiyūr a term used in the epigraphs to denote special kind of village; in the inscriptions a large number of village in the Tamil areas have been mentioned by the name *taṇiyūr;* the exact meaning of the term is hard to find. T.V. Mahalingam says, "it seems to have been an independent unit for political. purposes, and its status must have been at least equal to that of any large subdivision in the Empire.... The *taṇiyūr* may had a local treasury and may be compared to a modern *kaspā.*"

Taṇḍam fine, penalty or punishment; a punitive tax; a fine or tax payable as penalty.

Taṇḍu palanquin.

Taṇṇīr-kkāṇam (Tamil) water cess.

Taṇṭak-kuṟṟam a term used to denote a fine levied on those who had committed a crime.

Taṇṭam, taṇṭam-kāṇam a term used to denote judicial fines. As per the inscriptions it could be levied at atleast three different places viz. (i) at the *rājadhvāram* i.e. the king's court, (ii) at the *dhanmāśana* i.e. a court of justice, and (iii) at the revenue department on account of tax/revenue default. It could be imposed on different communities/ *jātis* like, brahmanas, Siva-brahmanas, *kaṇakkar, vyuāpāris, vellalar* or any other community. The same community was bound to pay this fine on which it was imposed.

The imposition of *tantam* was, by and large, imposed by the king alone as there are a very few instances of its imposition by the *dhaṇmāsana.* Moreover, this type of fine seems to have been imposed more in cases of the violation of an agreement rather than on the tax defaulters. In the event of a defaulter, as one can gather from several epigraphs, deviating from the same agreement, for which he had been fined once, he was again fined in terms of gold, and it was generally payable to the king. The inscriptions do not show much difference between this and another term, *maṉṟupāṭu.* Sometimes it has also been connected with the Sanskrit term *daṇḍa;* but it cannot be interpreted in the wider sense of *daṇḍa.* The term *tantam* was perhaps used in the restricted sense of 'fine'.

Taṇṭuvāṇ, taṇṭaluṭaiyāṇ a local officer who collected the revenue dues; 'one who is authorised to collect'; literally *taṇtu* means 'to collect'.

Taṇṭanāyakap-pēṟu a term used to denote the payment demanded for the army chief.

Taṅka a term used in the epigraphs to denote a private mint; according to one epigraph the provincial governors had the power to grant to private individuals the right of issuing coins and owning *taṅka.*

Tana grass.

Tanaikkan mānyam the *mānyam* granted to choultry sweeper.

Tandal collection; demand.

Tandal in'am held by a servant employed under the *monigar* of a village in collecting government revenue.

Tangal tank.

Tankhah, tankhwa (p.) salary, wages.

Tannir pandal in'am *in 'am* for the service of maintaining a water pandal where water and buttermilk were distributed to travellers during the hot season.

Tantravāya weaver.

Tantrimār members of the army crops; a class of persons who perform worship in temples; a priest; an officer or group of officers that cooperated with the assembly in its work; it also means a soldier; may refer to certain classes of people from whom men for the military were recruited; it is difficult to say if the *tantrimār* of the Vijayanagar days had anything to do with the military groups; *tantra* also means government in which case we may take the term *tantrimār* to refer to the officers of government in the local areas who controlled the working of the village assemblies and other local organisations, as such the term indicates fully the functions they discharged; the *tantrimār* made gift of land to the temple; made grant of a few taxes on lands for worship and repairs to the temple; the *tantrimār*, thus, appear to have been government officers in the local area.

One record has given the rate of taxes to be levied from, among others, the *tantimār*.

It says that on wet land on which dry crops were cultivated and dry land on which wet crops were raised, including the cultivation of plantains and sugarcane, the assessment was one *kalam* of paddy on each mā.

One inscription also gives the rate of property tax levied on the house of a *tantrimār*, the rate mentioned is 1½ paṇams. Moreover, since the inscriptions which refer to the *tantrimār*, as acting with the village asssembly in its work are largelly to be found in the Tamil areas, it is not possible to equate them with the Malabar *tantris* (a class of temple priests).

Tantrin this word was used in more than one senses, e.g. a soldier; a trooper; a leader of the army; a temple priest; a weaver.

Taqavi, takavi, tuccavee, etc. (Arabic) an advance or loan made to agriculturists to make improvements, buy seed, cattle, etc; The grant of this advance was regulated by the British government by Act XIX of 1883 and Act XII of 1884.

Tar one of the silver coins in circulation in south India; according to *'Abdu-r Razzāk* it was 1/6 of a *fanam*.

Taṟi-kkaḍamai one of taxes which according to the epigraphss accrued from the villages.

Taṟi-ppuḍavai (Tamil), tax on looms payable in the shape of cloth.

Taṟip-puṭavai lit. a cloth woven in a loom'; tax assessment on weavers; this assessment was on individual weavers.

Taṟi-taraku, taṟi-akkam, taṟri-iṟaik-kācu, taraku, taṟiyṟai different terms used to denote a tax on loom. *Acca-taṟi* and *tūcakat-tari* were also taxes on looms, but the significance of the words *acca* and *tūcka* are not clear. They perhaps refer to two kinds of looms used by the weavers. It may also be pointed out that the looms owned by different castes were taxed separately. For example, *cālikar-acca-taṟi and cālikai- taṟi* were levied on *cāliya* weavers; and *paṟait-taṟi* and *paṟaiyar-taṟip-puṭavai* were levied on looms possessed by *paṟaiyar* weavers. *Taṟi-iṟai,* in Tamil and *maggadere* in kanarese refers to a tax levied on loom used by a weaver.

Taṟa the term used in Malabār for a Nāyar's settlement or location; in the absence of large villages, the small hamlets and family settlements were grouped in to *tara*.

Tara street or hamlet (south Kānara); comparable to Tamil *teru* and Telugu *'teruvu'*.

Tarafdar an officer of government in charge of a *taraf*, collecting the revenue and exercising chief revenue and police authority in the area of his posting; holder of a *taraf* or portion of village lands.

Taraku, taraku-kūli, taragu brokerage a professional tax imposed on the brokers; levy charged on the merchandise brought in to a localtiy from outside. The term *taraku* has generally been taken as a brokerage. The context in which it has been used in the epigraphs, it seems to be a local cess, probably a variant of *cuṅkam*. An epigraph refers to *taraku* imposed on betel levies brought in to the locality.

Taram, terrim class, especially applied in south India to designate the different classes of villạge lands, and the heads under which they are arranged in the village accounts; classification to which a classified land belonged; assessment-classifications; however, it was fixed only when lands were reclaimed and brought under cultivation.

In the revenue administration introduced by the British administration the *taram* was the assessment-classification which grouped together lands bearing the same assessement rate though the lands might bear different classes and sorts. This was possible because the assessment rates were expressed in terms of a money rate based on the commuted value of grain, where as during the earlier periods this was not possible as the demand was both in terms of grain and cash and the rates under both had varied. The currency also had varying exchange value and even intrinsic value. In case a particular holder owned several parcels of land bearing varied assessment rates, they were reduced to a standard measurement. However, *taram* was certainly 'assessment-classification' and not a classification based on 'productivity'. There are number of instances noticed in the inscriptions where the *taram* has been arbitrarily adopted, pegged or reduced to limit the assessment on land. In fact in many an instance the quantum of demand had been fixed first, and then the *taram* worked out on that basis. In some instances the classification was argued on the basis of assessment and that the *taram* classifications would not *ipso facto* denote the productivity of land or other objective norms. Moreover, the assessment-classification was liable to revision, and at the time of such revision some lands were deliberately pegged at the *taram* rates assigned to them originally at the time of the grant to a temple or sale to a benefactor; revenue; each field in a village is classified for revenue purposes according to the colour, texture and fertility of the soil, facilities for irrigation, and distance from villages-site. The fields so classified fall in to a series of classes, or *tarams*, each class being assessed at an appropriate money rate; there used to be separate series for 'wet' and 'dry' lands; a scale of assessment rates under the Madras system; a table of rates pertaining to different *classes* and *sorts* of soil; sort, kind, rate classes or grades (of land).

Taram peṟṟa nilam assessment-classification.

Taramdar, terrimadar the assessor of land.

Taramidu lands classified on the basis of assessment.

Taramili a term used to denote unclassified land; non-classified lands; the tank water-spread and other areas not cultivable were also *taramili* lands and had no assessment classification.

Taramiṭṭa assessment-classification.

Tarapadi in'am *in'ams* granted at

original formation of a village for village purposes, comprising *grama manyams* the *in'ams* enjoyed by the village revenue, police, and private servants, and the village pagodas. The term *tarapadi in'am* is used in contradistinction to a *sanad in'am*, or an *in'am* held under a grant.

Tarappadi kanakku an account of the lands according to fertility grades.

Tarappaḍi mānyam (tarrabuddy manniam) ancient grants of *mānyam*.

Tarappottagam land register which showed such of those lands classified on the basis of the assessment rate charged for it.

Tarav–iḍu–nĕl (Tamil), paddy given in lieu of wages.

Tarawad, Taravād the term used in Malabār for the family groups or 'house–commisssion' managed by elders (*kāranavar*); the elders of the family or unit group of *taṛa* were called *taravād* and managed the affairs, and the managing elders were called *kāramavar;* a joint family unit.

Tarbands a grove or plantation of palmyra trees.

Tare a silver coin equal to 1/16 of a *fanam*.

Tarf side; quarter; district.

Tarfdar ruler of a district; one who has the superintendence of a small district.

Tari a term used for rice land.

Tari–cadamei lit. 'a weaver's reed', but used for the whole loom, and 'tax, due, fee'; it is paid in money and carried to the account of this fund; dues from looms.

Tari–iṛai a professional tax charged from the weavers.

Taṛip–puṭavai a tax levied on loom. However, it seems to have been collected in the form of cloth or a unit of *puṭavai* manufactured in a loom (*putavai*= a long cloth).

Tariśana–kāṇikkai (Tamil), presents offered to a king or a chief when one meets him; *nazrāna*.

Tarisee, tarisu waste lands; *banjar*; entirely barren and uncultivable (land); subdivided in to the *anadi carumboo*, or immemorial waste, and the *sheycal carumboo*, or waste land that has at some time been cultivated; each of these consists chiefly of tracts of common, on which the *mirásidars* graze the cattle employed by them in agriculture, or of jungle, in which they cut the firewood used by them for fuel, and both are held free from tax. Should the *mirásidars,* however, possess the means, they are vested with ample right to extend their cultivation to these lands, though it is understood that the consent of government is necessary before they can break up the *anadi carumboo,* or land that has never been under the plough; but the moment any part of either the *sheycal* or *anadi carumboo* is reclaimed, the nature of land is changed, and it ceases to be *tarisee* or waste, and no sooner it is converted in to cultivated land than it is transferred, as such, in the village accounts, to the head of *waraput* or *teerwaput,* and in common with all land of that description becomes, for the plain reason already given, liable to tax.

Tarōpādi productivity classification (of lands); assessment classification.

Tasadduq a fixed sum paid by government to a pagoda, a mosque or the officers in an establishment, as consolidated allowance in lieu of assumed land.

Tashkhis–i–jama the revenue assessment.

Taṭṭār goldsmith.

Taṭṭār–pāṭṭām, taṭṭāra-ppāṭṭam Tamil, tax on goldsmiths; Professions of various kinds were taxed and they yielded a good amount of revenue.

Taṭṭārpāṭṭam a type of professional tax imposed on the goldsmiths.

Tatan in'am held for the service of singing and beating a drum during matrimonial or funeral ceremonies in a village.

Tatchan in'am, tachchan in'am granted for the service of village carpented. Same as *badai in'am.*

Tatimma the remainder; the rest.

Tatoodarry a land tenure in the Northern Circars at a low unalterable rent.

Tattān goldsmith.

Taurh a silver coin of south India; it was 1/15 of a *fanam.*

Tavana-crayam *tavanei* signifies a term', and *tavana-craya-patram* is a deed by which land is transferred, liable to redemption within a fixed term, but becoming the absolute property of the transferree if not so redeemed; the word is Tamil as are many of those relative to the tenure of land used in similar deeds though written in Telugu.

Tavazhi branch of household.

Tayinati attendance; service; waiting.

Tēnpayilpodumbu groves where bees build honey-combs; the interpretation given by some epigraphists 'hollows where honey is stored' seems to be too literal to convey a definite idea.

Tēvai, tevai –a levy; a sort of payment collected as service charge; in some instances the village authorities on the basis of a royal order instructed that the *tēvai* should be in the form of a service for which a person may be deputed.

Tēvar-kaṭamai dues payable to the king.

Teddul punjah the highest land in the country, and dependent entirely on the falling rains, *Teddul punjah teerwa,* the rate or rent payable for such lands.

Tee iron.

Teeps billls of exchange.

Teerva jasti additional tax on dry and garden land converted in to wet.

Teerwa, teervah land tax according to the survey assessment; money assessment.

Teerwaput, Teervaput, teervapattu lands one of two classifications of the non-*mānyam* or *circar* lands during the Company's rule, and these were the lands wherein *mēlwaram* was in cash terms and was a predetermined sum; usually *teervaput* lands where *punjei* lands; lands the public revenue from which has not been alienated, but is paid to the state.

Tehsildars, tahsildar (H.) a native revenue official, in Madras presidency, the chief administrative officer of a *taluk;* revenue officer in charge of a *taluk.*

Tejo-mānya, teja-mānyam, tejaḥ-svāmyan the ownership of landed property with the *aṣta-bhoga* or eight kinds of enjoyment.

Tenai, thenai, thinai *setaria italica.*

Teppa in'am granted for supplying rafts to cross a river.

Terri the elevated lands of the village; mounds or mounds with trees used as a boundary of a village; ant-hills and other mounds; some epigraphists have translated it as 'hedges', and as 'big trees making the boundaries'; though this word is not found in the dictionaries, it is still in use in the Ramnad district in the sense 'mounds or elevated lands particularly in the midst of water.'.

Teruvelai in'am granted for the service of repairing and decorating a car belonging to a pagoda.

Teśa-kālam locality and time;

Teśa-kuḍimai tenancy under the

control of a temple

Teśa–vāḻi officer in charge of a village or district.

Tevadiyal in'am for the service of a dancing girl in a pagoda; the same as *dasi in'am*.

Thachchan mānyam the *mānyam* granted to the carpenter.

Thada an inflamed condition of the throat in cattle.

Thalkurniyan divisional accountants, *patwaris, karnams*, etc.

Thalpuchi (Tamil), *thal* stalk, *puchi* insect.

Thana, Thāna name of a geographical unit. A watch house; a police station; garrison in a fort; small fortified check–points to protect more settled areas against incursions from predatory tribal peoples.

Thanedar, Thanadar commander of one or more military check–points (*thanas*). Commander of a small for, a man who has the management of a district; an officer incharge of a *thana*; formerly an officer under *faujdar* employed with a small irregular force in protecting the area and enforcing payment of the revenue; a petty police officer subordinate to a *darogha*.

Tharāo 'to fix', an assessment introduced in to Kānara in 1819; it was called *sarásari* or average, because the assessment was based upon the average; collections of the years since British occupation.

Tharappadi manyakkanakku an account of *mānyams* granted before the Muslim rule

Tharavadu matrilineal household.

Thattans, thattars, tattans the goldsmith division of the *kammalam* or artisan caste.

Thattapair, tuttapire *cowgram; vigna unguiculata.*

Thellachida (Telugu), *thella* white, *chidda* pest.

Thiyyas, tiyyas the *toddy* drawing caste of the southern portion of the Malabar Coast, corresponding to *Bhillavas* further north, and to *shanars* in the south–east.

Thottakkal kanakku an account of the orchards.

Thovarai, tovaray, tovary redgram; (*cajanus cajan*).

Thravād tarwād the undivided family of the Nayars. As inheritance follows the female line, while a man has right to maintenance during his life from the property of his *tharvād*, he transmits no right to his children.

Thugai jabida a cash flow account.

Thukkiri, talayari mānyam the *mānyam* granted to *talayari*.

Tiguḷa–daṇḍa, āndhra–daṇḍa name of a tax; measuring rod, in Tamil and Andhra areas respectively.

Tila sesame.

Tilapeshakas oil pressers.

Tiṇai Italian millet.

Tiṇaik–kaṇakku an accountant incharge of land revenue.

Tippōkkuc–cempon a term used in the epigraphs to denote that a particular coin was corresponding or agreeing with coin (that had been tested by fire).

Tírvei each field.

Tiṛai a term used for tribute to be paid periodically by the conquered territories to the reigning king. This tribute could be in cash or in kind, even in the form of elephants.

Tirappu (the lands which were) resumed.

Tirast in'am held by a description of armed peons maintained by the hill *zamindars* of the Vizagapatam district for preserving the peace of the country.

Tirigai–āyam tax payable by the potter for his trade; *tirigai* being a potter's wheel.

Tiru–muga–kkāṇam (Tamil) expenses as wages, etc., paid to the person who brought the royal order to the village.

Tiru–mugam (Tamil), royal order.

Tirukkōyiluṭaiyāṇ vītu houses of temple managers.

Tirumāñjanakkuḷam scared bathing ponds.

Tirumal mandaghappadi in'am granted for the celebration of feast in a *mantapam* during the periodical festivals of a pagoda.

Tirumalai in'am granted for the service of supplying garlands of flowers in a pagoda.

Tirumēnikaval a general watchman of the temple; also *meykāval;* remunerated in the form of land grants or allowed a particular share in the income of the temple.

Tirumeni-kāval watchmen in a temple.

Tirumukam, Tirumugam royal order. Royal writ.

Tirumukat–tēvai a term used to denote payment collected as service charge for delivering the *tirumugam* i.e. royal order, of the king's government.

Tirumuṇpu–kāḷchikkum–niṇaipiṭṭu–taṇṭum–kācu a term used for payment demanded for getting an audience either with the king or a high level officer.

Tirumuṟṟam sacred courts.

Tirup–paṭṭam head ornament (of the deity).

Tirupani velai in'am granted for the service of keeping a pagoda in repair.

Tiruppudiyīḍu a tax in the form of 'holy first fruits' levied on people for the upkeep of temples.

Tiruvācalil–pōnta–kuṭimai a term connected with the revenue current during the Chola period.

Tiruvāykēḷvis same as *rāyasam.*

Tiruvadirai in'am granted for the service of offering an oblation in a pagoda on the day called *tiruvadirai.*

Tiruvanendal kattalai in'am granted for the service of performing the morning oblation in a pagoda.

Tiruvidaiyāṭṭam, Tiruvdidaiyāṭṭam (Tamil), a gift; a term occurring frequently in the inscriptions to denote land grants made to the temples.

Tiruviḷakkukudi servants incharge of lighting in the temples; they were remunerated in the form of land grants or a share in the income of the temples.

Tirwā rate of assessment; *tirwā–kamī,* reduction of assessment.

Tiryu–nāma–kkāṇi, tiru–nāmattu–kkāṇi (Tamil), land or village, generally revenue–free endowed to a *Śiva* temple; lit. 'the hereditary right of enjoyment in the sacred name'.

Tiṭṭum deficit, a term used in epigraphs to denote deficit in the collection of land dues.

Tiyar Islander; the term used in Malabār for an immigrant caste from south (traditional from Sri Lanka) who introduced to cocoa–nut tree.

Tōdai the rope that connects the handle with the yoke and the neck of the bull.

Tōṭṭa nilam a term used to denote garden land, on this category of land all fruit bearing trees, betel, vegetables etc. were cultivated.

Tōṭṭapuṛavu a term used in the epigraphs to denote a tax from garden lands.

Tōṭṭiyams one of the important group of people who colonised the south; originally shepherds and also became petty palegars in the south; epigraphs reveal that they were generally *vaisnavas* but their deities were Jakkanna and Bommakka who committed *sahagamana*; they had their own organisation; also called *kambaḷattārs.*

Tótam gardens.

Tótta–chittu a writing for the planting of a garden; though this type of deed conveys a permanent right but the right was limited by many circumstances viz. The grantee may build on the ground, and may transfer it by sale, gift etc., but the *mirásidar* retains his full share of *mirási* on the soil; if cultivated with field produce, paddy, dry grain etc. he may demand to be employed as the cultivator, and if be abandoned or fall in to decay, his entire proprietary right revives. These rights were frequently reserved in the deed itself, and it was safer to do so, but they were actually implied by the name.

Toḍā a tribe on the Nilgiri plateau; *Toḍās* lived by the produce of herds of buffaloes and were graziers only. They lived and some of them still live, in curious enclosed, domed huts, without doors or windows, and furnished with a small aperture in to which they creep at night. A group of such huts is called a *'mand'*.

Toḍā-girās, torā-girās this term has got nothing to do with *toḍā;* it was a customary payment to secure lands against the incursions of free booters (dispossessed chiefs and ruined families of *girāsiyas*, the old Rajput chiefs) who harassed the country; later it became a political allowance paid to some families as by prescriptive right; also called *'wol'*.

Toddy extracted from coconut palms, date palms, and palmyras. It is a sweet juice which ferments immediately unless fermentation is prevented with a view to conversion in to *jaggery* and sugar. It is usually drunk the day after it is gathered, being then a somewhat stupefying intoxicant. The next day it becomes vinegar, and then speedily decomposes.

Tola the weigtht of a rupee, .4114 oz.

Tolā a family; a crowd.

Toli the eighth of piece.

Tolkollans leather workers and dyers of the Malabar coast.

Tondaipuchi lit. 'throat insect', the paddy stem borer, *schoenobius bifunctifer*, a serious paddy pest.

Tondei–mandalam a tract in north Madras covering more than 18,000 square miles, anciently so called; the site of a great colonizing expedition, some held the opinion that the *vellālars* had colonized the whole presumably adopting everywhere the same principle of allotting and sharing the land.

Tondi–wáram, tonde warum lit., belly share. Share of the tenantry in the division of the crop.

Toni–kkaḍamai (Tamil) tax on boats.

Toomu a drain, water course, outlet; called *mercall* in Tamil being a variable measure equal to about 3 3/4 seers; a measure of land being 1/16 one anna less than acre.

Toondoowarum share of the peasantry in the division of the crop.

Tope garden land; the term means a grove of trees, properly of trees that bear fruit, as mango, tamarind. coconut etc. lands occupied by such trees and held free of assessment were treated as *in'ams*.

Tope in'am granted for the service of preserving a tope planted by a *zamindar*.

Topu gorves, orchards and plantations.

Topukaran in'am granted for the service of maintaining flower gardens and supplying flowers to temples.

Torai (Tamil), a standard linear measure of four fingers' breadth.

Toraṇa–kkāṇikkai presents or tax on gates for decorating the village with arches.

Toranam katti in'am held for preparing festoons of leaves and tying them across the street during pagoda procession.

Toṭṭa–ppuravu (Tamil), tax on garden land.

Toṭtam garden cultivation.

Toṭṭi cistern.

Totākāl garden land; applied to fields, whose original character, soil, etc., had been changed by long cultivation and care; came under the category of exceptional soils.

Totakal, tottakal, totacul garden produce; garden land cultivation.

Toti, totie, totier a caste of Telugu cultivators, village policeman, also guarded the crops and assisted in measuring them, the village watchman, messenger, etc.

Toti in'am granted for the service of village *toti*, a man of low caste who waits upon the village officers, generally assists in measuring land, carries letters to the *tahsildar*, acts as a guide to officers travelling on public duty.

Tottam, tottakal manually irrigated garden lands.

Tṛrparula salt officials; also called *kolakāndru*.

Tri–bhoga, Tri–bhōga beneficial grants made to institutions and individuals together–mixed grants; joint tenure enjoyed by a private individual, a god (or gods) and the Brahmans.

Tribhagam in'am *in'am* consisting of one–third share of the government revenue.

Tribhōg–ābhyantara siddhi a tenure enjoyed by a private person, a god or gods, and brahmans.

Trishvekam tenure *in'am* villages, two thirds of the revenue of which was payable to government, the remaining one–third being enjoyed by the *in'amdars*.

Tṛṇa–odaka the grazing tax.

Tṛṇa–yūti–gocara grass fields and pasture lands.

Tsalvadi in'am held by an officer who acts under the orders of the *setti*. His principal duty is to assemble the merchants on public occasions.

Tsakali, Tsavali in'am granted for the service of village washerman; the same as *dhobi in'am*.

Tsalivendra in'am the same as *tannir pandal in'am*.

Tsavadi in'am granted for the support of a building used for the accommodation of travellers. Such a building generally consists of a single hall and is less extensive than a *chattram*.

Tūcakattaṛi a professional tax charged from a kind of weavers.

Tūl length and width; the measurement of a heap of grain with a cord.

Tūm, Túm equal to four *mercáls* of Madras; 20 such *túm* make one *putti;* varied in different areas. A cubic measure in the Telugu areas; it also denotes the unit of land requiring a *tūm* of seed.

Tūmbu (Tamil) a measure of capacity; same as *tūmu*.

Tūmu a grain measure; also *tūmbu*.

Tūndū–teerwa lit. a part rent; varied from less than one per cent to 11 per cent; it was 11 per cent only in one village in Kanjeveram.

Tūndū–warum surplus rent of the *mirāsidars*; clear landlord's rent.

Tuḍava (Tamil), a liquid measure.

Tudumu in'am granted for beating a drum on public occasions, such as publication of a notice, the arrival at the village of high officials, etc.

Tufreek appointment of the assessment levied on a village; an extra assessment imposed upon cultivators holding an undue proportion of revenue–free lands.

Tuhul revenue peon.

Tuias or **tiyar** a class of persons who, according to Barbosa, were the only ones who were allowed to make wine.

Tukkiri in'am granted for service as head watchman of a village.

Tuḷai–pon a term used for the gold, subsequent to its being burnt, cut, melted, cooled, and found current, wanting neither in purity nor in weight.

Tulā (Telugu–Kannada), weight of a rupee, unit of the system of weights; fixed at 180 grains by the British; the weight of one rupee or 30 canteroy fanams; 1/3 of a *navaṭāku*; a measure or weight of gold and silver, being 100 *palas* or about 145 ounces troy. However, it varied a great deal during different periods and localities.

Tulā–bhāra the practice of weighing a king or an exalted person against gold or other precious stones and metals and distributing the same to temples etc., also called *mahādāna, tulāpurusa*.

Tulā–purusa 'weighing oneself against gold and precious stones'; a type of gift recommended for the brahmans.

Tuluvā a country anciently so called–mainly *'payín–ghât'*.

Tulya, Tulyam a true copy; lit. 'equal'; this term is generally found at the beginning or end of many of the inscriptions and it suggests that the engravings on stone and copper of the edict issued by the king were compared carefully with the original document on palm leaves.

Tumgha hereditary *jagir*.

Tuṇḍikerī a variety of cotton.

Tuṇḍu shortfall.

Tuṇḍu wāram, toondoo waurum same as *swāmibhōgam.*

Tundavaram landholder's share of cultivator's crop.

Tung copper.

Turai–miṇṇar–pon name of a coin.

Turavu large wells.

Turcaree pot–herb.

Turk a Musalman.

Tusrufat a term used to denote forcibly possessed.

Tyacut in the Dindigul province, land.

Tyasagari favourable assessment of the privileged castes.

Tycul a description of *jagir* grant to an individual for maintaining a military force, and other particular services, in the Northern Circars.

U

Ubbakavali in'am held for the service of head *kavalgar* or watchman.

Ubhaiyan one of the additional taxes collected over and above the usual land revenue collected for the maintenance of temples and brahmans, etc.

Ubhaya-nānā-deśi entire merchant community, i.e., including both the *svadeśi* and *para-deśi*.

Ubhaya-paliśai this term has been used in various ways, viz. a tax payable in gold; tolls collected on the highways-inward and outward; interest in two ways-in money and in kind; a gift to a temple or monastery.

Ubhayamukhī-dakṣiṇā special kind of religious present or fee; the gift of a cow at the time of giving birth to a calf.

Uḍaiyār (Tamil), lit. a possessor; a king or lord; the chief deity of a temple; owner; chief.

Uḍan-vāram-āt-kūli inclusive of wages, or cooly for labour.

Udarapattu in'am the same as *raktakanikai in'am*.

Uḍaya kuḍigal occupant tenants.

Uddha-grāma the village of which the revenue is fixed in lump sum.

Udghāṭana same as *araghāṭṭa*; however under this name it consisted of drum shaped wheel turning in a vertical plane over water, round which went a pair of endless ropes with *ghaṭa* or earthen pots tied to them at equal distances; the wheel had spokes at one end, and worked like a capstan; also called *ghaṭachakra*.

Udirapaṭṭi, udira-paṭṭi a plot of land given as compensation for some wrong done; in a quarrel, a certain person was punished by mistake and for the wrong punishment meted out to him, his son was given land as *udirappaṭṭi*, lit. bloodshed compensation; blood land; land given to the descendants of persons who fell fighting on king's behalf; see also *rakta-mānya*.

Udraṅga 'the fixed tax'; 'the land tax'; 'the principal tax'; the tax on the permanent tenants.

Udugaralu clothes and specimens of manufactures, presented to a superior.

Ujār depopulated, waste, deserted.

Ul paracoodie, ool paracoodie the fixed and permanent tenant of the *mirasidar* having no property in the soil.

Ul'lit'tár this term is used not for merely those possessing coparcenery rights with the principal, but 'all in any manner concerned or connected with him'; the Sanskrit term *dayāda* properly expresses the meaning of the word 'parcener'.

Uḻ-vari (Tamil), taxes, levied by the local bodies; same as *antar-āyam*; orders issued by the government fixing the amount of such taxes.

Ulai, ulaip-pāṭṭam, kollar-ulai-pāṭṭam different terms used to denote tax on blacksmith. It may be understood that the tax was levied on the furnace, which was the unit of assessment.

Ulakaḷanta it has been explained by some as a title conferred by the Chola kings on to the *sēnāpati* for his part in the revenue survey. But the epigraphs show that it was a part of the name, not a title as many other individuals also bore the name *ulakaḷanta*.

Ulkaḷanta Kuravaṇ Ulakaḷantāṉ was also a name of Lord Vishnu. *Kuravaṇ* i.e., a dwarf and *Ulakaḷantāṉ* is the one who measured the earth. The story of the *vāmanāvatāra* one of the ten *avatāras,* (incarnations) of Lord Vishnu, depicts an episode of humbling the prowess and pride of the Asura king Mahābali by Vishnu in the form of a dwarf brahman, thus indicating the above name. Also see, *ulakaḷanta* above.

Uḻamaiceytal (the service of) cleaning the premises of the temple.

Uḻapparaiyar a term used in the Tamil inscriptions to denote (sometimes) as a labour or slaves attached to the land.

Ularāi (Marāthi), a deed by which land is given at a favourable rent to merchants, etc., who helped the government with money.

Uḻaverudu the ox or bull that ploughs.

Uḻavukāni, uḻavukkāṇi a term used in the inscriptions to denote a lease which was consisted of a permanent lease of an uncultivated waste which the lessee was authorized to reclaim and to settle, to grow crops that suited him, wet or dry including plantain, sugarcane, turmeric, ginger, areca, and cocoanut and to pay the taxes in gold and grain; according to some inscriptions the lessee, holding lands under this tenure, had to pay the rent at an annually progressing rate; it was one of the systems followed by the temple.

Ulgu (Tamil), customs duties; tolls.

Ulku toll levied on the commodities passing through high roads.

Ulkūdī hereditary and permanent tenants or cultivators, who had doubtless aided in the founding of the village, were regarded as privileged and yet as inferiors, not co-sharers; a resident hereditary tenant of the 'landlord' *(mirāsī)* villages; such proprietors, 'to whom lands have descended by inheritance, and who hold them in their own right and transmit them in regular descent to their children, are declared unable to mortgage or sell them, on account of the reversionary right which is said to be vested in the *mirasidars*'.

Ullundu, oolundoo blackgram; *phaseolus mungo.*

Ulmanei inlands; lands within the site of the village.

Uḻugudi makkaḷ, uḻudān kuḍi, kuḍi makan, uḻudārkku Uḻukudigaḷ, uḻukuḍi, oolkoody, oolcooddy different terms denoting the cultivatiang tenants or actual cultivators or tenant–at–will; cultivating tenants or labourers; resident *payirkārar.*

Uḻukuṭikal a levy for desilting of the village irrigation tank of the cultivators.

Ulupha the term is an Arbic and signifies simply 'provisions', in Telugu means various articles of consumption, the produce of the area concerned.

Uḷvari mutation.

Umanar a group of persons specialized in salt manufacture and trade.

Umbaḷam, umbaḷikkai revenue–free gift of land, land granted revenue–free for the performance of specified service; same as *mānya.*

Umbali (Ṭamil), land granted revenue–free for the performance of specified service; revenue–free gift of land; same as *umbalam, umbaḷikkai;* in Coorg, lightly assessed land held for services mainly by village officers, etc.

Umbaḷige tenure, umbaḷi tenure terms used to denote revenue–free lands granted to persons for public services.

Umliga same as *amaram.*

Umliga tenure the same as *amaram* tenure, land granted for service rendered.

Umul fixed share of revenue.

Uṇbaḷi same as *umbali.*

Uṅdaṛuti a kind of mortgage in Malabār; in which both principal and interest were cleared off by the usufruct–same as *'lekhāmukhī'* mortgage common in some parts of India.

Upanum permanently cultivated land of high assessment; land under permanent cultivation; also *chali.*

Upasti for service, worship.

Upāti (Tamil), dues; anything payable as a debt or obligation.

Upāya minor taxes.

Uppam purthy, oopum purthee the annual cotton–sown generally in conjuction with other grains for the most part with *tenai* in October and November. The produce is gathered in March. It requires nine time ploughing, is not manured and has no contemporary sowing. *Gossypium herbaceum.*

Uppara in'am for the service of tank-diggers; the *in'am* under such name was for the service of executing the ordinary repairs of large government tanks; the same as *wadde-in'am.*

Uppāyam, uppuk–kācu, uppup–piṭi different terms used to denote duty levied on salt. It seems to have been levied like sales tax.

Uppilians salt manufacturers.

Uppu–kkāśu salt–tax.

Uprī, uparī, upri (Marathi), a term for a class of landholders, surviving from the times when a landlord class held the villages; indicating a land holder inferior to the *mirāsidār;* 'additional taxes'; 'unfixed taxes'; 'minor taxes'; 'tax paid by the temporary tenants'.

Ura koḍage a term used in the epigraphs probably denoting lands granted to be enjoyed by the whole body of villagers rent free on condition that they supplied fodder to the army.

Urala from *ūr* village, and *āl* headman.

Uralan manager of shrines/temples.

Urali caste name,.

Urani in'am *in'ams* for maintaining in repairs the village ponds for supplying drinking water.

Urdakarry where the shares remain as at first fixed, the village is called *urdakarry;* where shares are liable to periodical interchange among the partners, *pushoonkarry.*

Urdeekrayum a land tenure in *agraharum* villages; *urdi* would apear to signify permanent or irredeemable and *urdi krayum* an entire permanent sale, which the *agraharum* possessors have alone the power of making of whole villages, or of their shares in them.

Urk–kalancu a term used to denote dues payable by the residents of *Ūr,* it was collected as a tax and most of the instances of this tax, as one gathers from epigraphs, appear in the exemptions granted on lands of *dēvadāna* category.

Uṛmai township obligations.

Urodě, ūroḍeya (Kannada), the village headman.

Urū the term used in Kānara for a hamlet or group of family holdings; also see *grama manyam*.

Urudvé term used in Coorg for village forest–land.

Urzee (p.Arzi) petition; respectful statement or representation.

Uśāvaḍi the subdivision of the district.

Ustad in'am granted for the service of teaching the *zamindar* fencing and gymnastics.

Uṭaiyār 'the possessor'; the term generally used for the king; an appellation usually given to the presiding deity in a temple.

Utsṛṣṭa–paśsavaḥ the consecrated bulls; these bulls attained importance as they were specially reared for impregnation and had certain privileges; they were to be set free even if they trespassed in others' fields; cows let loose in honour of a deity according to the rites and consecrated bulls and the like; they were to be set free and should not be fined even when another's crop is consumed by them,

Uttāra a regular fixed payment.

Uttama–dōni a gift made without expecting any merit for the same; a superior kind of gift.

Uttara–vāda a guarantee; responsibility.

Uvacca–kkāṇi (Tamil) revenue–free land given to the drummers in temple service (*uvaccar*).

Uvaccaṇ –pēr–kaṭami a kind of poll tax paid by the *uvaccar*.

Uvaccaṇs there are different interpretations of this term, e.g. a tax on the temple drummers; they were the temple drummers; they were a low class of Muslims. However, the first two interpretations seem to be more plausible.

Uvaru brackist lands, not fit for cultivation; the term *uvaru* along with *kaḷaṟu* can be used in common parlance to mean barren or brackish land; in the inscriptions *uvaru* was intended to convey the idea of such lands as were also brackish.

Uvātti–vīṭu houses of teachers.

Uyāna gardens.

Uzhavadai uḷkuḍi an *uḷkuḍi* with long standing occupancy rights; *uḷkuḍis* of long standing, say four generations, came to be known as *uzhavadai ulkudi* and he became more privileged due to long period of cultivation; these individuals were virtually the masters of the soil they tended in the sense that the *swāmibhōgam* they paid was but a token amount, sometimes a mere fistful of rice; another term by which they came to be known as *kāṇikuḍi*.

Uzhavadai ulkūḍī an *uḷkuḍi* or *ulkūḍī* with long standing occupancy rights.

Uzhavadai ulkudi payirkarar *payirkarar* of long standing.

Uḷigam and uḷḷāyam two of the various taxes that, as the inscription of the first half of the fifteenth century shows, accrued from the villages.

Ūlkūdi paycarry, oocoodi paycarry where land for a certain period, which varies in differnet palces, has for several generations been farmed by the same family, the tenant is termed an *ūlkūdi paycarry*, and by prescription becomes possessed of an hereditary right to hold his farm in perpetutity, on condition of the regular payment of the *maumool* or customary *warum* or *teerwa*.

Like *mul–guenie* of Canara, the *ūlkūdi paycarry* and his descendents never can be ousted from their farm so long as this is paid, nor can the *warum* or *teerwa* be raised by the *mírásidar*; but they can mortgage, they can never sell these their hereditary privileges.

The Brahman *mírásidars* who do not follow the plough themselves, and many Shudras, leave their lands under the care of the *ūlkūdi paycarry*, who pays about fortyfive per cent of the produce of the land as revenue to the government direct, or through the Brahman; from twenty-two to twenty-five per cent, as landlord's rent to the absentee, and is content with twenty–eight to thirty–three per cent in remuneration for his labour, for seed, for cattle, and for his subsistence.

Ūlūngū, ooloogoo a method of revenue payment–a pre–British system; it prevailed in Tinnevelly and for a long time in Tanjore; a system of computing in money the actual grain–share for the year (valuing it by current prices); the trouble and uncertainty of this being progressively reduced by attempts to arrive at something more like an average produce and average price for assessment purposes. 'The system.. consisted in the commutation of an assumed or estimated quantity of produce, at a standard or fixed price modified by the current price of the day'. The average estimate of produce was calculated on the outturn of certain given years (according to the district circumstances), and the standard price on the average of certain specified years. If the current price was less than 10 per cent, above the standard, the standard was taken, if more, the excess only was added to the standard price to give the commutation, rate for the year. If the current price as not more than 5 per cent below the standard, the standard was taken; and if more than 5 per cent below, then the excess beyond the 5 percent was deducted from the standard and the balance formed the commutation rate. In short, a terribly complicated system. This system was abolished by the British.

Uñcha sort of tolls.

Ūr,oor, sabha, gramasabha the term 'township' is an apt rendering of the term *ūr*; the Cōla and the *Pāndya* inscriptions refer to the planting of prickly pear or/and stones to demarcate the boundaries of the *ūr*; in some cases, an earthen wall enclosed the habitat, an its appurtenances; it had the agriculturist occupants either directly paying land–dues to the state, or to the assignees in whose favour they were granted the whole or in part.

There is an exception in which in a particular *ūr* the agriculturist–land–holders therein had the obligation to render military services in times of war either to the chieftain to whom the land–dues or a portion thereof had been assigned as *jivitam* or to the king.

The term 'township' is certainly a generic term applied to any or all of these varieties.

It may be pointed out that *ūr* in Tamil was originally applied to villages in the agricultural tracts; *Ūr, pādi, cēri,* and *palli* to those in the pastoral tracts; *ūr, cēri, cēri, kudi* and *kuricci* to those in the mountainous tracts, *paṭṭinam* and *pākkam* to those in the coastal tracts and *paṛandalai* to those in the sandy tracts.

The term is invariably coupled with the *ūr–irukkai* or the *ūr–nattam* or *ūr–irukkai–nattam*, meaning village site; village council.

Ūr or the *sabha* had certain important functions to perform, such as, (a) supervise the maintenance of irrigation sources, (b) effecting sales and exchanging of lands, (c) supervising execution of charity (d) borrowing money from and lending to sabhas, (e) granting *mānyams*, i.e. agreeing to pay *mēlwaram* on behalf of a particular individual grantee, (f) intervention in case of forced labour, (g) supply of watchmen to public property such as temples, and (h) arbitration in case of complaints of harsh treatment of farm–servants.

Ūr was the assembly of non–Brahman villages, where as that of a Brahman village being called 'sabhā' or 'mathāsabhā',

Ūr–ēṭṭu (Tamil), taxes payable for the expenses of committee of eight members of the village assembly (*ūr*).

Ūr–iḍu–varippāḍu (Tamil); tax levied by the village assembly (*ūr*)

Ūr–kīḻ–iṟaiyili a phrase commonly used in inscriptions to denote the lands which were exempted from the payment of taxes by the village community generally on payment of capitalised money; tax free lands held by the institutions for religious instruction.

Ūr kīḻavan township leaders.

Ūr–kkaḍamai (Tamil) obligations and taxes levied by the village assembly (*ūr*).

Ūr-mányam lit. village rent-free lands; when differing from *cáni-mányam*, means such lands conferred by *sannad*, such as the *manyacar* or *reddi mányam*, which are sometimes held by the *mírásidars*.

Ūr-mutali village headman.

Ūr-oḷagana guildsmen of the town.

Ūr podu village common.

Ūrāṇmai a term occuring in the inscriptions from Travancore to denote lands held by the institutions free of taxes from the village community.

Ūrār residents; villagers.

Ūravar there is a mention of the term *Ūravar* in the inscriptions which denotes important officials; they acted as lease holders of the lands of the rulers; they granted temple honours to a cowherd for supplying kids to the temples during the festivals; some times some documents were also attested with their consent.

Ūriṟ, suṟukki township demand.

Ūriṭu-vari local bodies.

Ūrk-kaṇakku, ūrk-karṇam an official who maintained land revenue accounts at village level; he would maintain land records besides revenue accounts; sometimes he would also be attesting documents on behalf of the *Ūr*, in some cases he was also punished for misappropriation of temple funds.

Ūrkkal-śemmaippon corresponding or agreeing with the old coin that had been tested by fire; such types of mentions in the epigraphs indicate that the village assemblies were careful to receive gold coins of the proper weight and fineness in their transactions.

Ūṟṟāṇi a large nail which connects the plough-axe with the upper wood and makes it firm.

Ūruk-kīḻ-iṟaiyili the *iṟaiyili* remission granted by the *ūr*.

Ūrvāriyam a term used in the epigraphs to denote a committee of officers whose function was to see the lands of the village properly cultivated and to collect the produce.

Ūṭṭuppurai a term used in the epigraphs to denote the type of almshouse an important institution of poor relief and for feeding brahmans.

V

Vācalil–pōnta–kuṭimai lit. 'dues rendered at the royal door or palace'.

Vācittāṇ this term refers to the verification of the entry made in the (revenue) register.

Vāḍākkaḍan fixity of demand.

Vādākkaḍamai a term used in the epigraphs to denote tax on land for the maintenance of temples and brahmans.

Vāḍi a territorial term esp. in the Kanarese areas and certain contiguous tracts.

Vālamāñci a term comparable to *veṭṭi*; it was used to denote free labour; same as *amāñci.*

Vāmana–kkal boundary stone of lands granted for religious purposes

Vāṇikar–maṇai–iṟai a term used to denote tax on the house/place/shop occupied by the merchant communities. The term *maṇai* may be explained as shop, and *vāṇikar* as merchant communities.

Vāṇikar–pēr–kaṭamai a duty levied on traders (*vāṇikar* = merchant); the duty was assessed individually *(pēr* or *pērāl* = on individual).

Vāṇikkar–pērāṟ–kaṭamai dues on merchants.

Vāṇiyar merchants.

Vāṇiyar–pēr–kaṭamai a duty levied on oil merchants. The duty on these merchants was assessed individually since the word *pēr* is used in the term (*pēr* or *pērāl* = on individual). Same as *vāṇikar-pēr-kaṭamai* above.

Vāṇiyars oilmongers; those who plied this industry were subjected to a tax known as *śekku kaḍamai,*

Vāpatis, vyāpṛitas officials incharge of a gorup of administrative units.

Vāpī step–well; an irrigation well.

Vāra a share of the produce; system of letting land on an agreement to share produce (in Coorg); with the derecognition of 'slaves' being appointed to cultivate the lands owned by the *jenma* owners, the latter had no means of cultivating their lands, for they could not let or alienate them. It was ultimately determined that a portion of the holding, not exceeding one-fourth, might be sublet on the *vāra* plan (or paying half produce). This tenancy had to be offered to certain classes in order. The limitation was not, however, enforced in the case of widows, minors, and others incapable of cultivating land themselves.

Vāram, Wāram system of sharing the income from the land between the landlord and tenants; a share in kind; crop sharing; share–cropping basis; a share in the crops; the grain produce considered as the subject of division between the state, the cultivators, etc. Often in compound words as, *melvāram, kudī–vāram,* etc. The proportions were calculated in kind (*vāram*), and then commuted in to money values. This term represents the old plan of dividing the actual grain–heaps; same as the *batai* of North India; *mél–vāram,* the heap of the Raja or the owner, *kudī–vāram,* or cultivator's heap, etc.

Vārdhuṣin usury; the trade of a usurer was regarded immoral; a usurer was placed on the same footing as a thief; one who lives on illegal or prohibited interest.

Vāriyam (Tamil), a supervisor; an executive committee; appointment as a member of that body, an office of the supervision.

Vāriyar member of a committee in the village *sabhā*.

Vārtā lit. science of wealth; however, it includes in its scope any occupation or accomplishment that had an economic values; rules of agriculture, trade and the rearing of livestock which are the means of increase of one's wealth.

Vāśal–paṇam 'door–tax', periodical payment due to the palace; *vāśal* being the chief guard of the palace, this term has been explained as the door–money.

Vāśal–tiramam door-tax.

Vāśal–vari one of the taxes accruing from the villages.

Vāstu–kṛtya building work.

Vāstu–parivāra vacant site attached to house.

Vāṭikā defined as 5120 square *daṇḍas,* the length of the *daṇḍa* being 4 cubits; 4.48 acres; same as *veḻi* (in Tamil).

Vāy–kkeḻvi, vāy–kkeḻviyār an officer in attendance to the king, acting as the intermediary between the king and his subject; an officer who received the king's oral orders.

Vāyk–kēlvi receiver or recorder of king's oral order.

Vāykkāl the channels which pass through one village, obviously irrigating other villages also.

Vāykkāl–pāṭṭam (Tamil), channel cess, fee for keeping the channels in good repairs; channel tax; canal tax.

Vaḍḍa–vyavahāri a banker; the principal money–changer; the leader of a merchant guild; chief of *nānā–deśi* (non–local) merchants.

Vada–kaval the village watchman, whose duty it was to watch the bounds of the village, crops, sticks, heaps of grain, hay, and other property of the inhabitants in the village; got fee in cash and/or kind and/or in the form of land grant.

Vagainda–kāśu tax payable in cash for marking details of land etc,; fees for the division of land; also the fee for settlement of a dispute, etc.

Vaidā, vaidapattā, (Arabic), wayada; the term used in Kānara for the land allowed a lower assessment at first, but 'promising' to improve, and then pay the full rate; they paid by increasing rates till they became *bhartī*; i.e. attained the full assessment, *Vaidapattās* continued to be given by the British, though occasionally for waste land.

Vaidageni (Kanarese) lease for a term of years.

Vaidya in'am granted for the service of physician.

Vaidya–bhoga, vaidya–bhāga land set apart for the maintenance of the physician; also *vaidya–vṛtti*.

Vaidya–vṛtti same as *vaidya bhoga*.

Vaikāśi May–June.

Vaiśy–āgrahāra a privileged holding created in favour of members of the mercantile community.

Vaiśy–vāṇiya–nagarattār the guild of a class of merchants; a corporation of the merchants.

Vaiśyāgrahāra revenue–free holding in the possession of a *vaiśya*.

Vaita fertile, continuously cultivated land.

Vakil, vakeel, wakil (A.) authorized representative, attorney, pleader, lawyer.

Vaḻanāḍu (Tamil), a province; a district consisting of sub–divisions called *kuṟṟam* or *nāḍu*; an administrative division.

As per some inscriptions, in certain parts of the Vijayanagar empire above the *kūṟṟam* was a division called *vaḷanāḍu*, B.A. Saletore (*Social* and *Political Life in the Vijayanagar Empire*) doubts if the term *vaḷanāḍu* was used outside the Toṇḍaimaṇḍalam; however, it was in vogue in some other parts of the Vijayanagar Empire as is indicated by a few inscriptions; Saletore also thinks that it was a smaller division than a *kōṭṭam*; certainly there are a few inscriptions which mention that a *vaḷanāḍu* was a part of a *kōṭṭam* yet there are still others which mention the *kōṭṭam* as a division of a *vaḷanāḍu*; to add to the difficulty an inscription says that a *kōṭṭam* and a *vaḷanāḍu* indicated the same division; as such it is difficult to decide its relation with the *kōṭṭam* from the point of view of size; sub-divisions in to which a *maṇḍalam* was divided; in some areas *koṭṭam* was recognized as equivalent to *vaḷanāḍu*; it functioned as a revenue unit.

Vaḻi a term used in the Tamil inscriptions to denote the minor roads.

Vaḻi-āyam (Tamil-Sanskrit) toll levied on the commodities passing through high roads; tolls on the roadway.

Valitas, vaṇitas, vantyas administrative sub-divisions; the epigraphs do not give the exact nature of the divisions.

Vaḻiy-ayam (Tamil) 'tolls on the roadways'.

Vaḻudiy-accu-varggam a group of taxes payable in *Pāṇḍya* coins.

Valan a variety of coarse paddy.

Valanadu territorial unit.

Valangai the right-hand castes; lower caste occupations associated with agriculture; though treated as low but were integrated elements of the society; a group of communities, also called right hand group; the classes that comprised this group included – (i) *Banajigaru* of many trades, (ii) *Wodigaru* -cultivators of the sudra caste and of Karnataka extraction, (iii) *Jotiphana*-oilmakers who use one bull in mill, (iv) *Rangaru*- calico printers and tailors (v) *Ladaru*, and (vi) *Gujarati*.

Valaya (Telugu-Kannaḍa), an enclosure; a boundary; otherwise-a ring; a bracelet.

Valayan in'am held for the service of catching fish for the *zamindar*.

Valita, vaḷita a small territorial unit; a district or its sub-division; also *vaṇita*.

Valluva in'am granted for the service of *valluvan* who is a pariah, and is to low-caste persons what the *panchangi* is to the higher classes.

Valluvan mānyam the *mānyam* granted to the Parayar priest.

Vaṁśakāra bamboo-workers.

Vaṇ-pāṭṭam (Tamil), fixed revenue in kind due under a lease deed which does not provide for any relief against loss due to drought.

Vaṇika the trader.

Vaṇita (Kannaḍa), a small territorial unit; same as *valita*.

Vaṇṇak-kūli, vaṇṇarap-pārai terms used to denote tax levied on washermen.

Vaṇṇārpārai a professional tax collected from washermen.

Vanadurga forest-fort.

Vanan washerman; their number may vary from village to village and from time to time; they were essential component of most villages; remunerated in the form of a *mānyam* land or fixed share of the village output, and some got both.

Vancha a piece of sacking used for packing or baling a boat.

Vandra special land assessments for high castes.

Vaniers oil mongers.

Vaniya nagaram it refers to large organisation of oil-mongers which originated in the Tamil country around 10th century became a supra local trading organisation.

Vaniyam in'am granted for the service of supplying oil to a pagoda.

Vannan mānyam, Vannan in'am the *mānyam* granted to washerman; the same as *dhobi in'am*. He is also sometimes attached to a temple to wash the clothes of the idol and to supply rags for torches.

Vanpair ambalam in'am held for the service of collecting the assessment on garden lands.

Vanpyar, Vanypar it was a land of garden cultivated in backyard or in select spots and cultivated with sugarcane, tobacco, chillies, etc; lands yielding garden produce in Tinnevelly, cultivated in the backyards or select spots, consisting of plantains, sugar-cane, tobacco, chillies, etc.

Vantu a share, a part, a portion.

Vara-grāma village given as a gift to a temple or maṭha or a Brahman.

Varagaru the heavy crop; the great crop reaped after the rains.

Varagoo, varagu *paspalum scrobiculatum*.

Varagu koda millet (*pasphalum scrobiculatum*), a cereal inferior both as food and fodder, but very hardy and a useful famine reserve.

Varagū a millet; *panicum miliaceum*.

Varāha an indigenous gold coin in circulation in south India; it was a standard gold coin and weighed 52 grains; it was generally referred to as the 'pagoda' by the numerous foreign travellers of the period; the origin of this varnacular designation *varaha* or *varāgan*, (boar) applied to the gold coins of south India, must be traced to the boar device, characteristic of the *Cāḷukyan* coinage; the *Cāḷukyan* boar as well as the fish of the Pāndyas of the extreme south continued to appear during the eleventh century on the coins of the *Cōḷa* dynasty of Tanjore after it had absorbed those two lines; name of a gold coin called *pagoda*; the boar or rather Vishnu under that form, was the insignia of the Vijayanagar government; the coin being originally stamped with the figure of that animal.

Varaha pagodas, gold coins.

Varam (Tamil); share.

Vargdar (Kanarese) proprietor of a landed estate.

Vari (Tamil), tax; revenue register; order of the king and his officers fixing the revenue; land tax demand of the king; also used to denote other smaller levies; a term comparable with *iṛai*, in Cholamandalam it was suffixed in most of the cases and in few cases it was also used independently. The important terms to which it was suffixed were; *puṛa-vari*-land tax; *ūriṭu-vari*-tax demand of the local bodies. i.e. *ūr; cil-vari*-miscelleneous dues. However, in Tondaimandalam it was suffixed to more terms, e.g. *ampu-vari*-water dues, *cārikai-vari*-road-cess; *cōṇaka-vari*-cess on foreign merchant; *kaṭamai-vari*-land tax; *kōl-vari*-cess on balance (*kōl* = balance); *poṇ-vari*-tax on gold; *pū-vari*-tax on crop (*pū* = crop); *puḷuku-vari*-tax on incense articles etc.

Vari, varipottagam register of assessment of land showing the tenure of the land and the occupants from whom the land-dues in respect of each holding had to be collected.

Vari-ppottaga-nāyakam the head office of the revenue accounts; the chief officer of the same office.

Vari-ppottagam tax register; an officer maintaining the same.

Varicale the list showing the demand against each *rayat*.

Varip-pottakam seems to be an important officer in the revenue department. The name itself means a tax register as *vári* = tax and *pottakam*

= register or book. The officer seem to have enjoyed supervisory authority over the act of making entries in the tax register. In one of the epigraphs he is specifically mentioned as 'one who made the entry (in the revenue register) and read the document'; also *varip-pottaka-nāyakam* and *varip-pottakak-kaṇakku*.

Varip-pottakam kaṇakku an official in the land revenue department as denoted in the Chola epigraphs; other officials connected with this department were-*varip-pottaka-nāyakam, mukavetti, variyil-iṭu, paṭṭōlai, kīḻ-mukaveṭṭi, teṟippu, taravucāttu* and *paḷaniyāyam*.

Varipottagam a term connected with the land revenue current during Chola period in Tondaimandalam. Revenue register.

Variśai a graded scale; actual crop yields; the scale of land-dues; crop-wise scale of levy.

Variśai-kaḍamai the temples dues where an interest had been created in its favour.

Variyam in'am held for the service of watching the *melvaram* produce in the village.

Variyil -iṭu seems to be an officer who supervised the whole procedure of making entries on palm leaves; this term used in the epigraphs refers to the act of recording revenue accounts; *vari* would normally mean a tax or levy and *iṭu* is to make an entry; also *variyil-iṭṭattu* and *variyil-iṭuvittu*.

Variyilār the authorities in charge of land-tax register.

Vartanā prequisites due to an officer; periodical presents to be offered to an officer of rank by his subordinates and the people.

Vartanalu customary fees in money or in goods or grain to which the government servants and their menials were entitled, and which was collected periodically or seasonally.

Varuna Japan prayers to rain god Varuna. Generally parts of village output were assigned for this activity.

Varuṣa-kāṇikkai (Tamil), annual presents.

Vasad-bhoga-maryādā the term explains about the condition that the villages got as gift were to be enjoyed only by those who resided therein; relates the custom of the enjoyment of the gift land by the donee only by residing therein.

Vasad-bhogya-maryādā if has been interpretted as 'with the tenants' occupancy rights assured'; in other words it gives almost the same meaning as *vasad-bhoga-maryādā,* above.

Vasakaras bamboo-workers.

Vasanta garuvus rest houses; in the Telugu areas about A.D. 1520 customs were collected in *vasanta garuvus* (rest houses), watersheds, salt beds, market towns and roads frequented by people.

Vasantagaruvu a rest house.

Vastrarakṣakas tailors; one of the eighteen divisions of society.

Vaṭṭam trade discount, money-changer's commission.

Vatta murai the term used to denote a system of the distribution of spring channel water. The water was distributed in order of precedence, which was, (i) the temple, (2) the brahmin, and so on. Like wise the order of precedence of the distribution of water from rainfed tanks followed a similar pattern.

Vattiyar in'am granted for (i) the support of the village school master; and (ii) the support of the priest who conducts religious ceremonies in the houses of Brahmans.

Vayikkal in'am held for the service of preserving channels and other irrigation works in good order.

Vēli a standard unit of land; a *vēli* was

divided in to *mā* and *kuḻi*; a *vēli* was equal to 6.6157 acres; 20 *mā* made a *vēli* and 100 *kuli* made up a *mā*.

Vēlippaṇam levy of *paṇam* per *vēli* or levy of one *panam* per *vēlli* of land in cash.

Vētaṇai fees and presents. In inscriptions it is always found with *vetti*; a fee levied on the unit of land; the fee so demanded could have been for the remuneration of village or state servants. The inscriptions make it quite clear that it was assessed on a piece of land. Despite the fact that a number of items of fees could have been included in *vētaṇai*, it is not clear what other taxes were included. In due course of time, though the term *vētaṇai* had started disappearing, such tax remained prevalent in the form of fees.

Vētar–kummari tax assessed on the products of forest and hilly regions occupied by the hunters; a term used in the epigraphs of the Karnataka area.

Vĕṇṭhĕ an administrative division.

Vĕṭha (Kannaḍa) a small territorial unit; same as *vĕṇṭhĕ*.

Vecthyvadangan a type of paddy sown in May and reaped in September. It is dependent on the river freshes occasioned by the south–west monsoon during June and July. A slight rainfall is requisite in the end of April to admit of the ploughing of the land; but after sowing , the ground is left perfectly dry for three weeks, and it is considered that rain during that time is injurious.

Veda vadyar mānyam the *mānyam* granted to the teacher of vedas.

Veda–vṛtti revenue-free land set apart for meeting expenses of reciting the vedas; held for reading the vedas and teaching them to Brahman boys.

Vedar in'am granted to a hunter as a reward for the display of skill in the chase.

Vees equal to from 1.75 to 2 acres.

Veesum, vissum equal to two acres. It is also stated that a *vissum* of cultivated land was not equal to two acres as was commonly supposed by the farmers. There were two measures of *vissum–tauntla* or garden *vissum* was a rectangle measuring 200x160 cubits. Since a cubit measured 1½ feet, the garden *vissum* had an area of 72,000 square feet which is more than an acre. The other *vissum–chawk vissum* used to measure the ground under general cultivation. This was a square with an area of 1,12,500 square feet therefore exceeded 2 acres.

Vekkai (Tamil) hot; rinderpest.

Velā–durga–pāla a port officer.

Veḻḻāḻanparṟu peasant–occupants under the state; lands directly held by the *veḻḻālar*.

Veḻḻāḻas elders of the agriculturists.

Veḻḻān cultivator.

Veḻḻān vagai *rayatwari* villages; this term denotes holding in which an occupant has full rights on the land subject only to the payment of the land–dues direct to the king; through the collective agency of the *nāḍu* and the *ūr* or to the assignees in whose favour the king had granted his share of the dues; *veḻḻān vagai* holder could be equated with (i) where he holds the lands directly under the king, and the *kuḍi* or *kāṇiyāḻar* with (ii), where the land dues from the lands held by him had been assigned to a beneficiary; a direct holding of the occupants under the state; a kind of peasant proprietorship.

Veḻḻāṉvakai a term used to denote non-*brahmadēya* villages.

Veḻḻāṉvakai-mutal a term used in the epigraphs to denote the revenue collected in the non-*brahmadēya* villages.

Veli (Tamil), a big land measure; also see *vāṭikā*.

Veli–cenu, veli–polamu, veli–volamu

(Telugu), a field on a high level depending upon rain water; dry land.

Veli–kkāśu, veli–ppayaṟu (Tamil) tax payable in cash.

Vellai a vareity of sugarcane. The word *'vellai'* in Tamil refers to something which is whitish. The word *'vellai'* with reference to cane was perhaps used to denote a veriety which was not striped or coloured red, purple etc.

Vellaithal (Tamil) *vellai* white, *thal* stalk.

Vellalas the great farmer caste of Tamil country, corrresponding more or less to the Telugu *kapus*, or *reddis*, and ranking, among Tamils, next to Brahmans.

Vellarykuruvay a type of paddy of short growth the seedlings being transplanted in October when a month old and reaped in March. The soil is generally sandy regur and the crop is most frequently cultivated in the vicinity of hills and depends on the rain on the hills during August and September, as well as the north–east monsoon rains in October and November.

Vellavursay non–residents and not hereditary *rayats*.

Veṇī 're–united property after it was once divided'.

Veṇkāyam garlic.

Veppul red sandy soil.

Verasi total, entire.

Verpulu lit. 'root worm'; any sort of worm or grub that attacks the roots of plants.

Vertana means of subsistance, occupation, income, profit, fees, perquisites, especially of grains paid to the village records and papers and has lands perquisites assigned to him, for his support.

Verum patom ola karunum deed lease or mortgage on *patom*.

Verumpattakkaram (sl), verumpattakkar (pl.) one who holds a *verumpattam* tenure; cultivator, usually on wetlands.

Verumpattam tenancy at will; *verum* unqualified or unfavourable, *pattam* lease.

Veṭha, visaya, nirvṛtti an administrative division, same as a *koṭṭam*.

Veṭṭi it was used to refer to the maintenance service rendered to irrigation tanks and river banks; it was a form of unremunerated service rendered by the holders of land; tax demanded on a unit of land; the service was demanded for the maintenance of water courses in general. This type of service rendered to the state could also be considered as a form of revenue. Instead of collecting payments as tax the individuals were asked to execute certain public works for the state. The state, as such, was relieved from the burden of collecting taxes either in cash or kind, and subsequently spending the accrued income for execution of some public work. These services were usually entrusted with the local authorities and were utilised mostly for maintaining irrigational sources and guarding cities and villages.

The *veṭṭi* form of service seems to have undergone a change during the course of time for there is reference of *veṭṭi–puṭavai* a similar tax, prevalent in 1246 A.D. As such, it could be surmised that the paractice of extracting free labour was slowly given up and a payment of cash or kind or by way of land grant was demanded instead.

Waterman who attended to various menial tasks, kept a watch over the tank–*bund*, and regulated the flow of water for irrigating the fields; unpaid labour for public works in the village without time or other limits; free labour.

Veṭṭi–ccoṟu the obligation of feeding the veṭṭi labourers free of cost.

Veṭṭi–pāṭṭam (Tamil), 'a kind of tax'; tax in lieu of *viṣṭi.*

Veṭṭippuḍavai and **veṭṭitamyaḷ** two of the additional taxes on land charged, over and above the usual land revenue, for the support of and payment to the village officers.

Veṭṭiyāl unpaid labourers; village servant. Also see, *veṭṭi.*

Veṭṭiyān village servant, employed in measuring all the heaps of grain and carrying letters and money; he also burned the dead and did odd jobs of various kinds. Also see, *veṭṭi.*

Vetana wages; wages for the labourers in the public works of the village.

Vethupu rinder pest.

Vetti in'am granted for the performance of the lowest offices in a village, as those of a porter, grain watcher, scavenger, etc.

Vettis, vettiyan the lowest class of village servants, whose duty is to watch the burning-ground set aside for disposal of the dead; funeral attendant and watchman. Also see, *veṭṭi.*

Vettiyan those who looked after irrigation management; in certain villages, a *vettiyan* had vitally important ritual roles in temple functions, commensurate with the socio-economic role as irrigation attendant, village watchman and funeral attendant. Also see, *veṭṭi.*

Vettiyan mānyam the *mānyam* granted to funeral attendant. Also see, *veṭṭi in'am.*

Vettuvan Tamil caste.

Vīra–bhoga land assigned for the maintenance of a warrior.

Vīra–śāsana a grant made by the king in recognition of the heroic activity of a person; a charter recording the grant of land or other property to a warrior.

Vīra–śeṣai a tax; the provision made for the descendants of dead warriors.

Vīsa (Telugu–Kannaḍa), name of a coin 1/16 of a *haṇa* or *paṇa*; but 1/20 of the standard coin in value essentially; gold equal in weight to one grain of rice; 1/256 of a *hun* or *pagoda*; 40 *palas,*; a measure of land equal nearly to 2 acres; also called *visā, visya, visāmu.*

Vīsā–badi, visā–padī, veesapadi a method of dividing the revenue assessed under the village system according to customary shares in which the village body held their land. It involved the curious condition that if any one thought his share over–, and that his neighbour under–, assessed, he had a right to demand that the latter be made over to him at an increased rate, which he named, in exchage for his own. But should the neighbour assent to the enhanced rate, the exchage was not actually carried out but the complainant was allowed a proportionate reduction in *his* land. Also see, *visapadi villages.*

Vīṭu house.

Vibhūti–kāṇikkai (Tamil), originally it used to be voluntary contribution to a temple by the devotees while receiving the sacred ashes, later on, it was collected as a tax.

Vidha variety; kind.

Vidy–ānubhoga an endowment of land to a school for the encouragement of learning.

Vijāpya a petition; same as *vijapti.*

Vijñapti, vijñāpti petition to the king; an officer who brings petition of the subjects to the king's notice; also called *vijñāpya.*

Viḷakkal–taṇtam a fine levied on those who would fail to burn lamp in temple on the appointed days and hours.

Viḷantaikōl a measuring rod used in the revenue surveys; though it is difficult to calculate its length, its length could be equal to 16 *cāṇ* =12 feet appox. However, no perfect conclusions can be drawn about the actual length of the rods used in revenue surveys as they used to vary from area to area and period to period.

Vilai koṇḍa nilam grant of ownership of lands by purchase.

Vilai poruḷ price of land; also see *kāśu-koḷḷa-iṛaiyili.*

Vilai tuṇḍu, vellah toondoo 'price deficit'. Place felt that the *kāṇiyāṭchikārar,* by quoting low paddy prices, had derprived the *circar* of a part of the revenue. The *vilai tuṇḍu* amounted to less than 2% of the value of the crop, but Place insisted that this be included in order to preempt deception in principle; a penalty imposed by Lionel Place for under statement of paddy prices by the *kāṇiyāṭchikārar.*

Villéins en-gros a category of slaves who might be transferred without the land at the will of their lords.

Villeins regardant a category of slaves, attached inseparably to the soil.

Vimana pratishta in'am granted for the service of repairing the *vimanam* or pinnacle of a temple.

Vinamu (Telugu), a weight greater than a *cinna or cinnamu or sinna.*

Viniyōgam apportioned dues, or levy; distributed obligations.

Viniyoga an employment; use; expenditure.

Viṛpiḍi a professional tax charged from the hunters.

Virabhadra one belonging to a class of temple servants employed for protecting the properties and rights of the temples.

Viral-ariśi rice provided for gold smiths for amputating the last two fingers of the wives of cultivators.

Virivile, parappile a term appearing in the epigraphs to denote land-dues demanded on the basis of area measurement; standard measuring rod or pole in use.

Virivilē (land dues' demand on the basis of) area measurement.

Viṣa-vṛtti see *viṣahara-bhoga.*

Viṣahara-bhoga a land set apart for the support of a poison-doctor; also called *viṣa-vṛtti.*

Viṣaya a district; a kingdom or territory; *viṣaya* could be part of a *mandala* and also *vice-versa; mandala* and *viṣaya* were at times synonymous. Also see, *vishaya.*

Viṣaya-suṅka the tax of a *viṣaya.*

Viṣṭi unpaid or forced labour which the villagers were obliged to provide to the king or landlord on occasions.

Viśa-kkāṇam (Tamil), tax or share in produce as remuneration due to a village headman.

Viśeṣ-ādāya, viśeṣ-āya a special group of taxes.

Visam the fraction called one sixteenth.

Visapadi villages in the best days the Vijayanagar empire showed considerable activity in making improvements, building tanks and channels and in the settlement of new areas. To this period of settlement probably belonged the rise of the *visapadi* villages, a curious feature of the Cuddapah province, referred to by Thomas Munro. His description of such villages says,"There are many villages in which the Ryots settle among themselves the exact proportion of the whole rent that each individual is to pay. They are called Visapadi or 'sixteenth' villages from the land and the rent being divided in to sixteen shares, and they comprise a considerable part of the Cuddapah province, besides being scattered though more thinly over other parts of the country (Ceded Districts). When the season of cultivation draws near all the Ryots of Visapadi village assemble... ascertain the amount of the agricultural stock of each individual and of the whole body, the quantity of land, to the culture of which it is adequate and they divide it acordingly giving to each man the portion which he has the means of cultivating and fixing his share of the rent...' Government of Madras, Revenue Departemnt G.O.No. 2108, 21st August 1907. Also see, *vīsābadi.*

Visaya same as Telugu *visā, visāmu.*

Vishaya the most common designation of districts since the period of the Kadambas (4th cent.A.D. to the 10th century) in the south; subdivision of a *deśa* and *vishaya* seem to have been used as synonyms; *bhoga,* another administrative subdivision, sometimes occurs as part of a *vishaya,* while at times synonymous with vishaya. Also see, *viṣaya.*

Vishayapatis called *deśadhigārigal* in *Kannaḍa,* were royal officers; were custodians of the interests of the king whose authority they represented and exercised in their respective offices.

Viss a variable weight; in Madras 1 *viss* it was 120 *tolas,* or about 3 lb., in Ganjam 1 *Viss* it was 400 *tolas.*

Viṭṭukkuḍuttēn release or relinquishment of ones rights on the lands in favour of some one else.

Vittu mudal seed-capital.

Vivāha marriage.

Vivāha-ppaṇam the marriage fee; a tax on marriage; same as (Tamil), *kaṇṇāla-kkāṇan.*

Viyāyam (Tamil), expenditure; as opposed to *āyam* or income.

Vochchan mānyam the *mānyam* granted to upper non-brahmin *jati* priest who officiated in the pidari temple.

Vṛitti, Vritti, birt, birte the term *vṛitti* is usually employed to designate a service tenure, and adjectives are prefixed to it calculated to give some idea of the nature of the services implied; means; livelihood; occupation; grant of land for ones livelihood; land granted for service; share; share in village granted to a Brahman as a free gift; a maintenance. A small spot of land on which a dwelling is erected, generally with some ground around it, granted to brahmins; the sanskrit word used to express the idea conveyed by the Tamil term *carei,* a *mīrāsi,* share; one *carei* being generally considered as sufficient of one person or family; the term *swástyam* is often used in this sense.

Vrāyasam a variant of *rāyasam.*

Vralla from *ūr* village, and *āl* headman.

Vullah, bullah, equal to 3.82 acres.

Vullum equal to 4 *puddees*; 2 Madras Measures (one Madras Measure equal to 2.3 lb.). The same named land measure equal to 3¾ acres.

Vunnies, vanniyams Tamil caste; most of them 'were abject slaves before the period of British administration, incapable of owning property, or of cultivating on their own account. Others were thieves and robbers by profession, and existed on plunder. A wonderful change must have taken place in the last century to bring more than two-thirds of them in to the class of small farmers, or peasant proprietors.' (*Census Report, 1871*, p. 158).

Vyādha hunter

Vyākhyā-vṛtti land grant to meet the expenses of expounding the *purāṇas* and other *śāstras.*

Vyāpāra a trade.

Vyāpārin a trader.

Vyavasthai a term used in the epigraphs to denote 'conditions' imposed on the land grants made; regulations; a settlement or arrangement.

W

Wāra tuṇḍu, warah toondoo penalty imposed by Lionel Place for understatement of yield of land; 'share deficit'. It was intended to recover that portion of the *kaniyatchikarar's kudiwaram* which had resulted on the basis of false claims of *payirkarar* status and through false fictitious *mānyams*. Later on Place had incorportated in it the output of all lands that had been 'unjustly' claimed by the *kāṇiyāṭchikārars*, and not merely their *mānyams*.

Wāsil-bāqī one of the revenue accounts, showing payments of land revenue and balances due.

Wadla in'am for the service of village carpenter; the same as *badai in'am*.

Wajh-i-muqaarrari fixed revenue rate.

Waqf (plural auqāf) beneficiaries of such grants were institutions/ individuals on collection basis; for the maintenance of religious shrines, tombs and *madrasas*, – for their repairs, as also for the subsistance of their 'staff' and for charities disbursed through them. Though reckoned as heritable proprietary estates in nature, in practice it was always subject to alteration or even confiscation by the state.

Waraput village where the produce payable in kind was the traditional rule of assessment.

Waraput, warappattu lands one of the two classifications of the non-*mānyam* or *circar* lands during the Company's rule, and in these lands, the *circar's* share was in kind and constituted a fraction of the gross output; the *waraput* lands were *nanjei* lands with assured irrigation.

Warappattu kanakku an account of shares in the village output according to *melwaram, kudiwaram* and *swamibhogam* agreements.

Warariayat tenure certain lands in the Tinnevelly district held on a favourable assessment, the difference between the full and the favourable assessment being known by this term.

Waratanah an allowance in money paid by husbandmen on ploughs and by tradesmen on houses, shops and looms.

Warg, wargdar in Kānara, as many plots as appeared on one leaf (or *warg*) of the accounts, being held by the same family, formed a sort of unit-group, and each holding got to be spoken of as a '*warg*'; the holder was called, in revenue language, the *wargdār* or *mūlawargdār* (original or hereditary holder); in short, the land holding and owner of such a holding.

Warga bhumi landed property.

Warricum an allowance allowed by the government to the land holders to cover interest charges on the loans taken by them from the money lenders and this was followed only in cases where the land-holders paid interest direct to the money lenders.

Warum share of the produce, or the rate by which the division of it was made between the cultivator and government.

Wasulbandi roll or statement of payments remitted to the district treasury.

Waṭan, Watan Arabic-home, native;

name given under the Muhammadan kingdoms to the land–holdings (and privileges collectively) of hereditary *pargana* and village officers West, Central and South India, allowed them revenue–free; office or means of subsistence; hereditary duty with lands attached; same as *grāmamāniyam* etc.

Watandar–in'am land assignment and perquisites of village officials.

Watan jagir hereditary land or area held by the ruling class families, also place of residence.

Weights and Measures the inscriptions of South India contain reference to various units of weights and measures. The important feature of the system was its wide diversity. In due course of time foreign units of weights and measures also came in to existence in the principal centres of trade. The foreign merchants referred to the measuring units in terms of the foreign ones. Hardly any efforts were made to introduce any kind of uniformity in the prevailing systems of measuring units, particularly in the weight and surface measures. (No doubt the English government did take steps in this regard). The different units of measures usually bore the names of the local ruler or chief who introduced the measures and no serious attempt appears to have been made to standardize them. Following tables give different units of measures though there was difference between the same unit at different places :

(a) Measures of Land/Square Measure

(i) Tamil

576 square feet	=	1 *kuḻi*
100 *kuḻi*	=	1 *kāni*
5 *kāṇi*	=	1 *vēli*
1 *chei*	=	1¾ acres

(ii) In Thanjavur

144 Square feet	=	1 *kuḻi*
100 *kuḻi*	=	1 *mā*
20 *mā*	=	1 *vēli*
1 *vēli*	=	6.6 acres
1 *mā*	=	.33 acres
1 *kuḻi*	=	.0033 acre

(iii) Telugu

1 cubit	=	19.68 inches
32 cubits	=	1 rod
1 rod sqaure	=	2756 1/4 square feet = 1 *guntal junta*
1 *gunṭa*	=	0.633 acre
50 *gunṭa*	=	1 *gurtu* or *gorru*
	=	3.1637 acres
8 *gurtus*	=	1 *kuccala*
	=	25 acres

(b) Measures of Capacity/Cubic–Measures

(i) Tamil

5 *śeviḍu*	=	1 *āḻākku*
2 *āḻākku*	=	1 *ulakku*
2 *uḻakku*	=	*1 uri*
2 uri	=	*1 nāḻi* = 1 *paḍi*
	=	108 inches cubic capacity
8 *nāḻi/paḍi*	=	1 *kuruni*
	=	1 *marakkāl*
	=	½ cubic foot
	=	500 fluid ounces
2 *kuruṇi*	=	1 *padakku*
2 *padakku*	=	1 *tūni*
3 *tūṇi*	=	1 *kalam*

(ii) Malayalam

2 *ālākku*	=	1 *oḷaku*
2 *oḷaku*	=	1 *uri*
2 *uri*	=	1 *nāḷi*
4 *nāḷi*	=	1 *eḍangaḷi*
6 *nāḷi*	=	1 *nārāyam*
10 *nārāyam*	=	1 *para*

(iii) Kannada/Canarese

10 *paṇam*	=	1 *honnu* (*ponnu*)
4 *kākini*	=	1 *visam*
5 *vīsam*	=	1 *hāgam* or *pāgam*
4 *pāgam*	=	1 *paṇam*
10 *paṇam* (gold)	=	1 *gadyāṇa* (*honnu* gold)

4 *svarṇam*	=	1 *karṣam*
4 *karṣam*	=	1 *palam*
20 *palam*	=	1 *tole*
20 *tole*	=	1 *bhāram*
4 *jave*	=	1 *pāgam*
4 *pāgam*	=	*1* *baṇṇam*
4 *baṇṇam*	=	1 *kalpāyam*
4 *kalpāyam*	=	1 *kāñcanam*

4 *gidda*	=	1 *sollage*
4 *sollage*	=	1 *baḷḷam*
	=	2 seers
4 *mānam*	=	1 *baḷḷam*
4 *baḷḷam*	=	1 *koḷḷagam*
20 *koḷagam*	=	1 *khaṇḍugam*
8 *java*	=	1 *angulam*
12 *angulam*	=	1 *gēṇ*
4 *gēṇ*	=	1 *hasta*
4 *hastam*	=	1 *danḍam*
2000 *danḍam*	=	1 *krōśam*
4 *krōśam*	=	1 *yōjanam*

(iv) Telugu

4 *citti*	=	1 *śola*
	=	70 *tōla* of rice heaped
4 *śola*	=	1 *munta* = 280 *tōla* = 3½ *pucka seers*
4 *munta*	=	1 *kāiñcam* (*kuntsam*) = *1,120 tōla*
	=	14 *pucka seers*
4 *kūñcam*	=	1 *tūm, about a hundred weight*
20 *tūm*	=	1 *candy or puṭṭi or about a ton*

(c) Measures of Weight

(i) Tamil

10 *kāṇi*	=	1 *grain*
4 *kāṇi*	=	1 *mā*
2 *grains*	=	1 *kunṛi*
2 *kunṛi*	=	1 *mañjāḍi*
2 *māñjāḍi*	=	1 *paṇattūkkam*
20 *mañjāḍi*	=	1 *kaḷañju*

3 *tōlas*	=	1 *palam*
3 *palam*	=	1 *catca seer*
40 *palam*	=	1 *viss or* 3.0857 *lbs.*
20 *maunds*	=	1 *candy or bāram*

(ii) Telugu

1 *pagoda* weight	=	52 ½ grains troy
1 *tōla*	=	180 grains troy

10 *kurruck pagodsa* or 3 *tōlas*	=	1 *pollam*
8 *pollam* or 24 *tōla*	=	1 *pucka seer*
5 *seer* or 120 *tōla*	=	1 *viss*
8 *viss* or 960 *tōla*	=	1 *maund (100 pounds) troy)*
20 *maunds*	=	1 *candy* or *puṭṭi*

(Source : *South Indian Inscriptions,* ii, pp. 8 n. 36 n.' 65 n, 48 n.5, 75 n.1 and 2.338, 392; (i) p.92.; Allen Butterworth and V. Venugopal Chetty, A *Collection of the Inscriptions on Copper Plates and Stones in the Nellore District,* iii, Appendix III, pp. 1487–88.

Wet land see *nunjei.*

Witturnas agricultural slaves.

Wudders; wadde–in'am Tank–diggers; the *in'am* under such name was for the service of executing the ordinary repairs of large government tanks.

Y

Yātrā-dāna gift made for getting favours before starting on an expedition by the king.

Yátam engine for raising water.

Yadashut a memorandum; rough note.

Yadavas shepherds and cow herds.

Yadayan in'am held by cowherd for the service of taking out the cattle of the villages to graze.

Yajmān, yejamānah the term used in Coorg for the managing elder of the family group; he was the eldest member of the family group and also held the *sanad*, and the property registered in his name; master, called as *ecabhógam* sole enjoyment.

Yajman in'am the *in'am* is called by this name when its holder is the sole *mirasidar* of the village; the same as *grama-manyam*.

Yakki-accu name of a coin current in Kongu country.

Yalavarise tenure a term applied in the district of Tinnevelly to dry lands held by *kavalgars* on a favourable assessment.

Yantra a mechanical contrivance for diverting water.

Yatra-che-kathi land endowment supporting flag conveyance at fairs and pilgrimages.

Yava a kind of cereal.

Yavanas people of West Asian and Mediterranean origin.

Yenādi (s), kirāta, sikāri originally inhabitants of Nallamalai hill tract and led nomadic life. Labelled as 'criminal tribes' by the British administrators. The enactment of forest laws proved a death knell to the *yenadis*. Today most of Yenadis are employed for watching the peasants' crops and grannaries. (For details, see V. Ragavaiah. *The Yanadis*, New Delhi, 1962); had the duty of scaring away or destroying the wild beasts that might molest the village and its crops.

Yekhabhogum see *ekabhogum*.

Yeksal pattah *pattah* granted to poor *rayats*.

Yella boundary.

Yellu, yelloo gingelly; *sesamum orientale*.

Yennai vangi in'am held for the service of carrying oil from the oilmonger to the pagoda.

Yeomiahs charitable allowances in money or grain.

Yer aal attavanai kanakku a schedule or account of ploughs and ploughmen employed.

Yeri katta raman 'Rama who saved the irrigation tank'; it is the name of a temple situated at Madurantakam. There is a stone inscription which states that a certain number of oblations and rituals were funded by an endowment created by Lionel Place. According to the legend, Rama appeared in the form of a labourer and helped Place to save the irrigation tank. Having thus blessed with a *darisanan* (vision) of Rama, Place created an endowment for worship at the temple which existed there.

Yernaddies non-residents and not hereditary *rayats*.

Yeruckam *calotropis gigantea*, a bush specie.

Yilpah, illuppai *madhuca longifolia*.

Yojana a measure of distance, it is twelve miles and one thousand two hundred and eighty yards.

Z

Zabita a list, inventory, paper of names.

Zabita wāram a standardised revenue assessment imposed by Richard Deighton; 'general fixed standard for the division of the crops'; new distribution of shares, by all parties, renters as well as inhabitants; in other words, fixed *mēlwaram*.

Zakat a tax on merchandise imposed on the traders, travellers and citizens carrying goods.

Zamindar (p.) broadly speaking, the holders (of the rights over the produce) of the land. This term implied a range of highly variegated dominant rural classes and was inclusive of the so-called rajas who had an 'autonomous' control over the territories under their jurisdiction.

Zamindaran-i-zor-talab zamindars or palegars who would not pay the revenues unless demanded forcibly.

Zamindari in'am a general name given to a class of *in'ams* comprising the palegar, *nad gaud, desai, despandya,* desmukh, *kannugo, sanad samat gaud, nad karnam, majmudar, sirdespandya and samat karnam in'ams.* On the extinction of these offices and the resumption of the land and ready money emoluments attached to them, certain *in'ams* were granted for the support of the families of the holders. These *in'ams* have been treated as personal.

Zamindari, zamindary an office or jurisdiction of a *zamindar.* A settlement recognizing *zamindars* as hereditary proprietors of the soil.

Zamindari the various fines (*abwabs*), services aids, exacted by the *zamindars* from their tenants, resemble in all respects, 'feudal incidents' which the English terms denote; and the tenures, not of cultivating inhabitants, but the persons of their tribes, or their dependents, holding land under them, are nearly the same as 'feudal' tenures were at their origin.

Zamorin prince in Malabār.

Zillah an administrative district.

Zingar in'am granted for the support of a saddler in the service of a *zamindar.*

Zirat cultivation.

Zirat-zamin cultivated land.

Zudgar hired labourer.

Zunnardar a Brahman.

Bibliography

Primary Sources

A. Epigraphy

Report of the Mysore Archaelogical Survey, 1924.

Epigraphia Carnatica, Vol II.

Sewell, Robert, *The Historical Inscriptions of South India, collected till 1923,* edited by S. Krishnaswami Aiyangar. Madras, 1932.

Annual Report of Epigraphy (South India) for the years 1887-1944/5. Madras, 1887-1955.

Sewell, Robert, *Archaeological Survey of Southern India : List of tthe Antiquarian Remains in the Presidency of Madras,* compiled under the orders of government. 2 Vols. Madras, 1882-84.

Kundangar, K.G. (Ed.), *Inscriptions in Northern Karnataka and Kolhapur State,* Kolhapur, 1939.

Naik, A.V.(Ed.), *Inscriptions of the Deccan,* Poona, 1947.

Burnell, A. C., *Elements of South Indian Palaeography from the Fourth to the Seventeenth Century A.D. Being an Introduction to the Study of South Indian Inscriptions and Mss.* Second Enlarged and improved edition, London, 1878.

Travancore Archaeological Series Vol. I, Madras, 1910-1913; Vol. II to VII, Trivandrum, 1920-32.

Archaeological Survey of India, New Imperial Series, Vol. XXXIX *Coorg Inscriptions* (Revised Edition), by B. Lewis Rice, *Epigraphia Carnatica,* Vol. I. Madras, 1914.

Mysore Archaeological Series, Epigraphia Carnatica by B. Lewis Rice, 12, Vols., Bangalore, 1898-1905.

Archaelogical Survey of Southern India, Vol IV *Tamil and Sanskrit Inscriptions, with some notes on village Antiquities collected chiefly in the South of the Madras Presidency.* By Jas. Burgess with Translations by S.M. Natēśa Sāstri Pandit, Madras, 1886.

Krishna, K.G. *Studies in South Indian History and Epigraphy,* Madras, 1981.

Sivarama Murthy, C. *Indian Epigraphy and South Indian Scripts.* Reprint, 1966.

Desai, P.B., *Select Stone Inscriptions of Andhra Pradesh.* Hyderabad, 1962.

Ramesan, N. and Mukunda Rao, eds. *Temple Inscriptions of Andhra Pradesh.* Srikakulam District, Hyderabad, 1980.

Radha Krishna, B. *Early Telugu Inscriptions,* Hyderabad, 1971.

Kunduru Iswara Dutt, *Inscriptional Glossary of Andhra Pradesh*, Andhra Pradesh Sahitya Akademy, Hyderabad, 1967.

Karashima, Noboru, (Ed.), *Indus Valley to Mekong Delta : Explorations in Epigraphy*, New Era Publications, Madras, 1985, pp. 103-139.

Mahalingam, T.V. *Early South Indian Palaeography.* Madras : University of Madras, 1974.

Epigraphia Carnatica, Revised by B.R.Gopal, University of Mysore, Vols. III, IV, V, VI, 1974-77.

A Topographical List of Inscriptions of the Tamil Nadu and Kerala States, Vol-I, North Arcot District, (Ed.) T.V. Mahalingam, Delhi, 1985.

South Indian Temple Inscriptions, (Ed.), T.N. Subramaniam, Government Oriental Manuscript Library, Government of Tamil Nadu, (3 Vols.), 1953-57.

Inscriptions of the Pudukkottai State, (Translated into English by K.R. Srinivasan) Parts I, II, Pudukkottai, 1941-46.

B. Manuscript Sources

Madras Board of Revenue Consultations. (1790-1830) also known as *Proceedings of the Board of Revenue.*

Madras Revenue Consultations (1792-1830).

Revenue Dispatches from England (1792-1830).

Revenue Dispatches to England (1792-1830).

Madras Secret Consultations/Proceedings. Vol. I - 48.

Public Department : Sundries (Public Sundries).

Bellary District Records.

Revenue Department, Minutes of Consultations, Vol. 10-843.

Asafia Documents (Persian).

Hukam - Nama - i - Tipu Sultan (Persian).

Cuddapah District Records.

Hyderabad Residency Papers.

Survey of India Memoirs.

Home Department Revenue Records.

Fort St. George Records.

Mysore Records.

Inam Fair Registers

Statements Showing the Village Service Inams Fully Assessed.

Quit Registers of Personal Inams.

C. Printed Sources

Baramahal Records (1792-1799).

Col. Munro's Report Regarding the Poligars in the Ceded Districts (1801-1802).

Collector's Report on the Revision of Assessment, 1859.

Selections from the Records of the Bellary District - Political, Revenue and Agricultural Matters, 1800-1856.

Selections from the Old Records of the Bellary District, 1800-1807.

Papers Regarding Revenue Settlement, 1801-1823.

The Fifth Report from the Select Committee on the Affairs of the East India Company. Vol. I. *Bengal Presidency,* Vol. II. *Madras Presidency.* London : 1812. Madras: 1866 and 1883.

Selection from the Records of the Madras Government, New (Revenue) series, No. 1. A collection of papers relating to the Inam Settlement in the Madras Presidency. Madras, 1948.

Bundla Ramaswamy Naidoo, *Memoir on the Internal Revenue System of Madras, 1820.* Madras, 1908.

Correspondence Between the Collector, the Board of Revenue and the Government Regarding the Settlement of Fuslies 1230-1245 (1820-1835).

Col. Munro's Correspondence Regarding the Survey and Ryotwari Settlement of the Ceded Districts, 1802-1827.

Lushington, S.R. *Report Regarding the Tinnevelly Polegars and Sequestered Pollams.* 1800, Reprint 1919.

Graeme, H.S. *Report on the Polyams of Chitoor.* Madras 1893.

Khan, Yusuf Hussain (Ed.). *Farmans and Sanads of the Deccan Sultans.* Hyderabad : A.P.S.A., 1963.

Selections from the Records of the Bombay government, No.4. *'Report on the Village Communities of the Deccan'* by R.N. Gooddine, 10 October 1845.

Selections from the Records of the District of Cuddapah, No. 1. Cuddapah: Collectorate Press 1870.

'The Land Revenue in Madras', *The Calcutta Review,* 1852, 34. Vol. XVII, 1853.

Selections from the Records of the Mysore Commissioner's Office (Bangalore, 1864) contains-Wilks Report on the Interior Administration, Resources and Expenditure of the Government of Mysore, 1801.

Selection of Papers on Indebtedness and Land Transfer.

Aiyappan, A. *Report on the Socio-Economic Conditions of the Aboriginal Tribes of the Province of Madras.* Madras : Government Press, 1948.

Innes, *Note on Tenancy Legislation in Madras* (Madras, 1925)

Malabar Land Tenures (Madras, 1896)

Report of a Joint Commission from Bengal and Bombay appointed to inspect into the state and condition of the Province of Malabar in the years 1792 and 1793 (Madras, 1862) Reprint.

Report of the Malabar Tenancy Commission, 1940 (Madras, 1940).

Report of Malabar Tenancy Committee, 1929 (Madras, 1929).

Walker, *Report on the Land Tenures of Malabar* (Madras, 1801).

Gleig, G.R., *The Life of Major General Sir Thomas Munro, Bart. & K.C.B. Late Governor of Madras. 3 Vols.* (London, 1830).

Sastri, K.N. Venkatasubba. *The Munro System of British Statesmanship in India.* Mysore : University of Mysore, 1930.

Mahalingam, T.V.(Ed.). *Mackenzie Manuscripts : Summaries of Historical Manuscripts in the Mackenzie Collection.* 2 Vols. Madras : University of Madras, Vol- I, 1972; Vol- II 1976.

Bayley, W.H. and Hudleston, W. *Papers on Mirasi Right selected from the Records of the Madras Government.* Madras, 1862.

Arbuthnot, Alexander J. *Major General Sir Thomas Munro, Bart., Governor of Madras. Selections of his Minutes and other official writings.* 2 Vols. London, 1881.

Panikkar, K.N. (ed.). *Peasant Protests and Revolts in Malabar.* New Delhi ICHR and PPH, 1990.

Taylor, William. *Oriental Historical Manuscript in the Tamil Language, Translated with Annotations.* 2 Vols. Madras, 1862, 1935.

Crisp, B. *The Mysorean Regulations, Translated from the Persian.* Calcutta, 1792.

Dubois, Abbe. *Hindu Manners, Customs and Ceremonies, Trans. from the French and edited with notes by Henry K. Beauchamp.* London, 1924.

Heyne, Benjamin, *Tracts, Historical and Statistical, on India; with journals of Several Tours through various parts of the Peninsula. Also an account of Sumatra, in a series of letters.* London, 1814.

Gopal, M.H. *British Sources of the Economic, Political and Social History of the Mysore State* : Volume I, 1799-1812, *Purnaiah's Administration,* Volume II, *1813-1832, Raja's Administration.* Bombay: Popular Prakashan, 1993.

Elliot, H.M. *The History of India As Told by its own Historians : The Muhammadan Period.* Edited by John Dowson 8 vols. London, 1867-77, Reprint, Delhi, 1990.

Dua, J.C. (ed.), *British In'am Policy and Palegar Resistance in Ceded Districts : Select Documents Relating to Narasimha Reddy's Resistance,* Delhi, 1994.

Manuals and Gazetteers

Maclean, C.D., *Manual of the Administration of the Madras Presidency in illustration of the Records of the government and the Yearly Administration Reports,* 3 vols. (Madras, 1885-1893).

Gribble, J.D.B., *A Manual of the District of Cuddapah in the Presidency of Madras* (Madras, 1875)

Imperial Gazetteer of India : Provincial Series : Madras, 2 vols. (Calcutta, 1908).

Chetty, M. Gopala Krishna, *A Manual of the Kurnool District* (Madras, 1886).

Francis, W., *Madras District Gazetteers, Anantapur* (Madras, 1905).

Francis, W., *Madras District Gazetteers, Bellary* (Madras, 1904).

Hunter, W. W., *The Imperial Gazetteer of India,* vol. I (London, 1885).

Thornton, Edward, *The Gazetteer of the Territories under the government of East India Company and the Native States of the continent of India,* vol. III (London, 1854).

Brackenbury, C. F., *Madras District Gazetteer- Cuddapah* (Madras, 1915).

Maclean, C.D., *Standing information regarding the official Administration of the Madras Presidency in each department in illustration of the Yearly Administration Reports.* (Madras, 1877; 2nd edition 1879).

Rao, C. Hayavadana, *Mysore Gazetteer,* vol. IV, *Administration* (Bangalore, 1929).

Pate, H.R., *Madras District Gazetteer : Tinnevelly District* (Madras, 1979).

Stuart, J. A., *A Manual of the Tinnevelly District* (Madras, 1879).

Madras District Gazetteer, Bellary District, vol. II (Madras, 1930).

Sturrock, J., *Madras District Manuals, South Canara.* (Madras : Asylum Press, 1894).

The Imperial Gazetteer of India : The Indian Empire, Vol. III, Economic. Oxford : At the Clarendon Press, 1907.

Hemingway, F.R., *Madras District Gazetteers, Trichnopoly.* Madras, 1907.

Hemingway, F.R., *Madras District Gazetteers, Tanjore.* Edited by W. Francis. Madras, 1906.

Garstin, J.H., *Manual of the South Arcot District,* Madras, 1878.

Francis, W., *Madras District Gazetteers, Vizagapatam,* Madras, 1907.

Francis, W., *Madras District Gazetteers, South Arcot,* Madras, 1906.

Francis, W., *Madras District Gazetteers, Madras.* Madras, 1906.

Francis, W., *Madras District Gazetteers, Bellary.* Madras, 1904.

Crole, Charles Stuart, *The Chingleput Late Madras District, A Manual compiled under tthe orders of the Madras Government.* Madras, 1879.

Gazetteer of the Bombay Presidency, vol. I, Part II. *History of the Konkan, Dekkan and Southern Maratha country.* Bombay, 1915.

Dictionary and Glossary

Tamil Lexicon, 6 vols. (Madras : Madras Law Journal Press, 1934). University of Madras.

Yule, Henry and Burnell, A.C., *Hobson-Jobson : A Glossary of Colloquial Anglo-Indian Words and Phrases and of Kindred Terms, Etymological, Historical, Geographical and Discursive,* ed. by William Crooke (London, 1903, Reprint Delhi, 1968).

Wilson, H.H., *A Glossary of Judicial and Revenue Terms and of useful words occurring in official documents relating to the Administration of the Government of British India* from the Arabic, Persian, Hindustani, Sanskrit, Hindi, Bengali, Uriya, Marathi, Guzarathi, Telugu, Karnata, Tamil, Malayalam and other languages (London, 1855, 2nd edn. Delhi, 1968).

Sircar, D.C., *Indian Epigraphical Glossary* (Motilal Banarsidass, Delhi, 1966).

Sivaramaiya, C., *A Classified Glossary of Tamil Words with Explanatory Meaning,* Madras, 1908.

Modern Works

Abraham, Meera. *Two Medieval Merchant Guilds of South India*. New Delhi, Manohar Publications 1988.

Aiyangar, S. Krishnaswami. *Evolution of Hindu Administrative Institutions in South India.* Madras: University of Madras, 1931.

Aiyar, R. Sathyanatha. *History of the Nayaks of Madura.* Madras : Oxford University Press, 1924.

Appadorai, A. *Economic Conditions in Southern India (1000-1500 A.D.).* 2 vols. Madras: University of Madras, 1990 reprint.

Arokiasamy, M., *The Kongu Country*, University of Madras, Madras, 1956.

Ayyangar, S. Krishnaswami : *Sources of Vijayanagar History, selected and edited for the University of Madras, 1919.*

Baden-Powell, B.H., *The Land Systems of British India being A Manual of the Land-Tenures and of the Systems of Land Revenue Administration Prevalent in the Several Provinces.* Oxford 1892; Reprint Delhi, 1974.

Baden-Powell, B.H., *The Origin and Growth of Village Communities in India.* London, 1908.

Baliga, B.S. *Studies in Madras Administration.*2 vols. Madras : India Press, 1960.

Beaglehole, T.H. *Thomas Munro and the Development of Administrative Policy in Madras, 1792-1818 : The Origin of the Munro System.* Cambridge : University Press, 1966.

Bhandarkar, Ramkrishna Gopal, *Early History of the Dekkan down to the Mahommedan conquest.* Calcutta, 1928.

Chablani, H.L., *The Economic Condition of India during the Sixteenth Century.* Delhi, 1929.

Champakalakshmi, R. *Trade, ideology and Urbanization : South India 300 BC to AD 1300.* Delhi: Oxford University Press, 1996.

Chitnis, K.N. *Keladi Polity.* Dharwar : Karnatak University, 1974.

Coomaraswamy, Ananda K., *The Indian Craftsman.* London, 1909.

Das, Dipakranjan. *Economic History of the Deccan : From the First to the Sixth Century A.D.* Delhi: Munshiram Manoharlal, 1969.

Desai, A.R. (Ed.). *Peasant Struggles in India.* Delhi : Oxford University Press, 1982.

Dikshit, G.S., *Local Government in Medieval Karnataka*, Karnataka University, Dharwad, 1964.

Dua, J. C. *Agrarian System* in *South India: Some Aspects.* New Delhi: Radha Publications, 1990.

Dua J.C. *British Historiography Eighteenth Century Punjab :Their Understanding of Sikh struggle for power and role of Jassa Singh Ahluwalia.* Delhi : Radha Publication, 1992.

Dua, J.C. *British In'am Policy and Palegar Resistance in Ceded Districts : Select Documents Relating to Narasimha Reddy's Resistance.* Delhi : Triveni Publications, 1994.

Dua, J.C. *Palegars of South India : Forms and Contents of their Resistance in Ceded Districts.* New Delhi : Reliance Publishing House, 1996.

Frykenberg, Robert Eric. *Guntur District 1788-1848 : A History of Local Influence and Central Authority in South India.* Oxford : Clarendon Press, 1965.

Frykenberg, Robert Eric (Ed.). *Land Control and Social Structure in Indian History.* New Delhi : Manohar, 1979.

Frykenberg, Robert Eric (Ed.). *Land Tenure and Peasant in South Asia.* New Delhi : Manohar, 1984.

Fukazawa, Hiroshi. *The Medieval Deccan : Peasants, Social Systems and States : Sixteenth to Eighteenth Centuries.* Delhi : Oxford University Press, 1991.

Gopalachari, K. *Early History of tthe Andhra Country.* Madras : University of Madras, 1976.

Goshal, U.N., *Contributions to the History of the Hindu Revenue Systems,* Calcutta, 1929.

Goshal, U.N., *The Agrarian System of Ancient India,* Calcutta, 1930.

Govidaswamy, M.S. *The Role of Feudatories in late Cōḻa History,* Annamalainagar, 1979.

Guha, Nikhiles, *Pre-British State System in South India : Mysore 1761-1799.* Calcutta : Ratna Prakashan, 1985.

Gupta, K.M., *The Land System in South India Between c.800 AD. and 1200 AD. (in the light of Epigraphic and Literary Evidence).* The Punjab Oriental Series, No. XX, Lahore, 1933.

Gururajachar, S., *Some Aspects of Economic and Social Life in Karnataka (A.D. 1000-1300),* Prasaranga, University of Mysore, 1974.

Hall, Kenneth R., *Trade and Statecraft in the Age of Cōḻas.* Abhinav Publications, New Delhi, 1980.

Harriss, J., *Capitalism and Peasant Farming : Agrarian Structure and Ideology in Northern Tamil Nadu,* OUP, Delhi, 1982.

Hjelje, Benedicte, *Slavery and Agricultural Bondage in South India in the Nineteenth Century,* The Scandinavian Institute of Asian Studies, Monograph Series, Copenhagen, 1967.

Irschick, Eugene F. *Dialogue and History : Constructing South India, 1795-1895.* Delhi : Oxford University Press, 1994.

Iyengar, Sundraraja, S., *Land Tenure in Madras Presidency,* Madras, 1921.

Jha, D.N. *Studies in Early Indian Economic History.* Delhi : Anupama Publications, 1980.

Jha, D.N. *Temples and Merchants in South India (A.D. 900-1300),* New Delhi, 1976.

Karashima, Noborn. *South Indian History and Society : Studies from Inscriptions, A.D. 850-1800.* Delhi : Oxford University Press, 1984.

Krishnan, K.G. *Chittiramelip-Periyanadu–An Agricultural Guild of Medieval Tamil Nadu.* Madras : University of Madras, 1982.

Krishnan, K.G., *Studies in South Indian History and Epighraphy,* New Era Publications, Madras, 1981.

Krishnan,V.V. Kunhi. *Tenancy Legislation in Malabar (1880-1970) : An Historical Analysis.* New Delhi : Northern Book Centre, 1993.

Kumar, Dharma. *Land and Caste in South India : Agricultural Labour in the Madras Presidency during the Nineteenth Century.* New Delhi, Manohar, 1992 (Reprint).

Kuppuswamy, G.R., *Economic Conditions in Karnataka (A.D. 973- A.D. 1336),* Karnataka University, Dharwar, 1975.

Ludden, David. *Peasant History in South India* . Delhi : Oxford University Press, 1989.

Mahalingam, T.V. *Administration and Social Life Under Vijayanagar : Part I- Administration; Part II- Social Life.* Second Edition. Madras : University of Madras, 1969 and 1975 respectively.

Mahalingam, T.V., *Economic Life in the Vijayanagar Empire,* University of Madras, Madras, 1951.

Mahalingam, T.V. *Readings in South Indian History.* General editor S.P. Gupta, Editor K.S. Ramachandran. Delhi ; B.R. Publishing Corporation, 1977.

Mahalingam, T.V. *South Indian Polity,* University of Madras, Madras, 1967.

Minakshi, C., *Administration and Social Life under the Pallavas,* University of Madras, Madras, 1938.

Mohan, V.K. *Art and Architecture of the Telugu Cōḻa Temples.* New Delhi : Kaveri Books, 1996.

Mudaliar, Chandra. *State and Religious Endowments in Madras.* Madras : University of Madras, 1976.

Mukherjee, Nilmani, *The Ryotwari System in Madras, 1792-1827.* Calcutta : Firma K.L. Mukhopadhyay, 1962.

Myneni, Krishna Kumari, *Studies on Medieval Andhra History and Culture.* Delhi : Kanishka Publishers, Distributors, 1994.

Nagaswamy, R., *Seminar on Inscriptions,* Madras, 1968.

Nilkanta Sastri, K.A., *The Cōḻas,* University of Madras, Madras, 1955, Reprint 1984.

Om Prakash. *Early Indian Land Grants and State Economy.* Allahabad : Excellence Publishers, 1988.

Pandeya, B.K., *Temple Economy under Cholas : 850-1070,* New Delhi, 1984.

Prasad, Om Prakash, *Decay and Revival of Urban Centres in Medieval South India (c.A.D. 600 -1200).* New Delhi : Janaki Prakashan, 1989.

Raju, A. Sarada. *Economic Conditions in the Madras Presidency : 1800 - 1850.* Madras: University of Madras, 1941.

Ramesh, K.V. *A History of South Kanara (from the earliest times to the fall of Vijayanagar).* Dharwar, 1970.

Ratnam, R. *Agricultural Development in Madras State Prior to 1900.* Madras : New Century Book House, 1966.

Reddy, Nagolu Krishna. *Social History of Andhra Pradesh (Seventh to Thirteenth Century: Based on Inscriptions and Literature).* Delhi : Agam Kala Prakashan, 1991.

Richards, J.F. *Mughal Administration in Golconda.* Oxford : Clarendon Press, 1975.

Satayanarayana, A. *Andhra Peasants Under British Rule : Agrarian Relations and the Rural Economy 1900 - 1940.* New Delhi : Manohar, 1990.

Sewell, Robert. *A Forgotten Empire : Vijayanagar : A Contribution to the History of India.* Delhi, Publication Division, 1962.

Shanmugam, S. *The Revenue System of the Cholas, 850-1279.* Madras : New Era Publications, 1987.

Shantakumari, S.L. *History of the Agraharas, Karnataka A.D. 400 - 1300.* Madras, 1986.

Sherwani, Haroon Khan. *The Bahmanis of the Deccan.* New Delhi : Munshiram Manoharlal, 1985.

Shrinivas Ritti. *A Decade of Epigraphical Studies in South India,* Karnatak University, Dharwar, 1985.

Singh, Upinder. *Kings, Brahmanas and Temples in Orissa : An Epigraphic Study AD 300 - 1147.* New Delhi : Munshiram Manoharlal, 1994.

Sircar, D.C. *Landlordism and Tenancy in Ancient and Medieval India as revealed by Epigraphical Records.* Lucknow : University of Lucknow, 1969.

Sircar, D.C. *Studies in the Political and Administrative Systems in Ancient and Medieval India.* Delhi: Motilal Banarsidass, 1974.

Sivakumar, Chitra and Sivakumar, S.S. *Peasants and Nabobs : Agrarian Radicalism in Late Eighteenth Century Tamil Country.* Delhi : Hindustan Publishing Corporation, 1993.

Slater, Gilbert. *Economic Studies :* Vol. I, *Some South Indian Villages.* Madras : Oxford University Press, 1918.

Stein, Burton. *Peasant State and Society in Medieval South India.* Delhi : Oxford University Press, 1994.

Subrahmanyam, Sanjay. *Money and the Market in India 1100 - 1700.* Delhi : Oxford University Press, 1994.

Sundaram, K., *Studies in Economic and Social Conditions of Medieval Andhra (A.D. 1000 - 1600),* Machilipatnam, 1968.

Tirumalai, R. *Land Grants and Agrarian Reactions in Cōḷa and Pāṇḍya Times.* Madras : University of Madras, 1987

Veluthat, Kesavan. *The Political Structure of Early Medieval South India.* New Delhi : Orient Longman, 1993.

Venkatasubramanian, T.K. *Political Change and Agrarian Tradition in South India (C. 1600 - 1801): A Case Study.* Delhi : Mittal Publications, 1986.

Wade, Robert. *Village Republics* : *Economic Conditions for Collective Action in South India.* Cambridge: Cambridge University Press, 1987. Indian Edition : Bombay : Orient Longman, 1989.

Wheeler, J. Talboys. *Annals of the Madras Presidency...* 3 vols. Reprint, Delhi Low Price Publications, 1990.

Wilks, Lieut. Colonel Mark, *Historical Sketches of the South India in an attempt to trace the History of Mysore...,* (1810) Edited with notes by Murray Hammick, 2 vols. (Mysore, 1st vol. in 1930 and 2nd in 1932).

Wood, Conrad. *The Moplah Rebellion and Its Genesis.* New Delhi, People's Publishing House, 1987.

Yazdani, G. (Ed.). *The Early History of the Deccan.* 2 vols. New Delhi : Oriental Books Reprint Corporation, 1982.

Articles

Dirks, N.B., 'Terminology and Taxonomy; Discourse and Domination : From Old Regime to Colonial Regime in South India', in *Studies of South India.* Eds. Robert Eric Frykenberg and Pauline Kolenda (Madras : New Era Publications, 1985).

Dua, J. C. 'Comparative Position of the Village Headmen During the Early British Rule in the Punjab and the Madras Presidency', *Punjab History Conference,* Patiala, 23rd session, 1987.

– 'Landed Elites in Upheaval-Forms and Contents of Resistance by the Palegars 1800 - 1846', Dr. Kalaignar Thiru M. Karunanidhi Endowment Lectures, Madras University, Madras, 7th, 10th, 11th April 1995.

– 'Method of Land Measurement and Assessment in Northern Circars During the Pre-British Era as Reflected in the Chetri Ganitam', *Indian History Congress,* Dharwad, 1988.

– 'Nature of the Poligar Revolts in the Ceded Districts During the first Half of the 19th Century: A Case Study', *Indian History Congress,* Jadavpur, 1974.

– 'Review Article', on *South Indian Rebellion : The First War of Independence,* 1800 - 1801 by K. Rajayyan in *The Indian Historical Review,* Vol. II, No. 2, January 1976.

– 'Poligars : Their Rise in the Ceded Districts', in Proceedings of *Indian History Congress,* 33rd session, 1972.

– 'Position of the Patels and Karnams in the Ceded Districts during the First Quarter of the Nineteenth Century', *Indian History Congress,* Chandigarh, 1973. Also in Bhattacharya, Sabyasachi (Ed.), *Essays in Modern Indian Economic History* (New Delhi, 1987).

Grover, B.R., 'An Analysis of the Contemporary Revenue Documents and Correspondence Pertaining to Patiala Chieftainship *(Zamindari)* during the later half of the 18th Century', *Punjab past and present,* Vol. XXIV-I, April 1990.

– 'Nature of Land Rights in Mughul India', *The Indian Economic and Social History Review,* Vol. I, No. 1, 1963.

– 'Nature of *Dehat-i-Taaluqa (Zamindari Villages)* and the Evolution of the *Taaluqdari* System during Mughal Age', *The Indian Economic and Social History Review,* Vol. II No 2, 1965 and Vol. II, No. 3, 1965.

– 'Elements of Continuity and Changes in the Land Ownership and Rights from the Mughal Age to the Early British Administration in India', Presidential Address, Medieval Indian Section, *Indian History Congress,* 37th Session, Calicut, 1976.

– 'The position of Desai in the *Pargana* Administration of Subah Gujrat under the Mughals', *Indian History Congress,* Delhi, 1961.

– Hassan, S. Nurul, Three Studies of the Zamindari Systems, *Medieval India : A Miscillany* (Bombay, 1968).

– 'Aspects of Zamindari System in Deccan', *Indian History Congress,* Varanasi, 1969.

Jagannadham, A., 'Some Aspects of Socio-Economic Conditions in Ceded Districts : 1800-1810', *Itihas* (Hyderabad), Vol. IV, No. 2, 1976.

Komarov, Erik, 'Content and Principal Forms of the Evolution of Agrarian Relations in India in the 19th Century', *New India Studies by Soviet Scholars, - "Social Sciences Today",* No. 33, 1976.

Rao, B.S.L. Hanumantha, 'The Boyas in Andhra History; *Journal of Andhra Historical Research Society,* 38, 1983-84, pp. 77.

Rao, Diwan Bahadur T. Bhujanga, 'Rayalaseema', in *Journal of the Andhra Historical Research Society* Vol. XVII, Part 1-4, July-October 1946 - January-April 1947.

Reddy, M. Pattabhi Rama, 'Aspects of Agrarian Revolution in Andhra (1800 - 1820) : The Munro System - Extermination of Poligars', *Proceedings of Andhra Pradesh History Congress*, Ramachandrapuram, 1976.

Balambal, V., 'Sabha's Control over land during the reign of the Imperial Cholas', *JIH*, 1980.

Champakalakshmi, R., 'Growth of Urban Centres in South India : Kudamūkku - Paḻaiyarai, The Twin - City of the Colas', in *Studies in History*, Vo. I, 1979.

Champakalakshmi, R., 'Urbanisation in Medieval Tamil Nadu', in *Situating Indian History*, Delhi, 1986.

Champakalakshmi, R., 'Urbanisation in South India : Role of Ideology and Polity, Presidential Address, Ancient India Section, *Indian History Congress*, 47th Session, Srinagar, 1986.

Dharma Kumar, 'Private Property in Asia ? The Case of Medieval South India', in *Comparative Studies and History*, Vol. 27, 1985, pp. 340-366.

Indrapala, K., 'Some Medieval Mercantile Communities of South India and Ceylon', *JTS*, Vol. II 2, 1970, pp. 25 -39.

Karaishma, Noboru, and Sitaraman, B., 'Revenue terms in Chola Inscriptions', *Journal of Asian and African Studies*, No -5, Tokyo, 1972, pp. 87-117.

Karashima, Noboru, 'The Village Communities in Chola Times : Myth or Reality', in *JESI*, Vol. VIII, 1981, pp. 85-96.

Kasinathan, Natana, 'Sale of Land in the Chola Period', in *JESI*, Vol. IV, 1977, pp. 79-81.

Kesavan Veluthat, 'The *Sabha* and *Parisad* in early medieval South India : Correlation of Epigraphic and Dharmasastric evidence', in *Tamil Civilization*. Journal of the Tamil University, Vol.-3, No. 2-3, 1985, pp. 75-82.

Nandi, R.N., 'Feudalization of the State in Medieval South India', in *Social Science Probings*, Vol. I 1984, pp.33-59.

Nilkanta Sastri, K.A., 'Irai, Irai-Kaval and Iraiyili' in *Dr. S. Krishnaswami Aiyangar Commemoration* Volume, pp. 191-196.

Rajan Gurkkal, 'Aspects of the Reservoir System of irrigation in the Early Pandya State', in *Studies in History*, Vol - 2, No.2, (1986), pp. 157-164.

Shanmugam, P., 'Aspects of the Chola Revenue System in Karnataka', in A.V. Narasimha Murthy and K.V. Ramesh (Ed.), *Giridharasri : Essays on Indology* (Dr. G.S. Dikshit Felicitation Volume), Delhi, 1987, pp. 123-127.

Shanmugam, P., 'Tax-free Grants during the period of Rajaraja I' in K.K.A. Venkatachari, (Ed.), *Raja Raja - The Great*, Bombay, 1987.

Subbarayalu, Y., 'The Place of Ur in the Economic and Social History of the Early Tamil Nadu from A.D. 750 to 1350' in A.V. Narasimha Murthy, B.K. Gururaja Rao, (Eds.), *Rangavalli : Recent Researches on Indology*, pp. 171-177.

Subbarayalu, Y., 'Classification of Land and Assessment of Land Tax in Early Medieval Tamil Nadu from 950 to 1300', in *PIHC*, XXXVIII session (Bhubaneswar) 1977, pp. 341-346.

Iṇdex

A

A'bādāni 1

A-chammaṅgālaka, a-chārāsnana-charmāṅgāra 1

A-lavaṇa-khātaka 1

A-lavaṇa-klinna kreṇikhanaka 1

A-loṇa-guḷa-chchhobha 1

A-paramparā-balīvarda 1

A-paramparā-go-balīvarda, a-paramparā-balivarda-grahana 1

A-prāveśya 1

A-rāshṭrasāṁvinayika 1

A-vāra-siddhika 1

Ā-candr-ārkkam 1

Āḍa, aḍḍa 1

Ābhāvya 1

Ābhīra 1

Ābhoga 1

Ābhyantar-ādāya 1

Ācāra 1

Ācāra-pātra 1

Ācāra-sthiti-pātra 1

Ācārya-pūjanā 1

Ācāryas 1

Āchu 1

Āḍha 1

Āḍāṇaka 1

Āḍavallān 2

Āḍhaka 1, 2

Āḍi paccai 2

Āḍi-kārtikai-paccai 2, 75

Ādāna 2

Ādāya 2

Ādatta 2

Ādeya 2

Ādhavāpa, āḍhakavāpa 2

Ādirai-ppāṭṭam, attirai-ppāṭṭam 2

Āgāmin 2, 18

Āgama-nigama-dāna 2

Āhāras, hāras 2, 44, 156

Ājñā, Ājñapti, Ājñāpti 2

Āñjaṣṭa-sabhā, Āñjaṣṭa-śattu-sabhai 2

Āñjuvaṇṇam 2

Ājīvikas 2

Ājiva-kāśu 2

Āju-pācālattār 82

Ākāśa-pātāl-otpatti 2

Ākara-maṇḍalika 2

Ākarṣaka 2

Āḷ-vari 2

Āḷ-nĕl, āṇĕl 2

Āḷamanci 2

Āḷmañji 2

Āledere 2

Āmra 3

Āṇaka 15

Āṇḍārs 3

Ān-añju 140

Āṇimuttu 3

Ānanda-nidhi 3

Āndu, andoo 3

Āni 3

Ānita 3

Āpan-ājīvika 3

Āpaṇa 3

Āpaṇa-paṭṭakāra 3

Āṟṟaṅkarai-ttevai 3

Āṟṟu-kkulai 3

Āṟidupaḍugai 3

Āraycci, ārāya 3, 75

Ārdhika 3

Ārōgyaśātai 3

Āṣṭa-bhāgika 3

Āśuva-kkāśu, āśuvikaḷ-kāśu, āśuva-kkaḍamais 3

Āsana 3

Āsana-charman 3

Āṭṭivāriyam 164

Āṭṭuppāṭṭam 3
Ātaṇḍa, Ātoṇḍa, Atanda 3
Ātithya 3
Āturāvaḍḍi, āntarāvaḍḍi 3
Āvāra 3
Āvāta 3
Āvaṇam 3
Āvesani 3
Āvṛtti 3
Āya 3
Āya daṇḍam 4
Āyāga-sabhā 4
Āyagārs 3, 4, 47, 102
Āyam 4, 15, 202
Āyatanam 4
Āyudhīya 4
Áb-kárí, abkari, abkarry 4
Áltamghá, althamga 4
Ámání, Aamani 4
Ámishan, amshom, amsom, amsam, umsom 4, 103
Ására 4
Áwardah-navis, awurdah novis 4
Aagramandire 4
Abayam 4
Abhayaśāsana 4
Abhidhānacintāmaṇi 5
Abhinava 5
Abhinava-mārgaṇaka 5
Abhyantara-Siddhi, Abhyantara-Siddhika, Ābhyantara-Siddhi 5
Abohana, agovana 5
Abraiaman 5
Abwáb 5, 103, 208
Abwáb-i-Jáfar Khán-abwáb 5
Abwáb-i-kásim Khán-abwáb 5
Abwáb-i-Shujá Khán-abwáb 5
Abwáb-i-subahdári abwáb 5
Acala-pravṛtti 5
Acca-taṟi 5, 178
Accinaṭankaṣāla 5
Accu 1, 5
Accu-pannāya 5
Accu-taṟi, accu-ttaṟki 5
Accukkaṭṭu land 5, 108
Accupannāyadadhi-ṣṭhāyaka 5
Accutaṟi 5
Accuvari 5
Achandrarkam 5
Acharyapurusha in'am 5
Aḍaiōḷai, Aḍaiōlai 5
Aḍaipaḍi kadamai 5
Aḍaippar 5
Aḍaippu 5
Aḍappam 5
Aḍḍa-cinna 6
Aḍḍānaka
Aḍḍavaṭṭa-suṅkamu 6
Aḍimai (Tamil), Adumah, Adumy, Adima (Malayalam) adimai, adami 6, 94
Aḍimai-kkāśu 6
Adálat, Adalat 6
Adálat-i-díwání 6
Adálat-i-faujdári 6
Adamaana chitta 6
Adangal 7
Adangal olungu 7
Adavoo saathanum 7
Adḍaga, aḍḍuga 7
Addhikas 7
Addhiya-manussas 7
Adhaḥ 7
Adhi-kárí, Adhikari, Adhigari 7
Adhika-paḍi 7
Adhikāra-ppon 7
Adhikāra-varttāa 7
Adhirāṭ, ekarāṭ 7
Adhukāra-pperu 7
Adhyakṣa 7
Adhyayanam in'am, Adhyayana-vṛtti 7
Adi-kkāśu 7
Adirvedi in'am 7
Aditi 7
Adityuñcha 7
Adungul 7
Aerical 7
Aga 8
Agahara, agāhara, āgahara 8, 25, 105
Agapat (T) 8
Agara 8
Agara viniyōgam 8
Agara-brahmadeya 8, 32
Agara-pparṟu 8
Agaram 8, 32, 135
Agaras 8
Agathi 8
Agghāpaṇikaṭṭhāna, agghakāraka 8
Agnipuman In'am 8

Agra, agra-bhāga, agra-pratyaṁśa, agrapratyāya 8
Agráháram, Agrahāra 8, 9, 32, 59, 91, 94, 119, 151, 166, 167, 174, 189
Agrahāra-pradey-āṁśa 9
Agraháraváďei 8
Agrahārīṇa-mahattara 9
Agrahārika, Āgrahārika 9
Agrahārin, Agrahārīṇa 9
Agrahara vadakai, Agrahara vadiky 9, 31
Agraharamdar 9
Agran patun 9
Ahadi 9
Ahara 9
Ahkám-námah, akamnamah, ahamnamah 9
Ahasham, ahashaum, ahshám, asham, ahsham 9
Ahshám-i-amalah, asham omleh 9
Ahshám-i-sipáhi, asham sepaye 9
'Aín 9
Aimbadinmēlagaram 10
Aimmadaran 10
Airiṇadurga 10
Ajnapati 10
Akhrájját, akherjaut 10
Akhrájat-i-arang, akherjaut aurung 10
Akkam 10
Akka-Śālā 10
Akkarika-vṛitti 10
Akkaśālai-vari 10
Akkasālevari 10
Akṣaya-nīvi, akṣaya-nīvī 10
Akṣayanīkā, akṣaya-nīvikā 10
Akṣīṇin 10, 18
Akshadarśa 10
Al (Tamil, Malayalam), Alu (Kanarese) 10
Al-bahr al-kāhil 10
Al amanji al, 10
Aḷag-accu 10
Aḷḷāya-mānyam 10
Aḷantapaṭi 10
Aḷivu 10
Alahida 10
Alaktaka 10
Alal sherndakally 10, 79, 97
Alavan In'am 10
Aliyanasantana 110
Allodium 10
Almadia 11
Aloosa 11
Alotti In'am 11
Alpam-irai 11
Aṁśa-bṛhadbhogika 11
Aṁśapati 11
Amāni, Amání, aumany, aumani, aumanie (A) 11
Amadikarambu 11
Amal, amulu 11
Amanat in'am 11
Amañci, Amanci 2, 11, 193
Amaniya 11
Amañji 11
Amara, Amara-Māgaṇi 4, 11, 12
Amara-nāyaka 12, 124
Amarakar 12
Amaram 12, 189
Amaramāgaṇi 12
Amaranāyaka tenure 12
Ambalakaram in'am 12
Ambalam in'am 12
Ambalavasis 12
Ambali in'am 12
Ambaṇam 12
Ambattam 12
Ambigar in'am 12
Amil 12, 13, 62
Amildar, amal-dár, aumildar 12, 13, 117
Ammu-kaḍa-suṅkamu 13
Ammubaḍi-suṅkamu 13
Ampu-vari 13, 196
Amṛta-gaṇa, amirta-gaṇattār 13
Amṛta-padi, amuda-ppaḍi 13
Amukhyāhāra 13
Anubhoga-ppaṟṟ-ōḷugu 13
An-to-lo 13
Anādeśya, aniradeśya 13
Aṅgāraka 13
Aṇai 13
Aṅkāṭik-kūli, aṅkāṭip-pāṭṭam 13, 14
Anṟāḍu-kōmuṟṟavar 13
Anṟal-kōvukku 13
Aṅga-bhoga 13, 158
Aṅga-maṇi 13

Aṅga-maṇi-dravya 13
Aṅgāḍi-kkūli, aṅgāḍi-ppāṭṭam 13
Aṅgāra, aṅgāraka, a-carm-āṅgāraka 13
Aṅgaḍa-siddhāya 13
Aṅgula, aṅguli 13
Aṅkāṭi-kūli 13
Aṅkāṭi-pāṭṭam, kaṭai-pāṭṭam, uṟṟaṅkāṭipattam 14
Ana 14
Anādi carambu, Anādikarambu 14, 169, 180
Anāhārya 14
Anacchedya 14
Anádi, anadee 14
Anáth-banjar, anad-bunger, anod-bunjer 14
Anátha 14
Anáthi 14
Anaikatta 14
Anaikkaran in'am 14
Anakala in'am 14
Anantaravan 14
Anavamarśya 14
Anchana-kabuliyat 14
Anchumna, anchumma 14
Andharia kotha 14
Andi 14
Andi-samadhi in'am 14
Angazala in'am 14
Angazala kattubadi 14
Anicoody 14
Anicut 14
Aniyukta, niyukt-āniyukta-rājapuruṣa 14
Añjinānpugaliḍam 14, 15
Anjumana 2, 15
Anjuvannam 15
Anmosha 15
Anna 15
Anna shrotriyam 15
Annakavadi in'am 15
Anniyāyavavadaṇḍa viṟai 15
Anson Banjar 15
Anta mahāmātra 15
Antarāyam, Antar-āya, Antar-āyam, Antarāyām, Antarāyam 15, 187
Antar-ādāya 15
Antaḥ-kara, antar-ādāya 15
Antara-vaniyoga 15
Antarāya-kkāśu, antarāya-ppāṭṭam 15
Antarāyak-kācu 15
Antarāyam-pāṭṭam-utpaṭa-iṟaiyiliyāy 15
Antaralikaṃ 15
Anuga-jīvita, aṇuga-jīvita, aṇuṁga-jīvita 15
Anumodita 15
Anuvarttanā 15
Aparāntaka 15
Apparenjee Pagoda 15
Apradā 15
Apradā-dharma 15
Aprahata 16
Apratikara 16
Aputra-dhana, aputrika-dhana 16
Aputrika-veṇi 16
Aṟaccalai 16
Aṟaikāval 16
Aṟṟuk-karai, aṟṟukkulai 16
Aṟṟukkāl-amañci, aṟṟukkāl-veṭṭi 16
Aṟṟukkāl-veṭṭi 16
Aṟṟup-paṭṭam 3, 16
Aṟukūṟināl puravu 16
Ara 16
Ara-nír 16
Araghāṭṭa 16, 56, 157, 187
Arakkal 16
Aral in'am 16
Araṇya land 16
Araṇya-karshaṇa 16
Arang, aurung 10, 16
Araśu svatantaram 16, 77
Araśukāvalgār 16
Araśy-pēṟu 16, 105
Arasukaval 16
Aravadaṇḍam 16
Arcanā-bhoga, arcanā-vṛtti 16
Arcanā-vibhava-kāṇi 17
Archanabhagam 17, 160
Arcot Rupee 17
Ardha-namasya-vṛtti 17
Ardhamāanya, Ardhamanyam 17
Arikūli 17
Arimitikōl 17
Arimukkai 17
Ariśi-kkāṇam, Ariśi-kāṇam 17
Arrack 17
Arroba 17

Arthāruvā, andhāruvā 17
Arudi-carei, Arudikarei, Aṟudikarai (Tamil), Ardhachandrarkam 17, 136, 138, 144, 148
Aruhaṇa, āruvaṇa, aṟuvaṇa 17
Aruppampuchi 17
Ary koory (kooly) kanum karunum 17
Aryacut 17
Arz 18
Aṣṭa 18
Aṣṭa bhoga tejah svāmya, Aṣṭa-bhoga, aiśvary-āṣṭaka, aṣṭa-bhūti 2, 10, 18, 74, 162, 181,
Aṣṭādaśa-prakṛti 18
Aṣṭabhoga-tejaḥsvāmya 18, 166
Aśal 5, 18
Asadi in'am 18
Asal, assal, asil, ausil, auzil 5, 18
Asal-i-tumár jama, assual tumar jamma 18, 41
Asalminha gardens tenure 18
Asara 18
Asaris 18
Ashur-khana in'am 18
Askar 18
Asnad 18
Asof, Asoph (A) 18
Assāmikadhana 18
Astamba 18
Asti 18
Aṭaṅkal, aḍaṅga 18
Aṭavi 19
Aṭhavana 19
Aṭi 19, 30, 139
Aṭṭagam 19
Aṭṭagattar 19
Atalaya 19
Atchkutt 19
Athalai 19
Athals 19
Athoonee, athavani 19
Atikārap-poṉ 19
Atikāri 19, 124
Atsu-kavali tenure 19
Atti 19
Atti kempoorum 19
Atti kully kanum 19
Atti per 19
Attipett ola karunum 19
Atur in'am 19
Atvani 19
Auavagas 19
Audraṅgika 19
Aunakomban 19
Autoopachal (Tamil) 19
Avadāna, āvadāna, āvedana 19
Avanḍ-āya 20
Avanaku 20
Avani-randhra-nyāya 20
Avani-vetana, pādikāval 20
Avarai 20
Avarajat 20
Avaram, avarai 20
Avesanin 3
Avasaravarttanai 20
Awaraja 20
Ayam 20
Ayacret 20
Ayacut 20
Ayakaṭṭu 20
Ayaktakas, ayuktakas 20
Ayyagalu 20
Ayyam 20
Azmayish 20

B

B'il mukta 21, 27
Bāda 21
Bāhya, bāhy-ābhyantar-ādāya, puṟavāyam, Puṟa-kaḍamai 1, 21
Bānisa 21
Bághayat, bághát, bagahat, bajyhat, baugayher, baugayut 21, 24
Bákí, baky 21
Bákí kifáyat, baky keffyet 21
Báné 21
Bára-balúté 21
Báramahál 21
Báricudu 21
Bad 21
Baḍagá 21
Badai in'am 22, 181, 203
Badarkah, budrucka 22
Badernavis 22
Badi-bad in'am 22
Badulu 22
Bagayat 22
Bagh-mari in'am 22

Bahal 22
Bahattara-niyōg-ādhipati 22
Bail 22, 24
Baja-wala in'am 22
Bajerack 22
Bajra 22
Bakshi, Bakhshi (P) 22
Bali in'am 22
Balijas 22
Balla 22
Baṇḍi 22
Baṇṭula-āyamu 22
Banagar in'ams 22
Band, bund 22
Bandaikkai 22
Bandaloo 22
Bandar, bunder 22
Bandela in'am 22
Bandiman 23
Banjaras 23
Bants 23
Bantumana in'am 23
Bapatu 23
Barața 23
Barbast 23
Bariké 23
Bariki in'am 23
Bariz 23
Barr 23
Barut-goli in'am 23
Basa 23
Basivi in'am 23
Bati 23
Batta 23, 88, 125
Battai, hissa, warum 23
Batti 23
Bayinidi in'am 23
Bazí, bazee 23
Bazí daf-ah, bazee duffa 23
Bazí jama, bazee jamma 23
Bazí zamín, bazee zameen 23
Bazí zamín, daftar 23
Bazi-kharach, bazeecurtch, bazee-kurch, bazeh kherck 23
Be charagh 23
Bēdige, Bédige 23, 24
Bedabinugu 24
Bediga 24
Begari in'am 24
Begayet 24
Beldar in'am 24
Bellum 24
Beríz 24
Besa-vaga, besa-makkaļu 24
Bestas 24
Bettu 24, 106
Betunes, the 24
Bhāga, rājabhāga 24
Bhāṇḍara-pustaka, baṇḍāra-ppottagam 24
Bhágam, baugaum 24
Bhaikṣakạ 24
Bhakt-āya, bhatt-āya 24
Bhakta-grāma, bhatta-grāma 24
Bhakt-ādāya, pakt-ātāyam 24
Bhale-log 24
Bhaṁḍi, baṁdi 24
Bhaṇḍārin, Bhāṇḍārin 24
Bhandagarika 24
Bharati in'am 24
Bharti 24, 25, 194
Bhaṭās 25
Bhaṭṭa vṛttimānyams 25
Bhaṭṭa-grāma 25
Bhaṭṭavṛtti, Bhaṭṭa-vṛtti, Bhaṭṭa-bhāga, Bhatta-vritti 25
Bhaṭṭavṛtti-mānya 25
Bhatraz in'am 25
Bhatta, Batta 25
Bhaviṣya-kkiḍai-ppuṛam 25
Bhikhu-hala, bhikshu-hala 25
Bhōga-āyakam 25
Bhōgam, Bhógam, bhogum, bogum 25
Bhōgapatra 25
Bhógyádi, bhogyadhi 25
Bhógyam 25
Bhog-addharaṇika 25
Bhoga, Bhogas, bhāgas 1, 25
Bhoga-āyaka 26
Bhoga-janapada 26
Bhoga-patra 26
Bhogapati, Bhogapatika, Bhogikapāla, Bhogikapālaka 26
Bhogapatram 26
Bhogi-rūpa 26
Bhogika, Bhogin, Bhoktṛ 11, 25, 26

Bhogottara, Bhogatrā 26
Bhoja, Bhojaka pośar 26
Bhojiki 26
Bhoy 26
Bhū, bhūmi, bhūmī 26
Bhūmāṣakas 26
Bhūmi 26
Bhūmicchidra 26
Bhūmicchidra-nyāya 26
Bhūmicchidrapidhāna-nayāya 26
Bhūta-pāta-pratyāya, bhūta - pratyāya, bhūta-vāta-pratyāya, bhūt-opātta-pratyāya 26
Bhúdána-patram 26
Bhúlócam 26
Bhu-sakti 26
Bhukta, bugata (Telugu) 26
Bhukti, viṣaya, manḍala 27
Bhuktipati 27
Bhumi 27
Bhumi tottah 27
Bhúmi-vocalu 27
Bhumikreya sadanam 27
Bhumipa, bhūmīśvara 27
Bhuta-bail in'am 27
Biḷ-ānuvṛtti, biḷa-vṛtti 15, 27
Bīsva 27
Bibí-nazr, beebee nuzzer 27
Biabares, the 27
Bighā, bīghā 27, 28, 34
Bíjwár 27
Bilkoḍe 27
Billavas 27
Bilmaqta, Bilmakta, Bilmucta 27
Bilvarchana in'am 28
Bissoi tenure, Bissoi, Bissoy 28
Biswa 28
Bittuvaṭṭa, bittukaṭṭe 28
Blackgram, Black Pessaloo, oolundoo 28
'Board-sifárish' 28
Boddika 28
Boha 28
Boi in'am 28
Bommalata in'am 28
Bovenlanden 28
Bowries, Bāolī 28
Boyas, Bedars, Bōyas, bedas 28
Boyavandeloo, Bendars, 28
Brahdhala 28
Brāhmaṇa-rāśa (rāja) kkāṇam 28
Brāhmaṇa-viṁśati 28
Brahm-āṇḍa 28
Brahmadeya 7, 9, 28, 29, 32, 43, 112, 138, 147, 160, 198
Brahmadeya-kkiḻavar 29
Brahmandaya, Brahmadaya 8, 29, 112
Brahmapura, brahmapuri, agara-brahmadeya 29, 32
Brattis 29
Bubandu lekka 29
Bulla 29
Bulootch 29
Bulootedar 29
Burghers 21
Burki in'am 29
Buruj in'am 29, 93
Busa 29
Busi-bhaṁḍālu 29

C

Cālī 30
Cālikar-acca-taṟi, cālikai-taṟi 30, 178
Cāliyaweavers 30
Cāmara, cavala, cavela 30
Cāṇ 30
Cāni, Cowny 30, 37, 158
Cāturmāsya 30
Cārikai 30
Cārikai-ceṉvari 30
Cārikai-vari 196
Cāvaḍi, śāvaḍi, uśāvaḍi 30
Cáni-cuppatam 30
Cáni-mányam, káni-mányam 30, 192
Cáni-mérei 30
Cáni-peru 30
Cáni-sudantram 30
Cabaia 30
Cadjan 30
Cadvel, Carvel 30
Cairo 30
Caitya 30
Cakra-kāṇikkai 30

Calavasem marah 31
Calingulah 31
Callapay 31
Calvásám 31, 172
Caṇdeśvara-pperuvilai 31
Candareen 31, 140
Candayem, kandayam 31
Candrādittaval, candrādittavar, candrādityavat 31
Candy 31
Canji 31
Canti-āyam 4, 30, 31
Car 31
Carah 31
Carahatonilam 31
Coramboo 31
Caray 31
Careis, carays, carais 31, 202
Carī, carī - kṣetra 31
Caroo 31
'Carsy crop' 31
Caruveppillai 31
Cash 31
Cassada, cassava 32
Cathavany 32
Caturaka, catvara 32
Caturi, chaturi 32
Caturvēdimaṅgalam 32, 107
Cauḷūru 32
Cauri, Cāmara, Cavarālu 32
Cavathe, chavathā 32
Cawney, Cawnie, cáni 32
Cazhani 32
Cēris 32, 33, 191
Cēvakap-pēṟu 33
Cekkātāyam 4, 33
Cekkuk-kaṭamai, cekkiraip-pāṭṭam, Cekkātāyam 33, 87
Ceṉṉīr, nīr-amañci, ceṉṉīr-amañci, ceṉṉīr-vetti, ceṉṉīr-potuviṉai, Ceṉṉīr-veṭṭi 33
Ceṭṭiṟai 33
Ceṭṭiṟai-vari 33
Chārāsana 33
Chávadi 33, 94
Chaitya 33
Chaityagṛhas 33
Chak-bandi in'am 33
Chakkiliyans 33
Chakra, chakram 33
Chali 33, 189
Chalidomma 33
Chaligéni, Chaligeni (Kanarese) 33, 60
Chamar in'am 33, 104
Champane 34
Chamulu (Samulu), Samai (Panicum miliare) 34
Chaṇaka 34
Chandanavāri 34
Chaudhari in'am 34
Chaudharis 34, 36, 44, 55
Chandrāguru 34
Channel marah 34
Channel vary 34
Chanta 34
Charmakāra 34
Chaṭāh 34
Chatra, chutter 34
Chattram 34, 36, 102, 103, 122, 132, 185
Chatur bhagam in'am 34
Chauki, choky, chokie 34, 36
Chauravarja 34
Chauth 34
Chavadi 34, 36, 94
Chawkkissum 198
Chawar 34
Chazhi 34
Checári 34
Checcu-muttei 34
Chennapatam 35
Chentasawars, Chenchuvars, Chenchewars, Chenchus 35
Cherical 35
Cherikallu 35
Cheruman, Cherumar (pl.) 35
Cherumas 6, 35
Cheṭy, cetti, chitti, sheṭṭy, saiṭṭi, Chettis 5, 35, 93, 165, 185
Cheterys 35
Cheṭṭkaḷ-maṇai-iṟai 35
Chihra 35
Chili (chih-li-pu) 35
Chillary mānyam 35
Chiller, chillar, chitta 35
Chiller in'ams, or enaums 35
Chilleri 35
Chinna melam in'am 35, 106
Chittah 35
Chittari 35

Chodi 36
Cholam, cholum 36
Choradaṇḍaja 34
Choraḍrohakavarja 34
Choravarja 34
Choudari 36
Choultry, Cháwari 36, 91
Chowkie, Chowky, Chokie, 36
Chowrie 32
Chucker, chuckees 36
Chullaki 36
Chungadam 36
Churga 36
Cikāriyap-pēṟu 36
Cil-antarāyam 36
Cillāyam 36
Cilliṟai, Cilvari 36
Cina-kkanakam 36
Cinna 36
Cintriṇī 36
Ciṟṟaṅkātip 36
Ciṟumuṟik-kācu 36
Cira-khila 36
Cira-khila-śūnya 36
Ciravida 36
Circar (sarkar, government) land 36, 181
Cirikā, kraya-cīrikā 37
Ciṭalā, coṭāla, ciṭola 37
Citramēḷi, Citrameḷi, śittirameḷi, Cittirameḷi 37, 164
Citraméḷi periyamāḍu, Cittirameli periya nadu 37
Cōṇaka-vari 37, 196
Cōṟu, cōṟu-māṭu, eccōṟu-māṭu 37
Cól (large) 37
Cól (small) 37
Cóvil 37
Cody 37
Coilumin 37
Coir 37
Colingee 37
Collei 37, 149
Colly-chakram 37
Commewar, combies 37
Compte banias 37
Conicopillies, Kanakkapilla 37
Coolie 37
Cooll gootah 37
Cooll gootah shrotrium 37
Coolty, kulthee 37
Copra 37
Cora-daṇḍa-varjya, cora-varja, cora-varjya 37
Corambus, corumboos 38
Coray 38
Corga 38
Cortor 38
Cotay, kohti 38
Cott'adumei 38
Cottah 38
Country plough 38
Cowgram, thattapair, tuttapire 38
Cowle, Kaul (A) 38, 115, 159
Craya-sásanam 38
Croe 38
Cruzado 38
Cūnā 38
Cūrakāra, Cūṟakāra 38
Cucherry, Cusheri 38
Cuddapah and car, kadappu and kar 38
Cullum 38
Cully-chakram 38
Cumblies 38
Cumbu, cumboo, kumbu 38
Cuṅka-mērām 38
Cuṅkam 38
Cuppam 38
Cuppatam 38, 114, 137, 173, 174
Curnam, Curnum 38
Curracut 38
Curudu, kurundu 38
Cusbah, Cusba (A. Kasbah) 39
Cuzhi, kuzhi 39, 158

D

Dādaní, dadny 40
Dān-ādhikārin 40
Dāna-mukha 40
Dāna-ppuṟam 40
Dāna-pradānaka 40
Dāna-śālā 40
Dānādāya-dānībhoga 40
Dānam 40
Dānapuram 40
Dāṇi 40
Dānī, Dānin 40
Dāni-bhāga, Dāṇi-bhoga, dāṇi-bhogabhāga 40

Dāra 40
Dāradraṇaka 40
Dāśaris, Samayācāra, Samayācārya 40
Dāsaka 40
Dāsī 40
Dāyādas 40
Dánapatram 40, 119
Dab, dub 40
Dadhi 40
Daffedar, Dafadar, Duffedar (P) 40
Daftar gardens 40
Dahkala in'am 40
Dak'han-jama-i-kámil 41
Dakhila 41
Dakṣiṇāpatha 41
Dakshiṇa 41
Daksinasimpasandhipati 41
Dalavāy, Dalvai, Dalavay 41
Dalavāy agrahāra 41
Dalavāyi 41
Dala-adhikārī, Sainyādhikārin, Senāpati, Dalada-adhikāri, 41
Dala-vṛtti 41
Damdopat 41
Dana shasanum 9
Daṇḍa-āya 41
Daṇḍa-kkāṇam, daṇḍam-kuṟram 41
Daṇḍa-śulka 41
Daṇḍanāyaka 41
Daṇḍavāni 41
Daṇḍege umbaḷi 41, 138
Daṇḍa, Suṅka, Śulka 41
Daṇḍikā-jīvita 41
Daṇṇāik 41
Dandam 41
Dandasi in'am 41
Dandiya in'am 42
Danduga in'am 42
Dar-ul-jahad 42
Darbar (P) 42
Darbar-Khirch (P) 42
Darbha 42
Dargah in'am 42
Darkhwást 42
Darogha of sa'ir 42
Darśana, tariśana-kāṇikkai 42
Darśana-kāṇikkai 42
Darzi in'am 42, 175
Daśa-kriyai 42
Daśabandham, Daśabhandha, daśavandha, dasabandham, dasbhandam 42, 43, 44, 88
Daśavanda grant 43, 44, 76
Dasan 43
Dasi in'am 43, 182
Dastawiz 43
Dastu chitthas 43
Dastu kharchu chittha 43
Dastu-zabitas 43
Datti 43
Daunmuddy 43
Davandai in'am 43
Daya 43
Dayāda 187
Dayirya koḍage 43
Dēvāgrahāra 43
Dēvadāna 3, 43, 122, 138, 160
Déva-sthánam in'am, devasthanam in'ams 43
Dévarakádu 43
Dega in'am 43
Dehai 43
Dehangi-in'am 43
Dekhilu 43
Des-kulkarni 43
Deṣ-ádhíkárí 43
Deṣ-lekhak 43
Deṣ-pándyá (or-pándé) 43, 44
Deṣam 44
Deṣaválí 44
Deś-ādhikṛta, Deś-ādhipati, Deśāyi 44
Deśa 44, 170
Deśabandham in'am, dasabhandam in'am 44
Deśa kával, desha cavel, deshacawel, Desa kaval 44, 127
Deśadhigārigal 202
Deśādhikṛita 44
Deśabhōjaka 44
Desai 44, 45, 208
Desai in'am 44
Desaiyan 44
Deṣam 45
Desavazhi 45
Deshmukh, Desmukh 45, 61, 117, 159, 163, 208

Deshpande, Deshpandya 45, 61, 117, 159, 208
Deshmukh in'am 46
Despandya in'am 46
Deva-bhoga, deva-dāya, devabhoga-hala, deva-dāna, deva-deya, dev-āgrahāra, déva-déyam 8, 9, 46, 90, 91, 98, 124, 189
Deva-vihāra 46
Deva-vṛtti 46
Devāgrahāra 46
Devásthán, dewasthán 46
Devadāna-iṟaiyili 46
Devadasi mānyam 46
Devadayam 46
Devadurga 46
Devahala, devabhogahala 46
Devakula-puṣkariṇi 46
Devanga 46
Devaswam, devasam 46
Devata in'am 46
Deya 46
Deya-dharma 46
Deya-meya 46
Deyvamadi in'am 46
Dhāny-ādāya 46
Dhānya 46
Dhānya-hiraṇya, dhānya-hiraṇy-ādeya 46
Dhánya-mati 43
Dhānya-varga 46
Dhātuśila 46
Dhárekár 46, 90, 97
Dhaḻa-vādi, dhala-vali 46
Dhall, dholl 46
Dhamññikas, dhannikas 47
Dhanyadhikari 47
Dhára 46
Dharm-ādhyakṣa 47
Dharma-āsanam, durmasanam durmasenum, dharmāsana, dharmasanam 47
Dharma-chatra 47
Dharma-dāna 47
Dharma-deya 47
Dharma-dána-patram 47
Dharma-hala 47
Dharam-śālā 36
Dharma-śāsana 47
Dharma-vṛtti-iṟaiyili 47
Dharmadayam, dharma-déya 47
Dharmakaarta 47
Dharmaraja mānyam 47
Dharmikaḻ 47
Dharwiyan 47
Dheḍ, dherd, daird 47
Dher 47
Dhobi 47
Dhobi in'am 47, 185, 196
Dholl, redgram 47
Dhúlí-battá 47
Dhurya in'am 47
Dīnāra 47
Dīrgha-mānya 47
Dih, deh 47
Dih-dár, dehdar 47
Dih-kharch 47
Dih-kharchah, deh-khurcha 47
Dikshadar 48
Dikshatar in'am 48
Dirhem 48
Dirroas 48
Dittam 33, 48
Dittam in'am 48
Ditya 48
Divākaram 48
Divanottar, divánattár, dívánam 48
Diwan, Dewan (P) 48
Ḍoms 48
Dóni, doony 48
Dolabehara in'am 48, 116
Domala 48
Dombariapaṇṇu 48
Dommara in'am 48, 130
Dommaras 48, 130
Dommaripannu 48
Donthi 48
Dora 48
Dorasthanam 48
Doratanam 48
Doratanam in'am 48
Doruvu 49
Dowles 49
Drávid'am 49
Dracham 49
Dramma 49
Drōhin 49
Dubas 49
Dubash 49
Dudha 49
Dugalam 49
Dumbālah-dharná, dumbalah deron 49

Dumbálah, Dumbala 49
Durga-daṇḍanāyaka 49
Duswanah 49
Dvādaśaka 49
Dvijas 49
Dwadasi kattalai in'am 49
Dwi-bhashi 49
Dwitiya chokada in'am 49
Dyūta 49
Dzamilika in'am 49

E

Ēkabhōgum, yekhabhogum, Eka-bhoga, eka-bhogya 50, 64, 136, 144, 207
Ēr 50
Ēṟ-kācu 50
Ērāl-oru-kācu 50
Ēreḻupadu 51
Ēri-āyam 4, 51
Ērimīn-kāśu, ēri-mīṇ-kācu, ēri-mīṇ-pāṭṭam 51
Ērippaṭṭi, goḍage, kuḷappaṭṭi 51
Ētta, ēttam 51
Ēttamaram 51
Ēva 51
Eccōṟu 36, 51
Edangali, edangari, edangazhi 51, 125
Edigi-Gandlas (Ganigas) 51
Edroo pramanum 51
Ejoo tree 51
Ekabamhanasa 51
Ekabhogairaiyili 50
Ekkatlu 51
Ĕḻuttu-viniyogam 51
Elā 51
Elavai, ĕlavai 51
Ella in'am 52, 63, 149
Ellu, gingelly, gingelli 52
Eluvas, Ezhuvans 52
Eṇi-kkāṇam 52
Ĕṇṇĕy 52
Er-kkadamai 52
Er-ppŏn 52
Eraṇḍa 52
Eravari 52
Eri 52
Eri-ivu 52
Erikkāḍi 52
Erinīr-kōppu 52
Erivirappatanas 52
Erkádu 52
Erkkaṇikkai 52
Erukala in'am 52
Erukalai 52
Erumai-ppŏn 52, 105
Eruvaka in'am 52
Etchóru 52, 125, 169
Ettak-kaṭamai, eṭuttukkoṭṭi 52, 87
Ettugāṇa 52, 80

F

Fanam 7, 31, 33, 36, 53, 102, 134, 140, 175, 178, 181
Fanaos 53
Farash 53
Farman (P) 53, 116, 170
Faṣl 53
Faṣl-kamí 53
Fasal Jāsti, Fasl-jyástí 53
Faujdar 53, 59, 182
'Field lake' 53
Firka, Firqah 53
Florin 53
Fulooce 53
Fusgee 53
Fusli, Fasli (from A. fasl or fasal) 53, 170

G

Gāmuṇḍa, Gāmuṇda 54, 58
Gāndharva 54
Gāndhika 54
Gānuvuku-ari-suṅkamu 54
Gānuvula 54
Gānuvula-mudra-suṅkamu 54
Gāvuṇḍas 54, 56
Gángánah 54
Gáyál 54
Gadaba in'am 54
Gadabalu in'am 54
Gaddatiru in'am 54
Gadya, gadyana, Gadyāna 36, 54
Gahapati 54
Gal-puṭṭi 54, 56
Gaṇa 54
Gaṇa-bhoga, gaṇa-bhogya, gaṇa-bhojya, gaṇabhōgya, gaṇabhōgam 50, 54, 165
Gaṇaka 55
Gaṇapaṇa 55
Gaṇḍā 55

aṇikā 55
aṇin 55
aṇu 55
aṅgaikoṇḍa 55
anachari in'am 55, 60
andha 55
andha-Śāli 55
andum, godhuma 55
araḍi umbaḷi 55
aradi in'am 55
arhí 55
arige in'am 55
arise 55
arudakkal in'am 55
arudan samba 55
ass 55
at-kul 54, 55
atkul-miras 55
auḍa, gavuḍa, goud, gauda 55, 58, 171, 172
auda in'am 56
auda manda in'am 56
ava in'am 56
avadhyaksha 56
entoo 56
hās-dān 56
hát 56
hát-wál, gatwall 56
háts 56
haḍa-puṭṭi 56
hada-maṟuturu 56
hair dakhala 56
hale 56
haṭa 56
haṭachakra 56, 187
haṭi-yantra 16, 56
Ghaṭī 56
Ghaṭikā 57
Ghaṭikā-madhyastha 57
Ghaṭikaiyār 57
Ghee 57
Ghora-kṣetra, gṛha-kṣhetra 57
Gírás 57
Gidagauvel 57
Gidda 57
Giñjaka 57
Gingelly 57
Gingille oil 57
Girásiyá 57
Giraśal 57
Giri-durga 57
Girīndra 57
Giridurga 57
Go-gauḍa 57
Go-pracāra-bhūmi 57
Go-prachāra 57
Gō-saharra 57
Gōpracārabhūmi 57
Gōsthaka 91
Godugu in'am 57
Gocarman 57
Gola, Golla 57
Golakā, gulikā, goḷakkai, koḷakai, kuḷigai 57
Golawer 57
Golla in'am 57
Golla-vāru 57
Gomasta, Gōmāstāh, Gomashtah (P) 57
Gonchee Pattahs 57
Goortoo 57
Gooty 57
Gopaully 57
Gor in'am 57
Gorru 58
Gośīrsha 58
Goṣṭhi 58
Gosayeen, Gosain 58
Goud 58
Govallabhas 58
Govallava 58
Gṛha-kara, ilvari, manai-iṛai, manaippaṇam 58
Gṛhāḍḍanaka-patra 6
Gṛiha-sthāna 58
Grāma-bhogika 58
Grāma-drohin 58
Grāma-kārya 58
Grāma-kaṇṭaka 58
Grāmāgrāmabhojaka; Gramagrama-bhojaka 58
Grāmabhōjaka 58
Grāmakūṭakas 58
Grāmapraverticam 58
Grāmas 58
Grāmaṭikā 58
Grāsa-vāsas 58
Gráma-canaccu 58
Gráma-craya-sásanam 58
Gráma-otti-chittu 58
Gráma-uzhavadei-otti-chittu 58
Grámam 58
Grace 59
Grama kattubadi 59, 88
Grama kaval in'am 16, 59, 136

Grama kharchu chittah 59
Grama piada 59
Grama silavoo 59
Grama-maniyam, Grama-manyam, Grama maunium 59, 83, 116, 180, 190, 204, 207
Grama-shelevu 34, 59
Grama-vicraya-chittu 59
Gramabhagam in'am 59
Gramagarbha khandrika 59
Gramakuta 59
Gramam 59
Gramanis 59
Gramapanchaka 59
Gramawari system 59
Grammakantamu 59
Grammu-in'am 59
Gramuttam manium 50, 59, 119, 153
Grámátan, grammatan, Gramuttan 59, 119
Gramyakas 59
Green gram, green pessaloo, pire 59
Grīshmodaka 59
Grihastha 60
Ground-nut 60
Gúntu or déna-guntu, gootoo 60
Guda-yantrika 60
Guddad 60
Gudikattu 60
Gueny chalie 60
Gueny nairmul 60
Gueny shudmul 60
Guḷa 60
Gulies 60
Gulikā, pudu-kkuḻigai 60
Gullige 60
Gumastas 60
Gumika 60
Gunari in'am 60
Gundasala 60
Guñjās 60, 138
Guntaka, guntava 60
Guṟṟamu 60
Gurrapu in'am 60
Gurukkal in'am 60
Guṭṭige 60
Gutha 60
Guttagai, Guttige 60

H

Hāda 61
Hāga 61
Hakikat 61
Hajib 61
Hajjam in'am 61
Hakikat-i-jama 61
Hakim in'am 61
Hala, hāla, hali 61, 170
Halalkhor ina'm 61
Halu 61
Halut 61
Hañjamāna 2
Haṇa 61, 117
Hangami jodi 61, 71
Hanjumana 15
Haqiqat-i-jama'bandi 45
Har-sal-makta tenure 61
Haridrā 61
Haritaka 61
Hasala 61
Hásil 61
Hasta 62, 79
Hast-ó-búd 5
Hattavally 62
Havili, havelly, haveli 62
Havir-bali 62
Hawaldars 62
Haweli pargana 62
Hēma-garbha 62
Hĕggaḍĕ 62
Hĕjjuṅka, pĕrjuṅka 62
Heraṇika 62
Hingari 62
Hiraṇakāra 62
Hiraṇya 62
Hiraṇyasāmudāyika 6[illegible]
Hisa-i-zat 62
Hissa Shortriyam 15, 62
Hissah, hissa 62
Hobaḷi, hobḷi 62, 112
Holeya 63
Hommai 63
Hon 63
Hoṇa 63
Honnu 63
Hoolse nevise 63
Horsegram 63
Hūn 63, 136
Huggi manyam 63
Hukámi 63
Hukumnamah 63
Hul koḍage 63
Hulu 63
Hundi 63

Hunise-gadde 63
Huttalu 63
Huzur, huzzoor 63
Huzur sheristadar 63

I

Īḍara-vāru, iḍige-vāḍu 64
Īḻam-puñjai, iḻam-puṭci 64
Īḻavas 64
Iḍai-ppāṭṭam, iḍai-ppūṭci 64
Iḍaiyar-vari 64
Iḍaṅgai 64
Iḍaṅgaivari 64
Iḍaṅgaḻi 64
Idatorai 64
Idige in'am 64
Ijamana gramam 64
Ijara-darkhast 64
Ijarah, ijara, ijāra 4, 64
Ijaradhar 64
Ikrar 64
Ikshu 64
Iḻam-puṭi 143
Ilāqa, ilakh 64
Illadaarvar mel-saathanum chitta 64
Illadaarvar saathanum 64, 65
Illam, illom 65
Illuppai (Tamil), yilpah 65
Iman 65
In'am, Enam, Enaum (A) 5, 16, 17, 18, 24, 26, 29, 33, 34, 35, 40, 43, 44, 46, 47, 48, 49, 55, 59, 65, 71, 72, 80, 82, 86, 88, 89, 90, 94, 126, 130, 137, 139, 150, 168, 169, 177, 178, 179, 185, 208
In'am lands 15, 65
Iṇavari 65
Iṇṇilattāl-vanta-nirk-kiṟai 65
Ina-vari 65
Inamati Patti 65
Inamati mera 65
Inamati taffrik 65
Inami, Inaumy 65
Inavari-kkāśu 65
Inqiyad-nama 65
Iqrarnamah 65
Iṟai, iṟai 65, 87, 196
Iṟai-dravyam 66
Iṟai-kāval 66
Iṟai-kaṭamai 66
Iṟai-kaṭṭiṇa-kāṇik-kaṭaṇ 66, 75
Iṟai-porul 76
Iṟai-vāri 66
Iṟaikāval 66
Iṟaikaṭṭiṇa-nellu, kalarnilam 66
Iṟaikūli 66
Iṟaiporuḷ 66, 163
Iṟaiyili 66, 166, 192
Iṟaiyili-kkāśu 66
Irā madagu kāval śeri 66
Irāca-niyōkam 66, 145
Iraikudi in'am 66
Irasam 66
Iratta-kkāṇikkai 157
Irratta-mānya 157
Irsāl 66
Irsalnamah 66
Iruman 66
Irumḅukaṭṭi in'am 67
Iruvataṭik-kōl 67
Iswaran mānyam 67
Iṣṭāpūrtta 67
Iṭaip-pāṭṭam, iṭaivari 67
Iṭaṅka-śālai 67
Ivu in'am 67
Iwaz 67
Iyenberiz 22, 67
Izáfat 67
Izáfatdár 67

J

Jāgīr, Jagir, Jaghire, 4, 9, 11, 26, 62, 68, 113, 186
Jāti-siddha-āya 68
Jack 68
Jadimadu 68
Jagattumunūru 68
Jaghire, The 68, 174
Jagīrdār 26, 27, 44, 62, 68
Jakarai, jaggery 68, 184
Jala 18, 68
Jala-dvāra 68
Jaladurga 68
Jalaśāstra 68
Jalasūtra 68
Jam'i-kamil 68
Jamá, jama, jamma 23, 44, 61, 62, 68, 162
Jama'bandí, jamabandi, jummabundy 7, 68, 168, 173

Jama-i-tumari, jamma tumary 69
Jama-wasul-baki 69
Jamadar-khana, Toshe-khana 69
Jambu 69
Jaṅgama, jangam 69
Jana-pradhānin 69
Jangi Kattubadi 88
Janma 69
Janma-bhūmi 69
Janmabhogam 69
Janmam, jenmíkar, janmíkar 19, 69, 70, 83, 113, 118, 140, 169
Janmi, Jenmi 69, 70, 99, 111, 113, 132, 193
Janmí paimáish 70
Janmis 70
Janmisabha 70
Jaram 70
Jareeb muktusser 70
Jareebdars, jereebdars 70
Jari in'am 70
Jaríbiyán, jarebian 70
Jarib 70
Jase 70
Jatha 70
Jati pasungarai village 71
Jāti-siddha-āya 71
Jawabnaviṣ 71
Jayapāla 71
Jena 71
Jetti in'am 71
Jīraka 71
Jīvita, Jivita, Jivitam 71
Jīvita-kkārar 71
Jīvita -ppaṟṟu 71
Jinālayas 71
Jirar in'am 71
Jital 71
Jitavritti in'am 71
Jitotra in'am 71
Jivisthanam 71
Jivitam tenure 71, 191
Joḍi, jore 24, 65, 71, 72, 137, 161
Jodi in'am 71, 88
Jogida 71
Josi in'am 72
Jotiphana 195
Juari 36
Julah hatkar in'am 72
Jumla in'am 72
Jumta 72
Jyarum 72

K

Kācu-kaṭamai 73, 87
Kāḍu-kāval 73
Kādi 52, 73
Kākkunāyaka-viḷagam 73
Kāl-maṟuturu 73
Kāla dōṣam 73
Kālu 73
Kāma-dhēnu 73
Kānuka 73
Kāṇam 73
Kāṇi (cawney), kāṇiyāṭchi (cawney autchi), Kāṇiyāṭchikārar (cawney qutchikar) 6, 11, 30, 34, 36, 37, 38, 73, 74, 75, 83, 85, 92, 96, 102, 107, 112, 113, 117, 122, 137, 140, 142, 144, 149, 153, 165, 169, 173, 201, 203
Kāṇik kaḍan 74, 75
Kāṇik-kataṇ 66, 74, 75
Kāṇikĕ, kāṇiki 75
Kāṇika-kāṇé 75
Kānikĕ-kappa 75
Kāṇikuḍi 75, 190
Kāṇippiḍipāḍu 75
Kāṇiyākṣi 18
Kāṇiyāḷar, kārānmaiyāḷar 75, 107, 198
Kāṇiyāṭchi māṇyam 75
Kānchipuram (Conjevaram) 75
Kānika 75
Kānika Kārnika 75
Kāṇikkaṭaṇ 75
Kār crop 75
Kār-varaku 75
Kārāṇmai 75
Kāraṇavan 75
Kāriya-vārāycci, kārya-vārāycci 75
Kārpāśanam land 75
Kārpāsa 75
Kārtikai-arici 75
Kārtikai-kāṇam, kārtikai-kācu 75
Kārtikai-paccai 75
Kārttigai ariśi 75
Kārttigai kāśu 76
Kārttigai-ppaccai 76
Kārttika 76
Kāś-āya, Kāś-āyam, kāśu-āyam 62, 76, 139

Kāś-āya-vargam 76
Kāsú-vargam 76
Kāśāyam 76, 128
Kāśu 10, 31, 47, 50, 76
Kāśu pottagam 76
Kāśu-kadamai 76
Kāśukoḷḷa iṟaiyili, Kāśu-koḷḷā-iṟaiyili 66, 76, 201
Kāsa 76
Kāsākāras 76
Kāśāyam 129
Kāshṭhakāri-karmāra 76
Kāṭṭārampam 76
Kāṭṭu kōḍage grant 76
Kāval maṇyam 76
Kāval-kāṇiyāḷar 76
Kāvalgār, kāval kāvalgār 16, 76, 77, 135, 207
Kāvalgar in'am 77
Kāvalpperu 77
Kāvērik-karai-viṇiyōkam 77
Kāvērik kari-viṇiyōkam 77
Kāviri-kulai 77
Kāvitikāṇi 77
Kábulait 77, 78, 155
Kála-vásam, Kála-vasam, callavassum 77
Kánam (Malayalam) 77, 109
Kánam pátam, kanum patum 78
Kání (cawnie) 78
Kání-átachí kaurers, cawneyatchee caurers 78
Kání-átachí, kániádsí 78
Káriya, kárya, carreah 78
Kárya-káram, kariakaram, kárya-kárah 78
Kával-désa, kával désha, cawel desha, cavel desha 78
Kával-talam, cawel tallum, cawel tallum 78
Kávalkāni 73, 78
Kabúliyat, cabooleat 78, 91
Kach'hari 27, 38, 45, 78, 106, 162, 163, 174
Kaḍai iṟai 78
Kaḍaippū lands 78
Kaḍamai ūḻiyars 78
Kaḍamai, kuḍimai 78, 79, 84, 96, 111
Kadhichakas 79
Kaḍit-āmātya, kaḍita-vĕrgadĕ 79
Kadaiyan in'am 79
Kadambu 79
Kadarambam 79
Kadeem 79
Kadikaluthan 79
Kadir-kkāṇam 79
Kaharan 79
Kai 79
Kai-kánam-pátam, kay-kânum-patum 80
Kaigāṇa 80
Kaikkōḷas 80
Kaikkoḷar 80
Kaikolans 80
Kail 80
Kailu 80
Khairáti, Khairát 80
Kaittaḷaikai kūṭṭam 80
Kaivarta-bhoga 80
Kaiviṇaikkuḍi 80
Kal-velai in'am 80
Kaḷañju, Kaḷañju 80, 101, 130, 140
Kaḷa punjey 80
Kaḷam, kalaṭumēḍū 80
Kaḷani vāriyam 80
Kaḷanilam 80
Kaḷaṟu 80, 190
Kalagam 80
Kalai 80
Kalali 80
Kalam, collum 81, 104, 136, 178
Kalappai, alappadai 81
Kaliṅga-vāriyam 81
Kaliṅgam 81
Kalinga manyam 81
Kaliṅgu 81
Kalippanam 81
Kaliyuga 81
Kallāṇa kaṇikkai 81
Kallans 81, 82
Kallasaris 81
Kaliṅkattup-paraṇi, kulōttuṅika-choḷan ula; vikarama-chōḷāṉ ula, maṇṭalikaṇ, or maṇṭalikar 81
Kalum crop 81
Kāluve 81
Kalvay pannadi in'am 81
Kaṁsāli 81
Kamál, kámil 10, 81

Kamanisu 81
Kamati in'am 81, 94
Kamba, kamma 81
Kambakkaran in'am 81
Kambamkatti in'am 81
Kambaḷattārs 183
Kambangatti mānyam 81
Kambankatti 81
Kambharti in'am 24, 82
Kambu 82
Kamil, Kamal (A. = perfect) 82
Kammāra, 82
Kammāṇa, kammāḷar, kaṇmāḷar 82
Kammāra in'am 82
Kammaralas, kammalas, kammalans 81, 82, 120, 182
Kammas 45, 82
Kammayi vettu 82
Kampala, kampaṇa 82, 170
Kamsala in'am 82
Kamukukku-kaṭamai 82
Kaṇakka-kkāṇi 82
Kaṇakka-pperu 82
Kaṇakkavari 82
Kaṇakku 82
Kaṇḍuḷavu 82
Kaṇikkai, kāṇikkai 82
Kaṇkāaṇi, kaṇkāṇik-kaṇakkar-mutal, kaṇkāṇyār-nellu, kaṇmi-pēṟu 82
Kaṇkāṇiccu 82
Kaṇṇāla-kkāṇam 82, 202
Kaṇṇālak-kāṇam, kallāṇakkāṇam 82
Kaṇṇāṟu 82
Kanaga 82
Kanakkan mānyam 82, 85
Kanakkar (sl.), kanamdar, kanakkaram (pl.) 83
Kanakupilai, conicopoly 83
Kanam 83, 99, 111, 112, 174
Kanam patom ola karunum 83
Kanamkar, kanamdar, kanakkar (Malayalam) 69, 70, 83, 111
Kanchani in'am 83
Kañchara 83
Kañchuki 83
Kāñji, kāñjika 83
Kanda 83
Kandāyam, condoyam 83
Kandachar in'am 83
Kangani in'am 83
Kani, Kani-atchi, Kaniadsi (T.) 30, 83
Kani manyam 83
Kanians 83
Kaṇjud 84
Kanjurnoi 84
Kankāṇi 84
Kanni month 84
Kanomdar 84
Kanṟu mēyum pāḻu 57, 84
Kappa 84
Kapu 45, 84, 127, 199
Kapu' in'am 84
Kaṟenāḍu 84
Kaṟkkiṭai 84
Kara 84
Kara-grāma 84
Kara-śāsana 84
Karāṇmaiyāḷar 84
Karabādai 84
Karagrāma 84
Karai 84
Karai manyam 84
Karai-yidi 84
Karaikaran 84
Karaikkattu vaikkalkattu 84
Karaiyar 84
Karaiyedu, Karaiyīd 84, 85
Karaiyīḍu, Kareiyídú, Kareiyédú 85
Karanavan 85
Karaṇam, karṇam 22, 38, 85, 140
Karaṇas 85
Karaṇattān 85
Karaṇike 85
Karaṇikka-joḍi 85
Kaṟppūra-villai 85
Kareekar 85
Karisal, karasal 85
Karkoon 45, 85
Karkunan 85
Karnam, kurnam, curnam (K.) 7, 59, 85, 114, 168
Karnam in'am 86
Karnika-mirasi 86
Karpūra-mūlya, kappūra-vilai, Karpūravilai 86

Karpura-dipam in'am 86
Karshaka sangham 86
Karugal 86
Karumān field 86
Karuman 86
Karuman mānyam 86
Karuṇai 86
Karuppukittinoi 86
Karuvans, karumans 86
Karuvel (Tamil), cadvel 86
Karyasthan 86
Karzi in'am 86
Kasai in'am 86
Kasalu 86
Kasawurgum 86
Kassa 86
Kaṭai-ayam 14
Kaṭai-iṟai 13, 65, 86
Kaṭai-taram 86
Kaṭaippāṭṭattāl-vanta-kaṭamai, kaṭaip-pāṭṭam, kaṭaiyāyam, kaṭai-yiṟai 86
Kaṭaiyiṭu 87, 122
Kaṭamai, kuṭiamai 75, 87, 153
Kaṭamai-vari 196
Kaṭikai-kōl 87
Kaṭṭārampam 87
Kaṭṭaṇa 87
Kaṭṭe, kāluve, keṟe 87
Kaṭṭē 87
Kaṭṭha 87
Kaṭṭigevarttanai 87
Kaṭṭilērap-pōm-pōtu 87
Kaṭṭilērutal 87
Kaṭṭu 87
Kaṭṭu-kkuttagai, Kaṭṭugutagai, kaṭṭukkuttagai, Kaṭṭu-guttagai, Kattukuttagai 87
Kaṭṭumukkai 87
Katai-āyam 87
Katti (catty) 87
Katti-kkāṇam 87
Kattiyam in'am 88
Kattu kodige in'am 43, 88
Kattubadi in'am 88, 158
Kattubadis, Cuttobuddies 14, 42, 59, 71, 83, 88, 120
Kattugutta in'am 88
Kattuva 88
Kaul (Hindustani) 88
Kaulika-nikāya 88
Kaval 88
Kavale, kavaleḍu, kavaligĕ 88
Kavalgar, Kavalkaran 88, 172, 187
Kaveli russom 77, 88
Kaviraya in'am 88
Kavitai patam in'am 88
Kavu 88
Kawali 88, 119
Kayam jodi in'am 88
Kayam Pattah 88
Kazi in'am 88
Kēḻdavadhārisi 88
Kelvarku, Kēḻvaragu 88
Kedāra 88, 89
Kedaranarthy 88
Keppai 88
Kere 88
Kerya Saathanum 7
Ket-punjai, kate punjah 89
Keyār 89
Khādaka, khanaka, khātaka 89
Khās lands 89
Khāvandu 89
Khátedár 89
Khadim (Hindustani) 89
Khajan, khājan, khajjana, khajjaṇa, khajjāna, khajjaṇaka 89
Kham hissab 89
Kham wasual 89
Khaṇḍī, khaṇḍi 31, 89
Khaṇḍa 89, 90
Khanda Dasbhandam 43, 44
Khaṇḍaka 89
Khaṇḍuka, khaṇḍuga, khaṇḍika, khandikā khaṇḍi, Khandika Khaṇḍikā 89, 154
Khanduka vāpa 89
Khanah zadan 89
Khandi 89
Khandrika 89
Khandrika in'am 89, 149
Khandriká 89
Kharvaḍa, kharvata, kharvaṭa, kharvaṭam 89
Khas 89
Khas khail 89
Khas lands 89
Khasa in'am 90
Khassguṭ 90

Khaṭā 90
Khatib in'am 90
Kheḍa 90
Khetwar 90
Khichádi 90
Khoobash 90
Khot 90
Khulga in'am 90
Kīḻ kārāṇmai 90
Kīḻ kuḍigaḻitār, kīḻ kāraṇmai uḍaya kuḍigaḷ 90, 143
Kiatu 90
Kiḍangu 90
Kiḻān 90
Kiḻiṟaip-pāṭṭam 90
Kiladar, Qiladar 90
Killar-ulai-pāṭṭam 90
Kin 90
Kinaru 90
Kindi 91
Kiṟṟu vari 91
Kiramam 91
Kirana 91
Kirrit 91
Kiru-kula-viśeṣam 91
Kirukula 91
Kirūkulam 94
Kirukulaśunka 91
Kisan 91
Kisan sangham 91
Kist, Qist, Kisht 43, 91
Kistabandi 91
Kistu zabitas 91
Kḷipta-śulka 91
Klinna, klinnakreni 91
Knḍinīngakkārāṇmai 91
Knots 91
Ko-muṟai, ko-pada-vāram 91
Kōcceytu 91
Kōiltamarppēṟu 91
Kōl, kol 91
Kōḻvari 91, 196
Kōt-toṭṭuṇṇappālatevvakaip-paṭṭatum 91
Kōṭṭai magamai 91
Kōṭṭaipaṇam 91
Kōṭṭakam 91, 92
Kōṭṭam 92, 93, 107, 130, 141, 195
Kōyil 92
Kōyil-vācalaṟ-pōnta-kuṭimaikaḷ 92
Kōyilkaṇkku 92, 130
Kōyiṟṟamap-pēṟu 92
Kōyiṟṟamar 92
Kōḍi-kkaḍami 92
Kōḻmurai-ppāḍu 92
Kósham, kásha, koshan 92
Koḍagu 92
Koḍaga 92, 128
Koḍe 92
Koḍige 92
Koda-visa 92
Kodai vritti in'am 92
Kodali 92
Koday crop 92
Kodungone 92
Kol fields 92
Koḷaga, Kolaga 92
Koḷar-nilam 92
Koḷu 92
Koḻuvāṇi 92
Kola payko in'am 92
Kola-bhaṇḍālu, kolla-baṇḍi 92
Kolakāṇḍru 92, 185
Kolam kaval in'am 92
Kolīkanikāya 92
Kolika 92
Kolinji, kollingy 92
Kollai 92, 93
Kollaip-puncey 93
Kollan in'am 93
Komaṭi, Komatis 93
Kombú 93, 123
Kommu in'am 93
Kommu-maṟturu 93
Komutty 93
Kon in'am 93
Konda-kavali in'am 93
Kondapurirogam 93
Kondikar in'am 93
Kootshee 93
Koṟṟa 93
Korja 93
Korombo 79
Korra 93
Kośa 93
Kosham 93
Koss, Kaus, Coss (P. Karoh, S. Karosa) 93
Koṭai-āyam 4
Koṭṭagāram, Koṭṭāram 93
Koṭṭakāram 93
Koṭṭam 93
Kota in'am 93
Kota kodige in'am 93
Kota, kotah, kotai, kottai 93
Kota; Koṭadi in'am 93

Kottaḍimai 94
Kottam in'am 94
Kottam-vakai 94
Kotwal 94
Kotwal in'am 94
Kovai 94
Kovil, cóvil 33, 94
Kovil-antarāyam 94
Kovil gurukkal mānyam 94
Kovil kanakku in'am 94
Kovilakam in'am 94
Kovilakan 94
Kozhu 94
Kraals 22
Kramavittam 94
Kshetram 94
Kūḍai 94
Kūla 94
Kūlam 94, 143
Kūli 94
Kūlikku 94
Kūṟrams 94, 194
Kūra 94
Kūrait-taraku-āyam 4, 94
Kūrma 94
Kūṭṭum-vargattukku 94
Kúlikánam, kuyyikanam 94
Kumri 22
Kúnbhává 94, 113
Kucak-kāṇam, Kumāra-kaccaṇam 94
Kucakkāṇam 94
Kucava 94
Kuchal 94
Kuchela 94
Kuḍaimānyam 94
Kuḍi, kudi 75, 80, 90, 94, 95, 96, 191, 198
Kuḍi marāmattu, coody maramat 95
Kuḍi nīkki, kuḍi nīkkā 95
Kuḍi nīṅga dēvadāna, kuḍi nīṅgiya dēvadāna, Kudinīṅgādēvadāna, kuḍinīṅgādēva-dānam, kudnīkkā dēvadānam 95, 96
Kuḍi nīṅga iṟaiyili 96
Kuḍigal 96
Kuḍikalyāṇam 96
Kuḍikkāṇi 95, 96
Kuḍimai 96
Kuḍimaippāḍu 96
Kuḍimakan 96
Kuḍimakkaḷ 96
Kuḍinīṅgākārāṇmai 96
Kuḍipaṟṟu 96
Kuḍiwāram (coody waurum) Kuḍivāram 9, 95, 96, 97, 119, 193, 203
Kuḍiyiruppu kāṇiyākṣim 96
Kuḍuppōlai 96
Kuḍuppukūli 96
Kudi, Kudí, coody, 96
Kudian, kudiyan 96
Kudikidappukars 97
Kudirai kāśu 97
Kudirai-val 97
Kudivāraṭāṭkūli 97
Kudiyan sangham 97
Kudiyirippu 97
Kudukuduppai in'am 97
Kudumban in'am 97
Kudy (kury) irippa kury kanum ola karunum 97
Kul'am, cul'am 97
Kul-bab 97
Kul-qanum 97
Kuḷavaḍai 97
Kuḷam 90, 97
Kulai 79, 97
Kulai-veṭṭi, kulai-vaṭai, kurai-vauppu, kurappu-vetti 97
Kulam 97
Kulam vettu in'am 82, 84, 97
Kulargi, kularg 97
Kularika śreṇī 97
Kularikas 97
Kulavalay 97
Kulgootason 97
Kuli 94, 97, 135, 198
Kulika 97
Kullar, Kuller 97
Kultai 97
Kulwár 97
Kumāra-kaccānam, Kumara-kaccāṇam 97, 98
Kumāra-vrtti 98
Kumbharti in'am 98
Kummara in'am 98, 100
Kummaras 98
Kummarik-kaṭamai 98
Kumpini 98
Kumpli 98

Kuṇḍigai 98
Kuṇṭalu, kuccelu 98
Kunbhava 98
Kunbi 98, 158
Kunchamu 1, 98
Kunda 98
Kunds 98
Kunnal 98
Kunparars 98
Kunta 98
Kupadarśaka 98
Kupadarśakar 98
Kuṟṟam 98, 121, 195
Kuṟṟu-nĕl, Kūṟṟu-nĕllu 98
Kuṟangaṟu 98
Kuṟṟat-taṇṭam, taṇṭak-kuṟṟam 98
Kuṟṟattaṇḍam 98
Kura 98
Kurama 98
Kurinji tinai 98
Kuruba in'am 98
Kuruvaikalayn 98
Kuśa, Kuśa-kkāṇam 98
Kusa 98
Kushavan in'am 98
Kushem 98
Kusīda 98
Kuṭi 99
Kuṭi-kāṇam, kuṭumpak-kācu 2, 99
Kuṭumbha-vṛtti 99
Kuṭumbin 99
Kutchala 99
Kuthakai, kuttakai 99
Kuthugai (Tamil) 99
Kutimai 99
Kutlai 99
Kutta Towcoof 99
Kuttadi in'am 99
Kuttam 99
Kuttikkanam 99
Kuttumbitti 99
Kuyavan mānyam 99
Kuzhi 99
Kuzhikanakkar 99
Kuzhikanakkaran 99
Kuzhikanam (Malayalam) 99
Kyvedooth 99

L

Lābhālābhau 100
Lá-khiráj, lakeraje 100
Lánī 100
Lagayat 100
Laick daub 100
Lakṣána 100
Lambadies, lumbadies 100
Langarkhana in'am 100
Lankas 100
Larin or laris 100
Lavaṅga 100
League 100
Lekhāmukhi 189
Lella 38, 100
Leṅka, Leṅkā 100
Lenas 100
Ling Buljewars 100
Lópala-bhávalu 100
Loha-charmakāra 100
Loha-charmakār-āpana 100
Lohakāra, lohavaniya 82, 100
Lohar in'am 100

M

Ma'mūl 7, 101
Mā 101, 102, 178, 198
Māda 101
Māda-badi-pātuka 101
Māḍai 101, 138
Māḍalu 101
Mādārikkai 101
Māgāṇam, magam 101
Māgāṇi 101
Māgāni 101
Mañjāḍi 101
Mālākāras 101
Mālāris 101
Māliga-kkol 91
Māmaḍi 101
Māmūl-ādāya 101
Māmūlādāyam 101
Māṇikya-bhāṇdāra 101
Māna 101
Māna-pautava 101
Mānadaṇḍa 101
Mānasāra 102
Mānika 102
Mānya 17, 80, 102, 188
Mānyam 12, 35, 36, 46, 47, 59, 75, 76, 81, 89, 91, 102, 111, 112, 114, 120, 137, 140, 149, 159, 165, 166, 169, 171, 174, 175, 177, 180, 181, 182, 192, 195, 198, 202, 203
Mānyas 102

Māppaṇam 102, 105
Mārg-ādāya 5, 102
Mārgādāyam 102
Mārjavāḍa 102
Māshaka 101, 102
Māṭu 37
Māttu yēr, māttu yer, maththu-yer 102, 103
Māttu-āḷ, maththu-aal 102
Magane, mágánam, magamy maganny, magaum 103, 111, 168
Mángan, magun 103
Mávadei, maravadei 103
Mávina care 103
Mávu 103
Macchino 103
Machir 103
Maḍakku 103
Madakkuma, Maḍakku mā 103
Maḍappuṟam 103
Maḍippu 103
Madad-i ma'ash 103
Madadgar 103
Madaivetti in'am 103
Madam in'am 103
Madavadiyal in'am 104
Madham 104
Madhūka 104
Madhyastam 104
Madhyastha 104
Madiga 104
Madiga in'am 104
Madigaru 104
Madiyastam, madhyastham, madestrum 104, 165
Madras Candy 104
Madras Grace 104
Madras Marcal 104
Madras Measure 104
Magama 104, 146
Magamai maganmai, magaṇamai 104, 161
Magamey, magarry 104
Magani 104
Maganmai 104
Maggadere 104
Mahāmaṇḍaleśvara 104
Mahā-nāḍu 104
Mahā-nagara 104
Mahā-sabhā 104
Mahā-vyavasthā 104
Mahābhārata-vṛtti 104
Mahābhojas 104
Mahābhūmi 104
Mahābhūta-ghaṭa 104
Mahābhūtagahṭa-dāna 105
Mahādāna 186
Mahāgrahara 105
Mahājana 104, 105, 119
Mahāmātra 105
Mahāmaṇḍaleśvar-ādhipati 105
Mahānāḍ-prabhu, Mahānāḍprabhu 105
Mahānāḍu 105
Mahānāvika 105
Mahāpaṇa 105
Mahāprabhu 105
Mahāpradhānas 105
Mahāpradhāni; Mahá Pradána 105
Mahārāja-prayojana 105
Mahārājavāḍ 102
Mahāsāmanta 105
Mahāvaṇḍavyavahārin 105
Mahá-janam, mahajanum, maha-jana 9, 105
Mahájenam 105
Mahal (A) 68, 105
'Maharatta carnatic' 105
Mahattaras 105
Mahimai 105
Mahiṣa-kara 105
Mahōksa 106
Mahrattah tallabund 106
Mahsuldar in'am 106
Maikuruvay 106
Majal 24, 106
Majmu'-dar 106
Majhumu'-dar in'am 106
Makkaḷ-cēvakap-pēṟu 106
Makta 106
Mal 106
Maḷu 106
Maḷabraya 106
Mala 106
Malai-yidu in'am 106
Malakaran in'am 106
Malavadu in'am 106
Maldar 106
Maliahs, the 106
Malikana 106, 173

Malkiyat, Milkiyat 106
Mallāyi–maghami 106
Malli cariander 106
Malvandloo; Malvadu 106
Malzamin 106
Mamool–warum 106
Mamoti 107
Mamul 7, 107, 190
Mamutties 107
Maṇai–iṛai, manaiyiṛai 65, 107
Manṛuppāṭu 107
Maṇḍal–ādhipati 107
Maṇḍala 93, 107, 171
Maṇḍala-mudanmai 107
Maṇḍala–mutali 107
Maṇḍalam 107, 195
Maṇḍaleśvara 107
Maṇḍalika, Māṇḍalika, Maṇḍalīka 107
Maṇi–grāma 107
Maṇiam 107
Maṇikāra 107
Maṇṇāḷar 107
Manṛupādu-fine 143
Maṅgala 32, 107, 135
Man-kari 108
Man–pan 108
Mana 108
Manṅ–varei 108
Manai–kávali, munny cavelly 108
Manaikkaḍaiyār 108
Manaippaṇam 108
Manalvary 108
Manavāri lands 5, 108
Manavary 108
Manda varisei 108
Mandai–kanderram 108
Mandai–ppaṇam 108
Mandei varisei, mandei morei 108
Manei, maṇei, 108
Manei-craya-sásanam 58
Maneiollaver 149
Manen 108
Mangalams 32, 108
Mania sunkam, and mania ravesh 108
Maniac 108
Manikkattal in'am 108
Manivar 108
Maniyakaran 116
Manjanathi, 108
Manmaari 108
Mannalu 108
Mannans Vannans 108
Mannawurty 108
Mannevadu 88
Manneya, manniḍu, Manniya 108, 109
Manneya–svamya 109, 173
Mano–vritti, munnoverty 109
Manotti in'am 109
Manṛāḍi 109
Manṛam 109
Manṛu 109
Mantrin 109
Manvarti 109
Mānyam 109
Mauzawar 109
Manzur 109
Mappilas, Moplahs 109
Maqta 109
Maṛutu, maṛuturu, mattaru 93, 109
Maṛumanna 109
Marah 17, 109, 113, 174
Marakkaḍamai 109
Marakkal, Mercal 109
Maramut, Marammat 109
Maravaḍai 109
Maravadei 110
Maravalli 110
Maravars 110
Marah 31, 110
Margosa 110
Mari 110
Mark 110
Marumakkattayam, Marumakkathayam 110
Maruthu 110
Maryādā 110
Masab 110
Masala 110
Masalia, musala 110
Mashrut 110
Masjid in'am 110
Maṭhāpura lands 110
Maṭṭu 110
Matapati 110
Matapati in'am 110
Matham In'am 110
Mathas 110
Mattah, metta 110
Mattar 109, 110, 135
Mattaru 61, 81, 109, 110
Maund 110
Maunium 109, 110
Mauqub 111

Mawās 111
Mawashigiri 111
Mayadis 111
Mazkur 111
Mazra, muzera 111
Mēḷi 37, 111
Mēlātcuiḍayār 111
Melkuḍi 111
Mēlwaram (mel warum), Mēlvāram 9, 36, 95, 96, 102, 111, 119, 139, 143, 147, 167, 169, 181, 192, 193, 197, 203, 208
Médipālu 111
Mél-udenpadicai-olei 111
Mérá, merái 111, 112
Medi 37
Meeras; Miras (A.) 111
Meirei, merah, murah, marrah, murai 38, 111
Mel-vĕṭṭa-pperu 111
Melaḍi 111
Melagy 111
Melam in'am 111
Melcharth 111, 112
Melcharthdar 111
Meli 111
Melkāṇam, Melkanam 111
Melkanamdar 112
Melkoyma 112
Melviṭṭiya-vaaḍḍāravauḷa 112
Menewar 112
Menkaval in'am 44, 112
Menon 4, 85, 112
Mera 112
Meralu 112
Mere, mureh, merah, marrah, merai 111, 112
Merei sundantira padam 112
Meri 112
Meru 112
Meṭṭugana 112
Mete 112
Meti in'am 112
Mey-kaval in'am 112
Meykāval 112, 183
Mīṉ-pāṭṭam 112
Mikaṟp-pāṭṭam 112
Minha 112
Minnai 112
Mirās 3, 74, 111, 112
Mirāsī 8, 17, 26, 55, 58, 59, 74, 78, 84, 113, 114, 115, 119, 131, 137, 143, 144, 151, 159, 173, 184, 188, 202
Mirāsidār 8, 14, 17, 30, 31, 52, 55, 58, 59, 66, 78, 105, 108, 112, 113, 114, 115, 116, 118, 120, 125, 136, 137, 138, 143, 144, 148, 159, 165, 167, 173, 174, 180, 184, 185, 187, 188, 189, 191, 192, 207
Miśradurga 116
Misal 116
Mittadar 116
Mocassa 116
Mochai, Mochay 116
Modala-vāḍa 116
Modan 116
Mogeru 116
'Moghul Carnatic' 116
Mohtad, Mohatadi 116
Mohtad in'am 116, 127
Mohtarfa 116
Mohtasib in'am 116, 117
Mokāsā, Mokasa 116, 118
Mokāsadār 116
Moliko in'am 116
Momins 116
Monigār, Monigar māniyakāran 47, 116, 117
Monigar in'am 116
Moolumunishers 116
Moolvies 116
Moot 116
Mootahadar 116
Mootahdary 116
Mora 116
Morah 116
Morei-nir, moranír 117
Motapati in'am 117
Motarpah, Moturfa 117, 118
Motásthal 21
Mouza 111, 117
Mouzhawar 54
Mu'afi 117
Mu'azzan 117
Mu-ayyan zabitah, moyenzabitah 117
Mūḍai-kkūli 117
Mūla 117
Mūla-olai 117
Mūla-sadhana 117
Mūla-ratna-panṭārattār 117
Mūla-vīsa 117

Mūlāwargdār 117, 203
Mūladhana, mūladravya 117
Mūlgénī 33, 117, 190
Mūrdh–ādhikāra 117
Mūsara–vāru 117
Mūtt-ādikārama 117
Mūttāns 27
Mubbottu 117
Muchaaram 117
Muchalka 117
Muchalkah in dárad, muchelka in darud 117
Muctah 117
Mudal 117
Mudali, Mudaliyār 117
Mudam in'am 117
Mudavan in'am 117
Mudavandi palayam 117
Mudde in'am 118
Mudur 118
Mug Tiragee 118
Muggaḍu 118
Muhtarafah, moheterefa, Ṁuhtrfa 117, 118
Mujera 118
Mujra 118
Mujudat 118
Mukarrar 118
Mukaveṭṭi 118
Mukhadharakas 118
Mukhasa 71, 118, 159
Mukhasa, mokassa in'am 118
Mukhyasthan 118
Mukkal 118
Mukri 118
Mulada, muladalu (kanarese) 118
Mulaguena chitta 118
Mulawarga (Kanarese) 118
Mulawargadar (Kanarese) 118
Mulees 113
Mulgar 118
Mulgeni (Kanarese) 118
Mulk–i-jadid 118
Mulk–i-qadim 118
Muluḍa, Muḷuḍa 119
Mummeyvaydoo 119
Munneyvaydoo, manavadoo 119
Muṅgari 119
Mundala 119
Mundu 119
Munevet village 9, 119
Muniwar 88, 119
Munnims 119
Munshee, Moonshi 119
Muppatika–badi tenure 119
Muqaddam (A.) 44, 119
Muqarrar hasil 119
Muqasa (mukasa) 119
Muqasadar 119
Muqiman 119
Murṟṭṭu 119
Mura 119
Murattu mānyam 120
Murei 120
Mureicáren 120
Mureicárs 120
Murtuzanagar 120
Musaliar 120
Musaris 120
Musáḥarah–i–kụlkaranán, mushaira koolkernain 120
Mushrif 120
Muster 120
Musud 120
Muṭṭhai–āḷ 36, 120
Mutah, Muṭṭhā, mootah, mittah, mótai 120
Mutal 120
Mutalikan in'am 120
Mutasaddi 45, 120
Mutawattinin 120
Muthalali 120
Muthuvelly 120
Mutirigai 120
Muttaratsa in'am 120
Mutuḍa 120
Myrobalan 120
Mysore breed of cattle 120

N

Nāḍu, Nāḍ 92, 98, 105, 121, 122, 123, 125, 126, 127, 141, 143, 175, 194
Nāḍ–sēnabōva, Nāḍa–senbova 121
Nāḍa–gauḍa 121, 122, 208
Nāḍarasa 121
Nāḍu vagaiseydal 121
Nāḍu–cey, nāḍu–vakai–cey 121
Nāḍu–kāval 121, 143
Nāḍu–kaṇkāṇi–nāyakam 121
Nāḍu-kūṟu 122

Nāḍu-kūṟu-ceykiṟa-atikari 121
Nāḍu-talaiyārikkam 121
Nāḍukas, nāḍuka 122
Nāgarika 122
Nāhala 122
Nāḷ prabhu 121
Nāḻi, nāḻi 104, 122
Nāḷgāvuṇḍa 122
Nāla 122
Nāla-bhūmi 122
Nālān-taram 122
Nānādeśi 105, 122, 164, 173, 194
Nāndu 122
Nār-gāvuṇda 122
Nāttukkōn 122
Nāṭṭāmai 122
Nāṭṭār, nāṭṭavar, nautaur, nattaru, nattvar 122
Nāṭṭamai 122
Nāṭṭavar 122
Nāṭṭu viniyōgam, ūriniyōgam, Nāṭṭu-viniyogam 122
Nāṭṭu-kāṇikkai 122
Nāṭṭu-kkaṇakku-vari, Nāṭṭukaṇakku-vari 122
Nāṭṭunāyagam seyvār, nāṭṭunāyakam śeyvār, nāṭṭunāyakar 122, 123
Nāṭṭupati, nāḍu-upādi 123
Nāṭṭusammadam 123
Nātamkār 21, 123
Nāvalō-nāval 123
Nāyak, Nāyaka 123, 124
Nāyaka-wár, nāyakwár, naikwar 123
Nāyakavāḍis 123
Nāyaṅkara system 12, 123, 135
Nálá, nulla 124
Nár-pángellei 124
Nátam, nátha, naut, nautum 108, 124, 149
Nátam-kár, nautam kar 124
Nátawár, náthawár, nautawar 124
Náyak-wárí, náyakawárí, naikwarry 124
Naduvazhi 124
Naḍavumunai 124
Naḍu-vakai 124
Nadam or nadum purthy 124
Nadar 124
Nadavar 124
Naday olungu 124
Nad talari in'am 124
Naduwari, naduvazhi 124
Nagadali 124
Nagara 124, 125
Nagara-svāmin 125
Nagaram 125, 167
Nagarattār 125
Nagasarm in'am 125
Naidu 125, 158
Naikvariyan 125
Nair gueny 125
Nairmul gueny 60
Nakara 93, 125
Nakara in'am 125
Nakara parivāras 125
Nakarak-kaṇakku 125
Nakharadavāru 125
Nal'padi 52, 125
Nal-kiḍa 125
Nal-paśu 125
Nala 125
Nali, nari, nazhi 125
Nalinavāru 125
Nall-ĕrudu 125
Nall-ā 143
Nallāvu 125
Nallerudu 125, 143
Namaud 125
Nambi in'am 125
Nambiyars 125
Nambudri, Nambudiri 126
Naṇcey, nīrnilam, nīrārampam 126
Naṇcey-kaṭamai: 126
Naṇcey-puṇcey-Pottaka(m) 126
Nanadesi 126
Nanal in'am 126
Nanawutta 126
Nandavanam 126
Nandavanam in'am 126, 152
Nanjai taram-punjai, nunjah taum punjah 126
Nanjal-mel, nunjahmel 126
Nanjai-mel-punjai, nunjay mail punjah 126
Nanjei, nunjiah 36, 38, 114, 126, 135, 164, 170, 203, 206
Nankar 126
Nantangauls 126

Nāpita 126
Naqal 126
Nar pangellie 126
Nar-samatu 126
Nari-vetti in'am 126
Nashta, nesht, nisht 126
Nat ambalam in'am 126
Naṭṭiṛaiyili 126
Naṭṭupāḷ 126
Nata-silavu, nautsellavoo 126
Natcheny 126
Nattamai in'am 126
Nattangcál 126
Nattar 126, 127
Nattar in'am 126
Nattvar, Nāṭṭavar, nāṭṭār, nattaur, nautaur 126, 127
Naut karnam 127
Navarai 127
Navidan in'am 127
Nayadis 127
Nayadu in'am 127
Nayak-wadi in'am 127
Nayakars 127
Nayakwarian-i azam 127
Nayars, Nairs 127
Nayel kaveli, nayel cavelly 127
Nayudu 127
Nazar, Nazrāna 42, 127, 135
Nazūl 127
Něy 127
Neer moodut, ner moodut 127
Neerganṭee, nirgranthi 127, 129
Neernally 127
Negamā, naigamāḥ 127
Neguadee, nikuti 127
Nelevīḍu 127
Nelgutta in'am 127
Nell-āyam, Nellāyam, Něll-āyam 127, 129, 149
Nella yendagha chitto 128
Nellicoy 128
Nellore breed of cattle 128
Nelmudai 128, 129
Nesara koḍage, nettra koḍage, nettaru-paḍi mānyam, ratta-kuḍangai 128
Neṭṭāl 128
Neṭṭāl kūḷi 128
Nettara gōḍage, Nettara-goḍaga 128
Netti-velai in'am 128
Netturu-kattu in'am 128, 146, 157
Netturu-vettu in'am 128
Nharel 128
Nīr vilai, Nīr-kkāṇam, nir-vilai 128, 129
Nīr-nilak-kācu 128
Nīr-vilaik-kācu 128
Nīra-gṛha 128
Nīrāṇivari 128
Nīrguṇṭi 127, 128
Nīrk-kūli nīrkūli, nīrvilaikūli 129
Nīrkkīya-vilai 129
Nīrkkiṛai 129
Nīrkūli sarvamānyam 129
Nīrnilakkāśu 129
Nīru-nela, nīr-nela 129
Nīvī 129
Nír, nir 129
Nibarava 129
Nidāna 129
Nidhān 129
Nidhi-nikṣepa 129
Nidī, nidhi 18, 129
Nigama 129
Nikshépam 18, 129
Nila-craya-sásanam 58
Nilai-iṛai, vāḍākkaḍan 129
Nilak-kaṭamai 129
Nilam 129
Nilam aḷarpōr perumakkal 129
Nilamaḷavu-kōl, tiruvulakaḷanta-kōl 129
Nilam kalandapadi 129
Nilams 129
Nilamutal-pottakam 129, 150
Nilavari, Nilaviṛai 129
Nillāyam 129
Nilōpādi 129
Nimme badi tenure 129
Niṇraiṛai, Niṇrirai 129
Nir sarihadd in'am 130
Nir-attipper 130
Nirārampam 130
Nirarambam 130
Nirganti in'am 21, 81, 130
Nirmunaka in'am 130

Nirnilam 130
Nirpoku, nilam 130
Nirrlu–pandal 130
Nirūpa 130
Nirūpachchambaḍam 130
Nirvana manyam 130
Nirvṛtti 130
Niṣka 130
Nivāra 130
Nivanda, nimanda 130
Niyāyattār 130
Niyogas 130
Niyogi 130
Nizám, nizam 130
Nizámat, nizamat 130
Nizámat–adálat, nizamat adawlat 130
Nokkan in'am 130
Nondā–viḷakku 130
Nottan in'am 130, 166
Nūl–āyam 130
Nuckhood 130
Nukattāṇi 130
Nukattaḍi 130
Nukkattoṭai 130
Nunjei, nunjiah 126, 131
Nuri 131
Nyāsa 131

O

Ōḍakkūli 132
Ōlai 132, 175
Ōlai–eḻuttu 92, 132
Ōṭak–kācu, ōṭak–kūli 132
Obolus 132
Oḍaya 132
Odayaṁtrikas 132
Oddars 132
Odukkam in'am 132
Oduvan in'am 132
Oḻugu, Ooloogo 132
Oḻugu–nīrpāṭṭam 132
Olai–ccādanam 132
Olai–ccampaḍam, olai–ccambaḻam, olaiccammāḍam 132
Olai–nāyaka 132
Om ! 132
Onṭudāru 132
Onam 132
Oolcoodie, oolcoody, ooloocody 132, 137
Oolky 132
Oppers 132
Oouarkally 79, 97, 132
Opādi 132
Oṟṟi 132
Oranglaut 132
Oṭṭi (Malayalam), 132
Ottakaran in'am 132
Otty moory 133

P

Pañcālas 134
Pañca–kammālar 134
Pañca–karmara 134
Pañca–māśattam 134
Pañca–vāram 134
Pañcāla 134
Pañcālattār 134
Pañcamṛta 134
Pacahānamvāru or pāñcālamvāru (in Telugu) and pāñcāḷattār 134
Pāñcavāram 134
Pāñchāṇaṁvāru 134
Pācip–pāṭṭaṁ 134
'Pāḍi' 134, 191
Pāḍi–kāppān 134
Pāḍikāval, padikaval 16, 77, 134, 135
Pāda 61, 134
Pāda–padam–opajīvin, pāda–piṇḍ–opajīvin 134
Pādar 134
Pādava–kkāṇi 134
Pādika, pātika 134
Pāga 134
Pāga or hāga 134
Pāḷ 134
Pālaiyakkārar (Tamil), pālegāra (Canarese), Pālegādu (Telugu) Poligar 59, 71, 76, 88, 135, 148, 159, 208
Pālaiyam, Palaiyam, pollam 135, 148, 151, 168
Pānbuḍit, pāimāli, pāmālī 135
Pāra 135
Pārasi, pārasī, pārasika 135
Pāṣāṇa 18, 135
Pāśippāṭṭam, mīnpāṭṭam 135
Pāsārī 135
Pāṭaka 135
Pāṭikāval 135
Pāṭṭa–nēl 135
Pāṭṭam 15, 135
Pāṭṭamkār 135
Pātāsthal 21, 135

Pāvu ceỳdu 135
Pāvai 135
Pālyapati, pooliaput 135
Pán-málá, paunmala 135
Pát 21
Pátam, patam 135
Paccar 135
Pachalai 135
Paḍāgai, piḍāgai 135
Paḍaga, pāḍaga 135
Padaipāṟṟu 135
Paḍaiparṟu 136
Paḍalikai 136
Paḍayli-ānavaḷi 136
Padugaitākku 136
Pada śēṣa 136
Padakku 136
Padar 136
Padavāra, paduvāra, padavāram 136
Padi 136
Padi (Tamil) 136
Paḍi-viñjanam 150
Padia 136
Padikkaval manyam 136
Paditaram 136
Padiyal (Tamil) 136
Padugai 136
Pagalve-shakarar 136
Pagod, pagoda 30, 33, 54, 91, 101, 130, 134, 136, 138, 141, 143, 196
Pahikásht 33
Paiiki-guntaka 136
Paik in'am 136
Paikārar, pāikārī, parakūdī, poycarry, paicari, payeecari 31, 33, 52, 96, 113, 114, 115, 136, 137, 152, 153, 173, 188, 190, 203
Paikamu 137
Paili 137
Painers 137
Painth 137
Paisārī 137
Paitari in'am 49, 72, 137
Pakka 137
Paḷampuḷḷi-māḍai 138
Paḷḷi-ccanda, paḷḷī-grāma, pallī-cchanda 138
Paḷḷavāy 138
Paḷḷiccandam grant 138
Pala 138
Pala-kāya 138
Pala-rājākkaḷukku-iṟai-iṟuttu 138
Palabhōgam, pulbhhog, palabhógam, palabhogum 17, 138, 144
Palaki umbaḷi 41, 138
Palalu, paleru 138
Palampat 138
Palapati in'am 138
Palataḷi 138
Palaveli in'am 138
Pali 138
Palikiguntava 136
Palkalaykkundu in'am 138
Palkavadi in'am 138
Pallan 139
Pallan in'am 139
Palle kattu in'am 139, 171
Pallevadi in'am 139
Palli 139, 191
Pallivasal in'am 139
Palliyal 139
Palmyrah, palmira 139
Pambakkaran in'am 139
Pambala in'am 139
Pambatti pambu pamula in'ams 139
Paṅgu 139
Paṉniratik-kōl 139
Paṇa 17, 55, 117, 134, 139, 140
Paṇa-vāśai 139
Paṇavattam 139
Paṇḍāravāḍai 8, 139
Paṇi-kkŏttu 139
Paṇimakaṉ 139
Paṇṇai 139
Paṇṭāram (Tamil), bhanḍāra 139
Paṅa, paṇam or fanam 53, 102, 139
Paṅga, pāṅga 140
Pañca-gavya 140
Pañcavarṇa 2
Panāḍi 140
Panam 134, 140, 198
Panayam 140
Panchángen 140
Panchams 140
Panchanam 140
Panchangi in'am 140, 153
Panchayats 140

Pandárattar 140
Pandaram 140
Pandery 140
Pandluminu 140
Pandum 140
Pangali 140
Pangu 140
Pangu mālai (pangoo melah) 140
Panguvali in'am 140, 146
Pani seivan mānyam 140
Panika-seni, pārṇika-śreṇi 140
Paniar 140
Panikkan mānyam 140
Panikkans 140
Panipan in'am 141
Panisavan in'am 141
Panivaragu 141
Panjanga mānyam 141
Panji karnam in'am 141
Pannāya 141
Pannai 141
Pannaiyal 141
Pannasa, pannāsa, pannāsu 101, 141
Panniya 141
Pantoji in'am, pantulu in'am 141
Paoni 141
Paṟait-taṟi, paṟaiyar-taṟip 141, 178
Paṟaiya 141
Paṟṟaḍai 141
Paṟṟu, Paṟṟu 141
Para 141
Para-deśin 141, 173, 187
Para-manei, pira-manei 141
Para-tider 141
Paracheri, tider pareiyer 141
Paracheri 142
Paraḍai, Paraḍatti 142
Paradavar 142
Paraga nagaram 142
Paraikkauḷak-kuri 142
Paraittaṟi 142, 178
Paraiyans 142
Parakesari-kāl, Parakesari-kkal 142
Parakesari-nāḷi 142
Parakesari-uḷakku 142
Parambas 142
Parambu, paramba 142
Parameśvara-hasta 142
Parado (partab) 142, 143
Parao 142
Parasangs 142
Pareiyar 142
Pargana, parganah 3, 12, 34, 44, 45, 62, 105, 142, 204
Pariar 142
Paricharaka in'am 142
Parihāra, maryādā-parihāra 143
Parihara in'am 143
Pariharas 143
Parikāra 143
Parikara 143
Parikraya 143
Parinki 143
Parintirīss 143
Pariśu 143
Parisūtra 143
Parittivari 143
Parivarthanai 143
Parivṛitta 143
Parpattegār 143
Partāb 143
Partab 143
Paruḍal kudigal 143
Parutti in'am 143
Parwāna 143
Pasāitā 143
Pasang-carei, Pasangkareī 136, 143, 165
Pasankarei 144
Pashánam 144
Pashungherry villages 138, 144
Pasungarai (pashoonkarah), Pasungcarie 17, 71, 85, 144
Paṭai-mutalis 144
Paṭaiyilār 144
Paṭel, pāṭel, pāṭil 55, 59, 144, 159
Paṭṭa 144
Paṭṭāḍai-ayam 144
Paṭṭāḍai-nūl-ayam 144
Paṭṭāṁśuka 144
Paṭṭaka 144
Paṭṭakara 144
Paṭṭalekhin 144
Paṭṭana 144
Paṭṭanasvāmin 105, 144
Pṭṭaniga 144
Paṭṭana-svāmin 144

Paṭṭasāhiṇi 144
Paṭṭavaṭṭam 144
Paṭṭayam 144
Paṭṭe 144
Paṭṭi-kkāḍi 145
Paṭṭi-ppōn 145
Paṭṭit-taṇtam, paṭṭik-kācu 145
Paṭṭōlai, paṭṭlā, paṭṭolai, pāṭṭai 145
Paṭṭōlai-kacu, paṭṭōlaik-kacu 145
Paṭṭōlakāsu 145
Paṭṭolī 145
Patakdár, puttuckdar 145
Pátam tenure 71, 145
Patasala in'am 145
Patchei-vadam 145
Patel (k.) 112, 119, 145
Patel in'am 145
Pathạ 145
Patika-badi tenure 145
Patikaval 145
Patinaṛucāṇ-kōl 145
Patiṇen-cāṇ-kōl 145
Patiperadu 145
Patna setti in'am 145
Patomkar 145
Patra 145
Patram 135
Patta monigar 145
Pattā, patta, pattah 24, 25, 57, 88, 146, 152
Pattadar 146
Pattagar 146
Pattam 146
Pattanappagudi 146
Patti in'am 146
Pattī 65, 146
Pattinams 146
Pattivali in'am 146
Pattiwaris 146
Pattunūlkārar 146
Pattupadi 146
Payer-cudi 136, 137
Payercaren 136
Pazhikkani in'am 146
Pēmṭa-śuṅkamu 104, 146
Pēr, pērāl, pēril 146
Pēr-kaḍamai 146
Pēṭe, santhe, santepēṭe, pēṭa, pettah 146
Pĕdda-gadyamu 146
Pērjuṅka 146
Peddā kāpu in'am 66, 84, 146, 159
Peddā-kāpu 146
Pellettu in'am 146
Peon 146
Peṟike-edla-suṅkamu 147
Peṟike-edlu 147
Peṟu-varṭam 147
Perāṟu 147
Periḷamayār 147
Periya aramanai in'am 147
Periya melam 35
Periyanāṭṭān-śandi 147
Periyanadu 147
Perjjunka or peruśunka 147
Peru-nilac-celviyuṇ-taṇakke-urimaipūṇṭo 147
Perūñguḍi makkal 111, 147
Perukuli in'am 147
Perum-pādi-kāval 147
Peruṇguḍi-makkal 147
Perumāṇaṭigal 147
Perumál 147
Perumakkal 147
Perumboc, peramboke 17, 113, 137, 143, 147, 148, 153
Peruñ-kuṭikal-pērāl-katamai 87, 148
Peruṅkuṭikal-pēr-kaṭamai 148
Perunguḍi 148
Perunír 148
Peruvaḻi 148
Peruvari 148
Peshkar 148
Peshkash, peshkush 148, 162
Pessaloo, green or black 148
Peta gadu in'am 148
Pettah, petha, pettai, Peṭha 148
Pettendar 148
Phaiṇdi-āyāyi, phaiṇḍivāya-maṟuturu 148
Phala-sthirā 148
Phalabhogam 148
Phalia 148
Phuṭṭaka 148
Pīṭalikai-vari, piṭakai-ōpāti-iṟai 148
Piccottas 148
Piḍāgai 135, 148

Piḍāri, piḍāri-paṭṭi, ellai-amman 148
Piḍārivari 148
Piḍaligai 148
Pidára vaidyan in'am 149
Piḍari kovil, perumal kovil, amman kovil mānyam 149
Piḻḻai kaṇakkanār 149
Pillai in'am 149
Pilwări, pulwări, pillwany 149
Pippali 149
Pirāmaṇar-pēr-kaṭamai 149
Pirlu in'am 149
Piṣāraḍi 149
Piśānam crop 149
Pisanam, peshanum 149
Piṭi 30, 149
Pizhacadei, puzhacadei 37, 149
Plantain 149
Poā 149
Poduvāḻ 149
Pohal shrotriyam 149
Polichezhuthu 149
Polikōl 149
Polimera in'am 149
Politūṟṟun kūḍai 149
Pon, poṇ 149
Pon-mudal 128, 129, 149
Poṉmudal 149
Poṇ paṇḍāram 150
Pongal 150
Ponvari 5, 149, 150, 173, 196
Pooleyars 150
Poonas fussil, poonass fussil 150
Pooragoodies 150
Pooroopa 150
Poramboke 150
Porruppu in'am 71, 150
Portia 150
Porutpuṇai 150
Potaraz in'am 150
Pottakam, Pottagam 150
Potula in'am 90, 150
Prāṇāntika 150
Prāpti 150
Prativyañjana 150
Prabhu-svāmya 150
Pradhāna 150
Pradhāni-joḍi 150
Pradhānin; Pradhani 150
Pramāṇa 150
Prapā 150
Praśasti 150
Prasāda kāṇikkai 150
Pratigraha 150
Pratyāya 150
Praverticam 58, 150
Praveśa, prāveśa 150
Prayāṇa-daṇḍa 150
Pricchanda 150
Pū-vari 196
Pūgāḥ 151
Pūjā-vṛtti 151
Pūrv-ācāra 151
Pūrv-āgrahārika 151
Pūrv-maryādā 151
Pūṭṭānkayiṟu 151
Pú kizhar 151
Puḍā-nāḻicess 143
Puddee 151
Pugdi 151
Pujari in'am 17, 151
Puḻudi 151
Puḻudi lands 151
Puḻuku-vari 151, 196
Puḻḻipārta 151
Pulam 151
Pulattil-kuḻangal 151
Pulavar in'am 151
Pulavri 151
Pulbhog 138
Pulikattu in'am 151
Puliyamarum, paleamunaum 151
Pullari, poolary, pullavari 151
Pulleas 151
Puller 151
Pullu 151
Pully 151
Puṇcey, pūñcey, kollai-nilam 151
Puṇcey-kaṭamai 151
Puṇcey-puravu 151
Puṇpayir lands 151
Punam 151
Pundarah vadiky, pundarah vandiky, pundary vadiky 151
Pundarah-vadiky 151
Punganur breed of cattle 152
Pungoo bhogium muree 152
Pungs 31, 152

Punjah, punjei, punjah 36, 97, 136, 152, 170, 181
Punjah putcut 152
Punjei otty muree 152
Puntottam in'am 152
Punyam-patam, paunyam patram, poonyum patam 152
Puppotti in'am 152
Puṟa-kkaḍamai 152
Puṟāpaṟṟu 152
Puṟakkalaṇai-kaṭamai 152
Puṟakkuḍi 80, 86, 137, 152
Puṟav-āyam 21, 152
Puṟvari 152
Puṟamāgaṇi 152
Pura 152
Purakalam 153
Purakkadai, puzhakkadai 153
Purana in'am 153
Purav-āyam 4, 153
Puravari 153, 196
Puravu 153
Puravu-vari 107, 153
Puravu-vari-śrikaraṇam 153
Puravu-vari-tiṇaik-kaḷam 153
Puravu-vari-tiṇaik-kaḷak-kaṇkāṇi 153
Purbatty 153
Purkudy (poorah coody) 153
Purmbōkku, poramboke, purambok, puramboku, 153
Puro-nāyak, poṟṟu-nayak 153
Purohit in'am 153
Purohita 153
Purohita mānyam 153
Pushoonkarry 119, 153, 154, 189
Puṭavai 154
Puṭṭi 54, 56, 154, 185
Puṭṭi-dosillu 154
Putcut 154
Putla kattubdi in'am 154
Putti 154
Putti, pukti 154
Puttiam 154
Puttookaut lands 150
Puttookaut rayats 154
Puty 154
Puvika 154
Puvika-seni 154
Pykes, paykan, paikan 154

Q

Qabūlityat 77, 91, 155
Qadīm, cadeem, kadeem 79, 155
Qaul, Quoul, cowle 155
Qaul-nāma 155
Qist 155

R

Rāja-Vibhātan-kōl 156
Rāja-kārya 156
Rāja-kara, rāja-garam 156
Raja-karam, Rājakaram 156
Rāja-māna 156
Rāja-pradeya 156
Rājadrōhins 156
Rājakārya-bhāṇḍāra 156
Rājakara-upādi 156
Rājakaraṅ-kāṃikkai 156
Rājakīyabhūmi 156
Rājakulaṅ-kaṇi-ppaṟṟu 156
Rājanya 156
Rājarājap-peruvilai, Rājarājapperuvilai 156
Rājasva 156
Rājikā 156
Rājya 156
Rāmānuja kūṭa 156
Rāśi-paṇa, rāśī-ppon 156
Rāshṭra, raṭṭha 156
Rāshṭrakūṭa 156
Rāshṭrapati 156
Rāshṭrika 157
Rāyabhaṇḍāri 157
Rāyasa 157
Rāyasa-svāmin 157
Rāyasam 83, 157, 202
Rāyasavarttanai 157
Rāj-wár, rachewar 157
Ráj-kharch 47
Ráya-récha 157, 158, 170
Ra'iyati 157
Ragi 36, 157
Rahaṭṭa-ghaḍiya 16, 157
Rahdari 157
Raja 157

Rajabandhu in'am 157
Rajjuka 157
Rajjupratihāra 157
Rakṣā- bhoga 157
Rakta kodiga in'am 157
Rakta-kodage, ratta-kuḍangai 157
Rakta-mānya 157, 187
Raktakanikai in'am 158, 187
Raṅga-bhoga 158
Rangaru 195
Rangrizan 158
Ranuva kattubadi in'am 158
Rathākārs 158
Ratsavar 22
Rayaji cáni 158, 163
Rayalaseema 158
Rayalu 158
Ryat, ryot, raiyat 11, 19, 47, 65, 88, 99, 112, 130, 158, 171, 196, 199
Rayatulu 158
Rayatwari, ryotwari, raiyetwar 97, 109, 116, 139, 158, 198
Razeram 158
Razīnāma 158
Razu 158
Rēkai 158
Récha-sidd'hāyam 158
Reals 159
Reḍḍi 45, 127, 158, 159, 199
Reddi in'am 159
Reddy manium 159, 173, 192
Reddy, reddi 84, 110, 117, 159
Redgram 159
Regar 159
Regar banjar kayem cowle 159
Rekhā, reka 159
Rekai, rekai-ppon, irekai 159
Reveg jasti 159
Riaya, ri'aya 45, 159
Riayat 159
Riayat mukhasa tenure 159
Roap-nuts 159
Roghan-i-zard 159
Rokka gutta in'am 159
Rozina 159
Rusūm, Russom, russoom, rusum (A.) 109, 159
Rusum-i-zamindari 126

S

S-odraṅga 160
Śālābhōga 160
Śrībhanḍāram 160
Sāsan-ārdhika 160
Śālā-bhoga 160
Śālāvaṇam 160
Śālai, Śalai 160
Śālikattaṛi 160
Śānabhoga 160, 167
Śāsana-baddha 160
Śāśvatīya 160
Śāttvika-dana 160
Śāvi land 160
Śada-kkadamai 160
Śadiram 160
Saivācārya-kṣetra, Śaivācārya kṣetras 160
Śakkara-kāṇikkai, tirigai-āyam 160
Śalāgai 160
Śalāgai, śalākā 160
Śaṇa 160
Śaruppeṭi-maṅgalam 32
Śaṭṭu-vari 160
Śattige umbaḷi 160
Śēṇians 160
Śēṇigaru 160
Śēru 160
Śērvai 160
Śekk-āyam 160
Śekku-kaḍamai, śekkukkaḍamai 160
Śekku 161
Śelavaḍhaki 161
Śennel 161
Serī 161
Śetti 161
Śeṭṭi paṭṭaṇasvāmis, Śeṭṭi paṭṭaṇasvāmin 161
Śeṭṭi-iṛai, śeṭṭ-iṛai 161
Śeṭṭiyār-magamai 161
Śeviḍu 161
Śīmai-vivādam 161
Sirmai, Śīmai 161, 170
Sikhai 161
Silā-lekha 161
Śilliṛai 161
Śimēhabbaruva 161
Śirṛāyam 161
Śoḍaśī, śoḍaśika 161
Śodi 161
Śoḷaga 161

Śrāvaṇa 161
Śrēṇayaḥ 161
Śrēṇi 161
Śreṇi-bala 161
Śreṇi-dharma 161
Śreṇīs 161
Śreṣṭhin 34, 161
Śri-bali-bhoga 161
Śrī-mukha 161
Śrīballi-paṭṭi 161
Śrīpādakkol 91
Śrīy-ājñai 161
Śrotra 161
Śrotriya 161
Sūlavari 161
Śuḍ-kāṭṭu-ppāṭṭam 161
Śulka 162
Śulka-śālā, śuṅga-śālā 162
Śuṅgam, śuṅkam 162
Śuṅkada-adhikāri 162
Śunka-karaṇālu 162
Śunkarulu 162
Śuvāstiyam 162
Sa'ir 162, 163, 175
Sa-bhoga 162
Sa-pānīyam 162
Sa-tālaka 162
Sa-toṭṭam 162
Sādhya 162
Sāgu 162
Sāgavali-chitu 162
Sāhaṇkāṭi 162
Sālas 162
Sāliyas 162
Sāndhi-vigrahika 162
Sārthavāha 162
Sádir-wārid, saderwared 146, 162
Sávarah, sávaram, saverum 162
Sabhā 13, 163, 164
Sabhā-māñjikkam 163
Sabhā-madhyama 163
Sabhai-ppodu 163
Sabhā-viniyoga 163
Sabhaik-kaṇakku 163
Sachimattam 163
Sadbhāgin 163
Sadā-servai, sadā-sevai 163
Sadar 163
Sadavritti in'am 163
Saderwared 163
Sadwániyán, sadwannian 163
Saggio 163
Sagnally 163
Sagoobady daub 163
Sagoobady keyfeut 163
Sagoovaly 163
Sagubadi in'am 163
Sagupadi kanakku 163
Sagvaly 163
Sagwan 163
Sahib-i'iyar 163
Sahukar, sowkar, soukar, savukar (H.) 163
Saikalgar in'am 163
Sain 163
Saint Thome cāni 163
Sair 163
Sakkath 163
Salabhoga 163
Salada (Kanarese) 164
Salami 71
Saliya nagaram 164
Saliyana 164
Saṁvatsara-vāriya 164
Samāñjita 164
Samaba 164
Samai 164
Sāmantas 164
Samasta-sippiga-gottali 164
Samastanam peons in'am 164
Samatdar 164
Samavāsa 164
Samavāyah partnership 164
Samay-ācāra 164
Samaya cakravarti 164
Samaya-dharma 164
Samaya-patra 164
Samayakar in'am 164
Samba-kattalai in'am 164
Samba-peshanum 164
Sambandham 164
Samjhaish 164, 172
Sammat 164, 165
Samprati 164
Samprati in'am 164
Samudāya 165
Samudāya-prāpti, samudāya-ppirātti 165
Samudāyam, Samudāyanilam, Samudayam (Tamil), somadayem 4, 143, 165
Samudrāntā 165
Samudragāh 165
Samuta 165

Sanad, sunnud (A.) 165, 192
Sanad-i-milkiyat-i-istimrar 165
Sandai, shandy 165
Sandhivigraha-pperu, sandhivigrahi- paṇṇu 165
Sang tarash in'am 165
Sangitam in'am 165
Sangu-kulikaran in'am 165
Sanguical 165
Sankarappadi nagaram 165
Sankhanadam in'am 165
Sannad mānyam, sunned maunaim 165, 180
Sannad manyakkanakku 165
Sannad manyam (sunned maunaim) 102, 165
Santa 165
Santa basivi in'am 165
Santai 165
Santaka 165
Santati-praveśam 166
Santheya-śunka 166
Sappan 166
Sappani in'am 166
Sapt-āṅga 166
Sapta-santāna, sapta-santati 166
Sar tiram, ser terrim 166
Sar-i-lashkar, seir lascar 166
Saralai 166
Sararashtah 166
Sarbasta tashkhis 166
Sardar 166
Sarishtadār 166
Sarkár marammat, circar maramut 166
Sarkar, sirkar, circar 166
Sarkhel 166
Sarraf (corruptly shroff) in'am 166
Sarshapa 166
Sarv-ābhyantara-siddhi 5, 166
Sar-samatu: 166
Sarva manyam, Semman in'am 50, 166
Sarva-jātakam 166
Sarva-namasya 166
Sarvābhyantara siddhi 166
Sarvādhyaksha 166
Sarvajāta-bhoga-nirasta 166
Sarvamānya, Sarvamanayam Sarva-mānya 9, 102, 166, 167
Sarvamānyam villages 167
Sarvasva-harana 167
Sasanam, patram, chittu 115, 167
Sathāna-āchāryas 167
Saṭra-śāla 167
Sattra 167
Sattum parisatta nagaram 167
Satyamkāra 167
Savaram 167
Savarṇa-vṛtti 167
Sayer or sair 167
Sazzulu 82, 167
Sēnāpatya kaṇakku 167
Sētu 167
Seemai agathi 167
Seemai pala 167
Seer 167
Seh-bandi, sebundy 167
Sehbandi fasli, sebundy fusly 167
Seih 167
Sekhā 167
Sena-bhoga, Śeṇai-bhogam, senabova 160, 167
Senaiy-aḷṅgāḍika 167
Sendal, sendalai 167
Sendi in'am 167
Seni, śreṇi 168
Senkarisel 168
Seriyat 168
Seruvelly 168
Servai 168
Servaikkaram in'am 168
Seth 168
Setti in'am, patṇa setti in'am 168
Sevak-ttevai 168
Sevvel, seval 168
Seykāl karamb, Seykāl karambu, (sheycaul curramb) 168
Shaâmillut 168
Shāmil 168
Shamilat Dasbhandam 43, 44

Shāvī 168
Shánabhog, Shānabhogam 85, 168
Shahganj 168
Shakili 34
Shanan in'am 168
Shanars 168
Sharogar 168
Shava in'am 168
Shecal–carambu 168, 180
Sheccodu 169
Sheckizhar 169
Shem purthee, sarum purtee 169
Sheri or seri 169
Sheristadar 85, 169
Shevul, shewul 169
Sheycal carambu 169
Sheykal 169
Shikekayi 169
Shilotri 169
Shist, shistu 168, 169
Shistum 70
Shoru 169
Shotriyam, shrotriyam Shrōtrium (shotrum) 9, 91, 102, 169
Shroff 21, 169
Shudmul gueny 60
Shutta kreya shaasanum 128, 169
Shuhur san (Arabic) 170
Sīman 170
Sīmé 170
Sīrā 170
Sibbandi 170
Sibbandy fusly 170
Sibbendy police, sebundy (p.seh–bandi) 170
Sidd-āyam 170
Sitt-ayam 170
Siddh–āya, Siddhāya, Siddháya 18, 170
Siddhi 170
Sidi in'am 170
Sih bandi 170
Sikasth 170
Silakasu 170
Silvari 170
Ṣima 170, 171
Simt 170
Simt bandi 170
Sinna 36
Sippashari in'am 170
Siragu 170
Sirkār 14, 27, 170
Sirna gour, surnar gour 170
Sividi-praveśa-kandalivāḍa-grāma 150
Siwar 170
Siyahiwala in'am 170
Soap–nuts 170
Sotical 171
Sournadayam 171
Sripandáram 171
Sthāna–āchāryas 171
Srimukha 171
St'hanicas 171
Sthāṁkas 171
Sthānattār 171
Sthān–ādhipati 171
Sthāna–bhūmi 171
Sthāna–mānya, Sthānamanyas 171
Sthānapati 171
Sthalādāyam 171
Sthala 171
Sthala gaud in'am 171
Sthala–gauḍa 171
Sthala in'am 171
Sthala–kkāval 171
Sthala-karnam 171
Sthala–vṛitti 171, 176
Sthalādāyam 171
Sthalagauḍika 172
Sthalam 172
Sthalam kaval in'am 172
Sthanikam in'am 172
Sthanam 172
Sthanapati in'am 172
Sthulwār 172
Strīdhana 172
Stullawari chittah 172
Suba, subah (A.) 166, 172
Sūbadār, sūbedār, Subedar (p.) 19, 90, 162, 172
Sudantram 31, 172
Suddha–bhógyam 172
Suddha–craya–patram 172
Suddha–crayam 172
Suddha–vicraya–chittu 172
Suddula in'am 172
Sukhavasi 172
Sultān 172
Summádu 172
Sumohi 138
Suṅka-vĕrgadĕ 172
Suṅkamu 172

Suṅkapannāyadadhiṣ ṭhāyaka 172
Sunijaish 172
Sunkarulu 172
Surchasum 173
Suvarṇ-ādāya, Svarṇ-ādāya 173
Suvarṇ-āya 173
Suvarna-danda 173
Svāmi-bhoga 173
Svāmi-vāram 173
Svāmin 173
Svāmya 173
Svāmyam 173
Svadśin 173, 187
Svarṇakṣma 173
Svarṇa-vari, śoṇa-vari 173
Svarūpa 173
Swāmibhōgam, Swāmi-bhōgam 96, 137, 173, 186, 190, 203
Swāstiyam, Swāstyam 58, 113, 173, 202
Swámi-sudantram 173
Swástyacraya-patram 173
Swamy bhogium chitta 51, 173
Swatantra diṭṭam (swatantra dittam) 6, 12, 112, 173
Swatantram, soṭunterum, svatantra 14, 15, 59, 112, 148, 153, 173, 174
Swayampakam in'am 174

T

Ta'tifawali in'am 175
Ṭa-ahhud, toorhadi 175
Tāla 175
Tāla-patra 175
Tāmra-śāsanas 175
Tāṉ-vēṇṭu-kōviṉukku 175
Tāniya-varakkam, dhānya-varga 175
Tāqavi, Taccavi, tackavi, takavi 38, 175
Tār 175
Tāṟṟukkōl 175
Taaddi 175
Taajkaurs 175
Tabela in'am 175
Tacc-ācāriya-kkāṇi 175
Tacc-ācāriyam 175
Taccācārīyakkāṇi 175
Tachchan 175
Tadāga 175
Tael 175
Tafsil 175
Taherior 175
Tahwildar 175
Taiyalkaran in'ams 175
Takesim 175
Takhfif 175
Takid 175
Takkā 175
Takya, takia in'am 176
Taḷai-kkāṇam 176
Taḷarndu 176
Taḷavārikā 176
Taḷavṛtitti 176
Taḷmāri-kār 176
Tala-bhoga 176
Tala-dvṛitti 176
Tala-vāṭaka, tala-pāṭaka, tala-vṛtti 171, 176
Tala-vāṭaka-vāstunā saha kṣetram 176
Talāri, talaiyāri Talaiyari, talliari, tallari, (Tam), 21, 52, 76, 78, 114, 125, 172, 174, 176, 182
Talāri-pannu 176
Talārika 176
Talāṭi 176
Talab-diwani tenure 176
Talai ahappaḍi 176
Talai taram 176
Talai variśai 176
Talaivayccēri 33, 176
Talaiyārikkam, Talaiyārikkam 176
Talaiyari in'am 176
Taliccēru 33, 176
Taliqa 176
Tallabund 176
Tallagi 176
Talluqa 176
Taluk, talook, taluq (A) 27, 176
Taluqdaar 177
Tamalapakula in'am 177
Tamarind 177
Tambala tanure 71, 177
Tamidelu 177
Taṇiyūr 177
Taṇdam 177
Taṇḍu 177
Taṇṇīr-kkāṇam 177

Taṇṭak–kuṟṟam 177
Taṇṭam, taṇṭam–kāṇam 107, 177
Taṇṭuvāṇ, taṇṭaluṭaiyāṉ 177
Taṇṭanāyakap–pēṟu 177
Taṅka 177
Tana 177
Tanaikkan mānyam 177
Tandal 177
Tandal in'am 47, 177
Tangal 177
Tankhah, tankhwa (p.) 178
Tannir pandal in'am 130, 178, 185
Tantravāya 178
Tantrimār 178
Tantrin 178
Taqavi, takavi, tuccavee, etc. 178
Tar 178
Taṟi–kkaḍamai 178
Taṟi–ppuḍavai 178
Taṟip–puṭavai 178
Taṟi–taraku, taṟi–akkam, taṟṟi–iṟaik– kācu, taraku, taṟiyṟai 178
Taṛa 178
Tara 179
Tarafdar 179
Taragan 27
Taraku, taraku–kūli, taragu 143, 179
Taram, terrim 7, 179
Taram peṟṟa nilam 179
Taramdar, terrimadar 179
Taramiḍu 179
Taramili 179
Taramiṭṭa 179
Tarapadi in'am 179
Tarappadi kanakku 180
Tarappaḍi mānyam (tarrabuddy manniam) 102, 180
Tarappottagam 180
Tarav–iḍu–nēl 180
Tarawad, Taravād 180
Tarbands 180
Tare 180
Tarf 180
Tarfdar 180
Tari 180
Tari–cadamei 180
Tari–iṟai 65, 178, 180
Taṟip–puṭavai 180
Tariśana–kāṇikkai 180
Tarisee, tarisu 17, 113, 137, 143, 180
Tarōpādi 180
Tasadduq 180
Tashkhis–i–jama 180
Taṭṭār 180
Taṭṭār–pāṭṭām, taṭṭāra-ppāṭṭam 135, 180
Taṭṭārpāṭṭam 181
Tatan in'am 181
Tatchan in'am, tachchan in'am 181
Tatimma 181
Tatoodarry 181
Tattān 181
Tauntla 198
Taurh 181
Tavana–crayam 181
Tavana-craya-patram 181
Tavazhi 181
Tayinati 181
Tēnpayilpodumbu 181
Tēvai, tevai 181
Tēvar–kaṭamai 87, 181
Teddul punjah 181
Teddul-punjah teerwa 181
Tee 181
Teeps 181
Teerva jasti 181
Tēerwa, teervah 136, 150, 181, 190
Teerwaput, Teervaput, teervapattu lands 36, 114, 180, 181
Tehsildars, tahsildar (H.) 80, 85, 93, 174, 181, 185
Tejo–mānya, teja–mānyam, tejaḥ-svāmyan 181
Tenai, thenai, thinai 181
Teppa in'am 181
Teṟṟi 181
Teruvelai in'am 181
Teśa–kālam 181
Teśa–kuḍimai 181
Teśa–vāḻi 182
Tevadiyal in'am 182
Thachchan mānyam 182
Thada 182
Thalkurniyan 182
Thalpuchi 182
Thana, Thāna 182
Thanedar, Thanadar 182

Tharāo 182
Tharappadi manyakkanakku 182
Tharavadu 182
Thattans, thattars, tattans 182
Thattapair, tuttapire 182
Thellachida 182
Thiyyas, tiyyas 52, 182
Thottakkal kanakku 182
Thovarai, tovaray, tovary 182
Thravād tarwād 182
Thugai jabida 182
Thukkiri, talayari mānyam 182
Tiguḷa-daṇḍa, āndhra-daṇda 182
Tila 182
Tilapeshakas 182
Tiṇai 182
Tiṇaik-kaṇakku 182
Tippōkkuc-cempon 182
Tīrparulu 92
Tírvei 182
Tiṟai 182
Tirappu 182
Tirast in'am 182
Tirigai-āyam 30, 182
Tiru-muga-kkāṇam 183
Tiru-mugam 183
Tirukkōyiluṭaiyāṉ vītu 183
Tirumāñjanakkuḷam 183
Tirumal mandaghappadi in'am 183
Tirumalai in'am 183
Tirumēnikaval 112, 183
Tirumeni-kāval 183
Tirumukam, Tirumugam 183
Tirumukat-tēvai 183
Tirumuṉpu-kāḻchikkum-niṉaipiṭṭu-taṇṭum-kācu 183
Tirumuṟṟam 183
Tirup-paṭṭam 183
Tirupani velai in'am 183
Tiruppudiyīḍu 183
Tiruvācalil-pōnta-kuṭimai 183
Tiruvāykēḻvis 183
Tiruvadirai in'am 183
Tiruvanendal kattalai in'am 183
Tiruvidaiyāṭṭam, Tiruvdidaiyāṭṭam 183
Tiruviḷakkukuḍi 183
Tirwā 183
Tirwā-kami 183
Tiryu-nāma-kkāṇi, tiru-nāmattu- kkāṇi 46, 183
Tiṭṭum 183
Tiyar 183
Tōḍāi 183
Tōṭṭa nilam 183
Tōṭṭapuṛavu 183
Tōṭṭiyams 183
Tótam 183
Tótta-chittu 184
Todā 184
Toḍā-girās, torā-girās 184
Toddy 182, 184
Tola 184
Tolā 184
Toli 184
Tolkollans 184
Tondaipuchi 184
Tondei-mandalam 184
Tondi-wāram, tonde warum 184
Toni-kkaḍamai 184
Toomu 184
Toondoowarum 113, 155, 184
Tope 184
Tope in'am 184
Topu 184
Topukaran in'am 184
Torai 184
Toraṇa-kkāṇikkai 184
Toranam katti in'am 184
Toṭṭa-ppuravu 185
Toṭṭam 185
Toṭṭi 21, 172, 185
Totākāl 185
Totakal, tottakal, totacul 185
Toti, totie, totier 176, 185
Toti in'am 23, 29, 141, 185
Tottam, tottakal 185
Tṛrparula 185
Tri-bhoga, Tri-bhōga 185
Tribhagam in'am 185
Tribhōg-ābhyantara siddhi 185
Trishvekam tenure 185
Tṛṇa-odaka 185

Tṛṇa-yūti-gocara 185
Triṇayūti 57
Tsalvadi in'am 185
Tsakali, Tsavali in'am 185
Tsalivendra in'am 185
Tsavadi in'am 185
Tūcakattaṛi 178, 185
Tūl 185
Tūm, Túm 185
Tūmbu 185
Tūmu 101, 102, 185
Tūndū-teerwa 185
Tūndū-warum 185
Tuḍava 185
Tuddel punjah 152
Tudumu in'am 185
Tufreek 185
Tuhul 185
Tuias or tiyar 185
Tukkiri in'am 52, 125, 186
Tuḷai-pon 186
Tulā 138, 186
Tulā-bhāra 186
Tulā-puruṣa 186
Tuluvā 186
Tulya, Tulyam 186
Tumar jammah 9, 18
Tumgha 186
Tuṇḍikerī 186
Tuṇḍu 186
Tuṇḍu wāram, toondoo waurum 96, 137, 186
Tundavaram 186
Tung 186
Turai-minnar-pon 186
Turavu 186
Turcaree 186
Turk 186
Tusrufat 186
Tyacut 186
Tyasagari 186
Tycul 186

U

Ubbakavali in'am 187
Ubhaiyan 187
Ubhaya-nānā-deśi 187
Ubhaya-paliśai 187
Ubhayamukhī-dakṣiṇā 187
Uḍaiyār 187
Uḍan-vāram-āt-kūli 187
Udarapattu in'am 187
Uḍaya kuḍigal 187
Uddha-grāma 187
Udghāṭana 16, 56, 187
Udirapaṭṭi, udira-paṭṭi 187
Udraṅga 19, 160, 187
Udugaralu 187
Ujār 187
Ul paracoodie, ool paracoodie 187
Ul'lit'tár 187
Uḷ-vari 15, 187
Ulai, ulaip-pāṭṭam, kollar-ulai-pāṭṭam 187
Ulakaḷanta 188
Ulkaḷanta 188
Uḷamaiceytal 188
Uḷapparaiyar 188
Ularāi 188
Uḷaverudu 188
Uḷavukāni, uḷavukkāṇi 188
Ulgu 188
Ulku 188
Ulkūdī 113, 188, 190
Ullundu, oolundoo 188
Ulmanei 188
Uḷugudi makkaḷ, uḷudān kuḍi, kuḍi makan, uḷudārkku Uḷukuḍigaḷ, uḷukuḍi, oolkoody, oolcooddy 132, 188
Uḷukuṭikal 188
Ulupha 188
Uḷvari 188
Umanar 188
Umbaḷam, umbaḷikkai 188, 189
Umbali 189
Umbaḷige tenure, umbaḷi tenure 189
Umliga 189
Umliga tenure 189
Umul 189
Uṇbaḷi 189
Uṇdaṛuti 189
Upanum 33, 189
Upasti 189
Upāti 132, 189
Upāya 189
Uppam purthy, oopum purthee 189
Uppara in'am 189
Uppāyam, uppuk-kācu, uppup-piṭi 189
Uppilians 189
Uppu-kkāśu 189
Uppu-kocceyagai 143
Uprī, uparī, upri 189

Ura koḍage 189
Urala 189
Uralan 189
Urali 189
Urani in'am 189
Urdakarry 119, 154, 189
Urdeekrayum 189
Urk-kalancu 189
Uṟmai 189
Uroḍĕ, ūroḍeya 189
Urū 190
Urudvé 190
Urzee (p.Arzi) 190
Uśāvaḍi 190
Ustad in'am 190
Uṭaiyār 190
Utsṛṣṭa-paśsavaḥ 190
Uttāra 190, 160
Uttama-dōni 190
Uttara-vāda 190
Uvacca-kkāṇi 190
Uvaccaṇ -pēr-kaṭami 190
Uvaccaṇs 190
Uvaru 190
Uvātti-vīṭu 190
Uyāna 190
Uzhavadai uḷkuḍi 75, 137, 190
Uzhavadai ulkūḍī 190
Uzhavadai ulkudi payirkarar 190
Ūḷigam and uḷḷāyam 190
Ūlkūdi paycarry, oocoodi paycarry 190, 191
Ūlūngū, ooloogoo 132, 191
Uñcha 191
Ūr,oor, sabha, gramasabha 13, 124, 125, 163, 189, 191, 192, 196
Ūr-ĕṭṭu 192
Ūr-idu-varippāḍu 192
Ūr-kīḻ-iṟaiyili 192
Ūr kīḻavan 192
Ūr-kkadamai 192
Ūr-mányam 192
Ūr-mañjikkam 163
Ūr-mutali 192
Ūr-oḷagana 192
Ūr podu 163, 192
Ūrāṇmai 192
Ūrār 192
Ūrāṭci-tax 143
Ūravar 13, 192
Ūriṟ, suṟukki 192
Ūriṭu-vari 192, 196
Ūrk-kaṇakku, ūrk-karṇam 192
Ūrkāval 77
Ūrkkal-śemmaippon 192
Ūrkkaṇakkar-jīvitam 55
Ūṟṟāṇi 192
Ūruk-kīḻ-iṟaiyili 192
Ūrvāriyam 192
Ūṭṭuppurai 192

V

Vācalil-pōnta-kuṭimai 193
Vācittāṇ 193
Vāḍākkaḍan 193
Vādākkaḍamai 193
Vāḍi 193
Vālamāñci 193
Vāmana-kkal 193
Vāṇikar-maṇai-iṟai 193
Vāṇikar-pēr-kaṭamai 193
Vāṇikkar-pērāṟ-kaṭamai 87, 193
Vāṇiyar 193
Vāṇiyar-pēr-kaṭamai 193
Vāṇiyars 193
Vāpatis; vyāpṛitas 193
Vāpī 193
Vāra 193
Vāram, Wāram 193
Vārdhuṣin 193
Vāriyam 194
Vāriyar 194
Vārtā 194
Vāśal-kanakka 55
Vāśal-paṇam 139, 194
Vāśal-tiramam 194
Vāśal-vari 194
Vāstu-kṛtya 194
Vāstu-parivāra 194
Vāṭikā 194, 198
Vāy-kkeḷvi, vāy-kkeḷviyār 194
Vāyk-kēḷvi 194
Vāykkāl 194
Vāykkāl-pāṭṭam 194
Vaḍḍa-vyavahāri 194
Vada-kaval 194
Vagainda-kāśu 194
Vaidā, vaidapattā, (Arabic), wayada; 194
Vaidageni (Kanarese) 194

Vaidya in'am 143, 194
Vaidya-bhoga, vaidya-bhāga 194
Vaidya-vṛtti 194
Vaikāśi 194
Vaiśy-āgrahāra 8, 9, 194
Vaiśy-vāṇiya-nagarattār 194
Vaiśyāgrahāra 194
Vaita 194
Vakil, vakeel, wakil (A.) 172, 194
Vaḷanāḍu 121, 194
Vaḷi 148, 195
Vaḷi-āyam 195
Vaḷitas, vaṇitas, vantyas 195
Vaḷiy-ayam 195
Vaḷudiy-accu-varggam 195
Valamas 45
Valan 195
Valanadu 107, 195
Valangai 195
Valaya 195
Valayan in'am 195
Valita, vaḷita 195
Valluva in'am 195
Valluvan mānyam 195
Vaṁśakāra 195
Vaṇ-pāṭṭam 195
Vaṇika 195
Vaṇita 195
Vaṇṇak-kūli, vaṇṇarap-pārai 195
Vaṇṇārpārai 195
Vanadurga 195
Vanan 195
Vancha 195
Vandra 91, 195
Vaniers 195
Vaniya nagaram 195
Vaniyam in'am 196
Vannan mānyam, Vannan in'am 196
Vanpair ambalam in'am 196
Vanpyar, Vanypar 196
Vantu 196
Vara-grāma 196
Varagaru 196
Varagoo, varagu 196
Varagu koda 196
Varagū 196
Varāha 1, 130, 136, 196
Varaha 196
Varasha-putcut 152
Varam 196
Vargdar (Kanarese) 196
Vari 196
Vari, varipottagam 196
Vari-ppottaga-nāyakam 196
Vari-ppottagam 196
Varicale 196
Varip-pottakam 196
Varip-pottakam kaṇakku 197
Varipottagam 197
Variśai 197
Variśai-kaḍamai 197
Variyam in'am 197
Variyil -iṭu 197
Variyilār 197
Vartanā 15, 197
Vartanalu 197
Varuna Japan 197
Varuṣa-kāṇikkai 197
Vasad-bhoga-maryādā 197
Vasad-bhogya-maryādā 197
Vasakaras 197
Vasanta garuvus 197
Vasantagaruvu 197
Vastrarakṣakas 197
Vaṭṭam 197
Vaṭṭi-nāḷi 143
Vatta murai 197
Vattiyar in'am 197
Vayikkal in'am 197
Vēli 197
Vēlippaṇam 198
Vētaṇai 198
Vētar-kummari 198
Vēṇthĕ 198
Vĕṭha 198
Vecthyvadangan 198
Veda vadyar mānyam 198
Veda-vṛtti 198
Vedar in'am 198
Vees 198
Veesum, vissum 198
Vekkai 198
Velā-durga-pāla 198
Vellālanparṟu 198
Veḷḷāḷas 37, 184, 198
Veḷḷān 198
Veḷḷān vagai 84, 198
Veḷḷāṇvakai 198
Veḷḷāṇvakai-mutal 198
Veli 101, 135, 194, 198
Veli-cenu, veli-polamu, veli-volamu 129, 198

Veli–kkāśu, veli–ppayaṟu 199
Vellai 199
Vellaithal 199
Vellalas 199
Vellarykuruvay 199
Vellavursay 199
Veṇī 199
Veṇkāyam 199
Veppul 199
Verasi 199
Verpulu 199
Vertana 199
Verum patom ola karunum 199
Verumpattakkaraṃ (sl), verumpattakkar (pl.) 199
Verumpattam 199
Veṭha, visaya, nirvṛtti 199
Veṭṭi 11, 21, 24, 193, 198, 199, 200
Veṭṭi–ccoṟu 199
Veṭṭi–pāṭṭam 200
Veṭṭippuḍavai and veṭṭitamyaḷ 200
Veṭṭiyāl 200
Veṭṭiyān 10, 200
Vetana 200
Vethupu 200
Vetti in'am 106, 200
Vettis, vettiyan 200
Vettiyan 200
Vettiyan māṇyam 200
Vettuvan 200
Vīra–bhoga 200
Vīra–śāsana 200
Vīra–śeṣai 200
Vīsa 200, 202
Vīsā–badi, visā–padī, veesapadi 200, 202
Vīṭu 200
Vibhūti–kāṇikkai 200
Vidha 200
Vidy–ānubhoga 200
Vijāpya 200
Vijñapti, vijñāpti 200
Viḷakkal–taṇṭam 200
Vilantaikōl 200
Vil–paṇam 139
Vilai koṇḍa nilam 201
Vilai poruḷ 76, 201
Vilai tuṇḍu, vellah toondoo 22, 201
Villeins en–gros 201
Villeins regardant 201
Vimana pratishta in'am 201
Vinamu 201
Viniyōgam 201
Viniyoga 201
Viṟpiḍi 201
Virabhadra 201
Viral–ariśi 201
Virivile, parappile 201
Virivilē 201
Viṣa–vṛtti 201
Viṣahara–bhoga 201
Viṣaya 130, 201
Viṣaya–suṅka 201
Viṣṭi 200, 201
Viśa–kkāṇam 201
Viśeṣ–ādāya, viśeṣ–āya 201
Visam 201, 202
Visapadi villages 200, 201
Visaya 202
Vishaya 2, 44, 201, 202
Vishayapatis 202
Viss 202
Viṭṭukkuḍuttēn 202
Vittu mudal 202
Vivāha 202
Vivāha–ppaṇam 82, 202
Viyāyam 202
Vocalu 27
Vochchan māṇyam 202
Vṛitti, Vritti, birt, birte 5, 202
Vrāyasam 157, 202
Vralla 202
Vullah, bullah, 202
Vullum 202
Vunnies, vanniyams 202
Vyādha 202
Vyākhyā–vṛtti 202
Vyāpāra 202
Vyāpārin 202
Vyavasthai 202

W

Wāra tuṇḍu, warah toondoo 22, 203
Wāsil–bāqī 203
Wadla in'am 189, 203
Wajh-i-muqaarrari 203
Waqf (plural auqāf) 203
Waraput 36, 114, 115, 180, 203
Waraput, warappattu lands 203
Warappattu kanakku 203

Warariayat tenure 203
Waratanah 203
Warg, wargdar 203
Warga bhumi 169, 203
Warricum 203
Warum 190, 191, 203
Wasulbandi 203
Waṭan, Watan 203
Watandar-in'am 204
Watan jagir 204
Weights and Measures 204
Wet land 206
Witturnas 206
Wodigaru 195
Wol 184
Wudders; wadde-in'am 206
Wurgum 86, 113

Y
Yātrā-dāna 207
Yátam 207
Yadashut 207
Yadavas 207
Yadayan in'am 207
Yajmān, yejamānah 207
Yajman in'am 207
Yakki-accu 207
Yalavarise tenure 207
Yantra 207
Yatra-che-kathi 207
Yava 207
Yavanas 207
Yēnādi (s), kirāta, sikāri 207
Yekhabhogum 119, 207
Yeksal pattah 207
Yella 207
Yellu, yelloo 207
Yennai vangi in'am 207
Yeomiahs 207
Yer aal attavanai kanakku 207
Yeri katta raman 207
Yernaddies 207
Yeruckam 207
Yilpah, illuppai 207
Yojana 104, 207

Z
Zabita 208
Zabita wāram 208
Zakat 208
Zamindar (p.) 5, 23, 24, 25, 42, 43, 45, 52, 54, 56, 57, 59, 60, 62, 68, 69, 71, 78, 79, 88, 90, 93, 97, 118, 135, 138, 140, 143, 145, 147, 148, 151, 155, 157, 158, 159, 162, 163, 168, 169, 175, 176, 177, 182, 184, 190, 195, 208
Zamindaran-i-zor-talab 110, 208
Zamindari in'am 208
Zamindari, zamindary 92, 116, 126, 135, 152, 164, 208
Zamindari 208
Zamorin 208
Zar-i-wajib 45
Zillah 208
Zingar in'am 208
Zirat 208
Zirat-zamin 208
Zudgar 208
Zunnardar 208